THE
FIFTY-SECOND YEARBOOK

OF THE

NATIONAL SOCIETY FOR THE STUDY OF EDUCATION

PART I

ADAPTING THE SECONDARY-SCHOOL PROGRAM TO THE NEEDS OF YOUTH

Prepared by the Yearbook Committee

WILLIAM G. BRINK (*Chairman*), JAMES H. CHERRY, STEPHEN M. COREY, HARL R. DOUGLASS, WILL FRENCH, VERNER M. SIMS, AND RALPH W. TYLER

Edited by

NELSON B. HENRY

Distributed by

THE UNIVERSITY OF CHICAGO PRESS

CHICAGO 37, ILLINOIS

1953

Published by

THE NATIONAL SOCIETY FOR THE STUDY OF EDUCATION

5835 KIMBARK AVENUE, CHICAGO 37, ILLINOIS

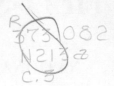
*The responsibilities of the Board of Directors of the National
Society for the Study of Education in the case of yearbooks
prepared by the Society's committees are (1) to select the subjects to be investigated, (2) to appoint committees calculated in
their personnel to insure consideration of all significant points
of view, (3) to provide appropriate subsidies for necessary
expenses, (4) to publish and distribute the committees' reports,
and (5) to arrange for their discussion at the annual meetings.*

*The responsibility of the Yearbook Editor is to prepare the
submitted manuscripts for publication in accordance with the
principles and regulations approved by the Board of Directors
in the "Guide for Contributors."*

*Neither the Board of Directors, nor the Yearbook Editor,
nor the Society is responsible for the conclusions reached or the
opinions expressed by the Society's yearbook committees.*

Published 1953
First Printing, 7,000 Copies
Second Printing, November, 1953, 5,000 Copies

Printed in the United States of America

OFFICERS OF THE SOCIETY
1952–53

(Term of office expires March 1 of the year indicated.)

WILLIAM A. BROWNELL (1955)
University of California, Berkeley, California

EDGAR DALE (1954)
Ohio State University, Columbus, Ohio

HARL R. DOUGLASS (1953)
University of Colorado, Boulder, Colorado

ERNEST O. MELBY (1956)*
New York University, New York, New York

WILLARD C. OLSON (1956)*
University of Michigan, Ann Arbor, Michigan

RUTH STRANG (1954)
Teachers College, Columbia University, New York, New York

RALPH W. TYLER (1953)
University of Chicago, Chicago, Illinois

PAUL A. WITTY (1955)
Northwestern University, Evanston, Illinois

NELSON B. HENRY (*Ex-officio*)
University of Chicago, Chicago, Illinois

Secretary-Treasurer
NELSON B. HENRY (1953)
University of Chicago, Chicago, Illinois

* Elected for three years beginning March 1, 1953.

iii

THE SOCIETY'S COMMITTEE ON ADAPTING THE SECONDARY-SCHOOL PROGRAM TO THE NEEDS OF YOUTH

WILLIAM G. BRINK (Chairman), Professor of Education, Northwestern University, Evanston, Illinois

JAMES H. CHERRY, General Assistant Superintendent, Joliet Township High School and Junior College, Joliet, Illinois

STEPHEN M. COREY, Professor of Education, Teachers College, Columbia University, New York, New York

HARL R. DOUGLASS, Director, College of Education, University of Colorado, Boulder, Colorado

WILL FRENCH, Professor of Education, Teachers College, Columbia University, New York, New York

VERNER M. SIMS, Professor of Psychology, University of Alabama, University, Alabama

RALPH W. TYLER, Dean, Division of the Social Sciences, University of Chicago, Chicago, Illinois

ASSOCIATED CONTRIBUTORS

MAURICE R. AHRENS, Director of Curricular Services, Corpus Christi Public Schools, Corpus Christi, Texas

GERTRUDE M. AITCHISON, Teacher of Unified Studies, Evanston Township High School, Evanston, Illinois

HAROLD ALBERTY, Professor of Education, Ohio State University, Columbus, Ohio

NADINE I. CLARK, Chairman, Social Studies Department, and Director, Curriculum Materials Center, Evanston Township High School, Evanston, Illinois

HOWARD CUMMINGS, Specialist for Social Sciences and Geography, Secondary Schools Section, United States Office of Education, Washington, D.C.

PAUL E. EISERER, Associate Professor, Department of Guidance, Teachers College, Columbia University, New York, New York

ROBERT J. FORBES, Instructor, Pasadena City College, Pasadena, California

ROBERT S. GILCHRIST, Assistant Superintendent in Charge of Instruction, Pasadena City Schools, Pasadena, California

J. DAN HULL, Chief, Secondary Schools Section, United States Office of Education, Washington, D.C.

v

WILSON H. IVINS, Associate Professor of Secondary Education, University of New Mexico, Albuquerque, New Mexico

CAMILLA M. LOW, Professor of Education, University of Wisconsin, Madison, Wisconsin

RUTH STRANG, Professor of Education, Teachers College, Columbia University, New York, New York

J. LLOYD TRUMP, Professor of Education, University of Illinois, Urbana, Illinois

J. G. UMSTATTD, Professor of Secondary Education, University of Texas, Austin, Texas

EDITOR'S PREFACE

The Society's committee for Part I of the Fourth Yearbook (1905) introduced its report on the training of secondary-school teachers with the statement that "Our secondary schools . . . have been called into existence by certain needs of the people." The series of yearbooks of the National Society now comprises a hundred titles, about two-thirds of which were specifically concerned with one or more of the currently challenging problems of the nation's secondary schools.

At different periods of time during these fifty years, different functions of the secondary school or different aspects of its program or procedure were the subject of review and discussion by representatives of the profession responsible for the preparation of one of the Society's yearbooks. It is fair to say that the relation of the school to the needs of the people it serves was properly reflected in the treatment of the problem as it was interpreted at the time of publication in each instance. To the committee for the Fourth Yearbook the need for competent teachers appeared to be "the most vital and determining factor" in the improvement of secondary schools of that time. In the discussion of the problem of adapting the schools to individual differences among students in the schools, the committee for Part II of the Twenty-fourth Yearbook declared, "Our profession is inclining more and more to the belief that education of maximal effectiveness is to be accomplished through the experiences of normal living."

In line with the observable trend of the earlier yearbooks, the committee for the present volume has expressed the view that "the most pressing problem now facing secondary schools is that of adapting their programs more specifically to the needs of youth" (p. 1). The publication was stimulated by a memorandum received from Professor Brink and presented to the Board of Directors in November, 1949. *Adapting the Secondary-School Program to the Needs of Youth* is a revealing treatise on desirable objectives and methodology for teachers and school administrators who earnestly desire to bring new knowledge to bear upon the solution of problems that might otherwise obstruct the normal adjustment of youth to life in school or might preclude their appropriate participation in the affairs of an adult society.

NELSON B. HENRY

vii

TABLE OF CONTENTS

CHAPTER I

INTRODUCTION: THE YOUTH-NEEDS MOTIVE IN SECONDARY EDUCATION

WILLIAM G. BRINK
Professor of Education
Northwestern University
Evanston, Illinois

PURPOSE OF THE YEARBOOK

This yearbook is devoted to a consideration of the problem of improving the education of youth in secondary schools. Although significant changes have been made in the scope and character of secondary education in the last half-century, there is still a widespread feeling shared by a considerable segment of the profession and of the lay public, and supported by considerable evidence, that further changes and improvements are needed.

Many factors have contributed to the growing demand for strengthening the education of youth. Secondary education is terminal for the vast majority of young people, and society has a right to expect that this period of schooling will contribute as fully as possible toward the growth and development of every student. This responsibility, although universally recognized, is by no means easy to fulfil. Indeed, the task confronting secondary schools has become more difficult and complex in recent years as a result of extensions in the functions and objectives of these schools, the increased heterogeneity of their population, and the growing impact of social and economic forces upon the world in which youth must seek adjustment.

In this yearbook no attempt is made to deal with all aspects of the problem of improving the education of youth. The yearbook committee recognized that significant proposals for the improvement of secondary education are constantly being considered or tested in the schools. Some noteworthy ones have been given considerable attention in recent years. It was the consensus of the committee that the most pressing problem now facing secondary schools is that of adapting their programs more specifically to the needs of youth. A consideration of ways in which this problem can be dealt with successfully constitutes the central focus of the yearbook.

1

Secondary education is here interpreted to embrace the education of youth between the ages of approximately twelve and twenty; these years are commonly referred to as the period of adolescence. In terms of grade levels, secondary education comprises Grades VII through XIV; thus it includes the junior high school, the senior high school, and the junior college. By *program* is meant all of the content, activities, and experiences that are organized and directed by the school to promote effective learning; this includes both the curriculum and the extraclass activities. The term *adapting* is here used to denote the continuous revision and reconstruction of secondary-school programs in order that they may become more effective in meeting the needs of youth. In view of the varied interpretations of the term *needs*, it appears desirable to explain more fully the sense in which the term is used in this yearbook.

The Broadening Concept of Needs

The term *needs* is certainly not a new one, nor is the assertion that secondary schools should meet the needs of youth a novel one. Teachers and administrators have always organized educational programs on the basis of some preconceived ideas as to the needs of the individuals who were to be served. However, the concept of needs as a foundation of curriculum development has broadened greatly over the years, and gradually a wider recognition of the implications of this concept for the education of youth is being achieved.

Emphasis upon Various Aspects of Needs

The history of secondary education in the United States records persistent attempts to discern the needs of youth and to expand and revise the curriculum accordingly. It reveals also the diversity of views which have been held at different periods as to the character of the needs of youth. This divergence of opinion is still evident in the expressed statements of the functions and objectives of secondary education today.

Early secondary schools devoted themselves primarily to meeting the needs of youth for college and the ministry. Stress was laid particularly upon intellectual attainments such as the needs of youth for facts and knowledge, for understandings and insights. This restricted conception largely characterized school programs up to the close of the nineteenth century. Recently, notable extensions have been made in the meanings associated with the term *needs*. Attention has been directed to various aspects of the needs of youth by many educators and professional groups For example, the citizenship needs of youth have been more widely emphasized since the United States has taken her place among the nations as a major power. Consequently, programs for youth have been extended to include opportunities for participation in the types of behavior associated with responsible citizenship.

Again, as science and technology effected revolutionary changes in economic and industrial life, increased awareness of the vocational needs of youth has led to the expansion of secondary-school programs to embrace preprofessional training, job preparation, and work-experience. The alarming status of the health of youth, as disclosed by the Selective Service System during World War II, made it abundantly clear that the schools should accept more responsibility in this area of needs. The findings of psychology as to the nature of the learning process emphasized the needs of youth as learners.

In recent years advances in our knowledge of the characteristics of adolescents have greatly influenced prevailing concepts of the needs of youth. Studies in this area have shed considerable light upon the nature of the drives and motives of adolescents and have, likewise, disclosed much relevant information concerning the types of "developmental tasks" with which youth are confronted. Recently, concern for the perpetuation of the democratic way of life has led to increased emphasis upon the need of youth to develop moral and spiritual values which will give direction to their choices, behavior, attitudes, and relationships.

Conflicting Concepts of Needs

Although these emphases have contributed greatly to a broadened concept of needs, conflicts and uncertainties as to the meaning of the term still exist. Some have viewed needs primarily from the standpoint of the demands placed upon the individual in adult life and have, accordingly, conceived of education as a preparation for life. Consequently, the immediate needs of youth were subordinated to probable future needs. In contrast to this position is the view of those who extol the primacy of the present life needs of youth, assuming that recognition of and provision for present needs are the best, if not the only, guaranties of satisfactory adjustment in adulthood. Although it is probable that no one has assumed that education should have its orientation exclusively in the present or in the future, nonetheless there has been a strong tendency to stress one or the other of these positions. This yearbook rejects the assumption of an antithesis between present and future needs. Rather, the position is held that many, if not all, of the basic needs of the individual persist in some form throughout his entire life, and that his future needs have their roots in the present.

A second source of conflict in regard to the conception of needs is to be found in the divergent viewpoints as to whether the emphasis in programs for youth should be upon personal needs or upon the broader needs of society as a whole. Some stress the needs that arise within the individual as concomitants of the process of growth and development. Modern psychology has contributed greatly to an understanding of the basic human needs and their pervasive influence upon behavior. They range from physical or biological needs as for food, shelter, and rest, to the need for such intangibles as social and economic security and harmony with reality. Another viewpoint is that the needs of the society in which the individual lives should give primary direction to programs for youth. Those who stress this position point out that the schools have been established by society for the purpose of perpetuating and improving the quality of living in society.

It should be clear that a defensible educational program for youth must recognize both the personal needs of youth and the broader needs of society. The personal needs of every individual are conditioned by the type of culture and society in which he lives. Even a universal physical need such as that for food is colored by the sanctions of society. Likewise, the needs of society can be fulfilled only as the personal needs of individuals are more effectively satisfied. Programs of education for youth should be based upon a continuous study of the changing needs of society and of their implications for the personal needs of individuals. Likewise, the school should give greater recognition to its task of so directing youth in the satisfaction of personal needs that they will be actuated by the desire to serve the interests of the society in which they live as well as their own interests. It is the viewpoint of the yearbook that in a democracy these needs are reciprocal in nature. The development of free and self-reliant men to the limit of their abilities is not only the best safeguard for the preservation and growth of our culture and society but also the only justification for the existence of a democracy.

A third source of conflict in the use of the term *needs* arises over the question of their specificity. Current statements of the needs of youth are frequently expressed in very general terms. Numerous lists of such needs have been prepared by various educational organizations and workers in the field of curriculum development. In most cases these lists do not differ significantly except in terminology and organization. For example, emphasis is almost always placed upon good citizenship, the development and maintenance of health and physical fitness, and the wise use of leisure.

It is the consensus of the yearbook committee that although such general statements of needs may serve a useful purpose, it is only when they are defined closely enough to indicate the specific types of knowledge, ability, skill, appreciation, and behavior to be developed that they can be of greatest value to teachers in selecting and organizing instructional materials. As will be indicated in the chapters that follow, teachers and administrators at the local level must give greater attention to the validation of their decisions concerning the specific needs of youth as a basis for defining instructional goals.

FACTORS CONTRIBUTING TO EMPHASIS ON NEEDS

In the preceding section consideration was given to some of the basic factors associated with the concept of needs. It is now our purpose to discuss some of the forces and factors that have stimulated the growing recognition of the function of the secondary school in meeting the needs of youth. The needs of youth can be perceived only in relation to the supporting culture; changes in conditions and values in society postulate new or altered needs. It is common knowledge that, during the past half-century especially, the rate of change in many aspects of our society has been greatly accelerated. It is not surprising, therefore, that the task of education in meeting the needs of youth has been made vastly more complicated and difficult. To survey and assess the significance of all of these changes is quite beyond the purpose and scope of this discussion. Consideration will be given only to a few of the insistent forces that are challenging the secondary schools to adapt programs more closely to the needs of youth.

Secondary Education for All Youth

The American people have committed themselves to the achievement of the ideal of free secondary education for all youth because of a firm conviction that this policy is essential to the strengthening of our democratic institutions and to the economic well-being of the people. This implies not only the retention of youth in school but also the improvement of programs in ways that will make school experiences more significant for youth. Much has already been accomplished in both of these directions. In 1951 all states required school attendance at least up to the age of sixteen. Certainly the growth in enrolments in our secondary schools has been nothing short of phenomenal. In 1890 approximately 360,000 youth of high-school age were in school; up to 1930 the high-school population more than doubled each decade; by 1940 an all-time high was reached when approximately 7,000,000 youth were in attendance. Largely because of the lower birth rate during the thirties, enrolments decreased to around six million in 1950. However, it has been predicted that by 1960 the high-school population will have increased by two and one-half million and that increases will probably continue until at least 1964–65. The significance of facts concerning enrolments is revealed more clearly when they are interpreted in relation to the total number of youth. For example, in 1950 approximately 73 per cent of the youth from 14–17 years of age were enrolled in school as compared with 11 per cent in 1900.[1]

As secondary schools have become less selective, the character of their population has become more heterogeneous in capacities, interests, and expectancies. Accordingly, the effort to adjust programs to the needs of youth has been intensified. That much remains to be done in achieving the goal of universal secondary education for youth is clearly evident from recent investigations of the holding power of secondary schools. These investigations concern themselves with the number of youth who drop out of school at various grade levels, the reasons for leaving school, and what secondary schools can do to improve their holding power.

The results of studies of retention indicate that for the nation as a whole only approximately 50 per cent of the youth complete high school. Wide differences are, of course, found in the holding power of particular schools.[2] Size of school does not appear to be consistently related to holding power. On the other hand, there is some evidence that a larger proportion of boys than of girls tend to drop out early.

Although many reasons have been alleged to account for the number of early leavers, there is as yet rather meager evidence to support some of the assumptions relating thereto. Recent surveys of student opinion concerning reasons for leaving indicate that a significant percentage of youth express dissatisfaction with various aspects of the program and life of the school.[3] Recently more dependable data have been obtained by studying the factors associated with early leaving. Although only inadequate information is yet available, studies indicate that drop-outs occur more frequently among students of inferior ability and from the lower socio-economic groups.[4]

---

[1] *Schools and the 1950 Census*. Research Bulletin of the National Education Association, Vol. XXIX, No. 4. Washington: National Education Association, 1951. See also *Statistical Summary of Education, 1947–48*. Washington: Federal Security Agency, Office of Education, 1950.

[2] Walter H. Gaumitz and Ellsworth Tompkins, *Holding Power and Size of High Schools*. Federal Security Agency, Office of Education, Circular No. 22, 1950. Washington: Government Printing Office, 1950.

[3] Harold J. Dillon, *Early School Leavers*. New York: National Child Labor Committee, 1949.

[4] Harold C. Hand, *Principal Findings of the 1947–48 Basic Studies of the Illinois Secondary-School Curriculum Program*. Illinois Secondary-School Curriculum Program, Bulletin No. 2, 1949. Springfield, Illinois: Department of Public Instruction, 1949.

Studies of Youth

During the past few decades there has been a steady increase in the number of studies of youth. These investigations have given additional impetus to the significance of adapting secondary-school programs to the needs of youth. For example, investigations of the reading interests and activities of adolescents have shown that a considerable proportion of youth are seriously handicapped in the basic skills involved in reading.[5] Far too often the reading of high-school students is poor in quality and limited in amount. This situation is especially distressing in view of the fact that there is little likelihood that students will change their reading habits and interests appreciably after they leave school. Comparatively few secondary schools have as yet provided developmental reading programs that will satisfactorily meet the needs of all youth.

Studies of youth in the area of vocations have revealed the serious inadequacy of the educational and vocational guidance provided.[6] Too often vocational interests are unrealistic and are arrived at by students without adequate understanding of their own capacities, the nature of occupations, or of available job opportunities. Follow-up studies of students indicate that occupational preferences often bear little relationship to the kinds of employment obtained. Moreover, such studies have shown that in some instances a large proportion of the students surveyed have reported that they received little or no help in choosing careers during their high-school attendance.[7]

Perhaps in no area has there been greater interest exhibited in the competencies of youth than in the field of citizenship. This is not surprising, for youth will fail in this area unless secondary schools develop in them the understandings, loyalties, and ideals that are essential for democratic citizenship. Studies in this area have dealt with a variety of problems.[8] Some have sought to discover the status of high-school graduates with respect to a knowledge of the essentials of citizenship.

---

[5] *Reading in the High School and College.* Forty-seventh Yearbook of the National Society for the Study of Education, Part II. Chicago: University of Chicago Press, 1948.

[6] R. W. Edmiston and C. H. Starr, "Youth's Attitudes toward Occupations," *Occupations*, XXVI (January, 1948), 213–20.

[7] S. H. Lorenzen, "Opinion Reactions in High-School Follow-up Studies," *Bulletin of the National Association of Secondary-School Principals*, XXXIII (Jnauary, 1949), 119–26.

[8] See, for example, "Education for Citizenship," *Review of Educational Research*, XVII (October, 1947), 257–98; and also "Education for Citizenship," *Phi Delta Kappan*, XXXIII (December, 1951), 166–99.

Others have emphasized the behavioral aspects of civic competence and the extent of participation in the civic activities of the school and the community. Although notable progress has been made in the adaptation of secondary-school programs to the citizenship needs of youth, there is some evidence that present accomplishments are not satisfactory.

Juvenile Delinquency

Further evidence of the importance of adapting secondary-school programs to the needs of youth is provided by recent studies of juvenile delinquency. Although there have been many alarming reports concerning the rapid increase in delinquency rates, it is exceedingly difficult to obtain objective evidence pertaining thereto. The definition of delinquency varies considerably from state to state, and there is no central agency to compile nationwide statistics. The evidence that is available is based very largely upon court referrals, which is obviously an inadequate source of dependable estimates. Although the number of court referrals appears to have increased up to approximately the close of World War II, there has been a decline in the number of such cases since that time.[9] However, it should be recognized that during the past few decades an increasing proportion of delinquents have been referred to agencies other than the courts. In any event the problem is still one of utmost concern to all agencies of society and particularly to the secondary schools.

As the result of numerous and extensive studies of many aspects of the problem by psychologists, sociologists, and welfare workers, much relevant information concerning the nature, causation, and prevention of deviant behavior in youth has been made available. Recent data point toward the necessity of re-examining many of the older assumptions in regard to the causes of delinquency and have laid a firmer foundation for effective programs of prevention. Investigations have also clearly indicated the multiple character of the conditions that invite delinquent behavior.[10] Although such factors as disintegration of home life, economic insecurity, war, lack of church ties, and low ability have long been thought to contribute to delinquency, it has been only in recent years that recognition has been given to the critical significance of the emotional conflicts, tensions, and disturbances that are often associated with preadolescent and adolescent growth. Of special significance, therefore, have been the recent attempts to discover the precise character of the

---

[9] *The American Yearbook.* Edited by W. M. Schuyler. New York: Thomas Nelson & Sons, 1950.

[10] See, for example, Martin H. Meumeyer, *Juvenile Delinquency in Modern Society.* New York: D. Van Nostrand Co., Inc., 1949.

problems and difficulties which youth face in their adjustment to school life. Deeper insight into the symptoms of maladjustment which are often associated with delinquency has challenged secondary-school teachers and administrators to re-examine many policies and practices of the school which may contribute to fostering and accentuating undesirable attitudes and behavior. Many investigations have disclosed that delinquent youth invariably evidence aggressive dissatisfaction with the program and services of the schools.[11] They also indicate that tendencies toward delinquency can often be predicted by the use of definable criteria and stress the crucial role of the school in the detection of atypical behavior.[12]

Perhaps the most salutary development in regard to the problem here considered is the emerging emphasis upon positive and constructive attitudes toward delinquent youth and toward the methods of treatment. Studies and publications such as those reported in the Forty-seventh Yearbook of the National Society for the Study of Education are of great value in clarifying the nature of the problem and in suggesting ways in which secondary schools can assist in promoting conditions that will favor the development of socially acceptable attitudes and behavior.[13] This publication and others have clearly indicated the desirability of guided group experiences, of adequate instructional and noninstructional services to youth, and of curriculum programs that are in harmony with the needs and interests of all students. Moreover, they have stressed the urgency of extending programs in areas that are as yet inadequately developed, such as guidance, education for home and family living, education in moral and spiritual values, and education for exceptional children.

Influence of Cultural Status

Another factor that has contributed to the growing emphasis upon the school's role in meeting the needs of youth is the growing awareness of the influence of cultural status upon the learning of pupils. By cultural status is meant the social group with which the individual is identified. Social groupings are dependent upon such factors as race, nationality, and social and economic class. Although the variability in the needs of youth with respect to differences in nationality and race have com-

[11] Sheldon Glueck and Eleanor Glueck, *Unraveling Juvenile Delinquency*. New York: Commonwealth Fund, 1950.

[12] D. P. Clarke and D. Gray, "School Surveys and Delinquency Prediction," *Journal of Educational Sociology*, XXIV (September, 1950), 21–29.

[13] *Juvenile Delinquency and the Schools*. Forty-seventh Yearbook of the National Society for the Study of Education, Part I. Chicago: University of Chicago Press, 1948.

manded some attention from educators in the past, it has been only in recent years that the implications of position in the social structure of communities have been studied.

American insistence upon the doctrine that "all men are created equal" has led to a virtual denial of the existence of social classes. The logical consequence of this assumption in attempting to provide equal educational opportunities for all American youth has been a strong tendency toward rigidity, uniformity, and standardization in school policies and practices. Recent investigations clearly disclose the reality of social stratification in contemporary culture.[14] Moreover, they reveal the pervasive influence of membership in the various groups upon the attitudes, personalities, and behavior patterns of youth. It is clear that the personality of an individual is already quite firmly established when he arrives at the period of adolescence. By this time he has developed a fairly clear conception of his place in the social structure of the community and of the approved forms of thought and behavior that are sanctioned or disapproved by his family and peers. Although there is considerable overlapping in abilities and interests among groups, significant differences are known to exist between adolescents of various subcultural groups with respect to the motivations operating in the satisfaction of even the most basic needs. Similarly, social status is known to have a direct bearing upon the value patterns and standards of conduct which control behavior directed toward the achievement of social recognition, security, and success. Moreover, youth from different social and economic groups differ somewhat in their educational and vocational preferences and expectancies.

Although teachers and administrators are coming to recognize the pervasive influence of cultural status upon the learning of youth, there is still considerable uncertainty as to what this implies for education. Clearly, recognition must be given to the serious danger of deepening and intensifying differences instead of developing common loyalties, appreciations, and attitudes. Certainly this whole problem offers a challenge to secondary schools and suggests the necessity of developing more appropriate methods and procedures for helping youth cope with the realities of modern society. In a democracy the school is concerned with the promotion of the welfare of all youth. In a democratic social institution it is expected that youth of various social groups will meet and intermingle on a basis of equality. The school cannot escape the dual task of

---

[14] See, for example, Allison Davis, *Social-Class Influences upon Learning.* Cambridge, Massachusetts: Harvard University Press, 1951; Robert J. Havighurst and Hilda Taba, *Adolescent Character and Personality.* New York: John Wiley & Sons, 1949; and August B. Hollingshead, *Elmtown's Youth.* New York: John Wiley & Sons, 1949.

reducing the anxieties, tensions, and frustrations of youth, which have their origins in social stratification, and of providing programs of education that will enable all youth to achieve their highest potentialities for personal happiness and social usefulness.

A Changing Social Order

The dynamic character of contemporary civilization has accentuated the problem of adapting secondary-school programs to the needs of youth. Education today operates in the vortex of powerful constructive and destructive forces. Youth face a world of unparalleled stresses and strains. Largely since the beginning of the twentieth century, scientific discoveries and technological advance have altered not only the material aspects of civilization but also the entire cultural system. Changes have occurred so rapidly that the peoples of the world have been challenged as never before by the complexity of the problems confronted. In large measure they have been unprepared for the decisions they have been called upon to make. In this same half-century the world has suffered two terrible wars and faces the prospect of an even more calamitous conflict. It is not surprising that the resultant strain upon the entire fabric of life has been greatly increased. The needs of youth have been significantly modified by these changes, and the distinctive characteristics of the present civilization have an important bearing on the problem of the secondary school program in relation to the youth of this generation.

Some Characteristics of American Civilization. During the past fifty years the world has become increasingly mechanized. Science and technology have enabled man to make great progress toward the conquest of nature and toward overcoming the limitations of his own physical make-up. The range of man's senses has been appreciably extended, and his energy multiplied enormously. As new sources of power have been harnessed and have been put to work, many different kinds of tools and machines have been invented. Increasingly man's habits have become mechanized as the kinds and number of machines have increased. In 1949, there were 44,670,588 registered automobiles, busses, and trucks in the United States; 103,000,000 radio and television sets; and 38,-229,800 telephones.[15] Add to this the number of boats, trains, and airplanes used in transportation, the power tools for work in mines, factories, construction projects, offices, and farms, the refrigerators, washing machines, sewing machines, and a host of other devices found in the home, and the total is astounding. Today we face the prospect of unlimited power as the result of discoveries in the realm of nuclear fission.

---

[15] *The World Almanac and Book of Facts for 1951.* Edited by Harry Hansen. New York: New York World Telegram and The Sun, 1951.

Even scientists are unable to predict the changes atomic power will make in the future.

With the expansion of machine power, the world has become more highly industrialized. Industrialization, in turn, has promoted urbanization, and science and technology have provided the means by which the conditions of urban life could be established. Improvements in building, in transportation, and in methods of marketing permit workers to congregate in cities where they are near their jobs. Consequently, the drift of peoples into metropolitan areas has become a trend in American life. According to the 1950 census, more than four-fifths of the national population increase of the last decade has taken place within metropolitan areas. Although outlying parts of cities have been growing faster than the central portions, the type of culture therein is definitely urban. This movement toward the cities has greatly influenced the character of the needs of youth. Congestion creates a hazard to health and safety; it greatly increases the chances of accident, fire, and disease. The concentration of people imposes greater demands for obedience to law, consideration of the rights and property of others, conformity to acceptable social usage, and effective participation in group life. The tendency of peoples of one race or nationality or social group to gather in one section of the city and to retain and deepen their distinctive characteristics augments the need for better interpersonal relationships and for closer social integration.

Scientific discoveries and technological advance have contributed greatly to the growing interdependence among peoples. This has become important not only at the local level but on a national and international scale as well. Telegraphs, telephones, radio, movies, television, and a greatly increased amount and variety of printed materials have brought the peoples of the world face to face. Differences in habits and customs, in beliefs and attitudes, have become more evident. Traditional standards of behavior and habits of thought are challenged in the light of those of other cultures. The utilization of world resources for an expanding technology is effecting a new world outlook. Sources of supply and potential markets are cut off by war, revolution, and disaster. Economic cooperation is imperative in the kind of world-scale developments that could and should be carried on in the future. In short, science and technology have made of the world a neighborhood. Potentially, intercourse among peoples of different cultures is unrestrained. In such a world, prejudice, suspicion, intolerance, isolation, and segregation are dangerous.

Home and Family Living. In a period of rapid change, it is inevitable that there will be concomitant transformations in the social agencies that serve youth. Among these institutions the home is potentially the most important, although the influence of the school and church is far reaching. The trends in family life which were already shaping before 1900 have persisted. The average family is small (3.4 persons according to the 1950 census). The number of broken homes is still increasing; in 1948 about 2,000,000 children under eighteen years of age were living with neither parent, and nearly 4,000,000 with only one parent. More and more women are working; in 1949 four million of the twenty-one million mothers with children under eighteen years of age worked outside the home.[16]

The home has changed significantly as it has adapted itself to an expanding technology. Especially in urban areas its economic function has been almost wholly lost. No longer do the members of a family work together to produce food or goods for their own consumption or to sell. Current economic life predicates separation and individualization in work. Very often children have no idea what their fathers' occupations involve. When mothers work also, the members of the family separate early in the morning and may not come together again until dark. This means that children and youth are largely unsupervised except during school hours. It means also a significant decrease in family unity.

Despite the changes that have occurred, the home remains the most powerful educative force in society, and the child is most significantly and irrevocably conditioned by its influence. The family is still the only "affectional" unit among social institutions. When death or separation or divorce deprive the child of the love and protection of two parents, or when discord and indifference characterize the home, the child is seriously handicapped in the development of a healthy emotional life. When parents are unworthy of love and respect, or when their striving for social and economic advancement leads them to disregard or exploit children, personality growth in children and youth is often distorted. When the home is unable to maintain a decent standard of living, the child suffers not only physically but socially and emotionally as well. In recent years increasing tensions and frustrations among adults have greatly impaired the function of the home in providing the security that is imperative for healthy personality development.

The reorientations in home life have many implications for secondary schools as they attempt to adapt programs to the needs of youth. Two trends in particular may be mentioned. Opportunities are being provided for youth to acquire the skills, knowledge, and attitudes essential for successful homemaking and for effective participation in family life

---

[16] *Children and Youth at the Midcentury.* Midcentury White House Conference on Children and Youth. Raleigh, North Carolina: Health Publications Institute, Inc., 1951.

through the addition of courses and units in home and family living. More recognition is being given to ways in which the school can supplement rather than supplant the home.

Influence of Technological Developments upon Work. The advance in technology has led to revolutionary changes in the world of work. Although the machine has largely replaced the unskilled laborer, many new jobs have been created by a greatly expanded industry and economy. The trend toward specialization has to some extent offset the displacement of workers by machines. Moreover, with the development of assembly-line methods by which commodities could be produced in mass quantities at reasonable cost, there has been a great increase in the consumption of goods. Specialization has also affected the professions and has led to an extension of opportunities for youth in these areas.

Industrialization and urbanization have influenced the growth of whole new areas of work concerned with the distribution of goods, advertising, and marketing. Moreover, industry is today using the skills of many professional workers, such as doctors and lawyers, nurses and dieticians, psychologists and counselors, accountants and efficiency experts. Perhaps the greatest increase in job opportunities have come to those persons in related service occupations, such as maintenance workers, insurance agents, realtors, bankers and brokers, restaurant employees, and government workers. Also, a much wider range of clerical jobs has developed in recent years.

Changed conditions in industry have decreased the opportunities for self-employment and greatly increased the interdependence of workers. Moreover, mass production has changed the emphasis from producing goods for use to producing goods for sale. Both these factors have tended to deprive many workers of a feeling of real achievement. Much work has become almost wholly impersonal; the worker does not know the employer or the consumer. The reward he receives for work is measured in terms of wages. He feels little responsibility for the quality of the product he is engaged in making and often can take little pride in it. He may have but a vague idea of the relationship of his particular job to the whole process. In many other occupations competition is great, and pressure upon workers is intense. Here again, success is frequently measured in terms of the volume of sales, or of the amount of goods handled, or of the number of subscribers. Stress is often laid upon quantity rather than upon quality, and in consequence work is not seen as service to others.

Secondary schools that are seeking to meet the vocational needs of youth must consider the implications of these trends for their programs. For example, for most youth the best job preparation is secured from a broad program which will lead to considerable flexibility in skills.

Changes are occurring so quickly in industry, especially in mechanized occupations, that a pupil may find that the particular job for which he has prepared has become obsolete or has been taken over by a new machine. Moreover, all youth need the understandings which will help them to be intelligent consumers as well as co-operative workers. They need to recognize interrelationships among various occupations and among the various forces which operate in modern industry and economy. They need to appreciate the dignity of all useful work and the contributions which various kinds of work make to the good of all.

Since many jobs provide meager opportunities for creative and artistic experiences, youth need to develop skills and interests in hobbies or avocations. The fact that modern technology has increased the number of specialized jobs for which youth can prepare predicates the need for more effective guidance in surveying occupational fields and in testing abilities and interests.

New Patterns of Leisure. Modern man spends less time in work and more in leisure, and the patterns of leisure are continuously being altered by the development of new media for recreation. Movies, radio, and television, especially, have contributed to the tendency to spend more time in entertainment and less in active participation in sports and in creative experiences. Passivity has become a characteristic of recreation; youth have become viewers and listeners who take no active part in the activities involved and no responsibility for them. Because recreational facilities are increasingly controlled by commercial agencies, the quality of the entertainment provided has often been questionable. Moreover, it has been planned for adults rather than for children and youth. On the other hand, these new media of communication have great potential value. Through the discriminative selection of movie, radio, and television programs, youth can become acquainted with the world's greatest music and drama, can participate vicariously in a wide range of sports, and can gain more realistic understandings of the world in which they live.

There is far greater uniformity in leisure-time activities than formerly, when various forms of recreation were characteristic only of certain sections of the country. The same books and magazines, films and records, radio and television programs are available from coast to coast and to people of all social and economic classes. Also there is more organization in leisure activities. Of course youth still spend a large part of their free time in loafing and visiting and "fooling around." But a much greater proportion of time is spent in activities that are sponsored either by commercial agencies or by community groups.

Recognition has long been given to the educative value of leisure-time activities. Greater attention has been given recently to the therapeutic value of recreation. Leisure-time activities can be made to contribute significantly to the stimulation of initiative, imagination, and invention, to the reduction of adolescent impulses toward aggression and rivalry, to the development of self-confidence and feelings of achievement and success, to the reduction of fears, inhibitions, and anxieties, and to the healthy expression of many of the pent-up emotions of youth.

In adapting programs to the recreational needs of youth, the secondary school should be concerned with (a) encouraging students to develop attitudes and standards which will lead to desirable choices among leisure activities; (b) offering youth many opportunities to acquire the skills, interests, and knowledge which will enable them to engage in creative forms of activity; (c) providing leadership for the kinds of extraclass activities that have educative and therapeutic value; and (d) co-operating with homes and communities in providing better facilities for wholesome use of leisure time.

World Order and National Security. The attempt to delineate in broad outlines some of the important factors that are challenging secondary schools to adapt their programs more closely to the needs of youth would be quite incomplete and unrealistic were no mention made of two interrelated problems that are commanding increasing attention—the problem of achieving world peace and order and the problem of strengthening our national security. Indeed, these problems overshadow in importance all others considered. Moreover, they have been conditioned to a great extent by the scientific and technological developments previously discussed. Never before in history has the human race had at its disposal as decisive a means of destruction; the problem of maintaining world peace and order is in no small degree the problem of survival itself. On the other hand, man has never had a more glorious opportunity to achieve world unity and to improve human welfare all over the globe.

People everywhere, tired of war and war's devastations, look to the future with mingled feelings of hope and despair—hope that the nations of the world may be able to resolve their conflicts and find effective ways of co-operation; despair in the face of mounting tensions and disagreements. But free men, men who realize their responsibilities as well as the benefits that come to them because they are free, do not easily yield to despair, nor do they indulge themselves in illusory hopes. Instead, they seek to apply their intelligence and creative imagination to such problems as peace and world stability in the same way that they have already applied themselves to the conquest of nature through science and technology. And this is precisely what the free peoples of the world are seeking to do. Already the foundations for achieving the objectives of peace and order have been firmly established. There have been mistakes; there have been difficulties and obstacles; but encouraging progress has been made.

In this great endeavor the American people have assumed unprecedented responsibility for leadership. That responsibility will undoubtedly increase in the years ahead. Whether or not the American people will be equipped to meet this challenge adequately will depend in no small degree upon the extent to which secondary schools develop in youth those qualities of mind and spirit that are so urgently needed. Certain it is that these frontiers of concern will demand young citizens who can think effectively, who have mastered the skills of communication, and who are cognizant of the role their country must play in world affairs.

The problem of national security is intimately related to the problem of world peace. In view of the ideological conflicts and tensions in the present world situation, and because of the powerful forces that now threaten the free world, it is possible that the present emergency may extend far into the future and affect very profoundly the lives of several generations of youth in our secondary schools. For example, instead of planning careers in line with chosen fields of interest, large numbers of youth will be looking toward some form of military service. The attendant disruptions of vocational plans will have far-reaching effects. Approximately four million workers will be needed in defense industries for every forty to fifty billion dollars of production. The demand for technically trained specialists for the Army alone will exceed 20,000 men annually. Although many of the highly specialized skills can best be developed on the job, secondary schools will be expected to equip youth with the fundamental understandings, abilities, and skills in the use of machines, tools, maps, blueprints, and the like.[17]

SECONDARY-SCHOOL PROGRAMS AND THE NEEDS OF YOUTH

The process of developing and implementing programs for youth in secondary schools involves several clearly defined tasks. Chief among these are: (*a*) the determination of objectives and goals that are in harmony with the age and maturity of pupils; (*b*) the selection and organization of appropriate content, activities, and experiences; (*c*) the guidance and direction of pupils in learning; and (*d*) the evaluation of the progress of pupils toward desired goals. It should be recognized, of course, that these tasks are not necessarily undertaken in the order in

---

[17] For a comprehensive analysis of the ways in which elementary and secondary schools can contribute toward national security see *The Schools and National Security*. (Edited by Charles W. Sanford, Harold C. Hand, and Willard B. Spalding. New York: McGraw-Hill Book Co., 1951.)

which they are listed. Not infrequently, for example, the evaluation of
the present status of youth may precede the determination of new objectives and goals. Moreover, it may give guidance to the selection of
content or learning activities.

The theme of this yearbook implies that secondary-school programs
should be based on the needs of youth. Let us now consider what this
approach to curriculum-building means in terms of the above-mentioned
tasks and thereby begin to indicate the scope of this yearbook.

Objectives and the Needs of Youth

Objectives or goals are generally conceived as the ends toward which
educational efforts are directed. Although the importance of objectives
has long been recognized, in school practice their relationships to actual
learning activities has often been indefinite and obscure. Not infrequently
objectives have been stated as broad generalities to which it was easy to
give lip service without perceiving clearly their significance for the guidance of learning. That is to say, the objective of good citizenship will in
all probability provide little guidance to the classroom teacher unless it
is analyzed to indicate more specifically the kinds of competencies and
behavior patterns considered desirable. However, even when objectives
have been analyzed in terms of specifics they have often failed to serve
a functional purpose because of any one or more of the following reasons:
(*a*) they may be completely inappropriate for a particular age-group of
pupils; (*b*) they may be pointed toward learning activities that have
little or no significance for pupils; (*c*) they may be chiefly academic in
character—the memorizing of facts or the learning of skills—without any
perceptible relationship to their uses; (*d*) they may be significant and
valid objectives, but textbooks or other materials used may have little
or no relationship to their attainment; (*e*) teachers may pay little or no
attention to them after they have once been stated; and (*f*) students may
not know what the objectives are.

The yearbook committee has no illusions in regard to the improvement
of educational objectives. There is no easy solution to this problem.
Nevertheless, it must be recognized as a task of paramount importance.
For unless objectives and goals are significant and valid, we may be
merely attempting to adapt youth to programs, which is obviously a
futile endeavor.

The determination of objectives on the basis of youth needs implies
that every reasonable effort will be made to discover what the needs of
youth are, both in general and in specific terms. It is believed that this is
a task that can best be performed at the local community level and in
relation to particular groups of learners. The needs of youth in one

community may differ significantly from those in another, and, as has already been suggested, differences will be found even within the same community and within the same classroom. In approaching curriculum development on this basis, the student becomes the focal point of concern. Otherwise, the subject, the content, the interests of the teacher, or some other factor may dominate the learning situation. How teachers and administrators can implement this approach is explained in the chapters that follow.

Curriculum Content, Teaching Procedures, and the Needs of Youth

Curriculum, teaching procedures, and objectives are inextricably interwoven and have meaning only as their relationships to each other and to the learning process are clearly perceived. It has been suggested that we may have more confidence in our objectives and goals if they are founded upon evidence in regard to the needs of youth. Here we wish to suggest that more effective behavior will result if the content and learning activities are in harmony with and are founded upon need-oriented objectives. The task facing the teacher and the curriculum specialist is that of making discriminative choices of the means that would appear to give the greatest assurances of enabling pupils to meet their own needs.

Brief consideration should also be given to the methods and procedures used in teaching as they are related to the task of meeting the needs of youth. Method is concerned with the *how* of teaching in contrast to the *what*. It raises the question, How can we most effectively guide and direct youth toward desirable educational goals? It involves not only the sequential order of the activities of pupils in moving toward goals but the quality of the activities as well. Here again a knowledge of the needs of youth is of basic importance to the teacher. The sympathetic and understanding teacher, for example, can do much to allay the fears and anxieties of the timid student and foster in their place feelings of security and personal significance. Through the use of appropriate procedures he can help pupils develop the abilities and skills of effective reading, problem-solving, and critical thinking, and thus assist them in satisfying their needs for self-reliance and self-direction. By carefully planned procedures he can enable students to develop enduring interests and satisfactions in reading, and thereby contribute richly to their wise use of leisure. Chapter xiii will consider more specifically ways in which learning materials and activities may be adapted to the needs of youth.

Evaluation and the Needs of Youth

Whether the term evaluation is used in reference to the over-all appraisal of secondary-school programs or in the more limited sense of its application to the measurement of learning in the classroom, it must be based upon knowledge of the needs of youth. There is abundant evidence of the widespread acceptance of this viewpoint. For example, the *Evaluative Criteria* developed through the Co-operative Study of Secondary-School Standards challenge teachers and administrators to focus their attention upon the needs of youth as a basis for determining the effectiveness of present programs and as a means of discerning needed improvements. Likewise, classroom teachers are gradually giving more attention to the appraisal of growth in terms of the needs of youth. This commendable practice is in sharp contrast to the traditional preoccupation with the testing of a narrow range of outcomes, chiefly of a factual character. In the evaluation of learning, the needs of youth, however they may be conceived, must serve as guiding criteria.

The appraisal of growth in terms of student needs is obviously a difficult task. Moreover, techniques for the evaluation of many types of needs, especially those in the realm of attitudes, appreciations, and behavior patterns, are as yet inadequately developed. That considerable progress has already been made in the development of techniques and devices for the appraisal of learning will be evident upon reading chapters iv and xiv. More effective preservice and in-service education of teachers is clearly indicated if further substantial progress is to be made in the appraisal of learning.

PLAN OF THE YEARBOOK

In the present chapter consideration has been given to the purpose of this yearbook, the broadened concept of needs, some of the factors that are challenging schools to adapt their programs more closely to the needs of pupils, and the implications of the needs approach in curriculum development. The fifteen chapters that follow have been organized under four major sections.

Section I contains five chapters which deal with basic problems involved in planning programs to meet the needs of youth. The first of these chapters might well be considered as basic to all others, for in this chapter consideration is given to the fundamental problem of how the needs of youth can be determined. Moreover, it will be of great value to teachers and curriculum workers at the local level who are confronted with the practical problem of breaking down broad categories of needs into the more specific ones that can serve as a basis for the establishment of teaching goals. Chapter iii, which is entitled "How Youth Learn To Meet Their Needs," develops the thesis that although teachers and administrators can set the stage, the actual learning (satisfying of needs) must be done by pupils themselves. Here is presented a refreshing viewpoint and one that will certainly be welcomed by teachers. Chapter iv deals with the problem of how a school can determine the extent to which needs are being met. The last two chapters of Section I will be of special interest to administrators and curriculum specialists, for they are concerned with the problems of leadership and planning.

In Section II five chapters are devoted to a consideration of the "Overall Design of Programs for Youth." Two of these chapters deal with various aspects of the problem of organizing programs to meet the common and special needs of youth. These broad areas of need are treated separately, although the writers of these chapters recognize clearly that there is no sharp demarcation between them. The last three chapters of Section II discuss various plans and procedures whereby extraclass activities, work and outdoor experiences, and guidance services can be made to contribute to the improvement of programs for youth.

Realizing the crucial role of the classroom teacher in adapting programs to the needs of students, it was decided early in the planning of the yearbook that considerable attention should be given to the problems of the classroom teacher in this regard. Although teachers will find many helpful suggestions throughout the yearbook, some of the problems which they especially have to deal with are given consideration in the first three chapters of Section III. The last chapter of the section considers the implications of the central theme of the yearbook for the education of teachers.

Section IV, entitled "Secondary Schools and the Future," contains the closing chapter. In it the reader will find a challenging description of the kinds of features and characteristics secondary schools will have when forthright efforts are made to adapt programs to the needs of youth.

BASIC CONSIDERATIONS INVOLVED IN PLANNING SCHOOL PROGRAM

CHAPTER II

DETERMINING THE NATURE OF THE NEEDS OF YOUTH

CAMILLA M. LOW

Professor of Education
University of Wisconsin
Madison, Wisconsin

INTRODUCTION

Problems Needing Clarification

Perhaps because the term "needs" is used in common English parlance without precise definition, professional educators have sometimes tended to employ it loosely with respect to curriculum. Just as glibly as the father says, "Bob needs a whipping" or the wife says, "I need a fur coat," so do many school people say, "Bob needs English" or "All students need algebra." The tendency to proceed upon such assertions to a course of action without checking the assumptions against valid criteria has led to a superficial, if not fallacious, approach to curriculum building and need-meeting. Under pressure of a busy life, many of us have tended to short-cut the logical line of analysis for determining needs by jumping in somewhere along the route with assertions which may be difficult to substantiate and have then used these untested generalizations as accepted premises.

Even though the foregoing difficulties can be ironed out as we become more precise in our definition of needs and more certain of their validity, teachers face other problems. Many have a sense of frustration as they attempt to break down a broadly stated area of need, such as "the need to make a living," into sufficiently specific needs to afford translation into actual classroom learning experiences. There is a long way to go in the process of analysis before a general need fans out into an array of contributory needs which have meaningful relationship to the lives of the boys and girls in question. As this fanning-out process takes place from several foci representing different areas of need, the resulting overlapping often presents a baffling problem to those responsible for guiding learning.

Purpose of This Chapter

The purpose of the present chapter is to set forth a defensible and usable concept of need for curriculum-building purposes and to suggest valid procedures for identifying the needs of high-school youth. No attempt will be made to present a full complement of such needs within the confines of a single chapter. Only a few illustrations can be included. The analysis aims to provide an acceptable rationale which may serve teachers and other curriculum-planners as a starting point for solving the more practical problems of curriculum building.

Assumptions

In any reasoned treatment of the nature of needs as they apply to curriculum building, it is necessary to make a clear statement of the important assumptions. Only in terms of their acceptance will the remainder of the discussion appear valid.

1. *The purpose of public education in this country is to induct the young into the American democratic culture within the ideological framework of that culture.*

Teachers have an unequivocal mandate not only to familiarize growing boys and girls with the social, political, and economic institutions characteristic of American democracy but to incline them to an acceptance of the ideals and values basic to these institutions. Only thus can there be sufficient identity of purpose and strength of loyalty to assure political and cultural survival. In the face of a shrinking world with heightened conflicts between opposing ideologies, there is no lack of evidence of the pressing nature of this social responsibility.

2. *Any problem the individual must solve in order to become more effective in furthering democratic ends constitutes a need for him regardless of whether he is now aware of this need or must be helped progressively to become aware of it.*

This assumption follows logically from the first. We are on firm ground in saying that the individual's needs include development of the habits and attitudes, the knowledge and skills, the values and ideals which help him become a supporting and useful member of the democratic community. He may be fully aware of some of these needs and already motivated to gain the experiences appropriate to meet them. If, however, there are some of which he is unaware or which he rejects, the obligation rests upon those who guide his growth to create the necessary awareness and acceptance.

3. *Since American democratic ideology embraces the belief that the individual is of supreme worth and the further belief that the preservation and improvement of society depend upon the full utilization of his potentialities,*

the methods employed for inducting him into the culture must neither deny his basic feelings of need nor be limited by his present feelings of need.

Fortunately, we are enabled, by the very nature of democracy, to avoid falling into the dilemma of failing to consider individual needs in the service of the group, or group needs in the service of the individual. It is through self-fulfilment that we believe the highest social aims can be achieved, and we, therefore, believe that there should be provided the largest possible measure of opportunity to develop the interests and talents of the individual and to give him feelings of personal satisfaction in the social role he is expected to play. That his activities may be channeled in a variety of ways, some more significant and in terms of higher purposes than others, we appreciate. The obligation again rests with teachers to encourage the boy and the girl to explore areas of activity which challenge the best that is in them and, thus, to foster the creation of new feelings of need on successively higher levels of maturity.

The Nature of Needs
Sources of Motivation for Need-meeting

On the basis of the foregoing assumptions we can examine more closely the nature of needs. First of all, it is quite apparent that there are two sources of motivation for need-meeting. One source lies within the individual, the other is external to him. Within the individual, the basic drives of self-preservation and the maintenance of personal integrity demand the satisfaction of very important needs. The needs for food and shelter, for love and friendship, and for successful achievement stem from this inner source. Such needs appear to be universal without respect to the type of culture or the special circumstances under which the individual may live.

A second and distinct source of motivation for need-meeting is the particular culture of which the individual is a part. He derives much of his motivation from the "outside" pressures exerted upon him. As stated in the assumptions, the survival of our American way of life and the continued application in human relationships of the beliefs upon which it was founded demand that every boy and girl gain an understanding of the social realities and develop skill in accepting a constructive role in the maintenance and improvement of group life. He must, of course, internalize these demands—"accept" them as his needs—in order to gain motivation for their realization.

Interaction of the Individual and Society

These two sources of motivation for need-meeting—that within the individual and that external to him—are clearly distinguishable but, unfortunately for any simple analysis, the needs themselves do not fit neatly into one or the other of these categories. Instead, they reflect the inseparable relationship between the individual and his environment. For example, while the individual is possessed of a strong feeling of need for food, society, in terms of its cultural preferences, imposes upon him the kinds of food he is expected to eat as well as the forms in which they are served. While there is an inner demand for the satisfaction of sexual urges, a given culture imposes its own restrictions and taboos which influence the ways in which such satisfaction can be gained. While the individual strives to be thought well of by his group, he cannot achieve the goal except through behavior which conforms to standards accepted by the group.

It is reasonable, therefore, to consider needs as an expression of the interaction between the individual-with-his-feelings-of-need and society-with-its-imposition-of-tasks. Society prescribes the special route or routes the individual must follow in order to achieve the satisfaction he desires. The individual is decidedly not a free agent. If he steps over the "cultural traces" to meet one goal, he diminishes his chances to gain another goal just as important. In our culture, for example, if he steals the food he eats or bathes naked in the public pool, while he may be satisfying certain of his physical needs, in all likelihood he will, in the process, find himself a social outcast and thereby forfeit his sense of belonging. The cultural "thou shalts" by which one gains social approval hold the individual rigorously in line. They insist that while he strives to satisfy a personal need he must employ behavior which likewise satisfies social requirements.

The Dynamic Nature of Needs

In understanding the needs of high-school youth, not only must we be aware of the interaction between the individual and his environment but we must also appreciate the dynamic nature of each. The individual grows and changes with consequent changes in his pattern of needs. At ten he may need membership in a one-sex gang and gain recognition through his role in group exploits. At fourteen his social life may no longer be adequate merely in the company of other boisterous boys. He begins to need friendship and acceptance by members of both sexes. By eighteen he may need a more permanent and intimate relationship with one member of the opposite sex in addition to the casual heterosexual contacts which fully satisfied him at a younger age.

Not only does the individual change as he grows and, therefore, exhibit new patterns of need but he changes as a result of shifts in fortune. If a high-school youth moves from a community where he is known and liked and has established a place for himself to one where he must start from scratch to gain acceptance, he will do many things which would not have aroused him to activity except for his present feelings of need. At this point his surroundings rather than his growth are primarily responsible for changes in his motivation.

A dramatic illustration in point is the manner in which group life in this country rapidly changes in response to international crises which call for extraordinary measures to safeguard national security. Every high-school Senior, for example, becomes the object of new and pressing demands which find their source in a changed social situation. In facing the prospect of active service in the armed forces and the imminent substitution of army life for family life, inner tensions develop which require the satisfaction of needs not conceived as probabilities even a short time previous. Similarly, adjustments in industry, in employment, in consumer habits, and in scores of other aspects of the culture in conformity to wartime economy present to high-school boys and girls, as well as to other elements in our population, new needs and new tasks.

While, as we have just noted, the particular environmental pattern influences the individual and creates in him a demand for the satisfaction of certain needs, we should not forget that group life itself goes through a continual process of alteration through the impact of individuals upon it. Thus, the changes resulting from such interaction preclude a static pattern of needs.

Needs Range from Universal to Unique

Mention has been made in preceding paragraphs of certain needs that are universal. Actually, needs represent varying degrees of commonality. For example, the individual appears to hold in common with all humanity the needs for food, affection, and self-esteem. They are no respecter of persons or of cultural groups. A member of the Bali tribe is just as strongly motivated as a resident of Boston or Seattle to gain these ends. At six or sixty with white or colored, rich or poor, the same personality needs serve to induce behavior responses.

There are, however, needs which the individual holds in common with groups representing varying lesser degrees and kinds of homogeneity, such as his sex group, his age group, his community, and his family. High-school boys as a sex group hold certain needs in common which differ from those of high-school girls. These dissimilarities relate both to differences in anatomical structure and function and to the cultural role each is expected to play. For example, adolescent boys, as a group, appear to enjoy and need opportunity to develop certain physical skills of a different order from those suited to adolescent girls. Not only do unlike cultural expectations account for this but so do structural differences, such as the sex difference in the angle at which the thigh bone is attached to the pelvis.

On the other hand, young people of both sexes at a similar level of development have certain common needs different from those at younger or older ages. Youth of high-school age need a degree and kind of independence from home control that they did not require prior to adolescence, for example.

Similarly, all members of a given community or, more intimately, of a given family, may be presented with common problems growing out of a combination of special economic, political, religious, ethnic, or other circumstances and thus experience common needs.

Finally, there are needs even within the smallest and most closely related group that are peculiar to the individual. Although he holds needs in common with groups of varying sizes and degrees of universality, he is still a unique personality reflecting needs which relate to his special combination of physical, social, and intellectual strengths and weaknesses and which grow out of a lifetime of responses to a unique constellation of environmental pressures.

Interrelationship of Needs

Another factor which must be considered in order to understand the nature of needs is their relationship within the matrix of a given personality. Needs are not discrete but are so intricately patterned that they cannot be singled out and met separately. Even the fundamental personality needs do not stay put in neat pigeonholes. The individual who has little sense of personal achievement and questions his own worth is at a disadvantage in making himself acceptable to others and, hence, in gaining a feeling of belonging. Conversely, an individual who is rejected by the group finds it difficult to experience a sense of self-esteem. Frustration in attempting to gain either or both of the above objectives may, in turn, have certain psychosomatic repercussions which interfere with the satisfaction of physical needs.

Not only are constellations of interrelated needs present at any given time in the life of an individual but there appears to be a kind of chain reaction throughout the life span of need-meeting and need-arousing activity. The tired man needs rest and retires early. Waking in the morning refreshed and full of energy, he now needs work to do. What he is then able to accomplish provides him with such a feeling of achievement that he sets himself higher goals which call for still other need-meeting experiences. And so it goes, ad infinitum.

The Hierarchical Arrangement of Needs

Needs also arrange themselves in hierarchies—one general need demanding the satisfaction of many subsidiary or contributory needs on different levels of particularism. Take, for example, the need for a feeling of membership in a group. This calls first for official membership in one or more particular groups, such as a gang, a club, or a homeroom. For admission to the group and, more important, for psychological acceptance by the group, the individual need to exhibit and, hence, to learn certain behavior. Thus contributing to the more general need may be such needs as the need for bodily cleanliness, the need for acceptable and attractive dress, the need for courteous and considerate behavior, the need to co-operate and share, the need to respect differences in others, and the need for a skill, a talent, or other asset which he can contribute to the group.

Each one of these needs, in turn, requires the satisfaction of needs still more specific, to the point where they finally become unique to a given individual. Illustrative is the need to dress acceptably and attractively. For some students on the secondary-school level this might well involve an understanding of style and color in relation to one's own body build and of the type of dress appropriate for various occasions. It might also mean that a given group of teen-agers need to learn how to get the best value for their consumer dollar in purchasing ready-to-wear clothing.

Thus, in the process of breaking down a need into the chain of needs which relate to it, we ultimately find needs which are so specific for the individual concerned that there is no difficulty in finding the appropriate learning experiences for him. The need itself is identified so closely with the experience that it virtually becomes the experience.

Use of These Concepts by Teachers and Curriculum Workers

The foregoing analysis is of value if it provides some clarification of the problems involved in need-meeting on the high-school level. Of course, the school is not the only need-meeting agency. Clear understanding of the nature of needs is as important to parents, social workers, and religious leaders as it is to teachers. We are interested here, however, only in tracing out for the school the implications of the foregoing concepts. We shall do this in regard to only the major implications.

In the first place, recognition of the dual nature of need-meeting guards against oversimplification. In planning the curriculum and in guiding learning it is necessary to help each individual satisfy his inner needs through experiences which concurrently satisfy social requirements.

The two are not necessarily antithetical. There must be sensitive awareness, nevertheless, that individuals differ in their tolerance to crisis and change and in the limits of their plasticity and growth and that what may reasonably be required of one individual by society may be quite unreasonable for another. Aware of these differentials, the teacher can give consideration to the problem of achieving an appropriate balance for each individual between the social adjustments which must be made in his behalf and the personal adjustments which he must make in society's behalf.

In the second place, a problem involving so many dynamic factors must always be in the process of being solved. While it may be disconcerting to be unable to determine the needs of youth once and for all, it is nevertheless important to appreciate that, though the substratum of basic needs is relatively stable, the contributory needs represent a kaleidoscopic pattern. Anyone seriously interested in providing high-school youth with learning experiences to meet their needs has the difficult responsibility for engaging in a continuing study both of the changing individual and the shifting cultural milieu in which he lives. He must see to it that the school curriculum, no matter how functional it may be at any given time, is never allowed to freeze.

In the third place, the intricate patterning of needs with its cross-currents of influence means that a given learning experience serves a multiple purpose which may, on the one hand, be wholesome in its entirety or, on the other, deny some needs in the service of others. In order that the total effect of a learning experience may be constructive in the life of the individual, its selection must be made with some understanding on the part of the teacher of the constellation of needs the boy or girl faces in his own life and of the relationships which appear to exist among these needs. A fortuitous approach to the selection of learning experiences denies their maximum use for need-meeting purposes, if it does not actually create more problems than it solves.

Finally, the foregoing concept of needs indicates that there is a sufficiently large common denominator of needs of adolescent youth to warrant considerable preplanning. In spite of the fluctuating features in the situation, the teacher does not have to rely primarily on improvisation in the selection of learning experiences. Research findings are available which enable him to anticipate with a fair degree of accuracy the nature and range of individual differences among a typical group of high-school youth. On the basis of this knowledge he can construct in broad outline, at least, a curriculum appropriate to meet these needs. What we know of the nature of needs, therefore, seems to justify at least three stages in planning:

1. Planning in terms of the common needs of youth of like developmental level, in a culture of like social requirements.
2. Planning with respect to a particular group of high-school youth in a particular community and school setting.
3. Planning with respect to a unique individual as a member of a unique family, neighborhood, and peer group.

Guidelines for determining needs for use in planning on each of these levels constitute the remainder of this chapter.

IDENTIFYING THE NEEDS OF YOUTH

Procedures for Identifying the Common Needs of Youth

Any significant long-range planning for secondary-school youth must proceed from an acceptable formulation of the common needs of youth.

A need assumes a present deficiency and anticipates a future change in the direction of a desired goal. It is something that must be satisfied in order to move from "here" to "there." Therefore, the first step in determining the common needs of youth is to know where adolescent boys and girls now are and where they either desire or are expected to go. In other words, it is important, first, to be clear on the present status of youth in terms of their level of growth and typical behavior and on the direction of desired individual development. It is likewise essential that we understand the present status of society and the goals representing social betterment. In both cases needs can then be identified which help to close the gap between present status and anticipated goal.

The Individual as the Genesis of an Analysis of Needs. High-school youth are at a level of development considerably short of maturity. They, therefore, have some distance to travel to achieve adulthood. A clear picture of just how far along the road they are can be gained from the so-called normative studies of adolescence. These tell us the range of individual differences, with respect to a large number of aspects of growth and behavior, which we can expect to find in a typical group of teen-age boys and girls. One of the valuable sources of such information is an earlier yearbook of this Society entitled: *Adolescence.*[1] Here are presented the findings of such important research as the California Studies of Adolescence, the Iowa Studies of Child Development, and the study of adolescents conducted under the auspices of the Progressive Education Association.

Other significant longitudinal studies, such as the Harvard Growth Studies,[2] have been reported. These studies describe in considerable de-

---

[1] *Adolescence.* Forty-third Yearbook of the National Society for the Study of Education, Part I. Chicago: University of Chicago Press, 1944.

[2] Walter F. Dearborn and John W. M. Rothney, *Predicting the Child's Development.* Cambridge, Massachusetts: Sci-Art Publishers, 1941.

tail various aspects of the physical, social, and intellectual growth of teen-agers and the psychological problems they face. For example, the typical adolescent is experiencing such physiological changes as rapid growth in height and weight, changes in body contour, rapid growth in organs of digestion and respiration, the appearance and growth of primary and secondary sex characteristics. For many, these changes are precipitous, bringing bewilderment and feelings of inadequacy. Individual differences in developmental status are very wide during high-school years and constitute a special problem for early and late maturers who want, above all, to be like their peers.

Socially this is a period when young people are struggling to break home ties and to exercise freedom in the choice of their friends. They are attempting, especially, to establish satisfying relations with the opposite sex. The ambivalent feelings which the adolescent often experiences as he thus grows socially reflect important needs.

Intellectually, adolescents are better able to think, reason, judge, and generalize than they were at younger ages. Their interests are expanding and maturing rapidly. They are capable of thinking about and dealing with appropriate aspects of the major problems which confront adults: problems of marriage and parenthood, employment, community welfare, and citizenship. They can pursue their interests with greater persistence and concentrate more efficiently than they did at younger ages on projects which they deem worth while.

When appropriately organized, these and many other such findings tell us where the adolescent is in terms of his level of maturation and of his behavioral reactions to cultural pressures.

It now becomes important to describe the individual that society hopes the adolescent will become. A number of such descriptions have been developed. The Educational Policies Commission several years ago, for example, subsumed the characteristics of an educated person under four major headings: self-realization, human relationships, economic efficiency, and civic responsibility.[3] Many state and local groups have attempted to set down the competencies that the school should strive to develop in its students.[4] Such descriptions, while usually presenting a "vision of possibilities" transcending the combination of qualities universally possessed by adult members of society, serve to define an endpoint for individual striving.

---

[3] *The Purposes of Education in American Democracy*, pp. 39–123. Prepared by the Educational Policies Commission. Washington: National Education Association, 1938.

[4] J. Paul Leonard and Alvin C. Eurich, *An Evaluation of Modern Education*, pp. 1–25. New York: D. Appleton–Century Co., 1943.

The objective thus established, the needs which adolescents experience can be identified as growing out of the disjunction between the behavior characteristic of their present immaturities and the behavior which society encourages them to exhibit. While a complete analysis of the common needs of youth goes far beyond what is possible in the present chapter, an illustration may help to make clear the procedure.

Characteristic of the typical adolescent is his almost slavish conformity to standards of the peer group. It is a matter of prime importance that adolescents dress alike, follow the same hair styles, use the same slang, rave about the same TV shows as others in the group with whom they wish to be identified. Even social behavior which is condemned by adults may be wholly acceptable to teen-agers if it is approved by the peer group. Fear of being called "chicken," for example, may prompt delinquent behavior if it seems the only means by which the adolescent can be assured recognition by his group. Adolescence is also a period in which differences in race, creed, financial and social status, and even slight discrepancies in physical characteristics may interfere with the individual's feelings of worth. There is nothing quite so disturbing as feeling different.

Such behavior, reflecting immature values and lack of self-confidence, is in contrast to behavior we wish to encourage. The mature individual distinguishes between reasonable conformity to accepted standards of behavior and taste and blind conformity where independent action is warranted. He realizes there are many superficial ways in which an individual may deviate from the group without forfeiting group membership. He has the courage of his convictions when it comes to important matters of right and wrong. He has sufficient self-understanding and self-esteem to accept his personal limitations without undue worry of their effect upon his status. He recognizes the need for all people to feel a sense of membership in the group and strives to give those with whom he associates a feeling of belonging.

To equip the adolescent to move toward this desired goal, certain needs now become clear. The adolescent needs to find opportunities in the school to "feel" like others in his age group, to gain reasonable success in his school work, and to participate in school activities on an equal basis with others. He needs to develop the skills and standards of behavior requisite for group acceptance: ease in conversation, cleanliness and good grooming, reliability, skill in dancing and playing active sports, etc. He needs to understand and accept differences both in himself and in others. He needs to discover and develop his assets to offset physical or other handicaps. He needs to receive understanding guidance if he is using unwise methods to gain approval, such as "buying" acceptance and show-off or antisocial behavior. He needs to be sensitive to the feelings of others who have difficulty because of social, financial, or physical disadvantage. He needs to learn to take a stand on important issues rather than being unduly swayed by group pressures.

Determining how to meet such relatively broad needs as those stated above necessitates their translation into many specific learning experiences and their allocation to appropriate subject areas. Such an analysis, if performed for every important growth characteristic of normal youth, would take much of the guess work out of a needs formulation by anchoring needs solidly to defined criteria. This time-consuming preliminary step in program planning should not, however, engage the efforts of every curriculum committee. Indeed, some useful analyses are already available in published form.[5]

Society as the Genesis of an Analysis of Needs. A second approach which is useful in identifying the needs of youth is to begin with an analysis of the American scene today—the respects in which society is functioning or failing to function in harmony with the democratic values and ideals we espouse. Just as a description of the typical adolescent tells us the level of maturity which he has already achieved and establishes the point from which he must make progress, so a description of the present state of affairs, so far as our social arrangements are concerned, tells us how far we have already progressed as a group in achieving satisfactory conditions for community living and, thus, where we begin in order to effect social improvement. Such a description of social reality when contrasted with a description of hoped-for social arrangements indicates, as did the preceding analysis, the distance which must be traveled to achieve community goals and thus aids in locating important needs of the individual. As stated in the initial assumptions (pp. 23–24), the individual must be the active agent for perpetuating the durable features of our cultural heritage and, at the same time, for improving group living through behavior which harmonizes with our democratic beliefs and values. His needs, then, would involve acquisition of skills, knowledge, attitudes, habits, and ways of behaving which would move us toward our community goals.

There are various organizing schemes which might be employed to establish this social contrast. Hand, for example, lists nine major social functions of an organized democratic state which may be used as a frame

---

[5] *Guides to Curriculum Building: Junior High School Level*, pp. 13–73. Madison, Wisconsin: State Department of Public Instruction, 1950. A detailed analysis of adolescent characteristics and the needs derived therefrom is presented in chart form.

of reference from which to derive the needs of youth. They are stated as social objectives, as follows:

To keep the population healthy
To provide physical protection and guarantees against war
To conserve and wisely utilize natural resources
To provide opportunity for people to make a living
To rear and educate the young
To provide wholesome and adequate recreation
To enable the population to realize aesthetic and spiritual values
To provide a sufficient body of commonly held beliefs and aspirations to guarantee social integration
To organize and govern in harmony with beliefs and aspirations[6]

A similar classification was derived by Frederick from thirty different listings of "areas of activity."

Protecting life and health
Living in and improving the home
Conserving and improving material conditions
Co-operating in social and civic action
Getting a living
Securing an education
Expressing religious impulses
Engaging in recreation[7]

In the case of each function or area it is possible to describe the social situation as it now exists and the characteristics of a society in which the objective is more adequately achieved.

Take, for example, certain features of our society as they relate to the field of recreation. Technological advance has served to increase leisure time. Concurrently, greater specialization has resulted in increased routinization and monotony which must be offset by varied and stimulating activities during nonworking hours. There is abundant evidence, however, that many individuals fail to find satisfaction in their leisure hours. The extreme appeals of radio, television, the motion pictures, and other commercialized amusements tend to exhaust and debilitate rather than recreate and invigorate. Alcoholism, delinquency and crime, nervous disorders, and traffic accidents are often evidence of misdirected energies in leisure time.

In contrast is the situation representing our social objectives. It is desirable that communities and neighborhoods accept responsibility for

---

[6] Harold C. Hand, "The Case for the Common Learnings Course," *Science Education*, XXXII (February, 1948), 5–11.

[7] O. I. Frederick and L. J. Farquear, "Areas of Human Activity," *Journal of Educational Research*, XXX (May, 1937), 672–79.

making adequate provision for the wholesome use of leisure; that they support well-balanced, nondiscriminatory and intelligently co-ordinated programs of both public and private recreation to appeal to individuals of widely varying interests and talents. An enlightened community, likewise, registers its demands that commercial amusements comply with acceptable standards of taste and of good physical and emotional health. It is alert to protect its citizens through law and the pressure of public opinion from undesirable influences which undermine and cheapen character. Citizens of an enlightened community plan their leisure hours as carefully as they do other aspects of their lives. They seek a healthful balance among creative, appreciational, social, physical, and spectator activities. They have developed acceptable standards of taste in terms of which they make intelligent choices among the commercial amusements competing for their time.

In order that the maturing adolescent may direct his efforts most effectively toward meeting the desired goal, he needs to gain some understanding of why the use of leisure time constitutes a social problem for the American people and of the kinds of responsibilities which communities must assume and pay for in this area. He needs to understand his role as a present and future citizen in participating in and providing for the recreational life of the community. He needs to become familiar with the range of leisure-time activities and to participate on an exploratory basis in a variety of recreational pursuits where he will experience feelings of achievement and satisfaction. The adolescent also needs to engage, under wise guidance, in setting up standards for the selection of movies, radio programs, television shows, and other commercial amusements and to gain many experiences in evaluating and in choice-making in terms of these standards. He needs to be encouraged to accept increasing responsibility for examining his own recreational activities and for thinking about whether they are wisely chosen and properly balanced.

This is merely the beginning of a complete analysis of the function of providing wholesome and adequate recreation and of the needs of the adolescent derived therefrom. If learning experiences were now identified to help the adolescent meet such general needs as those noted above, the contributions of various subject-matter areas—English, the social studies, science, mathematics, physical education, art, and music— would become quite clear.

If each of the social functions were exhaustively analyzed, the resulting curriculum would certainly not be lacking in content! A wide variety of needs would clearly and validly be identified. Fortunately, as with the needs derived from growth characteristics, such analyses can be performed by a central group and used by local groups. Reference should again be made to *Guides to Curriculum Building: Junior High School Level*, where needs derived from cultural characteristics have been identified in considerable detail.[8]

The Relationship between the Individual and the Social Approaches. In identifying the common needs of youth, it is important to consider both those that are derived from the growth characteristics of the typical individual of high-school age and those which stem from cultural factors. It is not an either-or proposition as some of the earlier schools of curriculum-thought would give us to understand.

If both of the foregoing illustrations of the derivation of needs were developed completely, there would occur considerable overlapping and repetition of needs. Actually one type of analysis serves partially as a check on the other and focuses attention upon certain needs which stand out "any way you look at it." It is not hard to understand the reasons for such similarity in the needs resulting from the two approaches.

In the analysis on page 32 it is impossible to describe the growth characteristics and behavior of the typical adolescent except in cultural terms. If we were describing a typical Icelandic teen-ager, the behavior norms would be quite different and the resulting description unrecognizable as an adolescent in our society. Similarly, in presenting our concept of the mature adult, it mirrors our cultural values and standards— what we consider "good" and "wholesome" in terms of our way of life. Finally, the derived needs likewise reflect tacit acceptance of a cultural setting. We say in the foregoing illustration that the adolescent needs to receive understanding guidance if he is using antisocial methods to gain approval. Yet, antisocial behavior means different things to different culture groups. We frown, for example, upon such behavior as lying. But the anthropologist, Herbert Passin, reports that the Tarahumara, a Mexican Indian tribe, systematically practices lying and other forms of deceit, especially as they relate to the denial of economic goods.[9]

Referring again to the same illustration, we say that the adolescent needs to develop the skills and standards of behavior accepted by the group: "ease in conversation, standards of cleanliness and grooming, skill in dancing and playing active sports." We know when we state this need that it does *not* include such things as dancing the hula-hula, becoming skilful in javelin-throwing, or wearing a nose-ring. Actually therefore, as already discussed earlier in this chapter, there is no such

---

[8] *Guides to Curriculum Building, op. cit.*, pp. 74–131.

[9] Herbert Passin, "Tarahumara Prevarication: A Problem in Field Method," *American Anthropologist*, XLIV (1942), 235–47.

thing as viewing the individual and assessing his growth status and his consequent needs apart from the cultural milieu.

In the second analysis (p. 34), wherein needs are identified as they relate to the characteristics of group life, they are, at the same time, selected against a background of understanding of what the typical adolescent finds interest in and is capable of achieving at this developmental level. If we were identifying the needs of the seven-year-old instead of the seventeen-year-old as they relate to the problem of leisure time, we would certainly not include the need "to gain some understanding of why the use of leisure constitutes a social problem for the American people." It is only because we feel reasonably sure from the normative studies of adolescents that these boys and girls have the background of experience, the intellectual development, and the requisite interest in community life, that such a need is included.

Thus we can see that each approach accepts, in its frame of reference, basic features of the other.

Classifying Common Needs. In the practical job of school organization and initial curriculum planning to meet the common needs of youth, needs determined in the manner indicated above may prove unwieldy to handle. Teachers and supervisors may, therefore, wish to employ some classification scheme for the hundreds of needs identified.

Havighurst suggests nine developmental tasks of adolescence which might be used as centers of interest for curriculum planning:

Accepting one's physique and accepting a masculine or feminine role
New relations with age-mates of both sexes
Emotional independence of parents and other adults
Achieving assurance of economic independence
Selecting and preparing for an occupation
Developing intellectual skills and concepts necessary for civic competence
Desiring and achieving socially responsible behavior
Preparing for marriage and family life
Building conscious values in harmony with an adequate scientific world picture[10]

The Illinois Secondary-School Curriculum Program has utilized an eight-fold classification as follows:

Earning a living
Developing an effective personality
Living healthfully and safely
Managing personal finances wisely
Spending leisure time wholesomely and enjoyably
Taking an effective part in civic affairs

[10] Robert Havighurst, *Developmental Tasks and Education*, pp. 30–55. Chicago: University of Chicago Press, 1948.

Preparing for marriage, homemaking, and parenthood
Making effective use of educational opportunities[11]

Some of these large areas of adolescent concern resemble the major social functions used on page 34 as the organizational framework for one of the suggested needs derivations.

Another even simpler classification will be used in a later chapter in this yearbook as a basis for ascertaining whether youth needs are now being met and what characteristics a secondary school should possess in order to meet youth needs. This fourfold classification is as follows:

Physical and mental health and fitness
Life work and economic literacy
Leisure interests and standards
Citizenship and group living

There are many other such problem centers which have been developed during recent years, all of which are helpful for certain phases of planning and appraisal but which cannot be substituted at other steps in planning for the more detailed analyses pointing up many specific needs which are readily translated into equally specific learning experiences. Moreover, the question often raised by teachers concerning what content goes into the curriculum dealing with such a needs area as "Life work and economic literacy," for example, can be adequately answered only in very specific terms. In such terms only, which reveal the richness and scope of the curriculum, can we also satisfy those who doubt that a curriculum based on needs has real substance.

Procedures for Identifying the Needs of a Particular Group of High-School Youth

The typical needs of youth provide a sound starting point for establishing curriculum content. As previously stated, such needs are identified in terms of a range of anticipated individual differences lying within the limits of normality and a similar range of differing local environmental settings.

The needs of adolescents who attend a given school or a given class in a given community setting can be identified within narrower limits. And it is at this point that a local group must accept the responsibility for identifying the needs of its own high-school youth.

The intellectual, physical, and social-growth characteristics of adolescents in a given school will be expected to fit the pattern in most respects of what is typical of a more universal population. However, at the local level the group may be more, or it may be less, homogeneous with respect

---

[11] Harold C. Hand, *Problems of High-School Youth.* Springfield, Illinois: Department of Public Instruction, 1949.

to certain group characteristics. Moreover, whatever the case may be regarding typical growth and behavior, it is necessary to discover the incidence of atypical characteristics if the needs of all boys and girls are to be adequately met.

For example, in a certain eastern suburban community the mean intelligence quotient of youth attending the public high school is 120. Certain needs of this group, therefore, as they relate to level of mental maturity and intellectual interests, are different from those of a typical group. The reverse of this situation might well obtain in other communities to the point where selected groups of mentally retarded boys and girls exhibit needs which call for special classes and specially trained teachers.

In similar fashion, a local study may serve to identify groups within the larger group whose physical or social disabilities (or exceptionally superior abilities) result in needs considerably different from those of the generality. To meet these needs, planning for special school services may well be involved.

Just as it is impossible to identify the needs of typical adolescents, except as we consider the impingement upon them of similarly typical characteristics of our American democratic culture, so it is impossible to study a local group of high-school youth apart from its community setting. The physical features of the community, the degree of concentration of the population, the percentage of home ownership, the ways in which the people earn their living, the level of income, the characteristics of the population with respect to racial and ethnic background, the stability of the family unit, and the place of religion in community life are some of the potent factors which influence the adolescent and, thus, serve to define his needs.

It may now be seen from the foregoing discussion that the identification of the needs of a given group of high-school boys and girls employs the same general procedures used to determine the common needs of youth. In fact the goals, as illustrated on pages 32 and 34, remain unchanged for the local study. They continue as the end-points toward which we want to help every boy and girl grow, regardless of the community in which he lives or his present growth status. The description of the local group of teen-agers, however, as well as the description of the cultural characteristics of the local community, would differ in conformity to the realities of Elmtown or Centerville or Middletown. Hence, the needs, representing, as they do, the distance this particular group of adolescents must travel to gain the desired goals, would be different in certain respects from those typical of a more universal population.

A much more specific discussion of what is involved in making appropriate school and community studies is presented in chapter iv which suggests techniques for appraising the degree to which youth needs are now being met.

Procedures for Identifying the
Needs of the Individual

It is fortunate for those who plan school buildings, purchase equipment, set up time schedules, develop resource units, and train prospective teachers that high-school boys and girls are similar in so many respects that their differences are somewhat predictable. It is only because a great deal of planning for a needs-centered school can go on prior to acquaintanceship with individual boys and girls that the school is ready for their entrance on September 2 or that a yearbook of this kind serves any purpose.

But a rigidly structured curriculum, built wholly in terms of anticipated needs, would fall far short of its objective. It is a truism to say that each boy and girl exhibits his own unique combination of characteristics and that special features of his environment operate uniquely upon him. Yet, in school practice we persist in falling far short of what such uniqueness implies.

Much of the responsibility for discovering the needs of the individual rests with the classroom teachers. Fortunately, each one of them does not have to start from scratch. There is opportunity for a good deal of pooling of information about individual pupils if the lines of communication are open and an adequate record moves along with the pupil from his early elementary-school years. Specialists, such as school social workers, psychometrists, and counselors can also help in the identification of needs, though at present very few schools have adequate services of this kind. Even with such services, however, a good share of the responsibility for understanding each boy and girl will always remain with the classroom teacher.

Observing the Individual. As a first step in studying a given pupil the teacher notes how he responds to a variety of situations and how these responses differ from those of other adolescents in the group. Whom does the boy or girl choose for friends? What role does he play in the peer group? How does he meet success and failure? How sensitive is he to the feelings of others? What, if any, nervous mannerisms does he exhibit? How much physical stamina does he display? How wisely does he expend physical energy? How well co-ordinated is he? For what kinds of activities does he display enthusiastic interest? How well does he read? What study and work habits has he developed? These are only a few of the questions which a good teacher seeks to answer in order to assess various aspects of the pupil's development.

To set up reasonable hypotheses from such observations necessitates viewing the boy or girl in a variety of settings. Often the most significant data are gathered in settings which are least prescriptive and in which responses are relatively uninhibited. Certainly, the observational data needed in assessing individual needs takes the teacher beyond his classroom.

Through such observations the teacher builds a partial picture of the adolescent's personality, compounded of what appear to be the durable and persistent features of his behavior. With such a picture of growth status the teacher can draw certain contrasts and arrive at certain tentative generalizations. He can judge in what respects the pupil is considerably different from or reasonably similar to his classmates and contemplate what these facts may mean regarding the present satisfaction of his basic needs for security, belonging, and self-esteem. He may judge how distant is the ultimate goal—how far the pupil has to go to be able eventually to function as a mature adult and to become an acceptable and contributing member of adult society. From these implications the teacher can gain a very general idea of the magnitude of the task of guiding the pupil's growth.

Searching for Causes. But knowledge of this disparity between "what is" and "what is hoped for" is not enough. It is only as the teacher gains some insight into the *reasons* for the pupil's behavior that he can understand the specific combination of factors which may be hindering him or helping him and know how far it is reasonable to expect that he can grow and change. The slow reader, for example, needs to "speed up." But the prior needs which must be met to facilitate improvement in reading relate to the causes of his difficulty. These causes also hold the key to determining how much improvement can reasonably be anticipated. As we study the individual, therefore, we adjust our general goal, set up for adolescents as a group, to harmonize with what we know about the special assets and liabilities of this particular adolescent. The group norm becomes relatively unimportant for him; and the group objective may represent an ideal toward which we can expect him to travel only part way.

Thus, only as such specific needs as relate to the *causes* of behavior are identified, can the school and the teacher realistically provide learning experiences to help the individual pupil solve his problems and make best use of what he has.

In his search for causes of the behavior and growth characteristics of a given individual, the teacher is led to an examination of the pupil's present environment and to a study of his developmental history. For example, the individual's daily regimen during nonschool hours—recreational pursuits, hours of sleep, regularity and adequacy of meals, hours involved in part-time employment, etc., will influence his behavior. Interpersonal relations within the family, especially the evidences of affection or rejection which the parents have for him, are extremely important in assessing his basic security. Characteristics which may bear a causal relationship to his social adjustment (race, religion, economic status, physical disability, language spoken or folkways practiced in the home, etc.) shed light on the degree to which he feels accepted. A study of the neighborhood to discover where and how he spends his spare time may reveal special problems of social adjustment or special interests and talents. In brief, the environment he lives in, with its principal ramifications, needs investigation to discover both the hazards and the constructive and supporting influences which affect his present adjustment and which indicate his present needs.

With this broad two-dimensional picture it is now important to give it perspective by pushing back to previous history. Individuals differ in rate of maturing and in the "ups" and "downs" in their patterns of growth. These show up only in longitudinal records of individual boys and girls. Moreover, experiences over the years often show revealing consistencies or inconsistencies in behavior. It is not so much *where the individual is* at any point in time as *how he has been growing* which helps us identify his needs. A well-devised cumulative record is an invaluable asset to teachers in revealing developmental trends as well as in highlighting the "growing edge" of the personality.

In learning the history of the pupil's development, it goes without saying that the parents are an important source of information. On the secondary-school level, especially, it is desirable to work with parents as partners and to pool information to the mutual benefit of both parents and teachers.

Finally, there is one other immensely important source of information concerning individual needs. That is the adolescent himself. The things he tells us which reveal the way he feels about himself, his family, his friends, his teachers; the goals he has set for himself, the things in which he feels he is strong or weak, the problems which he says are troubling him; his own ideas of what he needs—these may prove of greatest significance in causing the other pieces of information which variously describe his personality to fall into place.

The Complex Task of Assessing Individual Needs. In the attempt to discover individual needs, it is important not to lose sight of the fact that the adolescent is all-of-one-piece. We cannot dissect him to study him or remove him from his environment and study each separately. We cannot interpret any one item of information about him except in terms of all other known items. Since the evidence is never all in, we are never sure that we have really discovered his needs. We act on hypotheses with open minds, ready to revise a tentative diagnosis in the light of new data. The dynamic factors, both within the individual and within his environment, necessitate a continuing study of him and a flexible, constructive approach toward him. Short-cut methods to understand the infinite complexities of his personality are especially to be questioned. No battery of tests can ever substitute for the observations and investigations made and recorded by qualified and insightful teachers.[12]

Moreover, the teacher is always "in training" when it comes to the difficult task of assessing individual needs and acting intelligently upon what his study reveals. He learns to approach human problems with humility; he learns to be both cautious and courageous—recognizing the limitations of the diagnostic tools he has to work with and conceding to a given adolescent the "unknowns" in any picture he may be able to construct—yet willing to test hypotheses in constructive action.

SUMMARY

This chapter has attempted to do two things. In the first place, it has examined the nature of needs in order to show the complexity, yet rationality, of the needs-approach to curriculum building. In the second place, it has suggested a three-step process by which needs may be determined—the needs of adolescents nation-wide, the more definitive needs of groups of adolescents living in given communities, and the unique needs of the individual boy or girl. At no step have the needs actually been identified. What seem to be promising approaches to the discovery of needs have been illustrated, leaving the task of continuing the analysis to professional study groups and to individual teachers. The practical problems of school appraisal, curriculum organization, and administrative procedure, wherein the needs of adolescents are used as the point of departure, remain for discussion in subsequent chapters.

---

[12] John W. M. Rothney and Bert A. Roens, *Counseling the Individual Student*, pp. 83–178. New York: William Sloane Associates, Inc., 1949.

CHAPTER III

HOW YOUTH LEARN TO MEET THEIR NEEDS

PAUL E. EISERER

Associate Professor, Department of Guidance
Teachers College, Columbia University
New York, New York

and

STEPHEN M. COREY

Professor of Education
Teachers College, Columbia University
New York, New York

In the preceding chapter Miss Low developed a usable concept of needs. Then, as a basis for curriculum development she suggested procedures for identifying both the needs that are common to high-school youth and those that are unique to particular boys and girls. In the present chapter we will discuss the importance of trying to find out how boys and girls themselves perceive these needs as they learn to meet them. Some of their needs, of course, can be taken care of directly without appreciable change in understandings or habits or attitudes. The need for food, for example, is one that most high-school boys and girls can proceed to take care of immediately. They've already learned how. Other needs imply behavior that has not been learned. All young people need to make a wise choice of a vocation, from the point of view of both their own desires and the demands of society. A wise vocational choice involves many prerequisites in the form of understandings, skills, and attitudes that must be acquired—must be learned. How is this learning achieved? What is the process like?

THE NATURE OF LEARNING

Learning from the Point of View of the Aims of Instruction

We want to begin by trying to make somewhat clearer the sense in which we are using the word "learn."[1] The term is variously defined by

---

[1] If the reader is interested in a comprehensive treatment of learning, learning theories, and the relation between learning and instruction, he may want to see: *The Psychology of Learning* (Forty-first Yearbook of the National Society for the Study of Education, Part II. Chicago: University of Chicago Press, 1942); E. R. Hilgard, *Theories of Learning* (New York: D. Appleton-Century-Crofts, 1948); and *Learning and Instruction* (Forty-ninth Yearbook of the National Society for the Study of Education, Part I. Chicago: University of Chicago Press, 1950).

psychologists and has various usages in everyday speech. Any reference, however, to "learn" or to "learning" implies two observations of the learner, separated by some time interval. The parent who says his child has learned to climb the stairs is reporting that at one time when the youngster was faced with the stairs situation he could not climb them, but later on he could. Learning always means some change in the individual that makes him different now from what he was earlier.

Another aspect of learning that is common in most definitions and usages, and which we want to stress, is that this change is brought about by experience. Yet, the illustration about a baby learning to climb stairs does not call attention only to this experience element. One of the important factors that contributes to a child's ability to climb stairs is sheer physical growth and maturation. A better illustration of the role of experience in learning might be the statement made by a high-school girl that she had learned to understand the way the United Nations operates. This statement implies that at one time in her life, maybe just a few weeks earlier, she would have been hard pressed to explain the organization and operation of the United Nations. The fact that she now can do it more adequately has resulted from a number of experiences—reading books or bulletins about the United Nations, seeing motion pictures, possibly visiting at Lake Success, or listening to explanations made by her teacher or by her classmates.

The fact that learning results from experience makes it clear that we are learning all the time—not only in school but as we go about all of our activities. Learning does not necessarily mean that a teacher is involved. People are constantly changing their habits, the way they speak, the answers they give to questions, the way they feel about other people or other situations, the goals they seek, and the meaning they see in their own lives. Sometimes the change results in quite different and "new" behavior. Sometimes existing habits, understandings, and attitudes are reinforced.

Some of our experiences change us more noticeably than do others. The high-school boys and girls who spend a week visiting Washington, D.C., under the guidance of a sensitive teacher may learn more about the federal government than they had previously learned from many hours of reading and discussion. Certainly we do not all learn the same from what may seem to an outsider to be the same experience. For one high-school pupil a general-science course developed a lasting interest in science. The boy who worked with him on laboratory experiments was constantly bored and resolved to have nothing to do with science.

Many people who talk about learning imply that the term should be used only when a good or desirable or socially acceptable change has taken place. We are not using the word in this sense. The change in an individual that results from his experience may be either good or bad, adjustive or maladjustive, socially acceptable or unacceptable. Some pupils in an English class may learn to like Shakespeare while others may learn to dislike him. The "club" experiences children have in a high school may teach some of them not only how to get along with the members of the club but snobbishness and other undemocratic attitudes as well. All of these changes represent learning.

It is quite common for people who are talking about learning in connection with school situations to restrict the meaning of the term in another way. Because schoolwork historically has placed so much stress upon the acquisition of knowledge, it is easy to overlook the fact that changes in attitudes, feelings, work habits, discussion skills, and methods of thinking also represent learning. This problem is illustrated in the following conversation between a high-school student and an adult who is trying to find out what the student has learned from a core type of course which involved a great deal of teacher-student planning and student-initiated activities:

ADULT: What are you learning in this core course?

PUPIL: We're not learning anything very much.

ADULT: What do you do in class?

PUPIL: Oh, we sit around and talk and try to decide on something we all would like to do. Then we do it.

ADULT: Have you made any progress?

PUPIL: Yeah, at the beginning it used to take us two or three weeks to decide what we wanted to do, and now we ordinarily can do it in a day or so.

ADULT: Why is that?

PUPIL: Oh, we keep on the subject better than we used to. At first everybody popped off with any idea that came into his head; now we listen more carefully and keep on the subject better.

ADULT: Everybody doesn't talk at once any more?

PUPIL: Yeah, that's it. Last September, too, there were two or three kids who did all of the talking. Now almost everyone takes part.

ADULT: Do you have reports from the students in class?

PUPIL: Yeah, at the end of our units.

ADULT: Are the reports pretty good?

PUPIL: At first they were terrible. Nobody worked on his very hard, and we all were bored to death.

ADULT: Are they better now?

PUPIL: Yeah, I think the reports are a lot better. We pay closer attention, too.

ADULT: But you haven't really learned anything?

PUPIL: That's right.

This particular boy believed that he had not learned anything in the core class, even though he had been reporting for five or six minutes some rather significant changes that the class experience had brought about in him and in the other young people. He, however, did not consider these changes the sort that were called "learning" in a school situation. He thought that learning in school had to result in the ability to state new facts, dates, formulas, names, principles, or other kinds of knowledge.

Many laymen, too, think of learning in this restricted sense. Had this lad's father asked, "What are you learning in that core class?" he would only have been satisfied, probably, if his son had said that he had learned how to do long division, or had recited the names of the capitals of the states or certain chemical formulas or some generalizations and principles in physics, or the Spanish equivalent for the word "manufacture."

Many teachers, particularly when they are thinking of learning in relation to school, imply that they are concerned only with that kind of learning that has to do primarily with the memorization and understanding of subject matter. While this is, of course, one kind of learning, many other important changes occur in boys and girls as a result of their school experience. This stereotype of school learning has especially serious consequences when a curriculum is being developed which includes, but goes beyond, learning subject matter *per se* and is designed to meet a broad range of adolescent needs. One of the common limitations of these programs is that insufficient attention is given to intellectualizing and conceptualizing what is learned. By this we mean stating in verbal form the generalizations and attitudinal changes that grow out of the class experience and recognizing that they all represent learning.

Learning from the Point of View of the Learner

Learning is usually studied and described from the viewpoint of some "outsider" who is observing the learner. Most of the books on educational psychology or books describing the current status of learning theories are written from this point of view.[2] Consequently the evidence used for inference about learning is filtered through the particular assumptions and beliefs of the outside observer. In school, for example, it is usually the teacher who takes the responsibility for checking up on what has been learned by the pupils. Most of what teachers say about the way

[2] The two yearbooks named in footnote 1 are written from this "behavioristic" point of view, with the exception of one of the chapters in *Learning and Instruction*. This chapter, "Implications for Improving Instruction in the High School," by H. A. Thelen and Ralph W. Tyler, is an unusually provocative one and deserves careful reading by those high-school teachers who are reformulating their conception of the learning process.

in which their pupils learn is based upon their observations of this learning. The feelings and judgments of the pupils are generally not thought to have much pertinence to the work of the school.

This point of view has undoubtedly led to many insights into the way boys and girls learn in school, but the position taken in this chapter places major emphasis upon the way the pupils themselves look at the situations in which they find themselves. This orientation is neither novel nor original but is one which we feel has been neglected. It is not possible within one chapter to deal comprehensively with a topic as broad as learning, so we are singling out for emphasis the importance of trying to understand the teaching-learning situation as it is perceived by the pupils. We believe this must be done in order to gain additional insights into the way high-school pupils learn. We are not, of course, denying that we ourselves are outside the learners in a manner of speaking. But we are aiming to explore the understandings about learning which result if we try to perceive the experiences of learners through their own eyes.[3] As we approach the problem of helping boys and girls learn to meet their needs from this point of view, our discussion will center upon these four basic questions: (1) What is the motivation which impels boys and girls to learning activity? (2) How can we make sense out of the activity which we observe? (3) How can we account for the kinds of changes in activity which we have defined as learning? (4) What can teachers do to facilitate these changes? In the following section the authors will attempt to make clear the ways in which they would answer these questions. We give passing attention only to question 4 because it is the subject of chapter xiii.

MOTIVATION

If a typical high-school pupil were asked what needs he was trying to meet through his various activities, he would not be able to verbalize about "needs" the way some teachers and adults can. If, however, he were asked to tell something about his activities or the difficulties he was facing as he tried to get the most out of his life, he might mention that he was upset because he was so awkward in athletics, or because of his pimples, or his difficulties in getting along with some of his agemates, or his inability to do well enough in algebra, or irritations at home where he is trying to assert his independence and is running into trouble with his parents. A large number of specific concerns like these might be brought out as a result of talking to a group of youngsters of adolescent age, as-

---

[3] If the reader wishes to learn more about this "phenomenological" point of view, he may want to see these two references: Donald Snygg and Arthur Combs, *Individual Behavior* (New York: Harper & Bros., 1949); Nathaniel Cantor, *The Dynamics of Learning* (Buffalo, New York: Foster & Stewart, 1946).

suming that the atmosphere made it relatively easy for the boys and girls to speak freely. From these statements it would be possible to infer needs as they were perceived by the young people themselves. Whatever learning they engage in is to enable them to meet the needs that they perceive. One major job of the school, of course, is to help pupils see as important certain needs which at the present time do not concern them.

Boys and girls learn, or change their behavior, because they are uneasy about or dissatisfied with things as they are. In the case of a particular boy the uneasiness might result from the feeling that he is not getting along well with his father, or that he wants to be the star of the team, or that he would like to know more about woodworking in order to make a chair for his own room. He may either talk things over with his father or submerge his feelings so that his father will be more friendly. Or he may practice baseball or get someone to help him improve his skill. He may talk with a carpenter or learn some arithmetic in order to make a better chair.

In all these illustrations, whatever the young person does seems to follow from the way *he* sizes up the situation and the way in which he thinks he can best achieve what he is after. His success will be determined by the clarity with which he defines the problem and identifies the important factors that must be taken into account. In other words, the boy is driven to do something, not in accordance with the way somebody else defines his goals or needs, but in accordance with the way he himself perceives the situation and decides what must be done in order to get what he wants. People act in accordance with their perceptions of situations.

It may be helpful to remember that the individual is in the center of a world of many stimuli, some inside and some outside himself. The needs of the newborn baby are probably few though insistent. The processes of growth and maturation bring new powers, new capacities, and new differentiations. Those which can be attributed to experience, we are calling *learning*. At first, a mother is perceived as a source of comfort, then, as different from other women, and, later still, she may be seen by the child in a complex of relations to himself, to his father, to siblings, and to other adults. All of these increasingly complex perceptions of mother represent learnings, that is, they are more extensive differentiations in the world of stimulus possibilities. Most of these perceptions of mother may already be well known to the father. What determined the baby's behavior, at each stage, however, is his own perception at the time. At the age of six his behavior toward his mother is quite different from what it was at two.

No two people have *identical* perceptions of any situation. It follows that no two people ever have the same experience in a situation. It is in this sense that we may refer to the uniqueness of every human being.

As the young person acts to "meet his needs"—as we adults say—he selects from the world of stimuli about him certain ones to which he responds. Since his behavior always seems to imply some direction or purpose, we think of a *goal* toward which his activity is directed. These goals cannot always be immediately achieved. As we have said, many of the things that high-school pupils want cannot be gotten unless the pupils change, or learn. One boy must learn algebra because he wants to go to engineering school. A girl is not as popular as she wants to be with boys because she has not learned how to carry on small talk. These lacks are frequently referred to as obstacles or problems, and the point is made that learning results from trying to overcome them. This conception of obstacles is common in all analyses of learning. We want to emphasize the importance of relying upon the pupil's frame of reference to make clear what goal is perceived and what intervening obstacles seem to stand in the way.

Everyone who considers the nature of learning finds it necessary to refer to some concept of motivation. We want to know what impels the pupil to seek selected goals and to change himself, if necessary, in order to overcome the obstacles that stand between him and his goals. Motivation is extremely complex and subtle and inadequately understood even by psychologists who have spent a great deal of time trying to find out what causes people to persevere in their search for satisfactions. Admitting this complexity and subtlety, we find it helpful to assume as an overarching drive or fundamental motive the need the young person feels to maintain his position or defend his behavior and to enhance his social status or to improve himself in other specified ways.

Out of the vast number of stimuli which are always present, the boy or girl selects those which appear most likely to facilitate his maintaining and enhancing purposes. Maintaining and enhancing activities are not mutually exclusive. They are concepts we use to differentiate certain kinds of behavior. When a person perceives threat, his activities are likely to be mostly of the maintaining or defending variety. For example, a teacher noticed that Jim was making a computation in algebra by a method which in her judgment was rather laborious and inefficient. She pointed out the flaws in his method and suggested how he could solve the problem more readily. Her behavior was perceived by Jim in a negative way. He became defensive, and he thought of arguments for maintaining his way of doing the problem. The teacher's behavior was perceived as a threat to Jim's independence and ability to work things out for himself. Consequently, he had to defend his method. It was not the intent of the teacher to affect Jim that way, but she did not know him well enough to anticipate how he would respond to her efforts to be helpful.

On another occasion the teacher had a different experience with another pupil, Bill. She found him doing problems in much the same manner as Jim, and she reacted in the same way as she had previously. Bill, however, had quite a different perception of the teacher. He viewed her criticisms and suggestions as likely to help him solve his problem more efficiently. The new method was tried and proved to be more effective. When there was no perception of threat—no need to maintain or defend present behavior—when a new possibility was available, a new way was learned. Bill was able to improve himself.

If we can assume that the teacher behaved in the same way in the two situations, we may suggest that the instigation for maintaining (defending) or enhancing (improving) behavior came primarily from the perception of the learner. It is not easy to anticipate how one's behavior will be perceived by others. As the teacher's knowledge about pupils grows, the likelihood increases that anticipations will be more sensitive and more accurate. While behavior which can be called maintaining (defending), as illustrated here, is necessary from the individual's point of view, the teacher strives to keep this kind of behavior at a minimum. She directs her efforts toward creating the conditions which will make enhancing (improving) activities more likely.

Our reference to these comprehensive drives or motives—self-maintenance and self-enhancement—deserves further elaboration. We are implying that the most important things to the individual are his need, first, to preserve himself from harm, and, secondly, to improve his perception of himself as worthy and important. There have been many attempts to list and classify motives. Usually a differentiation is made between physiological drives—sex, hunger, thirst, and so on—and psychological drives like the need for affection, security, and recognition. We believe that these lists usually add up to what we are calling the basic drives for self-maintenance and self-enhancement. We will try to make our point of view clearer in the following section as we consider the task the teacher faces as she tries to understand more adequately the behavior of her pupils.

MAKING SENSE OUT OF THE BEHAVIOR OF PUPILS

As we have said, the young person selects and reacts to those stimuli, out of the vast number present, which appear to him to be most likely to help him meet his needs. His behavior is in accord with his perception of what the situation requires. These perceptions will not always be clear or sharply focused. Our point is that the interplay of internal need and perceived external forces determines behavior at a given moment. An outside observer, such as a teacher, cannot know at a given moment what the individual will consider most meaningful. He can get close, however, in the degree that he is able to see these forces in interaction as they are seen by the pupil. We are emphasizing here the effect that the individual's perceptions, including perceptions of himself, his needs, and the external demands, have on his behavior.

This is rather abstract, and we want to try to say much the same thing in a way that will relate more closely to school teaching. In the school situation the conscientious teacher is trying more or less continuously to make sense out of the variety of behavior which he observes in his students. He is aware that the boys and girls react differently in what to him seem to be the same situations. Such different behaviors are attributed to "individual differences," which have been greatly stressed in the training of teachers. They are implored to adapt their subject content and the other experiences they provide for students to the individual pupil. That this is no mean task is attested by every teacher who has tried to do it. It is easier to write about the importance of taking individual differences into account than it is to do something about them.

One reason for the difficulties teachers face as they try to adapt their instruction to individual pupils is the fact that every situation has unique meaning for the individual involved in it. This does not imply, however, that there is no possibility for understanding what the situation does mean to the individual. Probably the teachers who have had some success in promoting the development of their students as individuals have been able to get from them some picture of the way they look at things. We are reminded that the ways in which the situation, including himself, is viewed by the learner determine his behavior.[4]

Let us see further what this approach to learning means by looking at a high-school class. The teacher, whom we are calling Miss Jones, knows that the boys and girls in her class differ from each other in many ways. She observes differences in their physical characteristics, in the way they dress and deport themselves, in the preferences they have for each other, in the attitudes they express toward issues discussed in class. She knows that some of her pupils are brighter than others and that some are stronger than others. She suspects that some like her subject more than do others and that their interests vary. She can observe variations in the ways their personalities are expressed. Some are shy and reserved while others may be aggressive. Some seem to resist class activities while others seem to enjoy them.

---

[4] The teacher who wants to make faster progress in learning how the world looks to pupils will benefit from reading *Teacher Counseling* by Dugald A. Arbuckle (Cambridge, Massachusetts: Addison-Wesley Press, Inc., 1950).

We can get a better understanding of these differences among the students in Miss Jones' class if we can find out how they perceive the situations in which they find themselves. Mary hopes to go to college and believes that doing well in this class will in some way better her chances of going. Bill comes because he has to be in school or the law will be after him. He is willing to come for that reason. Susan is just happy to be with the gang—the rest of them are taking the course, so why not she? For Kate, the hour is more appropriate than other alternatives. Betty has developed a view of herself as an *A* student—she must get that mark in all her classes or she will consider herself a failure. Joe sees the class as one he must tolerate in order to play football.

It might be said of all these students that they are taking the course for different reasons. The class to them is a means for meeting quite different needs. The needs they are trying to meet, derived from the way the students perceive the situation, seem to influence their day-by-day activities in the class continuously and pervasively. Although the way each student behaves in a given situation is determined by his perceptions at the moment, there is a degree of consistency from day to day which seems based on a more generalized, probably more fundamental, personality orientation.

Students with unfavorable attitudes toward class are a source of annoyance to Miss Jones. Why is Joe so indifferent when it is clear from intelligence tests that he is brighter than most of the other students? Why does Joan always follow the line of least resistance, doing just enough to avoid censure but never working up to her obvious ability? The behavior and attitudes of these students and others like them disturb Miss Jones because she believes that they would learn more and be happier boys and girls if their attitudes were "favorable."

There are other complications in the situation. When Miss Jones gave an objective-type information test and studied the scores, she became even more puzzled. Some of those whose attitudes toward her class seemed most "favorable" scored lower than some with "unfavorable" attitudes. Even when she took intelligence into account, the rankings did not come up to her expectations. The problems Miss Jones faced trying to interpret achievement scores were multiplied whenever she tried to ascertain more subtle learnings, such as "attitude toward learning," "citizenship," "values," and "character learnings." And Miss Jones considers the latter very important.

As a conscientious teacher, Miss Jones wants every student to get something which she considers desirable from having been in her class for a semester or a year. She might settle for gains—she knows there will be differences among students—in the amount of information her pupils learn. This does not satisfy her, however, because she knows from other experiences in the community that people who seem to "know a lot" are not necessarily the best citizens. Yet most of them have attended high school and have made high grades. Miss Jones wants her subject to make a difference in the way her pupils live. She suspects that knowledge in itself is no guarantee of good citizenship; that feelings, attitudes, and values somehow come into the picture, but she is not sure how or where. As she looks around her she sees evidence that the schools of yesterday failed in large measure to achieve values that are involved in good citizenship. Miss Jones is no advocate of letting pupils do whatever they want to do. Yet she wants to do the best she can to make the school and her classes places where the young can learn in better ways than did she and others of her generation.

Miss Jones has discovered that the better she has known a student the more she has been able to help him develop. When she thinks about it, she discovers that her deepest appreciations and insights into students have come from "informal" discussions, from listening sympathetically to reports of what they think is important, what goals and aspirations they have. In these contexts Miss Jones sees her pupils not as tallies in a frequency distribution of scores but as whole persons. Once she discovers how much this process facilitates her teaching, she devotes more time to trying to help her students reveal the bases for their actions. She finds that her students, as they reveal themselves, are more different and more complex than any test ever suggested. The important lesson she has learned is that, when she understands what the pupils see in a situation, their actions make more sense to her. She does not necessarily agree with their actions, but she understands better why they do as they do.

How Can Learning Be Understood?

Miss Jones would probably say that she is not trying to understand the behavior of her pupils just for the sake of understanding it. She knows that her task is to bring about, in the behavior of her students, the changes in behavior that society and the school define as desirable. Her task as a teacher is to help boys and girls develop normally into socially sensitive people who want to promote the welfare of others. This is a large order, and Miss Jones' aspirations are not too unrealistic. She knows that what she will be able to do can be but a small contribution toward that end. She seeks improvement, not perfection, in what she does through her classroom and extracurricular activity.

We have said several times that the way boys and girls perceive a situation determines what they do. As their perceptions change, so does their behavior. We turn our attention now to this question: "How does Miss

Jones get an awareness that when perception changes so does behavior?" There is evidence in some of the books she has read that this is the case. What has convinced her more deeply, however, resulted from her reflections about herself. She has noticed that when she has changed her view of a student, she has acted differently because of the different perception. The change may have been in her attitude or in her feeling toward John when she discovered that he liked school but that her subject somehow did not make sense to him. She did not agree with John but realized that at least she had a better basis for understanding his behavior in a number of situations. She conveyed this understanding to John and noticed that his behavior toward her changed too. He seemed to understand her better.

John said once that he thought that teaching so many students must be hard. Miss Jones could warm up to someone who better understood and appreciated her own situation and its problems. Most of us are like that. As she examined her own experiences she could think of numerous times when she acted differently because she got a new slant on things, got a new way of viewing a situation. She had already discovered that no one ever "knows" another person completely. What you aim for is to understand him better. Miss Jones can be comfortable with such an aspiration. To expect to comprehend anyone finally and completely leads to futile perfectionistic striving. She knows some people who wore themselves out trying to achieve that goal. She is not complacent, though, for life will not let her be. The challenge to comprehend is always present.

Other evidence of the change in behavior that follows a change in perception comes to Miss Jones, too. She noticed that Joe was frequently getting into difficulty with other boys. He could not find a basis for getting along with them. When she talked the matter over with Joe, she sensed that he felt that the boys had it in for him and that he was not accepted. She sensed, too, that Joe did not like the situation as it was. He wanted a change but, seemingly, did not know how to bring it about. As long as he perceived the situation as he did, he acted on the basis of his perception.

Miss Jones decided to try to help Joe and the other boys see additional aspects of each other. She got them involved in a job which required cooperative action. Joe contributed something and so did the others. Out of that process Joe got a view of the boys as having other interests, some of them like his. He saw them, too, as interested in doing more than making his life miserable. When he saw them in this newer light, his old feelings changed somewhat and so did his behavior. The other boys, too, saw in Joe someone who could do more than get in a fight at the drop of a hat. As a result, Joe and the boys were looking at each other in a somewhat different light. They did not suddenly become different people—but the little changes meant a lot. They set in motion new attitudes that developed more generalizing value than one might expect from the initial situation.

Miss Jones remembered the time she caught Ralph copying on an examination. This incensed her because she felt that such behavior was unethical, at least that Ralph was learning to cope with life's situations the wrong way. She had a talk with Ralph in which she concentrated on trying to understand how he felt about the situation rather than to convince him that he had done wrong. From sympathetic listening Miss Jones got some new perceptions of Ralph. She had not realized what he was putting up with at home. She learned that he viewed his parents as continuously bickering and nagging each other. He felt that they had no interest in his welfare and talked to him only when they wanted him to do something for them. These changed perceptions of Ralph did not change Miss Jones' ideas about the undesirability of cheating, but she did feel that she could now understand that, from Ralph's point of view and from an appreciation of what he was up against, the learning of the subject she taught was not very important to him. She discovered her attitude toward Ralph changing as her perceptions of him and his situation changed. She still felt that her job as a teacher was to make her subject more meaningful for Ralph, but she was more realistic in her expectations. She concluded that when she expressed a favorable or unfavorable attitude toward her pupil's behavior she was less helpful than when she tried hard to see the world through his eyes. This changed perception led to a change in her own behavior.

Calling attention to the relation between the behavior of pupils and their perception of the situations in which they find themselves usually raises this important question: What reason is there to expect that changes in perception will necessarily result in better behavior, or in desirable learning? We believe that high-school boys and girls will learn to behave with increasing adequacy—that is, they will learn socially desirable behavior as they (a) enlarge the scope of their perceptions, (b) differentiate among these perceptions more expertly, and (c) generalize more objectively from the consequences of their actions. This implies that the person whose perceptions come increasingly to correspond with the world as it is will learn acceptable ways of reacting to the world as it is. The propositions building up to this implication might go like this:

What a high-school pupil does depends upon his perceptions of himself, his needs, the situation and its demands.

As these perceptions change, the pupil's behavior changes.

One of the major responsibilities of a teacher is to make it possible for her pupils to modify their perceptions so that more adequate behavior will be learned.

This last proposition raises at once the questions: When is behavior adequate? What kinds of perceptions lead to adequate or desirable behavior?

We find it helpful in our own teaching to think of adequate behavior as being relative. High-school boys and girls need help to increase the appropriateness of their behavior. Education is a process of becoming. Learning will be more desirable if it is based upon an enlarging of reality for the learner. He becomes able to perceive relationships that he was not formerly aware of. He comes to see and appreciate differences in events and in people. He discovers new complexities and aspects in the situations with which he must cope. He develops increasing skill at integrating all of this into more meaningful conceptions. His expanding perceptions and his deliberation about them provide him with more realistic data as bases for his choices and decisions, for deeper understanding, and for further experiencing. Now and then the ability of young people to make decisions that are wise and good or to take responsibility for their own choices is questioned. There is evidence that implies rather clearly that boys and girls are generally more capable in these respects than we give them credit for. Frequently it is the fear that young people will make decisions different from ours that makes us want to control their decision-making. Yet most of us realize that the power to make decisions that will reflect increasing wisdom can grow only through practice in making decisions, followed by reflective examination of their consequences. Learning entails risks. Often the good intentions of teachers and parents to keep young people from these risks prevent the learning of important lessons.

What assurances do we have that young people will base their judgments upon realistic grounds? Children, in their efforts to come into effective relationships with the world of objects and people discover very early that they get along much better when they take into account more and more aspects of their environment. For example, avoidance of hurtful objects is learned and respected early in life. Reactions are learned more slowly to the complexity of the demands of people. But the drive toward self-sufficiency and independence is strong, as one will see from observation of small children. They work at the business of learning how better to cope with things and people all their waking hours. They meet success and failure. They persist tenaciously in their attempts to overcome obstacles. They are not always wise, but they are always trying, and they grow in wisdom as they try.

The need to learn how to survive and to grow is inexorable. But it can be frustrated or deeply grooved by others, as the history of cultures demonstrates. In a rapidly changing society like ours no one can say that he knows the final ends of education—that what seems good for him is good for all. Yet most of us spend a great deal of time trying to force growth into the narrow paths of our own learning. We will not often face this fact so bluntly, but implied in our insistence is the assumption that if others become like us, everything will be all right.

Teaching and Learning

What a high-school pupil learns to do to meet his needs is determined by his perceptions, and changes in his perceptions lead to changes in his behavior (learning). Two implications follow which would seem to be of significance to high-school teachers. The first is this: Before a teacher can understand the way a high-school pupil behaves, he must have insight into the way the situation looks to the high-school pupil. What meaning does it have for him? The second implication is: High-school teachers who are most skilful in helping pupils extend or clarify their perceptions to the end that they will correspond more closely to reality will be the best teachers.

To find out how the world looks to another person is known to be difficult to any one who has tried it. Many people, of course, make no attempt. They assume that the way they regard a situation corresponds with its true nature, and anyone who does not perceive things in the same way is wrong or recalcitrant. The teacher who wants to understand and, if possible, comprehend how things look to the high-school pupil must work at it. Little progress can be made without the co-operation of the pupil himself. Perception is a highly personal matter. The boy who likes English and wants to improve his writing and who realizes that he can't get into college unless he does is going to learn quite different things than the boy who perceives his English class as a complete bore and sees little if any benefit in it to himself.

It is possible, of course, to make some rather shrewd and valid inferences regarding the way a particular pupil looks at a situation or at himself by just watching what he does and listening to what he says. A great deal of time and effort can be saved, however, if a situation is created in which the youngster not only feels free to communicate his perceptions to his teacher but is helped to do so. This will not happen if the high-school pupil is afraid of the teacher or has learned that frank expression of the way he feels and looks at things will result in punishment. Few high-school pupils, for example, are going to be explicit in their statements about their dislike for American history in conversation with a teacher who has let it be known that he values American history highly and has demonstrated that he can make boys and girls who say they do not like it very uncomfortable.

The behavior of boys and girls can only be understood if the teacher is able in greater or lesser degree to understand how they perceive themselves and their world. This understanding of the pupil's perceptions is greatly facilitated if the pupil feels free to report them. These are two strong arguments for permissive relationships between teachers and pupils. The establishment of these permissive relationships in many instances is quite threatening to a teacher. Our culture has taught most of us to expect a considerable degree of deference from our pupils. The deference in this country is undoubtedly less than the deference shown teachers by pupils in prewar Germany, but it is nevertheless substantial. Teachers must be more secure than most of us are in order to be able to tolerate and learn from a situation where pupils are encouraged to speak their real thoughts and identify real meanings.

A second implication of our analysis of the learning process has to do with the teacher's efforts to help his pupils extend and differentiate among their perceptions so that their behavior will correspond more closely with reality and, consequently, be more appropriate. The most common method employed by teachers is to try to broaden the child's verbal experiences so that he will talk about a greater range of factors bearing upon a problem and differentiate verbally among these factors in order to know which ones to attend to most particularly. These methods of facilitating pupil learning are considered to be time-tested and, hence, effective. Many teachers realize that mere modifications in the vocabulary of boys and girls do not necessarily imply any change at all in their perceptions or adaptability. It is possible, for example, for boys and girls to make great improvement in their ability to talk about democracy and democratic ways of behaving without changing to a noticeable degree the ways they behave in situations where democracy is at issue. Verbal exercises alone, in other words, do not give much promise for extension or better differentiation among perceptions.

The paragraph you have just read should not be interpreted to mean that verbalizing and intellectualizing are unimportant. They are necessary but not sufficient conditions for learning. Many teachers know well the bizarre meanings children associate with certain words because of limitations in their perceptual or first-hand experiences. Boys and girls should have a wide variety of direct experiences with objects, operations, and people. They need practice in perceiving, in testing their perceptions in action, and in generalizing about the consequences.

Another factor which makes it difficult for the individual to act upon and to develop the perceptions he has is the existence of threat. Threat almost always tends to restrict an individual's ability to perceive the factors in a situation that must be perceived if behavior is to be realistic. Threat leads in most instances to aggressive behavior or to retreat rather than to more realistic adjustment. This fact needs little elaboration because we all can recall instances of our own "stupid" behavior when we were threatened or scared. Our judgment is greatly affected, usually, and we do things that we never would do under more nearly normal circumstances.

We will mention one other difficulty that interferes with the extension of and differentiation among perceptions. It is inadequate symbolization. This problem has been studied by all students of communication and argues strongly for common experiences out of which terms will be derived which have more nearly common meanings for teachers and pupils.

The relationship between teaching and learning is by no means a simple one. There may be a great gap between what a teacher's learning objectives are and what is actually learned by students in a classroom. Learning results from the efforts of learners to achieve goals that are most insistent from their own points of view. Herein lies the danger when a teacher formulates specific learning tasks outside of an awareness of the learner's needs as he sees them. They are likely to miss the mark. Many young people today learn to dislike mathematics, for example, yet it is unlikely that anyone set out to teach them that attitude. Avoidance of participation in civic affairs is learned, too, yet no teacher would confess to having deliberately taught it.

The entire setting of teaching-learning needs constant critical examination. Much learning goes on without teaching. Much desirable learning proceeds from good teaching. And much bad learning—that is, learning with unfavorable consequences to the learner and society—goes on because of poor teaching. What is being learned by any particular student in a classroom situation is probably much more complex than we have ever imagined and far beyond our best efforts to predict today. Learning theories today are quite inadequate to explain most of what goes on in the ordinary classroom. This fact makes many teachers skeptical of books on learning because they seem to be pretentious in their implied claims. A conception of learning which is too restricted to fit the "complex reality" raises false hopes that understanding may be easily achieved. High-level abstractions and inferences too distant from observation help little. New observations, new conceptions, not restatement of the old, are needed.

CONCLUSION

Because of the limitations of space to which authors of chapters in this yearbook agreed to conform, we did not try to "cover" the field of learn-

ing. Many topics that usually appear have not even been named explicitly
—topics like transfer of training, whole and part learning, and retro-
active inhibition. We have tried to emphasize the importance of understanding how the world looks to high-school pupils as they learn whatever they believe they must learn to meet their needs. We have called
attention to the added insights teachers may gain into the learning process as they extend their efforts to find out how things look to the boys
and girls they are teaching. What meaning does school have to the young
people in the classroom? What are the goals that seem significant to
them? How do they perceive the obstacles that keep them from getting
what they want?

As we reread what we have written, it seems to us that most of our
argument can be summed up in four propositions. We are repeating them
below so that the reader may test them against his own experience as he
continues to work with boys and girls to the end that they will learn to
become better citizens: (*a*) Whatever boys and girls learn in school results from the way they perceive themselves and the demands of the
situations with which they must cope. (*b*) Changes in perceptions lead to
changes in behavior. (*c*) To the degree that these perceptions correspond
more and more closely with reality—physical and social—behavior becomes more appropriate. (*d*) A major responsibility of the high-school
teacher is to help boys and girls extend their perceptions, differentiate
cause and effect relationships among them, and generalize more effectively from the behavior that is based upon them.

CHAPTER IV

DISCOVERING THE EXTENT TO WHICH YOUTH NEEDS ARE BEING MET

J. Dan Hull

Chief, Secondary Schools Section
United States Office of Education
Washington, D.C.

and

Howard Cummings

Specialist for Social Sciences and Geography
Secondary Schools Section
United States Office of Education
Washington, D.C.

Purpose of the Chapter

Consideration has been given in previous chapters to two fundamental problems, namely, how to determine the needs of youth and how students learn to meet their needs. The purpose of this chapter is to suggest procedures for securing information concerning the extent to which youth needs are being met. Consideration is given to the securing of information about (a) individuals, (b) groups of youth in school and of those out of school, (c) the school and its processes, and (d) the communities in which youth are coming of age.

It goes without saying that with growing youth in a highly dynamic society the teacher who undertakes such a study will have before him, not a mosaic set in a fixed pattern, but a kaleidoscope which changes daily. Yet, a dynamic society as well as a static society must find places with full membership for maturing youth. Standards change in a dynamic society, but they are always present and are, in many cases, not less exacting because of their fluidity. Research has also established bench marks for youth's development toward maturity. It is toward the standards established by society for youth achievement that we first turn.

Standards for Youth Achievement

Standards for Growth Which Have Been Determined by Experts

Each individual has his own rate of growth, and in the past too much has often been made of norms. At the same time there are standards for adequate nutrition, for a balance between activity and rest, for personal cleanliness, and for other phases of development. These standards have come in large measure from laboratories and clinics. They have been approved by national, state, and local groups as significant statements of competencies that the school should strive to develop in its pupils. It is important that youth accept such standards and strive to reach and maintain them. The prevailing standards for physical and mental health are always subject to change when evidence from the laboratory indicates that other ratings should be recognized. In the regular health examinations, in the standards set by expert nutritionists, and in the diagnostic techniques of psychiatry, the schools have measures of how well youth needs are being met in these areas.

Standards Which Have Been Set by Society

Minimum standards for personal behavior are established by law. The statutes indicate the degree of responsibility which any individual must assume for his behavior at each age level—the child of four has no responsibility, the man of twenty-one has complete responsibility for personal acts which violate statutes. Youth needs to know and assume responsibility for observing the minimum standards prescribed by law. The juvenile delinquency rate of a community is an index of how well this need is being met. In addition to law, there is the whole field of convention. No legal punishment follows breaking a standard stated as a convention, but punitive action may take the form of loss of a job or social ostracism, either of which may be more serious than some forms of legal punishment. Conventions are standards which the individual may disregard, but at his own risk.

Probably the most serious aspect of the question of the needs of youth in this area is the need for being included. A birth certificate will admit him to most of the activities, but he may fail to meet the standards for driving an automobile, confirmation, or military service; and he may fail to find a job or a mate.

The adolescent, in his search for status, takes matters into his own hands and provides his own standards through cliques. The school is faced with the standards of a peer culture which must be taken into account. The value of the standards of the peer culture may be questionable for either the individual or the culture, but the school cannot ignore the fact that they exist.

STUDYING YOUTH IN SCHOOL
The Individual

In diagnosing the extent to which youth needs are being met, school staffs must work with individuals. When a school staff has clearly in mind the attainable standards which competent experts have set down for youth and those standards which society insists upon for its own welfare, the next step is to assess the resources which each individual has for reaching these standards.[1] This assessment can be made in at least five areas:

1. The health and physical status of the individual can be appraised by means of periodic physical examinations, tests of physical fitness, observations, nurse follow-ups of attendance records, and family consultations.
2. The intellectual development of the individual can be gauged by considering school marks earned and the results of intelligence (scholastic aptitude) and achievement tests. Tests of critical thinking and general educational development are examples of instruments which may be used in this area.
3. While the emotional and social development of the individual is extremely difficult to measure, estimates can be made through the indices secured through self-rating scales, problem check lists, adjustment inventories, and student questionnaires. Helpful in making such estimates are themes, autobiographies, observations, anecdotes, interviews, reports from employers, and parent conferences.
4. The personal interests and plans of the individual can be assessed by means of the records of previous achievement, interest inventories or tests, autobiographies, interviews, and a record of such out-of-school activities as leisure pastimes and work experience.
5. Special abilities of the individual can be appraised through special aptitude tests, products made by the individual, interviews, and a consideration of previous achievement or performance.

In no area are formal tests alone a substitute for the insight and intuition which come from observing the behavior of an individual in many different situations and over a considerable period of time. If there is enough freedom in the school to allow the pupil to reveal what he is like, he will exhibit his real resources by expressed interests and by his behavior in the classroom, in the corridors, in the lunchroom, and on the way to and from school. What he reads outside of school, how he spends his free time, how he behaves toward clerks and custodians as well as toward teachers, and how he behaves at home, all provide evidence which is helpful to a teacher in forming judgments about the resources of a student. Such judgments should consider the purposes of the individual and the experiences he has had, as well as the test data.

The purpose of all tests, inventories, anecdotal records, and other tools

---

[1] For outlines of procedures and selected references see:

Wilson H. Ivins, William H. Fox, and David Segel, *A Study of a Secondary-School Program in Light of Characteristics and Needs of Youth*, pp. 62–68. Bloomington, Indiana: Division of Research and Field Services, Indiana University, 1949.

J. Francis Rummel, *Know Your Pupils: An introductory Manual on Pupil Evaluation*. Salem, Oregon: State Department of Education, 1951.

of guidance is to measure the development of the individual toward physical, intellectual, emotional, and social maturity. Like all instruments, they are useful when in the hands of those who know how to use them. We cannot assume that secondary-school students are clearly aware of the conditions within themselves and in their society which make their road easy or difficult. The student must know what he is interested in and how these interests can be followed in the society in which he lives. He must learn how to think, a process which involves setting goals and selecting methods for reaching these goals.

The student needs to be aware of his strengths and to be prepared to make full use of them. He must also be aware of weaknesses and learn how to repair them or compensate for them. To help him conscientiously make a good beginning in these areas by using facts about himself and about the society in which he lives is the first task of the school. A larger task is to help him learn to think so that he can continue to solve problems pertaining to his social, economic, and political relationships in the future. In their guidance of students toward these goals, teachers should raise such questions as these: Is he growing into the kind of person he expects to be? Has he made the adjustments which should have been made in infancy and early childhood, such as developing a sense of trust and self-reliance? How well has he achieved the developmental tasks which equip him for mature adult living and for meeting the expectations of the community?

A list of important qualities and significant questions provides a framework for collecting information for the school records which should be kept concerning the resources of youth. The record of a student's activities will be a guide to his interests, his personal relations, his initiative, his stamina in reaching goals which he has set, and his qualities of leadership as judged by his peers. The records must be easily available to all professional staff members and be organized so that they can be readily used. The special value of the cumulative record is that it makes possible the viewing of the individual's status at a particular time against the background of his growth and development over a long period of time.

From the many items of information contained in the school record, predictions on future adjustment may be made. Always the total resources of the individual must be placed beside his aspirations and society's requirements. Will he be able to measure up to the kind of individual he expects to be? If not, then he must either increase his resources or cut down his aspirations. On the other hand, many students have resources which, if used, will carry them far above their present level of aspirations. Raising aspirations is as much a part of meeting the needs of youth as encouraging them to strive for lesser goals. Beyond the minimums established by society for all youth are the gradations where individuals will eventually arrive by developing their capacities through effort. Teachers help to discover the capacities, set the sights, and provide motivations.

Studying Groups of Youth

Evidences of progress toward many goals for youth lend themselves to objective treatment. It is possible to determine for the population of any local school and for component groups within the school the central tendencies and range of individual differences in numerous important respects such as indices of physical health, intelligence quotients, and results of formal tests of the fundamental skills. Such measurements indicate the degree to which characteristics of a local group vary from those of a more typical population and may point to particularly needed emphases in the school program, such as more systematic efforts to improve basic language or reading skills. Significant relationships may be revealed by examination of health and attendance records or by studies of retardation in the light of existing promotion policies. Even though such analyses may reveal no unusual needs, they will, in any event, aid teachers in understanding the ability and progress of the school population as a whole.

In the same way, information regarding such items as home backgrounds, leisure-time activities, vacation experiences, work experiences, and community relationships may be obtained from enrolment cards or from questionnaires submitted to pupils. Such evidence may indicate needs common to a considerable group of the high-school population. It may be that more searching and systematic studies will be indicated. In a rural area in a western state, teachers planned an investigation of the social and leisure-time activities of all seventh- and eighth-grade pupils in the area. The items to be covered in an interview were agreed upon, and ten pupils were interviewed by each teacher. It was found that about the only social activities available to the pupils were those sponsored by a new religious sect which had recently been introduced into the area.

Both simple and elaborate sociometric techniques have been developed and used to identify those who are in need of social skills and friendly relations with others.[2] A relatively simple device is a brief questionnaire by which young people may anonymously indicate those among their

---

[2] R. J. Havighurst and Hilda Taba, *Adolescent Character and Personality*, pp. 217–19. New York: John Wiley & Sons, Inc., 1949. See also *How To Construct a Sociogram*. New York: Bureau of Publications, Teachers College, Columbia University, 1947.

associates whom they would choose first and second as companions in a number of situations such as playing a game, eating lunch, going to a party, or working in the shop. The number of times each student is mentioned in each area and in all areas is easily found. Special opportunities can be devised for those most in need of developing social skills.

Social status of students can be determined by means of an index which involves the ratings by parents or guardians on (*a*) occupations, (*b*) source of income, (*c*) house type, and (*d*) dwelling area.[3]

In numerous schools investigations have been made of hidden tuition costs which strain pocketbooks and of the participation in extraclass activities of students who come from families in low-income groups. It has generally been found that incidental expenses involved in high-school attendance range from $75 to $175 per year per pupil and that participation in extraclass activities varies directly with the incomes of families. By means of comparatively simple and brief questionnaires, samples may be secured to test probabilities that these conditions exist in any school. For conducting systematic studies of both tendencies, there are available precise directions which were prepared for the Illinois Secondary-School Curriculum Program.[4]

There are available many problem check lists, questionnaires, and interest inventories which are used by schools to identify common problems and interests among youth.[5]

In Colorado a check list submitted to more than 1,800 boys and girls in Grades IX to XII indicated that a topic of most interest in each of the four grades was: "How to act—manners and etiquette for business, parties, dates, and so forth." A topic of least interest in each grade was: "Labor, management, unions, and related problems."[6] Another check list submitted to another group of high-school students indicated that more than half of them wanted to make new friends and wanted people to like them more. A questionnaire submitted to more than 4,000 youth, Grades VII through XII, indicated that most of them had worries concerning their own growth and health and that most of them did not know

[3] W. L. Warner, M. Meeker, and K. Eells, *Social Class in America.* Chicago: Science Research Associates, 1949.

[4] Harold C. Hand, *How To Conduct the Participation in Extraclass Activities Study* (Circular Series A, No. 51, Illinois Secondary Curriculum Bulletin No. 5); *How To Conduct the Hidden-Tuition Costs Study* (Circular Series A, No. 51, Illinois Secondary Curriculum Bulletin No. 4). Springfield, Illinois: Office of the State Superintendent of Public Instruction, May, 1949.

[5] "S. R. A. Youth Inventory" (Chicago: Science Research Associates); "Thurstone's Vocational Interest Schedule" (Yonkers, New York: World Book Co.).

[6] Stephen Romine, *Youth Interests and the Educational Program of the Secondary School.* Boulder, Colorado: Extension Division, University of Colorado, 1951.

how to be good committee chairmen.[7] In each investigation common centers of interest were identified for large numbers of youth. The results indicated the opinions of students concerning the extent to which their needs were being met.

STUDYING OUT-OF-SCHOOL YOUTH
Follow-up Studies of Graduates

Traditionally, high schools have accepted the responsibility for placing and following up students who planned to enter college. At the end of the first semester, many college registrars send the marks of midyear Freshmen to the high schools from which the students have been graduated. A compilation of reports from registrars tells the principal how many of the high-school graduates have entered colleges and the academic successes and failures of the first semester. Sometimes the principal pays a visit to the campus of a college attended by a number of his former students and questions them about the strengths and weaknesses of their high-school experiences. In many instances, over a period of years high-school principals and college admissions officers have shared experiences in counseling and observing students as they made the transition from high school to college. They have common understandings and insights as a basis for communicating with one another and for meeting this particular need of some high-school graduates.

By accepting a similar responsibility for job placement and follow-up, many school placement officers have built a similar rapport with the employers of a community. Employers have learned that many individuals who possess high-school diplomas do not have the personal qualities and skills they need on a particular job. Thus, employers have learned to inquire about the school records of employees. Teachers have learned to use the successes and failures which pupils have had on jobs as measures of the strengths and weaknesses of their pupils and as criteria for an evaluation of the educational experiences the pupils have had.

School placement officers are quite naturally most interested in young people who give promise of being successful workers. Students who show the least promise are often the last to be recommended for placement.[8] As a result, the school loses an opportunity to place and follow up many of those who are in need of work and whose experiences would throw light on the difficulties which other students have in making vocational

---

[7] F. L. Pond, "Determining the Needs of Youth," *Bulletin of the National Association of Secondary-School Principals*, XXXV (October, 1951), 88–97.

[8] *Why Do Boys and Girls Drop Out of School and What Can We Do About It?* Federal Security Agency, Office of Education, Circular No. 269, 1950, p. 29. Washington: Government Printing Office, 1950.

adjustments. At least when labor shortages exist, schools should extend their knowledge of how vocational needs are being met by following up a type of worker not eagerly sought by employers.

A few high schools, especially those emphasizing vocational training, make follow-up studies of all students—early school-leavers as well as graduates and those who secured employment with or without school assistance. If the follow-up is made one year after the students leave school, it may reveal comparatively little in terms of what they may do eventually. Many of them do not find regular employment within the first year; others attend college for a year or two and then enter the labor force. A number of high schools send a questionnaire to each former student five years after he has graduated or left school. One school requires each student, during a school-leaving interview, to fill in his name and address on a questionnaire which is to be mailed to him five years later.

Early School-Leavers

Extent of Leaving. High schools have assumed that students can make better adjustments by remaining in school, where they live in a peer society and have the help of teachers and counselors, than by dropping out of school and trying to make the adjustments alone. If this assumption is valid, the holding power of the school is a measure of the extent to which youth needs are being met. The latest available figures on school retention indicate that, of every 1,000 pupils who were in the fifth grade in our schools in 1943, there were 505 who graduated from high school in 1950.[9] This is the highest retention rate ever reported for American high schools. Undoubtedly many satisfactory occupational adjustments were made by the 495 youth of each 1,000 who dropped out of school. However, it is fair to conclude that, for the most part, they did not feel that their needs were being met well enough in school to justify the expenditure of time and money required to graduate.

Causes for Leaving. When early school-leavers have been questioned concerning their reasons for dropping out of school, their answers have most often been classified under low family incomes, failures in school, poor health, lack of interest in school, and lack of parental interest in education. Youth who drop out of school may not be completely aware of their reasons or they may be anxious to conceal them. Hence, wherever possible, investigations should be conducted by skilled interviewers rather than through questionnaires which are delivered by mail.

In general the studies of drop-outs indicate that this very large group, most of whom leave school soon after the law for compulsory attendance

[9] *Statistical Summary of Education, 1949–50.* Federal Security Agency, Office of Education. Washington: Government Printing Office, 1952.

permits them to leave, includes a considerable number whose needs are not being met either by the school or by other institutions in the community.

Every widely based study of holding power which has been made in American high schools also indicates that youth from the lower-income families drop out of high school in proportions greatly in excess of their relative number in the group of high-school age. The holding-power studies conducted in a number of Illinois high schools provide important evidence of this type.[10]

Other findings of the Illinois holding-power studies were that the percentage of students dropping out varied greatly among different schools (size of school alone did not account for this wide variation), more boys than girls left school before graduation, and most drop-outs ranked in the lowest quarter of their class.[11]

Probably many factors contribute to the high rate of early school-leaving on the part of youth from lower-income families. Some of the factors which may be contributing in any community are low incomes which force all family members to work, family goals which do not include high educational attainments, difficulties of teachers in communicating with youth from lower-income groups, the comparatively small degree of participation of youth of this group in extraclass activities, and hidden tuition costs which strain pocketbooks. The school cannot deal directly with some of these factors, but it can make adjustment to reduce the importance of any one of them. In most communities information is needed on all such possibilities.

Techniques of Study. Many state departments of education and some local school systems have prepared directions and schedules for conducting studies of dropouts. Complete directions have been published for conducting the Illinois studies.[12]

During 1948-49 the Virginia State Department of Education conducted a state-wide study designed to aid local schools in improving programs for youth.[13] The study was unusual in that it covered a range of ten years and included both graduates and early school-leavers.

---

[10] Harold C. Hand, *Principal Findings of the 1947–48 Basic Studies of the Illinois School Curriculum Program*, p. 15. Circular Series A, No. 51, Illinois Secondary Curriculum Bulletin No. 2, 1949. Springfield, Illinois: Office of the State Superintendent of Public Instruction, 1949.

[11] *Ibid.*, pp. 13, 14.

[12] Charles M. Allen, *How To Conduct the Holding-Power Study.* Circular Series A, No. 51, Bulletin No. 3. Springfield, Illinois: Office of State Superintendent of Public Instruction, 1949.

[13] *Virginia's High-School Graduates and Drop-outs of 1939–40.* Richmond 16, Virginia: State Department of Education, 1951.

It is possible to use what is known about school drop-outs to identify possible school-leavers in early grades so that the needs of these pupils can be met better and the likelihood of retaining them in school increased. Periodic interviews with such pupils should be conducted to determine their satisfaction with school and the particular difficulties they experience.

Teachers and administrators are often mistaken in their opinions of the holding power of the schools in which they work. Especially is this true if their estimates are based upon a comparison between the graduates in a given year and the number who were in the class when it entered the school. Mobility is so great that transfers to and from a school conceal many early school-leavers. The only way to secure a defensible estimate of the holding power is to follow the progress of individual pupils, taking transfers into account. In recognition of this and similar problems, representatives of school systems in cities of more than 200,000 population developed uniform accounting procedures which would enable them to make valid comparisons on different aspects of early school-leaving from their school systems.[14]

Depth interviews by persons trained in interview techniques are effective instruments for securing information from former pupils and their employers. A good example of the use of this method is the study of out-of-school youth in Louisville, Kentucky, made in 1947 by the United States Department of Labor.[15] Interviews were held with 41 representative Louisville employers and 524 boys and girls fourteen through nineteen years of age who were out of school and working or seeking work. Items of particular interest to those who are endeavoring to meet the vocational needs of youth are the following: (*a*) The majority of employers favored the practice of hiring, for full-time employment, only young people at least eighteen years of age, although currently most of them were accepting some applicants at sixteen and seventeen. (*b*) In general, the youngest workers had the poorest jobs, the greatest difficulties in getting jobs, and the fewest job satisfactions. These findings provide additional evidence for the point of view that the retention in high schools of all youth of high-school age is an important aspect of the task of meeting youth needs.

The interview techniques used, as well as the findings of the Louisville study, have some implications for youth education in most communities.

---

[14] *Improving School Holding-Power*, pp. 23–31. Federal Security Agency, Office of Education, Circular No. 291, 1951. Washington: Government Printing Office, 1951.

[15] *Hunting a Career: Study of Out-of-School Youth, Louisville, Kentucky*. United States Department of Labor, Labor Standards Bureau, Bulletin No. 115, 1949. Washington: Government Printing Office, 1950.

Probably in no school will resources be available for such comprehensive interviewing of employers and former pupils. However, in any school some high-school Seniors, after being appropriately instructed, can interview some employers or some workers who are former pupils of the school. It is not necessary to interview all employers or all school-leavers at one time. If some information is collected systematically each year it will serve as a valuable resource in helping pupils move from where they are to where they need to be in order to achieve reasonable adjustments on beginning rungs of vocational ladders.

STUDYING THE SCHOOL AND ITS PROCESSES
Check Lists for Experts

A number of devices have been used to study the school and its processes. In surveying a local school system, one professional staff developed a set of rating scales which was used to check the extent to which classroom practices were being adapted to the needs of individual pupils.[16] The scales, which were used by staff members in systematic observation of classroom activity, treated twelve distinct phases of learning situations in the classroom. For example, the first three phases listed were:

(1) Motivation. What is the motivational level on which learners are operating?
(2) Assignments. How are assignments handled?
(3) Problem identification. What practice is given in guided problem identification?

For each of the twelve phases, the scale consisted of seven identifying levels which were given ratings of one to seven. The ratings recorded by the observers were, in general, lower for classes in the senior high school than for those in junior high schools and elementary schools. In the same survey, the Illinois Pupil Inventory was used to secure responses of pupils to such questions as, "How well do you think you get along with your teachers?" and "Does your school give you enough help in choosing a vocation?"[17]

Opinion Polls

Several check lists and inventories have been developed to make possible the systematic registering of opinions by parents, teachers, and pupils concerning the extent to which youth needs are being met. A list of 160 statements has been developed from the "Ten Imperative Needs

---

[16] *A Look at Springfield Schools*, pp. 184 ff. Prepared by Illini Survey Associates, College of Education, University of Illinois. Champaign, Illinois: Stipes Publishing Co., 1948 (mimeographed).

[17] *Ibid.*, p. 189.

of Youth"[18] which, according to a professional jury, would identify any
school making great progress in meeting the needs of all youth. Such devices can be used to good advantage by any faculty or faculty committee
for the purpose of rating a school as strong or weak on each of the items
or characteristics listed. The weakest characteristics of the school can be
identified, and consideration can be given to raising these low points.

Self-appraisal check lists used in a survey of 169 participating high
schools in Texas included 120 statements of belief and 447 statements of
procedures.[19] Each school was appraised on the basis of its recognition of
the desirability of each belief and procedure and also of the extent to
which each one of the beliefs and procedures was being actually achieved.
The appraisals helped to identify weak points most in need of improvement.

A North Carolina study used a list of 300 curriculum practices and
conditions which, experts assumed, would aid greatly in meeting the "ten
imperative needs of youth."[20] This list was submitted in many communities of the state to teachers, parents, and pupils who were asked to indicate their opinions concerning the desirability of the practices. Next,
teachers of the local schools were asked to indicate their own judgments
concerning the extent to which the practices considered desirable were
actually being carried on. According to the teachers, especially in the
smaller schools, many of these desirable practices were not being carried
on. Thus, consensus was developed that a number of specific improvements should be made.

Similar techniques were used in each local school in Illinois which participated in the state curriculum-improvement program. This survey
was based on a list of 55 real-life problems of youth subsumed under the
following headings: earning a living, developing an effective personality,
living healthfully and safely, managing personal finances wisely, spending leisure time wholesomely and enjoyably, taking an effective part in
civic affairs, preparing for marriage, homemaking, and parenthood, and
making effective use of educational opportunities.[21] Inventories were developed to secure opinions from teachers, pupils, and patrons concerning

---

[18] William L. Ransom, "How Well Does Your School Rate on the Ten Imperative Needs of Youth?" *Bulletin of the National Association of Secondary-School Principals*, XXXIII (October, 1949), 8–46.

[19] John W. McFarland, "Life Adjustment Education in Texas Schools," *Bulletin
of the National Association of Secondary-School Principals*, XXXVI (January, 1952),
97–105.

[20] *Education in North Carolina*, pp. 149–63. Report of the State Commission,
United Forces for Education. Raleigh, North Carolina: The Commission, 1948.

[21] Hand, *op. cit.*

the amount of help the school should provide for pupils in meeting these specific problems. Other inventories were developed to secure opinions from teachers, patrons, and graduates concerning the amount of help the schools actually provided for pupils in meeting these problems. In most local schools, teachers, pupils, and patrons were agreed upon some approaches which they should make to meet the needs of youth. For example, in one school the inventory revealed that both teachers and parents believed that more attention should be given to preparation for marriage, homemaking, and parenthood. However, each group had been reluctant to move for fear of opposition from the other. The report of the inventory encouraged them to co-operate in developing the desired program.

In his report to the governor and legislature in January, 1952, the superintendent of public instruction in the state of Michigan included first returns from an opinion poll conducted on a state-wide basis to find out what the people thought of their schools and what they wanted from them. Most of the citizens believed the schools were doing a good job and most of them were agreed on the necessity of vocational education and education for home and family living. It is always possible to study systematically opinions concerning the extent to which the needs of youth are being met, and these opinions should always be taken into account.

STUDYING COMMUNITIES
Youth Needs in Relation to Community Resources

In this section we turn to the problems of the community to assess their sources of strength and weakness for meeting the individual needs of youth. Many of the needs of youth cannot be met by the school alone. Investigations of youth needs and the extent to which they are being met lead finally to problems of community and national concern. For example, in a contracting economy it will be difficult to meet the need that youth have for a place in the world of work. Outside the local community it will be more difficult for those youth who, as members of minority groups, are subject to various measures which are discriminatory. Community and culture are not synonymous, but the community exists within the larger culture; and there is always the need to keep both in mind when studying either.

Some of the important factors which influence adolescents are the number of persons in the different age and sex groups in the population, the concentration of population, the historical and geographical backgrounds of the people, the ways in which the people earn their living, the level of income, the percentage of home ownership, and the attitudes toward secondary and higher education. Many similar factors are frequently named and described in discussions of school and community relationships.

An example of the significance for youth of population characteristics is provided in many southern cities where there are as few as 85 males for every 100 females among the Negro population.[22] Certainly such situations are of concern to Negro girls who are looking forward to stable homes and family life. An example of the importance of vocational opportunities and of the historical background of the people is provided in a number of American Indian tribes which are largely non-English speaking. The needs which such Indian youth have for communication skills are quite different from those of youth from English-speaking homes; the vocational needs of the Indian youth may vary widely depending upon whether they plan to live on the Indian reservation where they face a contracting economy or to live in some industrial area where vocational opportunities are increasing but where some discriminatory practices may exist. In similar fashion the needs of youth in any local school may appear to depend upon different factors in the resources or the mores of the community.

Community Characteristics of Especial Significance to Youth

Social diagnosis, like medical diagnosis, is carried on by attention to symptoms. Some symptoms of social disorganization are divorce, illegitimacy, and venereal disease. If a community has a high rate in these three social disorders, it may be assumed that home and family living in the community are especially in need of improvement.

Nonvoting, crime and delinquency, and a high rate of accidents are evidence of a low level of citizenship. In a community where the economy provides full employment, the frequent appearance of the names of young workers on the lists of the local employment service office may indicate that such workers remain on the job only long enough to acquire compensation rights and then use up the accumulated benefits in periods of voluntary idleness. Frequent job changes by youth and failure to seek jobs which are available are other symptoms which may indicate poor adjustment of youth to work. Loss of time and loss of life from preventable diseases indicate that personal health is left to chance rather than guarded by intelligent personal vigilance or general community action.

It may be assumed that a community is meeting many important needs of youth if records regarding persons 15 to 24 years of age show a low rate of crime, a good state of health, full and regular school attendance dovetailed with full and regular employment, and a high rate of

---

[22] Gordon W. Blackwell in *1949 Work Conference on Life-Adjustment Education*, p. 29. Washington: Federal Security Agency, Office of Education, 1950.

marriage and childbearing. To the extent that the reverse is true, it may be assumed that many needs of youth are not being met. There is no implication here that complacency is warranted by a low rate of crime. The goal is the prevention of crime; and all the needs of all the youth are important considerations to the school.

Statistics as a Guide to How Youth Needs Are Being Met in a Community

Citizenship. When looking for evidence on the level of citizenship practiced by youth in a community, probably the place to begin is a study of the bare minimum which society requires, namely, observing the law. What are the statistics on delinquency and crime for the population group under twenty-four years of age? What crimes are most frequently committed? What are the trends? What are the relationships between the incidence of delinquency and property values in particular areas?

How do the rates of delinquency for boys and girls in that particular community compare with the rates in other communities? In using statistics on crime and delinquency, it should be kept in mind that on a national scale such statistics are often lacking in reliability. Uniform systems for accounting are not in use in the different towns and counties in the United States. Even with uniform accounting, the records of different governmental areas would not be comparable where policing practices are not uniform. However, in a community where police and court policies have been uniform over a period of years and the accounting system has not been changed, it is possible to use statistics to establish trends.

In addition to overt acts which bring youthful offenders into court, the school can study its own statistics for evidence of behavior which frequently precedes or accompanies delinquency. Truancy and vandalism are symptoms of apathy and revolt. The number of days of absence from school and the number of broken windows in a school building are clues to the rise and fall of adjustment to the civic aspects of school life.

Another measure of good citizenship is the amount of responsibility that youth are willing to assume for their personal safety and the safety of others. The accident rate for young drivers, young workers, and home members should provide some evidence on the growth of attitudes and habits which safeguard human life.

Finally, there is the question of participation in the civic life of the community as voters. How many youth at the age of twenty-one register and vote? How does this figure compare with other cities or with the national average of voting? These statistics are definite and can be used.

Home and Family Living. Stability and continuity are basic factors in good family life. While statistics on divorce and desertion are one measure of these factors, such over-all statistics are difficult to get, and the difference in state laws affects their use for comparative purposes. The age of marriage in the community is another measure. In general, local customs which encourage or permit youths of fifteen or sixteen to marry probably mean that young people in the community marry the first persons of the opposite sex who attract them. On the other hand, if the age of marriage is several years beyond the national average of 20.3 years for brides and 22.7 for grooms, the youth of the community are probably inclined to postpone founding a home until they have provided for other things which they consider more important. Promiscuous sexual relations are a threat to stable families, and illegitimacy and the venereal-disease rate are measures of promiscuity. Statistics in this area must be used with caution. Divorced couples may remarry and found stable families, and a high venereal-disease rate in one community may mean that more cases are found and reported there while less medical attention is given to the problem in other communities.

There are other measures of the quality of home and family living in a community. For example, what proportion of the adult population is married? What is the size of families in the community? Is there a tendency for parents with higher incomes and more years of schooling to have larger families? Has this increase been as large as the national increase from 1940-47 which indicates that mothers with the most schooling showed the greatest increase in fertility?

Leisure. Statistics on actually harmful uses of leisure are difficult to obtain. Alcoholism seldom afflicts youth, but drug addiction in youth has become serious in some communities. Statistics on gambling are frequently quoted but are over-all estimates which have no local significance. For measuring the quality of community recreation, statistics of a positive kind are more reliable and a better guide. For many years statistics have been gathered on the circulation of books at the public library, the circulation of magazines and newspapers, attendance at movies, concerts, and plays, and the number of radio and television sets, and the programs which are most popular in the community. Participation in games, sports, dances, and other organized social groups is another measure. A large part of the leisure time of many family members is spent in taking care of the home, the grounds, and the family automobile. Work done in the home and on the home is a contribution to high community standards.

In making any assessment of recreation in a community, the criteria for "good" recreation should be established. There are three general approaches:

1. Any recreation is good if the person enjoys what he is doing and if his activity is not harmful to himself or others.
2. Recreation is good when the activity engaged in is of some benefit to the health or personality of the individual.
3. At least some of the time spent in recreation should have some content which will help the person grow intellectually. This point of view has been advanced by those seeking better reading, better movies, better radio and television.

Probably a scale for judging recreation should include all three criteria. At a minimum, recreation should not destroy or degrade the person —at a maximum, it might improve his personality.

The Importance of Facts about Particular Communities

Personal judgments which are not based on knowledge of attainable standards and the status of the community in relation to these standards have little value. Whenever possible, facts should be secured as bases for judgments. The two questions to be answered are: (a) How well can a community meet the needs of its youth? (b) How does this community compare with the best communities? The following example illustrates the use of research to pin-point an area of child needs in a community.

In a national survey of infant mortality, a prosperous and proud American city appeared as second from the bottom in the group of cities with more than 200,000 population. The city with the highest infant mortality rate was admittedly unhealthful. The report convinced the citizens of the presumably healthy city that something was wrong, and a local survey was undertaken immediately to learn where and from what causes babies under one year of age had died. Remedial action which followed reduced the infant mortality rate 50 per cent in one year. Attainable standards may be established by reference to local as well as national statistics.

In a community settled by Swiss immigrants during the nineteenth century, only one homicide has occurred during the community's history. Many other communities of the same size have averaged one homicide a year during the same period. One community discovered that 250 young men and women, age twenty-one, had registered to vote for the first time. In the same community during the same period of time intervening between registration for voting, 1,100 liquor permits had been granted to citizens who had become eligible for these permits because they had reached their twenty-first birthday.

Securing Community Facts

Not only does securing of local statistics make possible the estimating of gaps between present status and future goals but it may also serve to enlist the interest of the community in further analyzing and meeting youth needs. Facts about communities often make it clear that there are many educational agencies in the community and that youth problems are the responsibility of the entire community.

By spotting the incidence of delinquency upon a map, school administrators in a midwestern city found that a definite relationship existed between juvenile delinquency and income levels. Juvenile offenses were most frequent where real estate values were lowest and where the fewest recreation facilities were available.

Teachers, administrators, and pupils should share in the experience of finding facts about the community. Often it is wise to share sponsorship of such an enterprise with some other agency in the community, such as a community council, a family-life council, or a service club. There should always be a clearly stated purpose and plan of action to follow up any community investigation which may be undertaken. Here and always, there is little point in collecting information about the present situation unless something is going to be done to improve it.

As the specific purpose of the investigation is defined and as the kinds of information to be gathered are determined, all data already available should be examined. Previous surveys, the federal census, community records, court records, market research agencies, and the local chamber of commerce are examples of sources from which pertinent data may be secured. The experience of other communities or agencies which have made similar surveys should also be helpful. Some of the outlines for making community surveys should be consulted.[23]

There should be developed a pattern of inquiry suited to the purpose of the investigation, the nature of the community, and the available staff. Instruction should be provided for the investigators, and this advance preparation should be supplemented by meetings during the survey, so that workers may have the opportunity to discuss problems and to exchange information as the work progresses. A calendar or schedule should be set for the progressive steps of the survey and each step should be carried out in logical order.

---

[23] Henry Harap, *Outline for Community Survey*, Nashville Curriculum Laboratory, Bulletin No. 64. Nashville, Tennessee: George Peabody College for Teachers, 1938.

Know Your Community. United States Office of Education, Leaflet No. 57, 1941. Washington: Government Printing Office.

M. M. Chambers and Howard Bell, *How To Make a Community Youth Survey.* Washington: American Council on Education, 1939.

Irving T. Sanders, *Making Good Communities Better*. Lexington, Kentucky: University of Kentucky Press, 1950.

Concluding Statement

This chapter has suggested procedures for securing information concerning the extent to which youth needs are being met. Because so many broad areas are encompassed by the purpose of this chapter, the suggestions we have offered for three of the areas discussed in the chapter are presented only in outline form. These areas are: obtaining standards for youth, studying individuals, and securing facts about communities. Community characteristics of significance to youth have been pointed out and sample studies of groups of youth in school and out of school have been described. Examples have been cited of the systematic gathering of opinions from both experts and lay citizens concerning the effectiveness of the school program. It has been assumed that the basic material from which teachers, parents, pupils, and administrators develop plans of action for improving instructional programs for youth is the information bearing on the extent to which youth needs are being met.

The task which faces leaders in education today is to help make clear to each pupil in the school the meaning which large political, social, and economic situations in his community have for him as an individual. American society with all its problems must be viewed psychologically. The pupil must see how these situations influence his career, his developing personality, and his inner life with its moral and spiritual values. With the facts bearing on problems in the community at hand, he can set his goals and devise methods for reaching them. These goals may be an adaptation of the individual to the pattern of life which the community offers him. The pupil may decide to remain aloof from a community pattern which he refuses to accept and feels that he cannot change. He and his generation may decide to build a new pattern for a healthier, more honest or more intellectual community. Another alternative in a mobile society like our own is to leave and search for another community more to his liking.

In acting as a guide in reaching these decisions, the school will have helped its pupils grow in understanding of themselves and of society and, most important of all, of the relationship of the individual to the society in which he lives. In a dynamic society such as ours, the individual must face a future in which he will have to solve problems as yet unseen by methods as yet undevised. Learning how to meet his needs is not a final act but a process which he will use all his life.

CHAPTER V

THE ROLE OF THE SCHOOL ADMINISTRATOR IN DEVELOPING EDUCATIONAL PROGRAMS FOR YOUTH

James H. Cherry

General Assistant Superintendent
Joliet Township High School and Junior College
Joliet, Illinois

Basic Factors in Effective Administration

Understanding Current Concepts of Educational Leadership

If education is to serve democracy, such service must be oriented by experience in situations in which democracy is practiced as a way of getting at all aspects of educational endeavor. Three generalizations are pertinent to this point of view where effective administrative leadership is to be exercised in adapting secondary-school programs to the needs and interests of youth in a democracy.

First, educational responsibilities in the public schools are both residual and delegated in nature. Some of the obligations in the educative process are retained by the people. Others are delegated by the people to the board of education, which in turn makes delegations to the school administrator. The administrator further commits certain functions to his administrative and supervisory staff, the teachers, staff specialists, or maintenance employees. Still other educational responsibilities are assumed by the learner. Effective administration can be more fully realized when all of these levels of responsibility are involved in the formulation of educational programs. Participation should be in terms of the inherent educational functions of each level.

Second, although meaningful education starts at the point of the learner's needs, interests, and capacities, it proceeds through purposeful activity to social ends. If there is a gap or inconsistency between the individual's developmental outlook and the requirements of the society, the educative process helps the individual learner to adjust himself to the standards of the society. If, however, the gap or inconsistency is so great that the individual cannot make a suitable adjustment without frustration or undue tension, then education should join with the society in the consideration of an acceptance of norms which are compatible with individual needs in a democracy. Effective administration, then,

81

implies a sharing of the responsibility of bringing together the representatives of those social agencies which should take part in studying evolving norms or cultural directives and, particularly, of formulating such educational programs as these norms and directives imply.

Third, the outcomes of education pertain to the whole child, the whole citizen, and the whole society. No one of these can be considered fully without reference to the others; nor can any one of them be dissected for isolated study without involving the related parts of the whole. In educational planning, therefore, artificial and imaginary segments of the program cannot be severed from the whole for separate planning and programming, for all parts operate as one. Administration, then, considers its responsibilities in the educative process as they relate to improving the ability of the school, in co-operation with the whole society, to provide for each learner the most favorable opportunities for the fullest realization of his potentialities.

These generalizations point to the planned participation of different levels of educational responsibility and different social institutions in situations in which effective leadership is to be exercised for the sake of proposed improvements in the program of the schools. Although the administrator has a definite legal status, he should be the first to recognize the fact that leadership in a democracy is concerned with the value of its services to society, not particularly with its authority under the law. An examination of the foundations of administrative responsibility may well reveal that they contain vestiges of authoritarian practices, either as a result of studied usurpation or through the failure of persons representing other levels of responsibility in the educational structure of the community to accept their fair share of the obligations of citizenship in a democracy.

In planning to meet a social situation of community-wide concern, the real leadership in that situation may appear in the person of an individual connected with any one of its facets, whether or not that individual happens to be in a position of legally established authority. Furthermore, the real leadership shifts from time to time, from person to person, or from group to group as the actual planning and the performance move through various phases. Because of this characteristic of leadership, confidence in group work is well-founded. The school administrator should realize that members of the group must be chosen for their sense of responsibility to education and to society. Also, he should understand the processes by which groups get work done. He should recognize responsible leadership wherever he finds it and put it to its fullest use; and when leadership is lacking he should nurture it. He should be constantly alert to the need for removing any barriers to full participation on the part of persons who are sharing in planning and carrying on the appropriate activities. He should point out evidences of achievement by group members at the earliest opportunity in order to foster group confidence and should point them up in such a way as to enable the participants to identify their own contributions and to recognize their worth.

At its basis, then, the leadership of the administrator is at once creative, consultative, and co-ordinating in nature. It is creative to the extent that it unassumingly sets up situations in which the leadership of others can be recognized and can flourish. It is consultative as it serves in the capacity of a friendly adviser. It is a co-ordinating leadership if the school and community are to function effectively in bringing their resources to bear directly on the problems of common interest to the learner, to the community, and to society as a whole.

Accepting a Consistent Philosophy of Education

The administrator himself must understand what democracy is and must believe in a philosophy of education which is consistent with basic concepts of democracy.

In a democratic society, two community-interest characteristics are manifest. First, those who are to live by a decision may share in making it. Secondly, those sharing in decisions will respect the points of view and the contributions of one another. These characteristics of the democratic society imply that all members of the society will be enlightened to the fullest extent of their capacities and that all will be kept fully informed, particularly about issues in which their own welfare is involved. They suggest that a democracy seeks to provide for all individuals a reasonable opportunity to attain suitable standards of living. They denote society's faith in the ability of the individual to develop more fully. They signify conviction with respect to the principle of the consent of the governed. They are predicated on a common reliance on rational and critical thinking.

In a democratic society, the school should be a place where democracy is practiced as a way of learning and as a way of living. If all human beings are believed to be of equal worth, then the schools have the responsibility of providing equal educational opportunities for all. The educative process should enable the learner to face up to the norms of living and to the basic issues of the day in such a manner that action for change can be taken where change is needed. The learner must acquire the ability to identify and analyze problems and must develop an understanding of where to find, how to evaluate, and how to use source materials. He must achieve the ability to think critically and must gain acceptable understandings, information, attitudes, appreciations, and skills that will enable him to share effectively in the society and culture of which he is a part.

If education is to keep abreast of a changing culture, the curriculum and all the procedures of the school should be developed through common counsel with the community and its social institutions. Objectives of the curriculum should be stated in terms of the needs of the learner as a member of a democratic society and should lead to the fulfilment of these needs. Both in the classroom and about the school there should be evidence of the use of community councils, community planning groups, and joint parent-pupil-teacher planning. An increasing number of the units of learning should be directed toward activity based on (a) identifying and exploring a situation, (b) formulating new modes of action or hypotheses, and (c) putting the formulations into practice. The classroom and activities programs should exhibit evidences of a competent identification of individual needs, interests, capacities, and abilities of the students; and the policies and procedures of the school should indicate a general alertness to the great problems confronting the culture, such as problems of conservation, national defense, and international understanding.

Understanding Sound Principles of Curriculum Planning

Educational engineering involves the reconstruction of social ideals, beliefs, and institutions. While it cannot repudiate all of the traditions of the past, neither can it always stand for the preservation of the existing order when that order clearly contributes to increasing cultural and individual frustrations or ignores basic biological drives. Of course, sound engineering seeks to preserve what is good, but at the same time it aims at the modification or elimination of what is inconsistent. The school administrator will find many opportunities for the exercise of effective leadership in the improvement of the secondary-school program if he has a good understanding of principles of sound educational engineering. Since the schools are a social institution there is a cultural relationship between the school and the community. Therefore, judicious curriculum planning will recognize the necessity for promoting community understanding of desirable curriculum revisions through community participation in the engineering of the changes to be instituted. Effective community participation cannot be expected without the aid of influential leaders of the organized civic forces of the community.

The engineering process should make use of the entire faculty, representative learners, and representatives of the lay community. With consistent emphasis on the values of group-planning procedures, the school administrator should aim at the broadest possible consensus of the participants with respect to decisions or actions on the problems under consideration.

There appear to be at least four distinct elements of social planning which have application to the school and its curriculum.

1. Before sound programs can be expected to result from efforts at improvement, there must be effective commitment to a common point of view about what should be done. The task to be undertaken must be corrective of cultural shortcomings and meaningfully related to the cultural norms. The point of view should be adequate so far as sociological factors are concerned, and it should be practical psychologically.

2. There must be a willingness of all participants to search out present cultural inadequacies, to recognize them when they are found, and to study their influences on the problems at hand in a forthright manner.

3. When deviations between practices and expectations are uncovered, a clear mental picture of adequate programs to meet the inadequacies must be developed.

4. Finally, programs must be carried out to make the mental picture a working reality.

Envisioning the Broad Outlines of an Effective Educational Program

By his training and experience the administrator should have acquired a point of view which will enable him to visualize the broad outlines of an educational structure that will provide administratively for the adaptation of school programs to the needs of youth. He should recognize that planning programs must promote administrative designs to accommodate two major kinds of needs, the common needs of all youth and the specialized needs essential to the attainment of individual goals.

The social setting presents certain requirements common to all, which ought to be in reality an influence binding the society together. Too, there are other needs which have their origin in the purely physical or biological needs of human beings and thus are common to all. These two types of needs are often called common needs. Moreover, certain segments of the society have specialized requirements, and certain individuals have specialized interests and capacities. These are often referred to as specialized needs.

In educational planning, analysis of needs results in another kind of classification of needs, which may be better identified by calling them generalized and particularized needs. Such a classification may well include in either category both common and specialized needs. Generalized needs are broad, general classifications of needs which give the educational program its major direction, while the more minutely diagnosed particularized needs may often be used as starting points of lessons or units to give the learning situation its motivation and drive. At every stage of thinking, care must be exercised to avoid confusing needs with ways of meeting needs. In the educational program both the common and the specialized learnings which are devised to enable youth to meet their common and specialized needs must be so clearly identified and so widely approved that each learner will acquire socially acceptable motives and goals.

The alert administrator should recognize the futility of attempting to implement needs-meeting programs by means of the traditionally compartmentalized secondary-school schedule. The educational experiences planned for the individual learner should be meaningful learning experiences which enable him to meet his common and specialized needs. Therefore, it would appear logical that the school day, the school year, and the total school experience should reflect a division of time in which one block of the learner's time is set aside for common learnings, which might well amount roughly to the time now spent in required courses. The remainder of the student's time should be spent in the exploration of individual interests and capacities leading into vocational and avocational pursuits. However, specialized learnings would be consciously oriented to common learnings, so that those special types of experience which contribute to social competence will not become detached from the society as a whole.

The ability of the secondary school to adapt its program to the needs and interests of youth undoubtedly bears considerable relationship to the grouping of students for longer blocks of time. With this kind of secondary-school schedule there will be greater opportunities for using community resources, for dealing with whole problems, and for making use of group planning.

UTILIZING THE INTEREST AND RESOURCES OF THE STAFF

Since most American educators agree that one of the main functions of education is to promote democracy as a way of life, the procedure by which the school adapts secondary-school programs to the needs of youth should be democratic all along the line from the earliest planning through the evaluation stage. Although the administrator can usually take it for granted that teachers are vitally interested in the welfare of youth, it will be discovered, as different situations are faced, that there are some differences in the points of view of staff members. One of the early purposes of improvement programs, therefore, should be to increase staff concensus concerning the points of view from which such work should be undertaken. Furthermore, the planning and implementing efforts of the

staff should be viewed as learning situations which will provide opportunities for growth on the part of the teachers.

Utilizing the Interest and Resources of Individual Teachers

The fortuitous occasions on which the administrator meets the teachers in individual conferences are legion. These situations, involving such
subjects as personal problems and aspirations, professional growth, and
teaching problems, provide opportunities for the alert administrator to
encourage staff members to do a planned program of study in higher institutions of learning. For teachers who are opposed to changes in the
curriculum, such a program of study will often change an attitude of
indifference to one of wholesome concern.

The reading of periodicals and books dealing with an idealized curriculum should be encouraged. The administrator should have a wide
selection of books and periodicals in his own library as well as a knowledge of what is in the professional library so that he may offer suggestions
to staff members in accordance with the particular problems or interests
of each teacher. A planned follow-up will often bolster the teacher's desire
to do something as a result of such professional reading.

Attendance at workshops and educational conferences should be encouraged. The school should provide an adequate budget for travel and
expenses for the largest possible number of staff members at workshops
and professional meetings. A faculty committee should share in planning
for the school's participation in workshops and conferences. Participants
may be recognized faculty leaders who are able to contribute to the workshops and conferences, or they may be teachers who might be encouraged
to assume more important local roles as a result of their participation in
such professional meetings. Reports by these participants to the entire
staff, or to appropriate staff groups, and the discussions which result often
stimulate teachers to more effective participation in the local developmental programs.

Staff members should be encouraged to engage in case studies. Informal or formal conferences about teaching and learning often turn on
the so-called problem child, the slow learner, or some unusual capacities
or contributions of class members. In these situations the possibilities of
a more complete case study of a particular pupil sometimes becomes apparent. The teacher who engages in a case study under adequate guidance
frequently becomes more sensitized to the problems of the learner in the
learning process, to the varying needs of youth, to the many influencing
factors in learning, and to the school and community resources which
may be utilized in improving needs-meeting programs. If each teacher
carries out only one case study each year and follows through on it, a

great stride toward the reconstruction of educational programs to meet youth needs and interests can soon be made.

Utilizing the Interest and Resources of the Faculty as a Whole

The administrator will need to work both with individual teachers and with the faculty as a whole. Most schools carry on a program of faculty meetings. Effective administration requires a planned program of in-service training, involving the staff as a whole, which envisages a constantly improving staff ability to deal with situations which obstruct development and progress. This program is best carried on if it is jointly planned, for in shared planning more complete engagement of faculty interest and effort is assured. The in-service training of faculty-wide scope, in a school which is planning and carrying out programs adapted to the needs of youth, should be focused on the following objectives.

1. *Continuing faculty participation in the development of a philosophy of education.* Divergence between beliefs and action programs leads to frustration and insecurity on the part of teachers who are honestly trying to move forward. Therefore, it would seem desirable that there be a continuing program aimed at stating beliefs about the functions of education in order to point up divergences between beliefs and practices. It is important that the divergences be stated finally as problems and that the staff as a whole develop action programs aimed at solving the problems.

2. *Faculty meetings on educational research and curriculum reconstruction.* Educational literature is full of reports of research dealing with teaching, learning, educational functions and objectives, group planning techniques, and successful practices. Unless a persistent effort is being made constantly to enable faculty members to acquaint themselves with latest research and thinking, there will be a wasteful lag between the contributions of the educational laboratory and prevailing educational practices. This problem is accentuated by the fact that in any faculty the training backgrounds will vary tremendously both as to time and point of view. Some faculty members will have experienced a much greater training emphasis on content and a much smaller training emphasis on understanding teaching skills. Faculty meetings planned to bring to the faculty the results of educational research and curriculum study should aim to acquaint faculty members with the practical values of such studies.

3. *Encouraging the study and discussion of recognized principles of curriculum construction and their relation to current practices.* There are many books and periodicals dealing with curriculum planning in idealized situations. Some of these works are the result of individual research, others have been written by selected commissions, and some originated as

reports of conferences. Such reading tends to increase the resourcefulness of the teaching staff in developing programs for meeting the needs and interests of youth.

4. *Carrying on surveys and studies basic to curriculum development.* Before effective curriculum development can take place, the problems, attitudes, and dynamics of the community must be explored and identified. The very act of engaging in school and community studies sensitizes the staff to situations which need study and attention.

5. *Faculty workshops on the interpretation of studies and surveys.* Even though the entire staff has been engaged in carrying on a study or a survey, there may be a lack of concensus about what findings are significant. A joint faculty study enables the entire group to come to an agreement on the proper interpretation of the findings.

6. *Faculty workshops on developing concensus concerning needs which should be met.* Action programs designed to adapt the purposes of education to the needs and interests of youth are well founded if they originate in a situation of general accord concerning what needs are paramount, as revealed by surveys. Unless there is considerable consensus, developmental programs may become confused through diversity of attack.

7. *Studying the effectiveness of the guidance program.* Guidance is a specialized service of the school which attempts to meet certain youth needs which are not being met in the regular teaching program. The guidance program of the school offers an excellent opportunity to alert staff members to the needs-meeting function of education. The emphasis in such a program of faculty study should be to improve teacher competency in an increasing range of guidance activities.

8. *Encouraging faculty participation in the development of administrative policies and practices.* Unless administrative policies are under constant study, they may become restrictive of developmental programs. Constant revision is necessary if administrative devices are to provide a free and permissive environment for continuing improvement in teaching. Such a program also provides an opportunity for teachers and administrators to work together. Often a joint teacher-administrator program of sharing in the development of desirable administrative policies provides a situation in which teachers can share in a feeling of satisfaction over the success of the newly established procedures.

Utilizing the Interest and Resources of Special Faculty Groups

It is axiomatic in developmental programs in education that the different curriculum and service areas of the school will be at different stages of progress at any given time. The administrative leadership of the school must recognize the need for giving working groups the opportunities for development which will challenge them in terms of their readiness to perform. Also, there is a level of participation in developmental programs at which a more specific pin-pointing of effort is required than faculty-wide endeavor can contribute. In still other instances administrative leadership will need to recognize the more specific interests of specialized-curriculum and service-areas personnel and to seize upon any readiness and willingness of individuals and faculty groups to take action. It is probable that all the points suggested in reference to engaging the entire faculty can be effectively used in more specific situations dealing with special groups of faculty members.

Supervisory Policies and Practices

Especially important to a continuing program of curriculum study is an emphasis by the administrative staff on teaching and learning situations which seem to have promise of meeting the needs and interests of youth. There should be an insistence on teaching-learning situations which are in keeping with the best research on child growth and development. Supervisory policies must anticipate developmental teaching programs by emphasizing teaching outcomes which will promote rather than obstruct curriculum revision. Supervisory practices must be under continuous study if they are to avoid conflict with developmental programs. Teachers who are sincerely trying to meet youth needs cannot teach effectively if their teaching is evaluated only in terms of the mastery of subject-matter.

Utilizing the Interest and Resources of Students and Community

Regardless of the type of community under consideration, there is a large amount of interest in education on the part of school youth and the lay public. Ideas of how the educational process should be administered may be quite diverse as to educational purposes, activities, and outcomes. The proper leadership of educational programs requires appropriate recognition of the interests of both students and the lay community as well as planned opportunities for them to participate in the discussion of needed improvements in the programs.

The school administrator in a democracy should recognize the right of every student in the school and every interested citizen of the community to expect the educational leadership in the community to keep him fully informed about educational issues and to provide the opportunity for him to share in making decisions which may affect him.

Keeping the Student Body and the Community
Informed about the School Program

The interest of students and community groups in curriculum development may be utilized to good advantage in the following ways.

1. *Newspaper and radio publicity.* An analysis of the coverage of curriculum and service areas of the school through newspaper and radio publicity may reveal that the major portion of the publicity is directed to such things as sports, dramatics, music activities, school finance, and building programs. Working through joint committees the administrator can help them search out and describe successful instructional programs and bring to the community a balanced diet of publicity which emphasizes first things first. All teachers should consider themselves publicity representatives of the school and should be encouraged to submit information about their teaching programs.

2. *Conscious emphasis in school publications.* School publications are often subject to the same sort of overemphasis of school news as newspaper and radio publicity. The administrator should urge the members of his staff who are in charge of school publications to secure the co-operation of the teaching staff, the students, and the community in planning and carrying out a program of publicity which will give recognition to all school programs and activities.

3. *Periodical school reports to the community.* Many schools use regular reporting procedures, such as periods when grade cards are sent home, as an opportunity to report to the community. Some of the school's activities do not lend themselves to publicity measures either through local newspapers and radio stations or in school publications. Such programs may need to be explained in greater detail than would make for readable news releases. In some cases, the administrator should select these activities or programs as the subject of special reports to the community. Perhaps this should not be a regular routine, since regularity makes it necessary for reports to go out whether or not the reports are needed. On the other hand, intermittent reports may also have a weakness in that the school may cease to be alert to its responsibility. Again, a joint committee of teachers, students, and community representatives could be of great assistance in determining what should go to the community in the form of special reports as well as the form in which it should be presented.

4. *School visitation program.* Although many schools designate special days or evenings when the public is invited for a visit, and, even though this is a most valuable way of keeping the community informed, the administrator should encourage individual staff members to report sig-

nificant or dramatic stages in their programs which would be of particular interest to parents and other citizens.

5. *Home visitation program.* The administrator will find it worth while to set up a program of home visitation under which the teachers will visit the homes of students at least once each year. In many communities this type of program would not involve a significant addition to the responsibilities of the school staff, since some curriculum and service areas are already carrying out a program of visitation which reaches a large number of homes. Teachers who are not used to making home visits would, of course, need training in the skills and amenities of acceptable home visitation as well as instructions on what to observe and report. Such a program, if effectively organized, will aid the teachers in securing important information about the needs and interests of school youth.

6. *Parent-teacher conferences on pupil progress.* Although it is not unusual for a teacher to carry on conferences in the event of student difficulties, the administrator should plan the teacher's schedule so that conferences can be carried on as a regular feature of the school program. Such a program, of course, has many desirable outcomes. Certainly one of these is the greater probability of the parent-teacher conference being carried on in an atmosphere of mutual respect, if the conference deals with pupil progress as a matter of course rather than as a result of difficulties which have arisen between teacher and pupil.

7. *Special reports to community agencies which have complementary responsibilities.* The community has many organizations which, by virtue of their interest in the welfare of the society, must come in contact with the school itself or with school youth. The school administrator should be alert to every possibility of reporting to those community agencies significant information or developments on problems with which they have complementary educational responsibilities.

8. *Special reports to the community.* Some phases of school programs are so important that it is often necessary for the administrator to go directly to the community to explain the school's purposes to every citizen. This is not a device which would have frequent use in most cases. It should be used only when deemed necessary by groups actively sharing in the determination of school policies and practices.

9. *Adult education programs.* One of the functions of the adult education program of the school should be to improve education. The administrator should provide competent instruction for adult classes in child care, child growth and development, principles of teaching, principles of school administration and supervision, principles of group dynamics, school organization, and school finance.

In every instance in which the school makes use of student and lay community participation in planning groups, committees, or councils, the administrator should encourage leaders of those groups to use every opportunity to instruct the participants on ways of accepting their full share of responsibility.

10. *Parent-teacher-student institutes on particular school problems.* The administrator may use the institute type of program for parents, students, and teachers to study school problems when there appears to be a need for both training on methods of promoting improvement in school services and opportunity for participation in decision-making. The institute can make use of outside consultants who can explain the purposes and the scope of the institute's program and give instruction on methods of determining the proper course to pursue. Such a program can be arranged to shift back and forth from lecture and demonstration to discussion, as the participating group shows readiness for each procedure.

11. *Regular day-school classes.* The administrator will find it advantageous to use classroom activities of the regular day school as opportunities to engage students and parents in planning and evaluating activities.

Utilizing the Interest of Students and Community as a Basis for Sharing in Making Decisions

A second principle the administrator should observe in utilizing the interest of students and community is that they should have the opportunity to share in making decisions about programs which will affect them. Joint planning groups will need to have a clear idea of the nature and scope of the work they are undertaking. Sharing activities should be carried on in an atmosphere of respect for the contributions of all participants. The school which carries on workshops on regular programs, special problems, and developmental projects will find these co-operative efforts successful to the extent that meaningful sharing is evident to all who take part. Meetings of parents, students, and the teachers of particular curriculum and service areas for discussion of the use of community resources in a unit of work on citizenship training, for example, will enable parents and students to contribute to the improvement of the educational programs with respect to the needs of youth. The learning which comes through more active participation in co-operative enterprises will become evident as a result of lay-learner contributions to the work of student councils, advisory committees, and planning groups. These increased understandings make not only for an enlightened community but also for a community which has an increasing sense of security because of its realization that it is actually taking part in the development of its educational program.

Making It Possible for the School Staff and the Community To Work Together in Co-operative Programs

Often there is a definite feeling throughout the school and community that something should be done toward developing better educational programs to meet youth and community needs. The starting point may not deal with curriculum at all but may deal with such issues as administrative policies and practices, improvement of salary schedules, or improvement of physical facilities.

Some schools have enabled the faculty to get developmental programs under way by organizing a problems-locating workshop. The most acute problems facing the faculty are apt to be identified in the workshop conferences. One method of approach would include some such general attack as the following:

1. Determining what the faculty believes the job of education is in relation to the problem of meeting the needs of youth.
2. Measuring the gap between what is being done and what ought to be done.
3. Identifying the most significant deficiencies as problems for attack.
4. Determining the order in which these problems should be attacked.
5. Analysis of personnel and other resources available for the tasks.
6. Selection of faculty production groups to do specific jobs.

As soon as a number of problems is identified for faculty attack and a number of production or working groups has been created, it becomes essential that some sort of steering device, preferably a representative committee, be created for developmental programs. If the developmental program has started within the school, the steering committee should be so organized that it can receive additional membership as community and student involvement occurs. The steering committee should deal primarily with policy-making and should have a clear understanding with the administration and the board of education as to the scope of its responsibility. Its functions within this agreed-upon framework should be:

1. To co-ordinate the work of production and working groups.
2. To furnish leadership to production groups.
3. To help keep production groups "on the beam."
4. To evaluate the work of production groups before such work is approved.
5. To analyze the opportunities for community co-operation.
6. To suggest opportunities for community participation in working groups.
7. To study consultant resources and suggest consultant personnel to work with production groups.
8. To analyze obstacles and difficulties and suggest ways of overcoming them.

The emphasis of the entire developmental program should be directed toward actually engaging the community and the students in both councils and working groups as well as the steering committee itself, since experience and actual participation in joint developmental programs is perhaps the most realistic way of developing community consensus about what the school should be doing.

To the extent that both the community and the student body are involved in the activities of the steering and the production groups, there will be a need for the orientation of student and lay members to the job which is being done and for the introduction of these groups to the principles of group process as they relate to the level of the responsibility in education represented by individual members. This is, of course, a crucial point in the initiation of developmental programs. If the situation at this point is not handled with extreme care, the student and community participants may well sense that they have little to do except to follow along a line already charted by the staff. At this point three things require consideration:

1. A redirection of developmental policies on the part of the steering committee so as to incorporate student and community viewpoints.
2. A redirection of the work of production groups to include lay ideas and aims concerning the job to be done.
3. Recognition of both lay leadership and student leadership as available resources for use by the production groups and the steering committees.

In order that improvement programs may be satisfactorily conducted, effective communication facilities must be provided so that the faculty, the students, and the community representatives may know what is going on. Whatever systems of communication are devised, they should be so planned that information will go out from the school to the community and reports of community reactions and ideas will get back to the school.

Within the school structure itself, provision should be made for both vertical and lateral communication, i.e., communication up and down the lines of the vertical organization of the school and laterally into the structural expansion areas involved in curriculum reconstruction and between production groups as well. A considerable amount of lateral communication can be accomplished by having some planned interlocking representation. A great deal of vertical and lateral communication can be accomplished through faculty meetings, school-community institutes, and student assemblies. The ordinary channels of public relations should be consciously made a part of the communications program to keep the community abreast of the programs as they evolve.

Whether work is being done by production groups, steering committees, or individuals, adequate records of all significant action and opinions should be kept. These should be produced in a sufficiently large number of copies to reach all groups or persons who are interested. At important points along the line mimeographed copies will need to go to the entire staff and to a large number of persons or organizations in the community.

Providing the Physical Means for Getting the Job Done

In adapting secondary-school programs to the needs of youth, the teachers, students, parents, and the lay public generally must come to realize that curriculum development is a part of teaching and should be going on wherever teaching is going on. There are, of course, some developmental jobs which must be done outside of the classroom. In these instances administration must provide leadership in setting up appropriate physical conditions through which developmental goals may be expressed. These would necessarily include adequate faculty time and school resources. In providing the physical means for getting developmental programs done, the administration will find the following measures helpful:

1. A steering committee or some other co-ordinating machinery should be provided as soon as the need for co-ordination is recognized.
2. Groups which have been functioning informally should be recognized as soon as their efforts can be identified as curriculum development.
3. Additional production groups should be set up as the need for detailed planning, intensive study, or the production of materials for teaching is recognized.
4. Adequate faculty time should be provided to get work done, through such means as:
   a) Regular release from daily teaching assignments.
   b) Intermittent release for shorter periods of time than a semester or quarter.
   c) Release of groups of teachers at the same time of day. This type of release is helpful when groups of teachers are engaged in studying common problems together with students in their classes.
   d) Long-term release for a specific production job.
   e) Leave of absence with pay for jobs which require absence from the school or community.
   f) Periodical school dismissal. In this case the developmental program should be of such scope that it can engage the interest and concern of the entire staff.
   g) Preschool and postschool workshops with pay.
5. Meeting places should be provided with facilities which lend themselves to all major phases of group work and all major activities in which the group will engage.
6. Provision will probably need to be made for research, testing, surveys, and consultant help.
7. Groups should have access to adequate professional curriculum libraries and will need certain basic materials in their possession constantly.

8. Meeting schedules should be set up so that all participants can attend.
9. Adequate clerical assistance must be made available.
10. Administrative assistance will be needed in the event control groups are used.
11. Administrative scheduling of completed developmental projects and programs should be prompt.

HELPING TO PROVIDE SECURITY FOR PERSONNEL INVOLVED IN IMPROVEMENT PROGRAMS

Participants in programs aiming at changes which depart from accepted ways of doing things may sometimes find themselves on the defensive in spite of careful planning. Schools and communities which are quite willing to generalize about change may show resistance when planning or action arrives at the point of specificity. The factors which contribute to a feeling of insecurity are cumulative as different groups sense that traditional methods and ideas are being evaluated in areas in which they are particularly interested. Careful joint planning, good communications, and early participation often preclude defensive tactics.

Administratively, effective leadership requires the development of policies and practices to enable the participants in programs which are calculated to end in change to have an opportunity to work in an environment of security. There are several ways administrative leaders can foster an atmosphere of security for those who are participating in programs for curriculum improvement. Some of these procedures are:

1. Providing adequate support for developmental programs.
2. Flanking curriculum development with an effective public relations program.
3. Defending changing programs against attack.
4. Helping to provide recognition to teachers who are conducting revised programs.
5. Assisting in taking stock of current educational effectiveness within the developmental area.
6. Demonstrating administrative interest and support by participating in curriculum revision.
7. Seeking effective ways of recognizing participants in programs which have shown progress.
8. Helping supervisory programs to sponsor worth-while changes in educational practices.

OVERCOMING OBSTACLES AND DIFFICULTIES

Those engaged in curriculum revision usually find that they must face many obstacles. While many of these problems stem from indifference or resistance to change, others arise through lack of understanding of educational procedures in a democracy. Many persons exhibit strong beliefs in traditional approaches to the teaching-learning situation. Others fear the consequences of shifting educational emphasis which might evolve from developmental programs. Some lack knowledge and understanding of recent research or basic factors in teaching and learning. Others have a dread of the results of experimentation because of unsatisfactory experiences with experimental programs which have failed to take hold or because of experimental work which has been rejected. Equally troublesome is a lack of knowledge of group-process principles.

Since fears and inadequacies may obstruct the way to programs of education, administrative leadership will be challenged at every point, and new roles of leadership in administration will present themselves with every forward movement. Space will permit calling attention to only a few of the measures which may anticipate or help overcome some of these more obvious difficulties in curriculum planning.

1. Early recognition and effective use of leadership in staff and community often avoids a situation in which aspiring leadership attempts to express itself through opposition tactics.
2. Continuing attempts should be made to involve the points of view and leaders of "pressure groups" in planning and working groups so that they will contribute to rather than oppose developmental programs.
3. Obstinate traditions and loyalties that seem to block progress should be identified and opposed, while loyalties that seem to accept the challenge of changed attitudes and progress should be fostered.
4. Constant attention and effort should be directed to measures which will enhance the status of teachers engaged in developmental programs.
5. Effective administration requires a keen sense of situations indicating that groups are baffled or lagging and a recognition of the kinds of assistance that will enable groups to renew their courage.
6. Every opportunity should be used to foster an awareness of progress through frequent evaluation.
7. Specialist and consultant help must be provided at the times and places that special competences and skills are recognized as being needed by the group.
8. Reference materials appropriate to group needs should be readily available.
9. Group meetings should feature "breaks" for social and recreational activities.
10. Recognition should be given to the fact that, in the main, steering groups should be responsible for general planning and co-ordinating activities, while detailed plans and materials are developed by production groups.
11. Faculty, student, and community participants should be truly representative of the significant groups which should share in the determination of program revision.
12. When group work is completed, the group should be encouraged to terminate activities promptly.
13. The creation of groups which duplicate the functions of other community groups should be avoided.
14. Use of persons who are neither interested nor ready should be avoided

generally, and participants who insist on leaving groups should be able to do so without loss of face.

15. The overburdening of willing leaders should be avoided.

UTILIZING LEADERSHIP OF NATIONAL, STATE, AND OTHER AGENCIES AND INSTITUTIONS

Although school programs to adapt secondary education to the needs and interests of youth depend in a large measure upon quality of administrative and supervisory leadership in the local school, there are many resources for leadership outside the local school and community. The well-planned program for improving the quality of educational efforts will analyze these outside resources in reference to ways of changing faculty outlook and attitude, the development of teaching and resource materials, the use of survey and research techniques, and the procedures of workshop and clinic planning.

Sources of Outside Leadership

Leadership may be found for developmental programs in (a) professional educational organizations; (b) state, regional, and national supervising and accrediting organizations; (c) colleges and universities; (d) other secondary schools where developmental programs are under way; (e) foundations and associations; (f) agencies with complementary educational responsibilities; and (g) leaders of organizations which have locals or chapters in the local community. Careful analysis of these various sources will undoubtedly reveal a large number of people who can do much to stimulate improvement in educational programs.

Types of Leadership

Within these sources of outside leadership not only are there persons with knowledge and experience who can render valuable consultant services but there are also research reports, publications, bulletins, and developmental materials from on-going programs that will be of great value to interested professional groups. The introduction of these types of leadership at just the right time will enable planning and working groups to overcome many obstacles which arise out of lack of knowledge about next steps.

Assisting in Making Effective Use of Consultants

In calling for consultant services, the local school should recognize that it has certain responsibilities which will enable it to make the most use of consultants.

1. The local school should establish some goals for work prior to the arrival of the consultant.

2. At least tentative determination should have been made about one or more beginning points.
3. The school should have developed a tentative organizational pattern to get at work to be done. Such a pattern should not be fixed but should be functioning and yet capable of extension and expansion to cope with problems and activities as yet unforeseen at the initial stages.
4. Plans should be made for local *rapport* with the consultants or consultant groups. The plan for *rapport* should include some study of consultant training, experience, qualifications, and special competences. In this way local expectations will be more reasonably geared to contributions which the consultants will actually be able to make. Meetings should be planned to make it possible for local groups to develop associations with consultants in social situations.
5. In conjunction with consultants or consultant teams, consultant competence should be weighed, and plans formulated for the consultant to make contributions in line with his field of specialization.
6. It should be recognized that the consultant is not to do production work except in an agreed-upon capacity for which no local person is qualified.
7. Consultants should be kept informed on local schedules and deadlines and should, of course, share in establishing schedules and deadlines when members of the consultant staff are to be involved.

The administrator should furnish leadership in preparing the way, in the name of the school, for all basic requirements in the situations in which consultants are to be invited to help. The administrator can help groups see to it that the consultant's service is selected or appraised by those persons best qualified to render judgment.

Helping To Make the Role of Outside
Leadership Understandable

The stage of developmental programs in which outside leadership is utilized is always a critical point. At this point local leaders may tend to exhibit a willingness to defer responsibility to the consultant group. There may also be a tendency to take a defensive attitude concerning the local situation when that phase is appraised by outside consultants. Administrators can plan an important role in making outside leadership understood through:

1. Encouraging attitudes of open-mindedness about the job under way.
2. Helping groups to avoid the "expert" types of survey-conclusion approach which fails because its "open-shut" method precludes effective co-operation locally.
3. Encouraging joint community-school co-operative evaluation of the entire planning program as well as the services rendered by the consultant.
4. Emphasizing that programs be jointly planned and that they be workable programs.

5. Encouraging the detection of special local obstacles to the accomplishment of the ideal.
6. Encouraging recognition of the relationship between the special competency of the consultant to the problem with which he is rendering consultant help.

SUMMARY

In developing educational programs to enable youth to meet their needs and interests, the nature of the leadership of the administrator is of utmost importance. Leadership roles should grow out of sound understandings of education in a democracy and a deep appreciation of the kinds of leadership a democratic society requires. These understandings and appreciations must result in administrative action, policies, and practices which encourage staff, students, and the community to participate in planning the improvement of educational programs. When promising practices and policies are proposed, ways and means must be found to incorporate them into the school program. In this way, each effort becomes a step on the way toward a kind of education that is intimately geared to the needs and interests of youth.

CHAPTER VI

DEVELOPING A PLAN OF ACTION FOR IMPROVING PROGRAMS FOR YOUTH

Maurice R. Ahrens

Director of Curricular Services
Corpus Christi Public Schools
Corpus Christi, Texas

Introduction

Not many years ago there was little recognition on the part of most educators of the need for planning improved educational programs for youth. The pattern of the curriculum was a rather inflexible one which had been passed on from generation to generation. The subject matter was determined largely by textbooks. The concept of the purpose of education, as that of passing on to each generation an accumulation of systems of knowledge, was exemplified in the content of these textbooks. Since both the curriculum pattern and the subject-matter content were accepted with little or no questioning, there was little need for planning.

During the past half century, new philosophical insights and new psychological studies reported from time to time have disturbed the complacency of such educators as were satisfied with a static curriculum. New ideas about the function of education in our modern society, new concepts about how young people learn, recent research on the acquisition and retention of facts, new findings pertaining to the needs of youth, and many other kinds of information have served to stimulate educators to re-examine both the pattern and the content of the curriculum.

With the new emphasis upon adapting secondary-school programs to the needs of youth, there has developed a desire to do something about it. As attempts have been made to improve instructional programs, many problems have arisen. In previous chapters, attempts have been made to present solutions to problems relating to the nature of the needs of youth and how these needs may be met. In this chapter, consideration will be given to the task of developing a plan of action for improving programs for youth. The purpose of the chapter is to bring together reports of experimentation and practices of promise which may throw light on local situations where plans of action are being developed to effect improvements in the educational programs for youth.

THE PRESENT STATUS OF CURRICULUM-IMPROVEMENT PROGRAMS

At the present time there are many different techniques and approaches to curriculum improvement in school systems. Among them, the following seem to be the most commonly used:

1. *The individualistic approach.* When this method is used, each teacher is given freedom to improve teaching in his subject field as he sees fit to do so. In this situation, some teachers stagnate, and many seek security by limiting curriculum changes as strictly as possible. A few teachers forge ahead through trial-and-error experimentation with little or no help from anyone. Changes that are made are usually not co-ordinated with the total school program.

2. *Maintaining the status quo.* When this situation prevails, the existing curriculum is not disturbed. Textbooks and courses of study are followed with little or no flexibility. Constant vigil of administrators and supervisors demands that teachers teach a predetermined curriculum. The watchword is "keep the lid on."

3. *The lip-service technique.* There are some school systems that involve personnel in study groups, workshops, and other planning procedures in which statements of a modern philosophy and the objectives of education are discussed. Sometimes materials are produced for classroom use which implement these statements. Often these statements and materials may be found in storage closets and desk drawers collecting dust. Although lip-service is usually given to them, no curriculum changes have resulted from the activities carried on.

4. *The central-office approach.* When this technique is used, the central office staff determines the curriculum. It may be done on a planned basis, where administrators and supervisors write courses of study, or on a haphazard basis, where the central staff works with varied groups of teachers telling them what to teach and how to teach it. Teachers are usually "at sea" because they have had no opportunity to participate in the study from which the new curriculum evolved.

5. *The committee method.* This approach involves the appointment of small committees, usually by the administration, to revise programs in existing subject fields. The committee produces courses of study or teaching guides which are foisted upon the teaching staff with the expectation that the changes will be made in the classroom. Again, the fallacy of the method lies in the fact that teachers cannot effectively change practices unless they experience a change in thinking similar to that which the committee experienced in its group meetings.

6. *The subject-matter approach.* Perhaps the most widely used procedure in curriculum improvement is that of reorganizing subject matter in the various subject fields. The teachers in specific fields are organized to work

together in rearranging and revising the subject matter which they have already been teaching. Little attention is given to the real needs, problems, and concerns of youth.

7. *The segmentary technique.* On nearly all faculties there are teachers who are willing and anxious to make improvements in the curriculum. Principals sometimes single out these teachers and encourage them to study and experiment in specific subject fields or in new curriculum areas. Often the work is done without the rest of the faculty knowing about it or without relation to the rest of the program. When this is done, jealousies arise, and, not infrequently, faculty discord results.

8. *The existing pattern approach.* In this approach, full opportunity is provided for curriculum improvement in existing subject fields. In several school systems where this has been done, the subjects were reorganized and revised to include consideration of the problems and concerns of youth. No attention or consideration of the curriculum pattern was afforded. The assumption that the existing curriculum pattern is a suitable basis for a program to meet the needs of youth and society is questionable.

It will be recognized that there are other approaches being used to improve programs of instruction for youth. It is also evident that some school systems employ more than one of the approaches described above. The contention here is that none of those discussed, singly or in combination, is adequate in carrying on a plan of action for curriculum improvement. For this reason, the remainder of this chapter will be devoted to the presentation of information based upon the modern concept of curriculum development—the democratic method.

A Plan of Action Should Be Developed through Democratic Procedures

There is little disagreement today in the belief that the major function of education is to foster, develop, and preserve democracy as a way of life. Teachers are being encouraged to provide learning experiences for boys and girls which will help them acquire democratic attitudes and habits along with social skills, interests, and ideals. To facilitate this kind of teaching, it is important that all phases and aspects of program improvement be based upon democratic methods. Teachers need opportunities to participate in every step of program planning so that they may experience the kind of working relationships which exemplify their work with youth in the classroom. Certainly there is little encouragement and desire to practice democratic concepts in the classroom if teachers are denied the opportunity to participate in making decisions which have significance in their work with boys and girls. In developing a plan of action for program improvement in a democratic atmosphere, the concepts and practices described below seem to be significant.

All concerned—administrators, supervisors, teachers, parents, and students —should participate from the very beginning of the project. Too often status leaders err in making certain decisions before others are invited to participate. When this is done, limitations are imposed which thwart full and free opportunity for co-operative planning and action.

Any plans for curriculum improvement should be based upon a census of problems obtained through co-operative planning of teachers, parents, students, and administrators. No one wants to work on problems which are deemed important by one or a few individuals. The care exercised in arriving at significant problems is of utmost importance.

Where it is found necessary to use small committees to do special kinds of work in problem-solving, the committees should not make decisions for the total group. The reports of such committees should be given to all who should be participating, with ample opportunity for everyone to discuss and suggest modifications in the findings. Decisions should be made by all who are concerned.

Any improvements or changes made should be in relation to and with full consideration of the total school program. The secondary program today is a "hodge-podge" of courses which have been added from time to time with little or no thought of how they fit into the total school program.

The right of each school unit to develop a program to meet the needs of its youth should be respected and protected. The varying needs, concerns, and problems of young people, from city to city, school to school, and class to class, should be recognized. City-wide or central planning often fails to consider these differences; and hence, opportunities for practicing democratic concepts are greatly reduced.

A plan of action should provide for flexibility in the program so that teachers in the classroom will have many opportunities to employ democratic methods such as those involved in co-operative planning with pupils and to deal with problems which cannot be anticipated. Rigid, inflexible curriculums impede rather than encourage democratic practices.

A plan for curriculum improvement should give consideration to the status of thinking and practices of teachers, parents, and students. This does not mean that the best thinking and practices should be ruled out. It does mean that recognition should be given to individual differences so that teachers, parents, and students may grow toward the ideal with a reasonable sense of security.

In the foregoing discussion an attempt has been made to stress the concept that a plan of action for improving programs of youth should be conceived in a democratic atmosphere and developed through democratic processes. Democratic ways of living and working are learned as they are practiced. Schools have a unique responsibility in furthering the democratic way of life; and hence, they should seize upon every opportunity to improve programs through co-operative participation of all concerned. The achievement of this goal involves an answer to this question: "Where shall the responsibility for improving the program for youth be focused?"

The Individual School: The Primary Unit for Improving Programs for Youth

Until comparatively recent times, the unit for improving curriculum programs was the state or county or, more frequently, the central offices of school systems. In any of these approaches classroom teachers who were charged with the responsibility of implementing the programs rarely had the opportunity to participate in their formulation and development. Those who prepared the programs usually examined the research and studied the literature which resulted in the acquisition of new concepts and new ways of thinking about content and methods. Teachers who were required to use the materials produced had no such opportunities; hence, the materials were often meaningless and unusable.

In recent years the literature has given much credence to the approach of making the individual school the primary unit for improving programs for youth. There are at least four assumptions which have prompted educators to propose this focus for curriculum development. First, the curriculum can be improved only as teachers experience changes in their thinking and subsequently in their practices. Second, changes in thinking and practices are more sure to take place if teachers participate actively in improving the curriculum. Third, the organization for planning must reach the grass-roots level where all concerned have an opportunity to participate. The individual school is the unit which makes this possible. Fourth, one curriculum cannot serve the needs of all youth in a state, county, or city system. In individual school planning, it is possible to come nearer to meeting these needs.

New Responsibilities. When the individual school becomes the primary unit for improving the instructional program, the principal and the faculty must take on many new responsibilities. The principal assumes an active leadership role in improving the instructional program through providing opportunities for teachers, pupils, and parents to plan co-operatively. He becomes a master of group process in addition to being a master of the mechanics of administration. He assists teachers, pupils, and parents in the identification of problems and determines co-operatively how these problems may best be solved. He facilitates the work of the planning groups through seeing that all human and material resources are readily available. He works with teachers, students, and parents in identifying and encouraging creative leadership.

The faculty, in turn, must assume the responsibility for developing the best possible program for youth, planning with parents and students, being willing to give time and leadership to the work to be done, and carrying on experimentation which will lead to improvements in the curriculum.

There are also certain changes which should be made in the services of the central office. If the principal and his faculty are to assume responsibility for improving the program, it is essential that the central offices do everything possible to facilitate the work in the individual school. The budget should be decentralized so that faculties may have freedom in choosing materials and equipment and in deciding upon desirable maintenance projects. Supervisory service should be provided at the request of the faculty. All other services should be provided so that the principal and faculty may use them to further the plans for curriculum improvement.

Organizing for Program Improvement. In small schools with faculties of twenty-five or fewer, the total faculty can often work together as a group in planning for improvements. It may be necessary at times to select small committees to do special jobs, such as to synthesize the research related to a problem being considered or to formulate concise statements distilled from discussions of the total faculty. Whenever a small committee is used, it is important that the committee submit data sufficient to give the faculty a background of experience equal to that of the committee. The committee may make recommendations, but the decision should be the prerogative of the faculty. Thus a faculty committee through careful study of the literature and through contacts with other school systems may feel confident that a core curriculum should be instituted in the school. This may be recommended, but it is still the responsibility of the committee to present to the faculty the complete data, preferably as it is being unearthed, allowing for full and free discussion so that the total group may act intelligently.

When a faculty numbers more than twenty-five or thirty, the opportunity for full participation in planning is greatly reduced. At least two methods of organizing have been used effectively in a number of schools. In one type of organization, the faculty selects a representative group of teachers to serve as a curriculum council or a committee on instruction. A method used in selection is that of including a representative from each department in the school. This approach often results in a struggle for vested interests. A procedure which has proven to be more workable is that of selecting those members of the faculty who are particularly able and interested in co-operative planning and curriculum development. The second type of organization is based upon utilization of the planning period provided each teacher in most secondary schools. Teachers who have the same planning period meet together and select a chairman or leader. The total faculty identifies the problems to be considered, and each group gathers evidence regarding the problems and presents its data and findings to the total faculty. In many cases the group leaders meet together to iron out differences and present a unified, co-ordinated report to the faculty.

In either plan of organization, it is important that the functions of the faculty and the curriculum council or planning groups be clearly outlined and understood by everyone. In no case should the faculty be relieved of considering all the data related to the problem. The final decisions should be made by the total faculty.

The organization for parent and student participation should be carefully planned. The method of calling a mass meeting of parents which has been widely used has not proved to be effective. Parents and students need the same opportunity as teachers of participating in small groups. A number of school systems have accomplished this goal through focusing parent and student planning in homeroom or core groups. Each homeroom or core class organizes the parents and students and carries on the same kind of planning which is done by teachers in their groups. A parent and student from each group may be selected to serve on a central council. The planning at the grass-roots level with parents and students can be co-ordinated with the teacher planning by the classroom teacher. In many instances it is desirable to have joint meetings of the teacher, parent, and student central councils to consider certain aspects of the improvement plans. It may also be necessary to have some large meetings of parents and students.

The importance of involving both parents and students in curriculum improvement cannot be overstressed. The organization described above is only one way of doing it. There are many others. Parents are prone to evaluate education, and rightfully so, on the basis of the philosophy, objectives, and practices which were in effect when they went to school. Boys and girls usually interpret as their parents do. Hence, it is the responsibility of educators to involve both parents and students in planning so that they may be conversant with new ideas, practices, and developments in education. In this day of educational unrest, few changes will survive unless parents and students participate in making the changes. It is their privilege to do so.

Any plan of organization should provide a maximum amount of help for teachers. In large secondary schools, principals do not have time to provide all the assistance needed. Some schools select a well-qualified teacher to serve as a helping teacher or as a co-ordinator of instruction. This teacher is released for full time or half time through the school year to give specific help to teachers in implementing the plan of action agreed upon by the faculty. Such an arrangement should not in any way be construed as releasing or removing the principal from his role as an instructional leader. Help of this kind is similar to that provided by an assistant principal in dealing with administrative problems. Other teachers who work with the principal and instructional co-ordinator are freed for two or three periods a day to provide these services: to help teachers identify, evaluate, and use materials effectively, including audio-visual materials; to assist teachers in developing methods and techniques of appraising growth toward objectives; and to work with teachers in dealing with vocational problems of youth, including placement in part-time jobs.

In addition to these services which are made available in the individual school, plans should be made to utilize the central supervisory services. Supervisors are especially skilled and equipped to work with planning groups and with individual teachers on problems of instruction. If they are not used, one very important resource is being overlooked.

Time for Planning. Planning has assumed such a significant role in improving modern secondary-school programs that time for group planning on the part of the faculty should be provided within the school day. In most secondary schools individual teachers are allowed an unassigned period which, in some schools, is regarded as a "free" period but is used in many schools as the means of promoting curriculum planning. Many principals have found ways of building schedules so that groups with common interests may have their planning time at the same period. In addition, many budgets now include appropriations to provide substitute teachers during the school day for the release of small groups of regular teachers who need to work on a curriculum problem in a concentrated way for a day or more.

A great majority of teachers are willing to supplement in-school planning with group work before or after school, but it is unreasonable to expect them to do all the planning outside of school hours. In one school where provisions for group planning have been made in the schedules and where small committees are released occasionally for work during the school day, the teachers agreed to give an hour and a half of their time two afternoons a week for planning. In another school with similar provisions, teachers work one hour before school starts two days a week.

SUGGESTED STEPS IN PLANNING FOR CURRICULUM IMPROVEMENT

There is no one way in which all programs for curriculum improvement are to be initiated; nor is there only one pattern of procedures for carrying on such projects. For this reason, the discussion which follows is not an attempt to set a pattern but rather to present a composite of successful practices being used in a number of individual schools.

Agreeing upon a Philosophy and Objectives. Many schools and school systems have developed statements of philosophies and objectives of education through extensive study and elaborate planning procedures. Frequently these statements are "shelved" and consequently little use is made of them. In any plan for curriculum improvement it is essential that changes be made in relation to an accepted philosophy and to well-defined objectives. Where statements have been formulated, it is important to use them in obtaining leads for curriculum improvement and also as a frame of reference to evaluate the soundness of proposals which do not come from the professed philosophy and objectives. A frame of reference will not only unify the efforts of all who are participating in curriculum improvement but will also serve as the medium for evaluating efforts and plans for changes.

Taking a Census of Problems. It is usually desirable to employ some method of identifying the problem or problems which the faculty considers of prime importance. One way of doing this is through a census. Several ways of carrying on this activity have proved successful.

1. The discussion-group technique has proved to be very effective. One school with a large faculty uses the groups formed by those teachers who have a planning-period assignment at any given period of the day. Ample time is provided for each group to identify the most pressing curriculum problems. Teachers are asked to do the same thing with their students and with parents in core classes or homerooms.

2. An "open-end" questionnaire may be used. The council in one school asked all teachers, room parents, and students to respond to these questions· "What are we doing in the program we have for young people in our schools that you consider good?" "What are we doing that you feel could be improved?"

3. Where the faculty is small, the census may be made in a series of meetings of the total faculty. This, of course, should be supplemented with a census of parents and students. The discussion-group technique can also be used in these situations.

4. In large schools, the curriculum council, the parents' council, and the student council are sometimes used for the census. A disadvantage is that all concerned do not participate in the first step.

Whatever method is used in identifying significant problems, the administrator may determine the success or failure of the project. In the first place, he has the responsibility of suggesting problems which he thinks are important as he views the total program. Secondly, he should be willing to have his suggestions evaluated in the same manner as those made by teachers, parents, and students. Unless this is done, the process will break down since the other participants will soon sense that a predetermined plan has been formulated. The development in one school will illustrate this assumption. The principal had attended a summer workshop and had become enthusiastic about teaching American history through the current-problems approach. In working with his faculty in identifying curriculum problems he used the "selling" technique of impressing upon the faculty the importance of his pet project. Since a permissive atmosphere did not prevail, the teachers did not feel free to evaluate his suggestion as they evaluated their own. Hence, the principal's problem was selected as the one of highest priority. Although a committee was authorized to plan a new approach to teaching American history, there was little or no enthusiasm because the teachers were not ready for this step. They did not have the principal's background of experience to help them understand why the change should be made. The result was a year of confusion, a mediocre job of teaching American history, and almost complete failure of the project.

Obtaining a Consensus. It is obvious that no faculty could work simultaneously upon all the problems unearthed through a census-taking activity. The question then arises, "Which problem or problems have highest priority in the minds of the faculty, parents, and pupils?" Before this is determined, it is important that every person concerned understand the significance of each problem. This can be done in an open, free discussion. Sometimes it is desirable to have the person who proposed the problem make a statement about it.

There are several methods which have been used successfully to determine the priority ratings of a list of problems.

1. The problems may be listed and each teacher, parent, and student asked to select a first, second, and third choice. After tabulating these choices, the top selections are brought to the various groups to select one or more for consideration.
2. The list of problems may be sent to selected discussion groups to reach an agreement on top priority problems. Such groups would include the unassigned-period groups of teachers and the core or homeroom groups of parents and students.
3. The faculty, parents, and pupils may select a small number of representatives who are given the responsibility to suggest the few most pressing problems.

Planning for the Solution of the Problems. Assuming that full opportunity has been provided to reach an agreement on the relative urgency of the different problems and how many problems can be studied simultaneously, it is the responsibility of participants to set up a plan and organization for the solution of the problems. The work of many faculties has "bogged down" because they have chosen to study too many problems. It is usually preferable to work toward the solution of one or a few problems and complete the work within a reasonable length of time rather than to dilute and scatter efforts to the point where little or nothing is accomplished. The following ways of organizing for the solution of problems are commonly used:

1. The total faculty, particularly if it is small, may study and work as a group on the same problem. At times, it may be desirable to divide into small groups for intensive work. Parents and students may be brought into these groups; or the same problem may be discussed by them in groups in which teachers participate.
2. The faculty may divide into small groups, each of which works on a different problem. Each group assumes a responsibility for keeping the total faculty informed of its progress and uses the faculty as a sounding board and for the purpose of receiving criticisms, points of view, and suggestions. Representative parents and students are usually regular participants in these groups.
3. The faculty may designate one or a few committees to work on specific problems agreed upon. This plan is often used when the problem is of particular concern to a certain group of teachers. For instance, the faculty, parents, and students may decide that the English curriculum should be reorganized. In such case, the faculty might designate the English teachers as the basic group to do this job. The committee should then assume the responsibility for the following procedures: having all members of the faculty participate in some of the work; keeping every member informed; making recommendations for faculty action instead of making decisions; and providing for participation on the part of representative groups of parents and students.

Whatever the method used in planning for the solution of problems, there are certain practices which are important to consider. First, ways of involving the total faculty as active participants should be employed. Second, research studies and other information should be gleaned from the literature. Third, materials which show trends and describe promising practices should be utilized. Fourth, group work should provide full opportunity for everyone to participate. Fifth, the culmination of the study of a problem should be a plan of action which will result in improvement of the program.

CENTRAL CO-ORDINATION OF INSTRUCTION

In the foregoing discussion the primary responsibility for developing a plan of action for improving programs for youth has been placed upon the principal and faculty in the individual school unit. Suggestions have been made for ways in which a faculty may work together with parents and students in assuming this significant responsibility.

Although the individual school should be the primary unit for improving instruction, school-wide or city-wide co-ordination is desirable and essential. Without such co-ordination, a school system could well become a series of individual units with little or no relation to one another. Such a situation often results in the virtual isolation of certain schools. In the development and improvement of any program for youth, there is a need for policies and services which will encourage and facilitate the work in the individual schools. If these are determined and provided centrally through democratic methods, a school system can function smoothly as a unit and yet provide the needed autonomy for each school to develop a program to meet the needs of the youth it serves.

Organizing for Central Co-ordination. In recent years a number of school systems using democratic procedures have developed effective organizations for the central co-ordination of instruction. Most promising among these is a central council on instruction or a committee on instruction. Principles which may be used in organizing such a central planning body are:

1. Each school should have one or more representatives chosen by the faculty.
2. Representation should include administrators and supervisors chosen by their respective groups.
3. The council should be small enough so that every member has full opportunity to participate. Participation is greatly reduced when a group is larger than twenty-five.
4. If at all possible, the council should meet regularly and on school time.
5. A clear statement of the functions, duties, and responsibilities of the council should be developed by the group. This statement should be made through participation of the total personnel and should be understood by them. It should be subject to revision as the work proceeds.
6. The work of the council should in no way restrict or hinder the individual school in its efforts to develop a program to meet the needs of its youth and its community.

In small school systems of twenty schools or less, the problem of the composition of a central council is rather simple. Each faculty can elect one representative, supplemented with an elementary, junior high school, and senior high school principal, a supervisor, and a member of the central administrative staff. In very small systems, it may be desirable to have faculties choose two representatives. In either event, the council would not be larger than twenty-five which provides ample opportunity for full participation.

In large school systems the organization becomes more complex. There is great need for experimentation in decentralizing the central planning so that all personnel can participate. It is the suggestion here that the school system be divided into regions or communities, such as might be formed by a senior high school, its contributing junior high schools, and their contributing elementary schools. In most cases, this division would make possible a reasonably small central planning committee with each school represented. The chairmen of each regional group could serve as an over-all co-ordinating group. It is quite possible that a grouping of schools on the basis of some other criterion than that of contributory relationship would prove more effective in some situations.

Where regional or community councils are developed, it is desirable that central instructional staffs be decentralized. Each regional group of schools should have access to a supervisory or consultant staff which could provide needed services.

Another plan employed in a large city is a horizontal organization with a senior high school committee on instruction, one for the junior high school, and regional elementary committees. A central body composed of a few representatives from each committee serves as the city-wide co-ordinating committee. The disadvantage of working with this type of organization lies in the difficulties involved in articulation.

Participation of Parents and Students. Ways of involving parents and students in central co-ordination vary considerably. Some school systems have no parent or student representation but rely upon each school to involve these two groups when the reports and other considerations of the council are referred to the faculty. Other systems have a small representation of parents and students on the central body. Reports from these schools indicate a low interest because so many matters of little concern to parents and students take up a sizable portion of the council's time. One system is considering the formation of two additional councils, one of parents who are chairmen of the P.T.A. curriculum committees in each school, and the other of students composed of a representative from each school selected by the student council. In this type of organization only matters of real concern will be discussed with parents and students. There will be committees composed of members of all three groups, and some combined meetings should be held.

Initiating a Central Council. The way in which a council is initiated is of great importance. If it is conceived by the administration and foisted upon teachers, it is often unsuccessful. In one school system the curriculum director called together the principals, explained the many needs for co-ordination of services, and proposed a central council as one means of solving some of the problems. The principals were asked to discuss this suggestion with the teachers and to explore other functions of such a body. Also, they were asked to receive suggestions of other ways to approach the matter of taking care of the needs of the school system. Principals were requested to bring back a report on whether the teachers felt that a central council would be of any value in improving instruction in the school system. Still better, in another school system each faculty was asked to select a representative to meet with the central curriculum staff to discuss the feasibility of a central council. The teachers in turn reported back to their buildings and, after extensive discussion, met again to make a decision.

Ways of Working. The way in which a council works will determine its usefulness and effectiveness. Few such organizations survive unless democratic ways of working are employed. A council which becomes a group of self-sufficient decision-makers is little better than an administrator or a small committee employing like procedures. Members of the council should be representatives of their faculties, and decisions which are made should be those of the faculties. It is important that all instructional problems be dealt with by the council. Councils often fail because of the feeling of futility which members have when administrators make decisions involving instruction without referring the matter to them. The council exists as an organized group through which the needs, desires, and concerns of all personnel are dealt with in a way which facilitates and improves the work teachers and administrators are doing.

It is useless for a council to be working on problems that are of little concern to teachers, parents, and students. Consequently, the first step in the work of this body is to identify the problems which have system-wide significance. A council in one system did this through having its members go to their faculties and, with ample time for discussion, determine problems of most concern. These were brought together centrally, and the total list referred again to the faculties. The procedure was continued until the problems of highest priority were identified. The following list includes the needs which teachers and administrators felt were most important for consideration.

1. Help in the organization of a comprehensive audio-visual program, including improvement in central services and more effective use of materials.
2. Assistance in evaluation of classroom activities, with emphasis on methods of evaluating behavioral growth.
3. Aid in lessening conflicts in meetings involving teachers.
4. Help in teaching through the co-operative development of teaching guides.
5. Help in teaching academically retarded children.
6. Assistance in the organization of elementary libraries, including the selection and effective use of materials.
7. Development of resources which would be available to teachers so that they could have them at hand when working on an instructional problem.
8. Development of an in-service program.

Since the solution of each of these problems would involve delving into the findings of research and gathering much information, committees were appointed to begin the study. As the committee work progressed, reports were brought to the council and in turn were taken to the faculties. In addition, information needed from teachers was requested by committees through the council. This back-and-forth procedure was deliberately planned by the council so that every teacher would have a chance to participate as the committee work progressed. Decisions made were those in which all personnel participated.

Functions of the Council. The functions of a curriculum council will vary from system to system. A general statement which applies is that the council determines co-operatively any policy and performs any service which facilitates the work of teachers in individual schools but which does not block the efforts of each school faculty in developing a program that meets the needs of its students and its community. When a criterion such as this one is used by a council in determining its responsibilities and its work, there is every reason to believe that the organization will assist materially in improving the program for youth.

SERVICES FOR TEACHERS

In developing a plan of action for improving programs for youth such as has been described heretofore, services to teachers have a very important role to play. Since these services will be discussed in later chapters of this publication, only brief mention of them will be made here.

The principal and the faculty in each school are the first resources for assisting teachers in improving instruction in the classroom. Next comes the supervisory or consultant service which is usually available in a central staff. In the approach to curriculum improvement described here, the supervisor no longer assumes a role of authority but rather identifies himself with a service function. He works through the principal and provides help to teachers, individually and in groups, based upon their needs. He is, in fact, a resource person.

There are many other services which can and should be provided by the council on instruction. Teachers need opportunities to participate in workshops, both in the summer and during the school year; they need post-session and pre-session planning time; they need a resource laboratory where all materials are centered which may be needed when they are working on curriculum problems; they need provisions for interschool and intraschool visitation; and they need opportunities to attend professional meetings, both state and national. These and other services are part and parcel of a comprehensive, effective plan of action for a curriculum-improvement program.

SUMMARY

In developing a plan of action for improving programs for youth, it is important to examine present practices critically to ascertain whether desired goals are being achieved. Since we are living in a democratic society, it follows that a plan of action should be developed through democratic processes in which administrators, teachers, parents, and students participate.

In improving programs for youth, the focus for planning and action should be determined. It has been suggested here that the primary unit for improving instruction should be the individual school. All other curriculum activities and services should be planned and developed to serve the individual school in providing better instruction for youth. Although the organization effected for improving the program is a means to the end rather than the end itself, some type of organization in each school is essential if improvement goals are to be attained. The organization should be developed co-operatively, and the planning should be carried on through participation of teachers, parents, and students under the leadership of the principal. School-wide co-ordination of instruction is necessary and desirable and should be made possible through a democratically conceived organization which assumes responsibility for dealing with problems of city-wide significance while providing the opportunity for each school to develop a program to meet the needs of its pupils. In a democratic approach to curriculum improvement, all available resources should be utilized. There should be recognition that achievement in this way of working requires co-operative effort and a willingness to experiment.

REFERENCES

Action for Curriculum Improvement. Yearbook of the Association for Supervision and Curriculum Development, 1951. Washington: National Education Association, 1951.

ALBERTY, HAROLD M. *Reorganizing the High School Curriculum.* New York: Macmillan Co., 1947.

CASWELL, HOLLIS L., and ASSOCIATES. *Curriculum Improvement in Public School Systems.* New York: Bureau of Publications, Teachers College, Columbia University, 1950.

Education for Life Adjustment: Its Meaning and Implementation. Edited by Harl R. Douglass. New York: Ronald Press, 1950.

Group Planning in Education. Yearbook of the Department of Supervision and Curriculum of the National Education Association, 1945. Washington: National Education Association, 1945.

HORACE MANN–LINCOLN INSTITUTE OF SCHOOL EXPERIMENTATION. *Co-operative Planning in Education.* New York: Bureau of Publications, Teachers College, Columbia University, 1947.

KELLEY, EARL. *Workshop Way of Learning.* New York: Harper & Bros., 1951.

KRUG, EDWARD A. *Curriculum Planning.* New York: Harper & Bros., 1950.

MIEL, ALICE. *Changing the Curriculum: A Social Process.* New York: D. Appleton–Century Co., 1946.

STRATEMEYER, FLORENCE B., and OTHERS. *Developing a Curriculum for Modern Living.* New York: Bureau of Publications, Teachers College, Columbia University, 1947.

WILES, KIMBALL. *Supervision for Better Schools.* New York: Prentice Hall, Inc., 1950.

SECTION II
OVER-ALL DESIGN OF PROGRAMS FOR YOUTH

CHAPTER VII

DESIGNING PROGRAMS TO MEET THE COMMON NEEDS OF YOUTH

HAROLD ALBERTY
Professor of Education
Ohio State University
Columbus, Ohio

INTRODUCTION

It is the thesis of this yearbook that the secondary-school program should be based upon the immediate and predicated needs of youth which grow out of the interaction of the individual and his environment. This chapter is concerned with that part of the program which is designed to meet the *common* needs of youth. By this is meant the learning experiences which are required of all students on the ground that they provide primarily for the development of the attitudes, understandings, and basic skills needed by all students to make them effective citizens in our democratic culture. By program design is meant the over-all plan or organization of learning experiences, considering both scope and sequence of the experiences contemplated.

PLAN OF THE CHAPTER

This chapter is based on the assumption that common needs of youth may be distinguished from those which are engendered by the peculiar interests of selected small groups or individuals. Since analyses have been made of these common needs, and techniques have been proposed by which a school may identify the common needs of its own students as a basis for reorganizing the program of general education, the present discussion is confined to an examination and evaluation of the various types of programs which are designed to meet these common needs.

It is helpful to consider the various programs in terms of their departure from the conventional pattern of required subject-matter courses. In other words, the programs may be placed on a scale. At one end is the conventional subject-centered program, organized in terms of systems of knowledge set up in advance. At the other end of the scale is the experience-centered program with learning activities determined by the immediate needs of the group. At intermediate points on the scale are to be found programs which deviate more or less from the extremes.

This chapter identifies six different program designs, each of which is regarded by some people as being the most effective plan of providing common preparation for democratic citizenship. These designs are presented in the order of their deviation from conventional practices, and each one is evaluated critically in terms of the basic thesis of this yearbook. A case is made for the design which seems most promising.

In discussing the various designs, use is made of the various concepts of the core program in current use. It is hoped that this treatment of the core curriculum will help to clarify the confusion in the use of that term. There seems to be one common element in programs that are referred to as the core. The term is applied in some fashion to *all or part* of the total curriculum which is required of all students at a given level. In other words, the core is used to designate all or part of the program of general education. This important concept is utilized as the point of departure in presenting the six designs.

The various interpretations, presented in the order of their deviation from conventional curriculum organization, are as follows:

1. The core consists of a number of logically organized subjects or fields of knowledge each of which is taught independently.
   Example: English, world history, and general science are required at the ninth-grade level. They are taught without any systematic attempt to show relationships.
2. The core consists of a number of logically organized subjects or fields of knowledge, some or all of which are correlated.
   Example: American history and American literature are required of all twelfth-grade students. When the history teacher is dealing with the Civil War, the English teacher introduces the literature of that period.
3. The core consists of broad problems, units of work, or unifying themes which are chosen because they afford the means of teaching effectively the basic content of certain subjects or fields of knowledge. These subjects or fields retain their identity, but the content is selected and taught with special reference to the unit, theme, or problem.
   Example: "Living in the Community" is selected as a unit of work for the tenth grade. The unit is then organized in terms of such subjects as science, art, and social studies and may be taught by specialists or by one teacher.
4. The core consists of a number of subjects or fields of knowledge which are unified or fused. Usually one subject or field (e.g., history) serves as the unifying center.
   Example: American history and American literature in the eleventh grade are unified through a series of epochs, such as "The Colonial Period," "The

Westward Movement," "The Industrial Revolution." The unification may be extended to include other fields, such as the arts, science, and mathematics.

5. The core consists of broad, preplanned problem areas, from which are selected learning experiences in terms of the psychobiological and societal needs, problems, and interests of students.

   Example: A Unit on "Healthful Living," in the twelfth grade, stresses the health problems of the group and how they are related to the immediate and wider community. The unit is teacher-student planned, but in terms of a basic curriculum structure.

6. The core consists of broad units of work, or activities, planned by the teacher and the students in terms of needs as perceived by the group. No basic curriculum structure is set up.

   Example: An eighth-grade group, under guidance of the teacher, decides to landscape the school grounds. The activity meets criteria decided upon by the group.[1]

CURRENT CONCEPTIONS OF PROGRAMS DESIGNED TO MEET THE COMMON NEEDS OF ADOLESCENTS

In this section each of the types of core programs presented above will be analyzed, illustrated, and evaluated in terms of their appropriateness in meeting the common needs of adolescents.

Type-One Core: Program Design Based upon Separate Subjects, Each Taught Independently

Critical readers may object to designating a general-education program which is made up exclusively of separately taught subjects as a core program. However, this is what is meant by many people when they use the term. No less an authority than the Harvard Committee on the Objectives of a General Education in a Free Society[2] refers to a "continuing core for all" made up of required subjects in the humanities, the social sciences, the sciences, and mathematics. After all, the general-education program, however organized, is the center or heart of the curriculum, and there is, therefore, a certain appropriateness in calling it the core—if we don't confuse the separate subject organization with types representing more significant departures from convention. If we always refer to such an organization as a *Type-One* core, there should be no confusion.

Even a casual look at current offerings in secondary schools reveals that all or nearly all of them by implication give considerable attention to

---

[1] See the somewhat similar analysis made by L. Thomas Hopkins, *Integration: Its Meaning and Application*, chap. xii. New York: D. Appleton–Century Co., 1937.

[2] *General Education in a Free Society*, p. 99. Report of the Harvard University Committee on the Objectives of a General Education in a Free Society. Cambridge, Massachusetts: Harvard University Press, 1945.

the problem of meeting common "needs." By and large, needs, in the sense that the term is used generally, refer to the knowledge, habits, and skills which all individuals should possess in order to function effectively as adult citizens in our society. These learning products are expected to be mastered through the study of systematically organized subjects or fields of knowledge. Since the vast majority of secondary schools rely upon an officially adopted set of textbooks for the basic materials of instruction, the so-called common needs are met largely by means of "lessons" assigned from textbooks.

The program design then consists of the enumeration of a number of time units which are defined in terms of subjects pursued for a given number of periods per week for a specified number of weeks.

In the typical program design, three types of courses may be identified: (a) courses required of *all* students, (b) courses required of certain groups of students, and (c) courses which are required of no one but may be elected by any student who can fit them into his program. On the basis of this analysis a school might *require* all students who graduate to complete three or four units of English, about an equal number of units in the social studies, one or two units in mathematics, possibly one unit in science, and perhaps continuous exposure to physical education for which they would receive one or two units of credit. In terms of our definition, these requirements are thought of as the core.

A closer look at these required areas would reveal that they are made up of a number of short courses, each one quite independent of the other. Thus, a student's program of general education in the typical four-year high school would probably consist of semester or year courses in English composition, English literature, American literature, world history, world geography, American history, American government, algebra, general science, and physical education. *These required units reveal what those who prepared the program believe to be essential for meeting the "common needs" of students for democratic citizenship.*

Wright estimated that 96.5 per cent of all public secondary schools in the United States are organized on the basis of separate subjects.[3] In other words, nearly all secondary schools may be said to have a *Type-One* core—and this in the face of three decades of successful experience of a number of schools in breaking down the barriers between subjects!

Now let us turn to the strengths and weaknesses of this design for meeting common needs.

---

[3] Grace S. Wright, *Core Curriculum in Public High Schools: An Inquiry into Practices, 1949.* United States Office of Education, Bulletin 1950, No. 5. Washington: Government Printing Office, 1950.

Strengths. Many claims are made for the separate-subject design. Among them are the following:

1. Systematic organization of knowledge is essential to the effective interpretation of experience.
2. The organization of a program based on separate subjects is simple and easily understood by teachers, students, and laymen.
3. The program is easily changed, since subjects may be added, dropped, or revised without disturbing the general pattern.
4. The program is easily evaluated by means of standardized tests which have been developed in all or nearly all of the subject fields.
5. Such programs are generally approved by the colleges since college-entrance requirements are usually based upon subjects.
6. Such programs are generally approved by teachers, and laymen, since they represent the pattern in general use in high schools, colleges, and universities.[4]

Weaknesses. Since the separate-subject program has been under attack for many years, many weaknesses have been pointed out. Among them are the following:

1. Such programs are far removed from the common needs of adolescents as defined in this yearbook. All programs are defended by those who advocate them on the basis of meeting "needs," but, in the case of this type of design, needs are defined in terms of logical systems of subject matter. "Needs" are presumed to be met through the mastery of these systems of knowledge. Therefore, needs are derived from an analysis of knowledge rather than from an analysis of the student. It is not to be denied that the skilful teacher may meet many of the psychobiological needs proposed in this yearbook, but the acquisition of bodies of subject matter must necessarily be the primary consideration.
2. Such programs perpetuate the evils of specialism which long have been the concern of educators. The general-education program turns out to be largely a miscellaneous and unrelated collection of specialized bodies of knowledge. The Harvard Committee states the situation succinctly in the following passage:

    The impact of specialism has been felt not only in those phases of education which are necessarily and rightly specialistic; it has affected the whole structure of higher and even of secondary education. Teachers, themselves products of highly technical disciplines, tend to reproduce their knowledge in class. The result is that each subject, being taught by an expert, tends to be so presented as to attract potential experts. This complaint is perhaps more keenly felt in colleges and universities, which naturally look to scholarship. The undergraduate in a college receives his teaching from professors who, in their turn, have been trained in graduate schools, and the latter are domi-

---

[4] For an elaboration of these arguments see: Harold Alberty, *Reorganizing the High-School Curriculum*, chap. iv. New York: Macmillan Co., 1947.

nated by the ideal of specialization. Learning is now diversified and parcelled into a myriad of specialties.[5]

The committee is probably correct in stating that the situation described is more applicable to the colleges than to the secondary schools, but it must be remembered that specialism, especially in the senior high schools, is the rule rather than the exception. Even the junior high schools have tended to follow the pattern of the senior high schools and colleges rather than that of the elementary schools.

3. The separate-subject design of general education is psychologically unsound.[6]
There is a wide gap between the experience of the student and the logically formulated experience of the race. While logical relationships are essential in the organization of experience, they cannot be imparted ready-made to the student. Dewey pointed this out many years ago in the following often-quoted passage:

"Facts are torn away from their original place in experience and rearranged with reference to some principle. Classification is not a matter of child experience; things do not come pigeonholed. The vital ties of affection, the connecting bonds of activity, hold together the variety of his personal experiences. The adult mind is so familiar with the notion of logically ordered facts that it does not recognize—it cannot realize—the amount of separating and reformulating which the facts of direct experience have to undergo before they can appear as a "study," or branch of learning. A principle, for the intellect, has had to be distinguished and defined. Facts have had to be interpreted in relation to this principle, not as they are in themselves. They have had to be regathered about a new center which is wholly abstract and ideal. . . . The studies as classified are the product, in a word, of the science of the ages, not of the experience of the child."[7]

Type-Two Core: Program Design Based upon Informal Correlation of Subjects

When schools break with the organized-subject tradition, the simplest deviation is known as correlation, which, reduced to its lowest terms, means the showing of relationship between two subjects. Thus, when the history teacher is dealing with the Civil War, the English teacher might have the students read *Uncle Tom's Cabin* or *Gone with the Wind*. When such correlation is quite informal and casual, it does not, of course, affect the design of the curriculum at all.

Strengths and Weaknesses. In general the Type-Two core has the same strengths and weaknesses as Type One. It does, however, have the ad-

---

[5] *General Education in a Free Society, op. cit.,* p. 56.

[6] See Alberty, *op. cit.,* pp. 106–8, for an elaboration of this criticism.

[7] John Dewey, *The Child and the Curriculum,* pp. 10–11. Chicago: University of Chicago Press, 1902.

vantage of enriching the courses affected, and it stimulates a certain amount of co-operative planning on the part of teachers. Obviously teachers have to get together to discuss their respective programs in order to provide for even a minimum of correlation. It is referred to as a new type of design, since it is a movement away from the rigidity and compartmentalization of the separate subject organization.

Type-Three Core: Program Design Based upon Systematic Correlation

A few schools have experimented with a more systematic type of correlation. For example, the teachers of English, social studies, and science might agree that for a given period of time, say six weeks, each would emphasize the same overarching theme. Such a theme might be "Living in the Home." The second six weeks of the semester might be given over to "Living in the Community," and so on through the year. In this scheme, each teacher would continue to teach his particular subject in a separate period but would try to relate it to the overarching theme agreed upon by the group of teachers. This plan was used quite extensively in the early years of the Eight-Year Study of the Progressive Education Association.

A good illustration of such a design is reported by Pierce.[8] The faculty of Wells High School in Chicago chose the following "centers of interest" for Grade IX A: "Conservation of Cultural and Material Resources," "Our Changing Methods of Production and Consumption," "Government and Other Social Agencies in Co-operative Living," and "Work in Relation to Daily Living." The following is the initial breakdown of one of the centers, in terms of "unit loads . . . for the three major core fields."

SOCIAL STUDIES: *How Conservation Improves Daily Living.*

Learning objective: To make effective use of our possessions and avoid needless waste.

Unit elements: Why we should avoid waste; obtaining and using capital; need for conserving forests; conserving fuels and other natural resources; services of the Civilian Conservation Corps; eliminating waste in child labor; conservation through minimum hours and wage provisions; eliminating waste through unemployment; accident and retirement compensation; conservation of school supplies and property.

ENGLISH ARTS: *Conservation in the Development of American Civilization.*

Learning objective: To improve reading and expressional skills through the study of conservation needs in our country's development.

Unit elements: How the pioneers used the forests—girdling; the destruction of buffalo and other game; devastation of forests for timber and turpentine; waste

---

[8] Paul Pierce, *Developing a High-School Curriculum*, p. 47. New York: American Book Co., 1942.

in past and present mining; oil and other fuels in our country's growth; how Americans have made use of their land; beginnings and growth of conservation movements.

SCIENCE: *How Science Aids in Conserving Natural Resources.*

Learning objective: To understand and appreciate better how science aids in preserving our natural and material possessions.

Unit elements: How science aids in conserving soils; science and the protection of vegetation and livestock; conserving the energy of air, water, and sunlight; how science is utilized to conserve our fuel supply.[9]

The general curriculum design which finally emerged at Wells High School retained the subject fields as the basis for the program, but these fields were related or correlated through the use of the following functions of living: (*a*) ethical and spiritual character, (*b*) work, (*c*) leisure, (*d*) thought and its communication, (*e*) health, (*f*) social relationships, and (*g*) economic consciousness.[10]

Strengths and Weaknesses. It will be noted that the Wells program described above does not break cleanly with the subject-centered design. Rather, it retains subjects but seeks to enrich them through the showing of relationship to life activities in the school, home, and community and to the functions of living carried on by students. This type of core is a further step away from specialism and tends to move in the direction of making vital problems of living at least co-ordinate with subject mastery.

Type-Four Core: Program Design Based upon Fusion or Unification of Fields of Knowledge

A more significant departure from the conventional design of general education is the unified-studies or fusion concept of the core. It is more difficult to develop, since separate subjects tend to lose their identity, and the problem of sequence becomes more difficult. Scheduling is also more difficult because of the larger block of time which is required when subjects or fields are unified.

Probably most of the public secondary schools of the United States that are included in the recent report of the United States Office of Education[11] as having core programs fall into this category. The criteria set up would exclude the schools having program designs which have been designated as types One, Two, and Three. The following quotation makes this point clear:

High-school principals were asked to report as core those courses which "involve the combinations of two or more class periods from subjects that would ordinarily be taught separately." . . . A further restriction imposed upon the inclu-

---

[9] *Ibid.*, pp. 47–48.

[10] *Ibid.*, p. 134.   [11] Wright, *op. cit.*, pp. 5–6.

sion of courses as cores was that they cut across large areas of the curriculum. That is, a double-period class in language arts or a double period in social studies was not counted.[12]

On the basis of the criteria set forth above, it was discovered that approximately 3.5 per cent of all public secondary schools may be said to have a core which cuts across subject lines and utilizes a large block of time in the daily schedule. Also included in the 3.5 per cent of schools are those which have programs which we shall describe as Type-Five and Type-Six cores. The following are examples of a Type-Four core.

The Culture-Epoch Approach. A simple illustration of the unified-studies concept of the core is the fusion of American history and American literature in the eleventh grade. Instead of teaching these fields separately, they are brought together in a larger block of time—usually two consecutive periods. A favorite way of organizing the combined content is to divide the course into a series of epochs, such as "the colonial period," "the westward movement," "the industrial revolution," etc. The literature dealing with a particular epoch is studied along with the economic, social, and political aspects. English composition and spelling are taught functionally as tools for developing the basic understanding of the epoch. Sometimes the block of time is extended to three periods to provide sufficient time to bring in art, music, science, or other required subjects. A similar organization may be built around world history. The best example of such a program was that of the Horace Mann School of Teachers College, Columbia University.[13]

The course was organized around the general theme of the progress of man through history. The program began in the seventh grade and extended through the twelfth. Successive culture epochs were studied and all aspects of a given period were brought in as needed to understand that particular epoch of history. Approximately one-half of the school day was given over to this program. Most of the teaching was done by a "co-ordinating" teacher, who was free, however, to call upon specialists in the various subject fields for assistance. The co-ordinating teacher usually represented the fields of English and the social sciences.

The curriculum design of the various grades was as follows:

1. *The Story of Man through the Ages*
   Grade VII. From the beginning through the ancient period
   Grade VIII. To the discovery of America
   Grade IX.   From the discovery of America to life in the modern world
2. *Modern Civilizations and Cultures*

---

[12] *Ibid.*, p. 3.

[13] *Adventures in American Education*, Vol. V, *Thirty Schools Tell Their Story*, pp. 406–28 *passim*. New York: Harper & Bros., 1943.

Grade X.   American civilization and culture
Grade XI.   Other civilizations and cultures (e.g., Russia, Germany, China, Great Britain, France)
Grade XII. Modern problems and issues in America

The critics of the culture-epoch approach to general education claim that the scheme devotes entirely too much time to the past and that it is far removed from the needs of youth. On the other hand, its proponents defend it on the ground that the present and the past are interwoven and that the needs of the students are met as they compare present-day problems of living with those of the past.

Undoubtedly it has the advantage of providing a ready-made sequence, i.e., chronology, and provides the opportunity of bringing in subject matter from all fields of knowledge.

Contemporary-Problems Approach. A glance at the design of the program of the Horace Mann School indicates that as the student moves to the upper-grade levels, particularly the eleventh and twelfth, the orientation shifts to modern cultures and contemporary problems. Thus, a unit on "communication" might be the means of unifying language arts, social studies, and science. A unit on "housing" could easily be the vehicle for teaching basic language skills, the fine and applied arts, social studies and science. Current practice in the unified-studies program follows both the culture-epoch and the contemporary-problems approach. Broad comprehensive units are developed around areas or problems of living at certain grade levels while at others, ostensibly to meet the requirement of a year in American history, the units might be developed around the usual chronological periods of American history.

Strengths and Weaknesses. It is important to keep in mind that none of the various curriculum designs for general education discussed thus far breaks completely with the organized subject-matter tradition. They are employed for the purpose of making subject matter more meaningful. The *nature* of the subject matter is not basically different. There are bodies of content in English, social studies, and science that are, from some points of view, regarded as essential. All individuals growing up in our culture are assumed to "need" this content. Correlated and fused programs are held to be more effective ways of dealing with it. It is not claimed that such programs are constructed upon the basis of common needs or problems as defined in this yearbook.

Type-Five Core: Program Design Based upon a Preplanned Structure Determined by Adolescent Needs

We now turn to a program of general education which deviates sharply from those which have been described. This design is based upon the conviction that the secondary school should make a direct attack upon the common problems which youth in our society face and that it should help them to identify and meet their common needs. Subject matter from all pertinent fields of knowledge is drawn upon to clarify persistent common problems of living and to provide data for solving them. No preconceived bodies of subject matter are set up to be "covered." If particular subject matter is needed to achieve the goals set up, it will come in—otherwise it is left out. From one-third to two-thirds of the school day is set aside for this part of the curriculum. The remaining time is devoted to instruction in special-interest areas elected by students on the basis of their particular interests and needs (see chap. viii). In practice, mathematics and physical education are required of all students in addition to the two- or three-hour block of time devoted to broad comprehensive common problems of living. Studies of the possible contributions of these two areas to the core are now under way.

There have been many formulations of problem areas for this type of design. Perhaps the following analysis prepared by the writer[14] will serve as an acceptable illustration:

1. *Orientation to the School.* Problems relating to the school program and the role of the pupil in understanding, interpreting, and improving it; understanding and practicing democratic values in school relationships.

2. *Home and Family Life.* Problems relating to the role of the family and the relationships among members of the family.

3. *Community Life.* Problems relating to the structure and functioning of communities and the role of the individual in understanding, interpreting, and improving community living.

4. *Contemporary Cultures.* Problems relating to the understanding of different world cultures and their potential contributions to civilization.

5. *Contemporary America among the Nations.* Problems of determining the contributions of America to world unity; understanding the American tradition; reconciling national sovereignty with a world order; defining the role of the American citizen in developing world understanding.

6. *Competing Political, Social, and Economic Ideologies.* Problems of orienting the individual to conflicting ideologies, on the local, national, or world scene; modes of reconciling or reducing conflict.

7. *Personal Value Systems.* Problems involving the way people acquire beliefs and values and how they are woven into systems of value that direct behavior; role of critical thinking in making value judgments; democratic values and attitudes.

8. *World Religions.* Problems pertaining to an understanding of the major reli-

---

[14] Harold Alberty, "A Proposal for Reorganizing the High-School Curriculum on the Basis of a Core Program," *Progressive Education*, XXVIII (November, 1950), 57–61.

gions of the contemporary world and their influence on civilization; relationships of personal, moral, and ethical beliefs to religion; the impact of modern science upon religion.

9. *Communication*. Problems relating to the various modes of communication and their influence upon human welfare; developing skill in communication.

10. *Resource Development, Conservation, and Use*. Problems pertaining to the conservation and use of human and natural resources in relation to the enhancement of human personality at all levels; developing consumer literacy.

11. *Human Relations*. Problems relating to the factors which promote or defeat co-operation among individuals and groups; understanding the techniques of group action; securing unity through diversity; implications for dealing with racial and ethnic groups.

12. *Physical and Mental Health*. Problems bearing upon healthful living on the part of the individual, community, and world; ways of securing and maintaining good physical and mental health at all levels.

13. *Planning*. Problems relating to the need for and techniques of planning on the part of individuals, communities, nations, and the world.

14. *Science and Technology*. Problems bearing upon the use of science and technology in promoting or destroying civilization; the lag between technological "know-how" and its application to the solution of human problems.

15. *Vocational Orientation*. Problems pertaining to the understanding of the way the work of the world is carried on; determining the individual's capacities in relation to particular occupations; provision for first-hand experiences in work.

16. *Hobbies and Interests*. Problems pertaining to the role of hobbies and other interests in mental health; developing skills in hobbies and other interests, developing appreciation of art, music, and literature.

17. *Public Opinion*. Problems relating to the influence of various factors upon the molding of public opinion; propaganda analysis; role of emotional appeals; public opinion and international co-operation; use of critical thinking in forming public opinion.

18. *Education*. Problems pertaining to the role of education; securing an education; the maintenance, extension, and improvement of educational agencies at all levels; education and international understanding.

19. *War and Peace*. Problems pertaining to the causes of war and how they may be eliminated; understanding the relationship between scientific advance and security; understanding and appraising organizations and agencies for promoting world peace; examining and trying to reconcile the conflicts between national sovereignty and a world order.[15]

These problem areas, here stated without any implications for sequence, provide the scope of the program design for meeting the common needs of adolescents.[16] In practice, the definition and scope of the problem

[15] *Ibid.*, pp. 60–61.

[16] For similar formulations see the following:

Prudence Bostwick and Chandos Reid, *A Functional High-School Program* (New York: Hinds, Hayden & Eldridge, Inc., 1947); William Van Til, "A Social Living Cur-

areas would be determined on the basis of the formulation of common needs accepted or worked out by the faculty. The sequence would also be determined by the faculty. It is proposed that a block of two or three periods per day be set aside for this aspect of the program. In most of the schools using this type of core, units of work from these areas are to be selected, planned, and carried out co-operatively by the teacher and students. The group identifies the particular problems upon which it wishes to work, draws upon all available resources, and organizes itself for an intensive study of these problems. When help is needed, specialists on the faculty are brought in. For example, in a unit on "home and family life" in the eighth grade, the home economist might be brought in to help identify family problems; the science teacher might help in a study of technological advances in the home; problems of health might require the assistance of the teacher of health and physical education or the school doctor or nurse; the teachers of fine and industrial arts might be utilized in connection with house planning and interior decoration; and the mathematics teacher might help in problems of family budgeting.

In addition to the block of time devoted to the core or general education, students would be enrolled in elective courses in the fine and practical arts, music, foreign languages, advanced science, and mathematics, vocational subjects, and other special-interest areas.

The problem of determining the sequence of units or learning activities in a general-education program, based upon common needs and problems of adolescents, presents difficulties not encountered in the subject-centered program. In such programs, sequence is usually determined by the logic of the subject or field, which takes precedence over the immediate felt needs of the students. The assumption is that common needs are met as students secure mastery of the subject or field of knowledge.

Schools that have developed programs based upon preplanned problem areas have solved the problem of sequence in several ways, none of which is entirely satisfactory.

In Harford County, Maryland, problem areas were allocated by the faculty to the various grade levels, and resource units were developed in each area, with suggested learning activities based upon the maturational levels of the students. Dorothy Mudd explains the plan as follows:

With the arrival of the millenium, when master teachers people ideal classrooms in school plants with unlimited resources, in communities where the best efforts of all laymen and all the professional staff are co-operatively addressed to

riculum for Postwar Secondary Education" (Unpublished doctoral dissertation, Ohio State University, 1946); Lucile Lurry, "The Contribution of Home Economics to Selected Problem Areas in the Core Curriculum of the Secondary School" (Unpublished doctoral dissertation, Ohio State University, 1949).

the problem of providing the best educational experience for all children, we shall undoubtedly abandon many of the curricular methods which serve us now. While we await that golden age, we face realistically the problems which confront us. To meet one which stems from the dual cause of (1) insecurity on the part of many teachers conditioned by preservice and in-service training to expect a fixed curricular pattern, and (2) the need for many and varied instructional materials which demands some preplanning as to areas in which classes will work, we have dared to propose the following sequence of resource units as a possible pattern:

Grade Seven

1. Living in the junior high school; exploring my educational opportunities
2. Knowing Harford County
3. Discovering Maryland as America in miniature
4. The finest machine; keeping physically fit; preventing accident and disease

Grade Eight

1. Relating our land and resources to our history
2. Conservation of our natural resources
3. Finding fellowship with Americans North and South
4. Our physical environment shaping our living

Grade Nine

1. Appreciating the contributions of other cultures
2. Our shrinking world
3. How science and technology affect our lives
4. Finding one's place in the world of work

It will be readily apparent that we are thinking in terms of an expanding community concept developing out of learning experiences in this sequence. We do not propose this as an ideal pattern—not even as a desirable one. It is, as we indicated above, our attempt to meet a specific problem which confronts us.[17]

This extended quotation indicates that practical rather than psychological considerations played the major role in determining the scope and sequence of the problem areas.

Another illustration of a fixed sequence program is that of the New School of the Evanston Township High School. This program probably approximates what we have defined as a Type-Five core, although some of the areas set forth might be more accurately described as Type Four —or unified studies. The areas utilize a two-period block of time and are developed in the following sequence:

Freshman Core—Orientation:

1. Finding myself in school and community
2. Choosing a vocation
3. New horizons through literature
4. The United States and world affairs

---

[17] Dorothy Mudd, *A Core Program Grows*, pp. 23–24. Bel Air, Maryland: Board of Education of Harford County, 1949.

Sophomore Core—World Mindedness:
1. The atomic age
2. War and peace
3. The development of law and justice
4. Theaters, motion pictures, radio, and television
Junior Core—American Life and Culture
1. The American people
2. America in literature
3. The United States Government, its structure and development
4. The development of an American economic system
Senior Core—Life Adjustment:
1. College and careers
2. Our literary heritage
3. Consumer education
4. Marriage and family living.[18]

Garrett County, Maryland,[19] is also an example of a fixed scope-and-sequence design for general education. These problem areas evolved from the basic philosophy developed by the teachers and an analysis of the basic needs of the students. Each problem area is implemented by a resource unit developed by a group of teachers. Learning units, based on these resource units are planned co-operatively by teachers and students. In addition to the core, students are required to take mathematics in the seventh and eighth grades and physical education at all levels. The program utilizes three periods per day in the junior high schools, and two periods per day in the senior high schools. The problem areas, arranged in terms of scope and sequence, are as follows:

GARRETT COUNTY, MARYLAND
CORE PROGRAM
1950–51

Grade VII
School living
Health and safety
Transportation
Communicating ideas

Grade X
Intercultural relations
Living in one world
Leisure and recreation
Communicating ideas

Grade VIII
Knowing Garrett County
Natural environment
Leisure and recreation

Grade XI
American heritage
Personal development
Establishing beliefs

[18] Reported by Ellsworth Tompkins, *The Activity Period in Public High Schools*, p. 4. Federal Security Agency, Office of Education, Bulletin 1951, No. 19. Washington: Government Printing Office, 1951.

[19] For a brief description of this program, see C. B. Mendenhall and K. J. Arisman, *Secondary Education*, pp. 267–71. New York: William Sloan Associates, 1951.

Grade IX	*Grade XII*
Making a living	Family living
Establishing beliefs	Role of education
Consumer problems	Making a living
Personal development	Health and safety
American heritage	Consumer problems
	Technology of living

It must not be concluded that the programs set forth are completely fixed, leaving no place for teacher-student planning. Within limits teachers are free to plan with students in terms of the particular problems of the group. The resource units which have been developed are intended to be suggestive rather than prescriptive. They contain many more suggestions for learning activities than could possibly be carried out by any one group. While it would be difficult to defend psychologically the placement at the particular grade level of most of the problem areas, it must at the same time be admitted that a psychologically sound learning unit might be developed from any one of them at the grade level specified.

A more flexible program design is that which has been developed in the Ohio State University School. This program is based upon the philosophy of the school and the needs, problems, and interests of students at the various maturational levels. The general design of the program follows:[20]

THE OHIO STATE UNIVERSITY SCHOOL CORE PROGRAM

Problem Areas—Grades Seven, Eight, and Nine

1. Understanding my body
2. Beliefs and superstititions
3. Hobbies
4. Managing my personal affairs
5. Sports and recreation
6. Living in University School
7. Living in the home
8. Living in the neighborhood
9. Personality and appearance
10. Earning a living
11. Housing
12. Natural resources

---

[20] *The Philosophy and Purposes of the University School* (Columbus: Ohio State University, 1948); Norma Albright *et al., An Inventory Study of the Personal and General Social Problems of 256 Students in Grades Seven to Twelve, Inclusive* (Columbus: Ohio State University, 1940); *How Children Develop: A Report by the Faculty of the University School* (Columbus: Ohio State University, 1946).

13. Community agencies and services
    a) Recreation
    b) Protection
    c) Government
    d) Education
    e) Welfare
14. Communication
15. Living in Columbus
16. Living in Ohio
17. Living in another country or other countries

Problem Areas—Grades Ten, Eleven, and Twelve
Tenth Grade

1. School living
2. Problems of healthful living
3. Problems of living in an urban society
4. Problems of the family as a basic social unit
5. The development of the American scene

Eleventh Grade

1. School living
2. Problems of living in the Atomic age
3. The problems of establishing beliefs
4. The problems of making a living (exploring vocations)
5. Current world problems
6. Driver and pedestrian education

Twelfth Grade

1. School living
2. Problems of producer-consumer economics
3. Implications of scientific advancement
4. Major conflicting ideologies
5. Bases for determining values by which to live
6. The American heritage

These problem areas are suggestive only. There is perhaps a presumption that learning units be selected co-operatively by teachers and student groups from the list of problem areas approved by the faculty. However, any learning unit which has the approval of the grade faculty may be chosen by the teachers and students. It is probably fair to state that in the main the units selected are closely related to the problem areas listed. When the problem areas were set up several years ago, some of them were "pegged" at certain grade levels, which meant that learning units based upon such pegged problem areas were required. Gradually the program has become more flexible.

Between the two extremes represented by the Maryland programs de-

scribed above and the Ohio State University School program, many variations are possible. Probably the general tendency is to start with a rather
fixed program to provide for teacher and student security. As resources
are developed and the faculty and students gain experience in the co-operative selection, planning, and carrying out of learning units, there is a
tendency to relax requirements and to permit wide discretion in choosing
learning activities.

What are the strengths and weaknesses of a program design for general education based upon preplanned problem areas?

Strengths:

1. Such a program makes possible a direct attack upon the needs of youth and
the problems which beset them in our present-day culture. The traditional program is based upon the assumption that once young people have gained some degree of mastery of the so-called fundamental subjects—English, history, science,
and mathematics—they will then be able to cope successfully with their problems. The program under discussion reverses the process. Common problems of
youth are identified; they are studied intensively, drawing upon appropriate subject matter, and solutions are reached through individual and group thinking.
The so-called fundamentals are learned functionally, and there is usually plenty
of evidence that this learning is effective.

2. Such a program is the means of bridging the gap between education and
guidance,[21] between the curriculum and the extracurriculum,[22] between general
education and special-interest education. Homeroom activities and individual
and group guidance become an integral part of the educative process as the
teacher and students go about the solving of problems. Likewise, many of the informal student activities, such as class projects, school business, clubs, and organizations are absorbed in the block of time devoted to the core or the general-
education phase of the instructional program. Special interests of students are
cultivated in the core up to the point where laboratories and studios and specialized instruction are needed.

3. The problem-areas design tends to break down the class barriers which so
frequently are maintained in the traditional program. The use of the broad, comprehensive units of work makes possible provision for individual differences in
abilities and in rates of learning, thus obviating the necessity for sectioning, or
ability grouping. Moreover, students of all social and economic levels work together in the solving of common problems, thus exemplifying democratic living
at its best.

4. It facilitates the unification of knowledge. Subjects are no longer taught in
water-tight compartments. Problems of living refuse to be straight-jacketed into
logically organized systems of knowledge. Interrelationships among subjects and
fields are established as the various disciplines are drawn upon as needed.

---

[21] See Alberty, *Reorganizing the High-School Curriculum, op. cit.,* chap. xiii.
[22] Tompkins, *op. cit.*

5. Such a program is consistent with the newer theories of learning and transfer. For the most part, traditional instruction is based upon the atomistic approach to learning. On the other hand, the core, with its emphasis upon broad comprehensive units of work and vital problems of living, stresses the organismic approach. Transfer of training takes place through the enrichment of meanings and their use in a wide variety of life situations.

6. A program of this type encourages the teaching staff to plan and work together. In the compartmentalized program of general education, each teacher works more or less in isolation from his fellows. The English teachers have no need to co-operate with the social studies or science teachers. Each group plans its own program out of relationship with the others. Such situations cannot exist in the type of program which we are considering. Teachers of *all* areas have contributions to make, and they have a stake in the outcome. If it is to be successful, such contributions must be elicited and utilized. Thus, the teaching staff must work together as a whole.

7. The procedures of this program encourage the use of democratic practices in the classroom. The subject-centered program, with its fixed quotas of subject matter to be mastered is not conducive to teacher-student planning. Really there is little about which to plan! The problem-centered approach changes the scene completely. The student has a role in identifying problems, in planning the attacks upon them, and in evaluating the effectiveness of the work. These practices are the essence of the democratic process.

8. The study of problem areas encourages the use of the community as a laboratory for learning. The common problems of youth grow out of the interaction of the student and his immediate and wider environment. They do not exist "under the skin" of the individual. Problems of home and family living, for example, cannot be isolated from the environmental conditions surrounding the home. Thus, the classroom takes on the character of a meeting place for planning the attack on the problems. The activities of the students, as they go about discovering pertinent data, are bound to take the class out into the community. Incidentally, the larger block of time set aside for the core makes such community exploration possible without encroaching upon the time allotted to other school activities.

9. Such a program makes it possible for teachers to reduce materially the student loads which they are required to carry in a traditional program. Loads of 175 students per day are not uncommon. Obviously the teacher who carries two core groups of three periods each would have only one-third as many different students per day as the teacher who handles six separate classes. The core organization, in cutting down the student load, makes it possible for teachers to know students more intimately and hence to guide them more effectively.

Weaknesses.

1. The program requires a vast amount of work on the part of teachers and as a consequence many groups are unwilling to undertake such a drastic reorganization.

2. There is danger that the scope and sequence may become "frozen" and thus fail to meet the changing needs of youth.

3. Teachers are not well equipped through training to carry out such a program. Consequently they may feel insecure and defensive.

4. The public may be slow to accept a program which breaks so completely with the familiar subjects.

In spite of these weaknesses, there is evidence to show that a school system with good leadership and a teaching staff that is willing to work co-operatively may develop a successful Type-Five core. The programs described here are proof of this claim.

Type-Six Core: Program Design Based Exclusively upon Teacher-Student Planning

The discussion of program design based upon broad preplanned problem areas should have made clear the point that there are wide differences in practice in the use of the structured problem areas. Programs were presented in which the problem areas actually determine all of the learning units developed in the classroom. At the other extreme, one program was presented in which all of the problem areas are to be regarded as suggestive. The next logical step would be to *eliminate problem areas entirely*, leaving the choice of learning activities exclusively to the teacher and his group of students.[23] In such a program, criteria as to what constitutes a satisfactory unit of work would be arrived at co-operatively. Proposals of units or problems would be made by the students and teacher. These proposals would be evaluated in terms of the criteria, and decisions would be made. The actual design of the program would simply be a record of what had been undertaken at each grade level during the course of the year. The argument for this procedure is very simple. The teacher and students are most competent to determine the common needs of the particular group and, hence, to determine the learning activities best suited to meet these needs. Structuring the program in advance is just another way of imposing subject matter. The method of determining problems, goals, and ways of working is more important than the actual subject matter that makes up the program.

Some so-called progressive elementary schools are organized on this basis. It is impossible to find any design or structure in the program. This does not mean that there are no agreed-upon values or objectives or that teachers are not sensitive to the need for developing certain recognized

---

[23] See William H. Kilpatrick, *Remaking the Curriculum* (New York: Newson & Co., 1936); L. Thomas Hopkins, *Integration: Its Meaning and Application* (New York: D. Appleton–Century Co., 1937).

skills of living. It does mean, however, that no design for meeting common needs is set up in advance.

Few if any secondary schools are organized wholly on this basis. Probably the nearest approach would be that of the Gillespie Junior High School in Philadelphia as described by Gertrude Noar[24] and limited segments of the program at Denby High School in Detroit.[25]

It is possible to find individual teachers in high schools operating on this basis. For example, a number of schools have provided administratively for a double or triple period for meeting common needs, giving wide discretion to the teachers as to what shall be taught. In such a school some teachers will teach traditional subject matter, say English, history, and science, in successive periods; some will correlate these subjects; some will fuse them on the basis of contemporary problems or culture epochs; some will set up their own individual problem areas; still others will discard all preconceived subject matter and base units of work upon the immediate felt needs of students. Thus, the same school might illustrate all the types of core programs which we have discussed. Needless to say, such a school cannot be said to have a program design.

Strengths:

1. This plan recognizes the dynamic character of the learner and the learning process.

2. The procedure provides optimally for teacher and student initiative.

3. The design guards against the "freezing" of programs in terms of problem areas, or subject to be mastered.

4. The use of the democratic process in the classroom is facilitated.

Weaknesses:

1. The program may be opportunistic, with little or no continuity.

2. It may lead to teacher-student insecurity.

3. Teachers in specialized-interest areas may become dissatisfied with the program because they see no pattern which is being followed and, hence, have little faith in what is being taught.

4. The public is likely to question a program which departs so radically from conventional practices and which at the same time appears to be opportunistic in character.

---

[24] Gertrude Noar, *Freedom To Live and Learn.* Philadelphia: Franklin Publishing Co., 1948.

[25] Roland Faunce and Nelson Bossing, *Developing the Core Curriculum.* New York: Prentice-Hall, Inc., 1951. See especially chap. vi, "A Core Class in Action" by Dr. Rosalind Zapf. See also a film strip prepared by Dr. Zapf entitled: "A Core Class in Action," produced and distributed by College of Education, Wayne University, Detroit, Michigan, 1948.

Concluding Statement

We have now completed our survey and evaluation of the leading trends in curriculum design to meet the common needs of secondary-school youth. It must be evident to the reader that only a relatively few schools have departed from the traditional subject-centered program that has been under attack for a long time. The senior high schools have changed their basic design hardly at all in the past three decades. Only a handful have revised their programs in terms of the needs or problems approach—and this in the face of significant research in the area of adolescent needs and problems and of considerable successful experience in curriculum reorganization.

Why can't we put into practice what we know how to do? We have the knowledge necessary to rebuild our secondary schools. Why don't we utilize it? Why did the *Eight-Year Study* have so little impact on the high schools? Why did the publication and widespread distribution of *Education for All American Youth* cause hardly a ripple on the surface of curriculum development? Why, in a period of history which demands a more dynamic and functional program of secondary education geared into the vital problems of living, are the forces of education in retreat?

The answers to these questions are not hard to find. Some of the more important forces which block the development of a psychologically sound program of general education are noted here.

1. Teachers and administrators tend to be complacent and satisfied with the traditional program.
2. Teacher-education institutions have perpetuated the traditional pattern. Only a few have developed programs for training core teachers.
3. State and regional accrediting agencies have not provided leadership in breaking the lock-step.
4. State certification requirements continue to be stated in terms of credits in subjects and fields of knowledge. Very few state departments of education have any plan for certifying teachers outside of the traditional pattern.
5. Many schools are intimidated by well-organized pressure groups and are afraid to launch the kind of program which is demanded by the crucial times in which we live.

In spite of these blocks, there are observable trends which indicate that they may, with concerted effort, be removed. We close with a mention of a few of them.

1. There are deep stirrings in higher education. Many colleges and universities are reorganizing their programs of general education in the direction of greater functionality.
2. A few teacher-education institutions are experimenting with new programs designed to prepare teachers to meet needs rather than to teach subjects.

3. Curriculum experimentation is going forward in a few schools, and the results are being made known.
4. Professional organizations are aroused to the need for action in meeting the insidious attack upon the schools.
5. An increasing number of schools are using laymen effectively in curriculum reorganization.

There is at least a chance that educators will capitalize on these significant trends and within the next decade transform our static and ineffective programs of general education into programs that will really prepare youth for living in a democratic world.

CHAPTER VIII

DESIGNING PROGRAMS TO MEET THE SPECIAL NEEDS OF YOUTH*

Robert S. Gilchrist
Assistant Superintendent in Charge of Instruction
Pasadena City Schools
Pasadena, California
and
Robert J. Forbes
Instructor, Pasadena City College
Pasadena, California

Purpose of the Chapter

In designing programs to meet the special needs of youth, educators usually think in terms of specialized offerings. Those who determine curriculum generally assume that special needs of youth are met if the school program includes appropriate vocational and college-preparatory courses and a relatively few other special subjects. Such courses are important and will be treated in this chapter. Other means, possibly more fundamental, by which schools can meet the special needs of students will also be discussed. The purpose of this chapter is to develop a design for that part of the program which is different for various students and to point out phases of the total program that are important to the success of the

* In developing the contents of this chapter the authors received suggestions from the following group of Southern California educators: Anna Davis, Co-ordinator of Guidance and Counseling, Pasadena City Schools, Pasadena; Elmer J. Erickson, Principal, South Pasadena-San Marino Senior High School, South Pasadena; Rebecca D. Farley, General Supervisor, Burbank Unified School District, Burbank; Mildred L. Finnerty, Director of Student Activities, Whittier Union High School District, Whittier; Youldon C. Howell, Head Supervisor of Art, Pasadena City Schools, Pasadena; Howard E. Marvin, Head Supervisor of Vocational Education, Pasadena City Schools, Pasadena; William B. Melchior, Supervisor of Curriculum Development, Long Beach Unified School District, Long Beach; Fredericka Moore, Co-ordinator of Corrective Physical Education for Women, Los Angeles County Board of Education, Los Angeles; Claude E. Nihart, Head Supervisor, Vocational and Practical Arts, Curriculum Division, Los Angeles City Schools, Los Angeles; Reuben R. Palm, Director of Secondary Education, Los Angeles County Board of Education, Los Angeles; Lee W. Ralston, Director of Trade and Industrial Education, Los Angeles County Board of Education, Los Angeles; and Gunnar Wahlquist, Director of Guidance, El Monte Union High School District, El Monte.

specialized offerings. It is recognized that the manner in which a school meets common needs of youth has important implications for the design of the program to meet special needs.

Basic Considerations in the Designing of Programs To Meet the Special Needs of Youth

Teacher Participation in Curriculum Development

Chapter vii has pointed out several weaknesses in secondary education. In our judgment, the most important explanation of these weaknesses is that curriculum designing is carried on too much by educators far removed from the schools of a community where the program is applied.

College professors, textbook writers, experts from state departments of education, and central-office supervisors in large cities have important functions to serve in helping local school faculties design programs. But in the last analysis, if the actual needs of youth are to be met, those who know the boys and girls have by far the most important role to play. These persons should be led and stimulated by the local school administrator who must be a curriculum leader in his own right. The reasons that a school faculty should be involved deeply in designing its curriculum are obvious, yet the importance of this basic principle of curriculum improvement is often ignored.

This chapter is presented with the hope that individual teachers and local faculty groups may find help as they attack problems of designing programs to meet special needs of youth. In a sense we are indicating a design which we believe is an ideal toward which to strive. We recognize, however, that the specific elements of a design can only be determined in relation to a local school unit. Therefore, specific practices mentioned are only illustrative.

The Guidance Program

Guidance programs are frequently separate from instruction in a school and often represent efforts of the school to fit students into the existing curriculum offerings. If a guidance program is a good one, we believe it will have these four characteristics:

1. Every student will be known well by someone on the school staff.
2. Provisions will be made in planning the teacher's "time" and pupil load for individual conferences as well as the group guidance in classes.
3. Secondary-school plants will be built or redesigned to include conference offices where teachers and students can meet privately.
4. A premium will be placed on the development of a faculty which is guidance-conscious and trained in guidance techniques.

If either the general or the special needs of youth are to be met, it seems obvious that students must do things at school that seem worth while to them. Too often, young people regard time spent in the regular curriculum of the school as a necessary evil. If the real needs of youth are satisfied, the young people themselves will have to sense the relationships of school experiences to their lives outside of school. Johnny Jones and Mary Smith will respond with enthusiasm to classroom opportunities only to the degree that activities are clearly related to what they recognize as their own needs. All of this means that a successful guidance program must underlie the program offerings of the school if that program is to meet general and specific needs of youth.

Of the programs to meet common needs of youth outlined in the previous chapter, Type Five (core consists of broad preplanned areas, from which are selected learning experiences in terms of the psychobiological and societal needs, problems, and interests of students) and Type Six (core consists of broad teacher-student planned units of work, or activities, in terms of the expressed wishes or desires of the group) would best promote the development of an instructional program in harmony with a sound guidance program. Even with Type One (core consists of a number of logically organized subjects or fields of knowledge, each of which is taught independently), it would be possible for a school to do much to relate its offerings to the guidance program if the principle that every student should be known well by someone on the school staff is accepted. A step in this direction might be to make the first-period teacher the guidance teacher for students in this class. It is often said that some teachers are not cut out to be good guidance workers. However, if this is true, they probably are not as effective as teachers as they might be, and involving them in the guidance program may help them grow as teachers and guidance workers. It is probably correct that in most secondary schools there are a few teachers who should not be involved in the guidance program. But we feel that most of the faculty must participate if guidance is to be of value to the students. There should be well-trained guidance personnel on the staff to give leadership. These experts ought to work primarily with those teachers who are sufficiently acquainted with students to help them on their problems.

Good Teaching

A good guidance program alone will not assure classes which meet the needs of youth. In fact, students will probably not be very enthusiastic about conferences with teachers unless the results of the conferences make a difference in classrooms. The difference between good teaching and poor teaching is so pronounced that one can say that good classroom teaching will do more to insure the meeting of special needs in a school than any other single factor. Without good teaching, special offerings to meet special needs often fail, not because the offering is unsound, but because the basic atmosphere of the school is not one of effective living and learning.

Good teaching demands that each student feel that he is being treated as an individual. He must sense that his difference and his uniqueness are respected. More and more literature is becoming available to indicate the underlying needs of human beings which, if not met, block the satisfaction of other needs. The last White House Conference highlighted these needs.

A recent pamphlet[1] gives specific suggestions to teachers on things to do and not to do in meeting the need for belonging, the need for achievement, the need for economic security, the need to be free from fear, the need for love and affection, the need to be free from guilt, the need for self-respect, and the need for guiding purposes. If every classroom is an environment in which these needs are considered, the school will find it easier to meet the special needs of youth.

Though a good guidance program makes it possible to bring together a group of students who understand why they are in a class and are interested in its possibilities, this step alone may not satisfy the needs of the group. Good teaching also provides the opportunity for students to help plan the contents of their courses. Educators recognize the importance of a citizenry able to participate in group planning, executing, and evaluating. It is not hard, therefore, to justify taking time in every class for student participation. If teachers permit students to help develop goals for the course, to decide what experiences offer the greatest promise of achieving these goals, and to evaluate how well the goals are achieved, students should leave high school able to participate effectively in group planning, whether it be in the home, church, or community.

Through the guidance program and student participation in planning the work of classes, students will be helped to establish personal goals as to the kinds of people they wish to be. With good leadership, adolescents grow up wanting to be healthy, to be effective members of families, to earn a living honestly and successfully, and to participate in the affairs of the community. If students and teachers are both concerned over the attainment of these broad goals, subject matter can be used more effectively as a means of achieving them.

Interrelatedness of Programs To Meet
Common and Special Needs of Youth

Several illustrations of the interrelatedness of programs to meet common and special needs of youth will be presented. With sound guidance and good teaching we believe that these two phases of a school program

---

[1] *Do's and Don't's of the Needs Theory.* Edited by Louis E. Raths and Anna P. Burrell. Bronxville, New York: Modern Education Service (Box 26), 1950.

will complement and supplement each other to the end that the total school program will be evaluated as more than the sum of its parts. In fact, we doubt whether the common needs and special needs of youth can be met in a school unless the faculty co-operates closely and unless the school has good guidance and good teaching throughout. Let us turn to some illustrations of interrelatedness:

1. Classes well taught often meet both common and special needs. A class in auto mechanics may be the one place in the school where a boy will start taking an interest in learning to read better. Any of the special offerings where adolescents respond enthusiastically because they sense their needs are being satisfied is an ideal environment for the development of citizen traits. There is no better place for a poor reader to get help than with his social-studies teacher, providing that teacher wants to help him and has the proper materials to do so. Though the class may be primarily one to meet common needs, an English teacher, well trained and well advised, may do much to assist a student who stutters—a special need.

2. In classes designed to meet common needs, the teacher has many opportunities to help students sense the importance of correcting a weakness, start to learn a salable skill, and plan ways to enjoy leisure hours more completely. As they work in programs designed to meet their special needs, boys and girls will often discover that subjects which once bored them are important. This often happens when teachers assist students to clarify their purposes and to evaluate their progress in achieving goals.

3. No sharp lines can be drawn between offerings designed to meet the common and special needs of youth. In the same class, one student may be satisfying a special need while another is meeting a need common to all youth. A shop is a good illustration. Many students are in the class because of the opportunity provided to learn a leisure-time activity or to become adept in the use of their hands—general-education purposes. To some, however, the shop course is the beginning of vocational preparation.

In another sense sharp lines cannot be drawn. In the earlier secondary-school years much of the program should be exploratory in nature. As students mature, these programs justifiably become less general and exploratory. Special needs of groups of students commence to be met by special offerings. The arts program or the physical-education program are good illustrations. Surely no one would question that practical and fine arts in the junior high school should be a part of the program to meet the common needs of youth. The same would be true for physical education. By Grades XI and XII, however, these programs often have specialized offerings in order to meet the varying needs of young people.

Perhaps the most fundamental manner in which the programs of meeting common needs and special needs are interrelated is that the special-needs program can be designed effectively only in relation to the kind of program which the school has designed to meet the common needs of youth. Most of secondary education should be general education to meet the common needs of all. The school with a Type-One program as outlined in the previous chapter must necessarily have a vastly different special-needs program from Type Five or Type Six.[2] An illustration will help to clarify this point. If a school has an academic program with separate subjects taught without any attempt to show relationships, there is likely to be little opportunity for individualization of work for students who vary in ability, background, or plans. In such a school it would be absurd for those designing the special-needs program to assume that vocational students were getting adequate preparation in English or mathematics in their common-needs program. On the other hand, with the Type Five or Type Six common-needs program the vocational people could assume with some degree of confidence that the English and social-studies classes were meeting the needs of vocational students for functional English and arithmetic.

Appropriate Program Designs for Special Needs
Over-all Designs

Secondary schools have traditionally offered special curriculums for students with different vocational goals. The most common patterns have been "college preparatory," "commercial," and "general." Homemaking and agriculture, and the breakdown of college-preparatory work in terms of the kind of college to which the student plans to go, illustrate variations of these patterns.

The authors feel that the recommendations stated in *Planning for American Youth*[3] are sound. A block of time in the school day, possibly one hour in length in Grade X, two hours in Grades XI and XII, and half-time in Grades XIII and XIV, is set aside for vocational and prevocational subjects. Vocational and prevocational subjects include the preprofessional or college-preparatory subjects as well as those set up for students to develop salable skills for use immediately upon graduation from secondary schools. In other words, college preparatory is considered prevocational. One hour a day throughout Grades VII to XIV is allotted to health and physical fitness. Two hours in the junior high school and an hour in Grades X through XIV are provided for the pursuit of special interests.

This design consists of required courses and electives. It proposes that all students would engage in the common-learnings program and the

---

[2] These types were explained earlier in this chapter (p. 143).

[3] *Planning for American Youth: An Educational Program for Youth of Secondary-School Age.* Washington: National Association of Secondary-School Principals, 1951.

health program throughout their secondary-school experience. All students from Grade X through XIV would be engaged in some phase of vocational preparation although the specific subjects would vary. The same would be true in regard to special interests. The experiences of students in health and special interests are common experiences (at least the students are enrolled in the same classes) in the earlier years of the secondary school. In the more advanced grades students would be in separate classes in terms of their special needs. In this design it should be recognized that there is a decrease in time given to common needs (the common-learnings program), as the student proceeds through the secondary school, and an increase in vocational preparation. Differentiation also occurs in the offerings in health and physical fitness and in special interests as the student progresses from Grade VII through XIV.

Earning a Living

The need to develop a salable skill by which to earn a living is common to all youth, even those whose economic circumstances might permit them to continue throughout life without earning. All persons need to feel economically competent in order to be well-adjusted human beings. Even though this vocational need is common to all people, the secondary schools must develop specialized offerings to satisfy the need since, obviously, the roads to development of salable skills are various.

How can a school be effective in helping students choose and prepare for a vocation? This is a double-barreled job. One group may have a fairly good idea of what they want to do or become. Some of these are rather certain that they must go to college to prepare for their jobs, and they must have the facilities for getting college-preparatory training. There are others who intend to end their education with high school or junior college and who are taking vocational or business courses or some specialized offerings which they feel will qualify them for their chosen work. They rely on the school program to train them to get a job. Students in these categories know, at least temporarily, what they are going to do vocationally.

A second group, unfortunately larger, is composed of students who are not sure what they want to do for a living. This is one of the big problems with which they are struggling. A recent study[4] of the nature of occupational choice and the process through which a decision is made shows that choice of occupation results from many factors occurring over a rather long period of time, that it is a very complex thing in which many conscious and unconscious forces operate, and that there is great variability

---

[4] Eli Ginzberg *et al.*, *Occupational Planning.* New York: Columbia University Press, 1951.

in the times at which young people are able to make decisions about occupations.

This points up the need of young people for opportunities to explore the world of work and to be exposed to different types of work in a realistic atmosphere. In addition, students need the opportunity, under competent leadership, to talk about vocations with other young people. It may do a great deal of good for students to talk together about these problems and to see what their contemporaries are thinking about. Young people are under tension at this time to decide "what they are going to be." Though teachers and parents prod them in many ways to hurry their decisions, many of them are not prepared to make the decision. By and large, schools do very little to help students evaluate themselves in terms of the type of work they might choose. Some information is given them about opportunities and salaries, but there is little attempt to assist them to discover whether their interests and ideals and other personality characteristics fit into the type of work they are considering.

Parents sometimes make it difficult for a school to provide for a boy or girl in terms of his abilities, needs, and the opportunities in the world of work. The prestige factor in occupational choice is very important to parents, and they are wary of school people who suggest that their children try out a "vocational" subject or that perhaps it would be wise for them to give up the idea of studying medicine or dentistry. Unfortunately, it is the student who suffers in such a conflict. The school staff should ascribe equal importance to all phases of its offerings and should carry on a parent-education program to help parents analyze the value of such subjects. If this is not done, students will be apt to select courses without relation to their actual needs and interests. Culture patterns change slowly, but, in a democracy which respects the dignity of all work, progress should be made toward enabling an individual to feel that he is a success doing the kind of work for which he is suited. Our society is burdened by many frustrated people who are unhappy because they do not have white-collar or professional positions.

Vocational educators sometimes let their enthusiasm for vocational education keep them from recognizing that vocational preparation is only one of the objectives of secondary education and that vocational success depends on personal characteristics as well as on skill. At its worst, this enthusiasm of vocational educators has resulted in separate programs or schools of vocational education where general education is given far too little emphasis. Separate schools and separate school systems for vocational education must contend with the same problem of probable unbalance as the academic high school which does not accept vocational preparation as one of its purposes. Possibly a separate vocational school can be justified in cities of one-half million or more people where the special school can provide specialized equipment which will enable it to offer subjects which the comprehensive high schools cannot. However, in most communities a secondary school is called upon to offer programs to meet both common needs and special needs. The authors of this chapter contend that this is a desirable situation. When teachers of vocational- and general-education subjects are on the same faculty and have an opportunity to work together in designing a total program to meet both common and special needs, there is more assurance that a successful secondary curriculum will evolve. It must be remembered that all students need general education, and, equally important—all students need vocational orientation and opportunities for vocational exploration. Separate schools run the decided risk of overemphasizing their specialty.

Every boy and girl should be treated as an individual case in deciding how his special needs can best be met. How long will he remain in school? How clear are his vocational goals? How sound are these goals in relation to his abilities and in relation to employment demands? Not only should the school be clear on the answers to these questions but the student must be taking courses appropriate to his circumstances. Grades VII, VIII, and IX should provide many exploratory opportunities which will give students sensitivity to areas of vocational choice in which they may have an interest and an ability. More and more as the world of work is requiring maturer people, and as thirteenth- and fourteenth-year offerings are provided in local communities, Grade X is becoming a year for exploration rather than for specific vocational preparation. The suggestion is made, however, that students be allowed to elect vocational courses even though it would outwardly seem better for them to wait until a later grade. If a student does not feel that his general-education program is meeting his needs, if he is disinterested and wants to quit school because he thinks it has nothing for him, he ought to have the opportunity to select whatever vocational subjects give promise of being important and useful to him.

Offerings of a secondary school for vocational and prevocational preparation divide themselves into three groups: first, vocational subjects offered in the school building; second, co-operative, part-time work programs; and third, precollege subjects.

Vocational Subjects Offered in the School Plant. The secondary school should have shops and laboratories in which to teach auto mechanics, radio, electricity, carpentry, and similar subjects. Agricultural communities, particularly, need farm shops and rooms designed for the teaching of agriculture, as well as suitable facilities for industrial shops. Secondary schools also need rooms designed specifically for business-education courses—typing, shorthand, bookkeeping, and accounting.

These industrial, agricultural, and business subjects might best be delayed until Grades XIII and XIV if the holding power of the secondary school and the economic circumstances of families permitted. There is another group of offerings which ideally ought to be provided in Grades XIII and XIV. Courses for practical nurses, dental assistants, television technicians, refrigeration and air conditioning technicians, and cosmetologists often should be offered in the thirteenth and fourteenth years. Perhaps they should be given earlier in some communities where employment opportunities, labor laws, and size of school justify. In each secondary school it would be sound for the faculty to plan vocational-subject offerings for those years immediately preceding employment. The school does have an obligation, however, to make a careful estimate of its holding power and to be sure that offerings are available before students drop out of school.

In smaller schools the same facilities will undoubtedly have to serve both general education and vocational purposes. As the size of the school increases it becomes possible to justify more highly specialized facilities and equipment for vocational purposes.

Co-operative, Part-Time Work Programs. Many vocational skills can be learned best on the job. Generally it is not a question of either offering vocational subjects in school or of providing for co-operative part-time work programs in which the skill will be learned on the job. Often the first part of the preparation can be secured at school with this training being supplemented by practical on-the-job experience properly supervised to assist students to relate this work experience to school subjects.

Subjects which should be part of a co-operative part-time work program depend on many factors. Whether or not the program can be financed is a major consideration. State and federal reimbursement possibilities must be explored. Can people of the community, including both employers and unions, be sold on the desirability of such a program? It seems probable, however, that any school which aims at providing its students with salable skills will have some type of co-operative, part-time work program. Under most circumstances, auto mechanics, radio repairmen, bookkeepers, salesclerks in stores, and those in many other occupations will learn best in actual situations where they will later work.

In schools where both vocational education and general education are offered there is a question as to the need for separate and related courses in mathematics and other subject fields. Unless clear-cut reasons exist for separating students into groups for instruction in subjects related to the vocation for which they are preparing, these students should remain in general-education classes with the college-bound students. If this policy is not observed, the school is likely to be weak in its offerings for citizenship, homemaking, and leisure activities.

Precollege Subjects. Studies show that a very large percentage of students who take college-preparatory courses in high school or junior college do not go on to college. They form a great middle-class group between the relatively small number who do actually continue university or college studies and the similarly small group who, at the end of high school, have a reasonably good background for getting a job. In general, they are the students who wish they had taken a different course in high school. One implication of this is that students ought to think very realistically about *why* they are taking certain courses. Assisting them would be one objective of the guidance program. The "one-shot" guidance that characterizes most scheduling certainly is not enough. A good program would consist of continuous personal evaluation in conjunction with classroom work, specialized counseling, and consultations of parents, students, and teachers. After the student has selected a college-preparatory subject, teachers of these classes should attempt in as many ways as possible to individualize the content in terms of the particular needs of the student with respect to his college plans and his abilities. The content of a course in physics should be quite different for a student who is definitely planning to be an engineer than for a student who is taking the course because it is merely the best way of meeting an academic requirement.

In large high schools specialized courses, such as physics for engineers, are justified. In the smaller high school, however, it is probable that a physics course should be set up primarily for general-education purposes for all students—college preparatory and terminal. The burden of proof should be on the college to show why this general-education kind of physics isn't the best preparation in science for the student who is going on to college but not into a specialized field requiring highly technical science. For the student who is going to be an engineer, work should be individualized within the class. For many years, elementary-school teachers have taught groups within their classes, rather than giving the whole class the same learning experiences. Many secondary-school teachers are already varying the work of students within their classes. This practice should characterize more secondary classrooms. The high school ought to avoid the trap of offering a college-preparatory course in science, social studies, English, or mathematics in order to be sure that a few may become prepared to go to the university which has the most stringent requirements. In such instances, most of those in the class have experiences which are not best for them in terms of their abilities or their plans. It is more likely that high schools are completely justified in a reverse procedure—that is, providing general-education offerings to meet the needs for life of both the college-bound and those who will be employed immediately on leaving high school.

Secondary-school educators must not justify course content in their classes because of college-entrance requirements. Throughout the country, colleges are revising their standards of entrance. Many are tending to place higher premium on skills, abilities, and understandings, rather than covering all specified subject matter. If enough high-school educators base their school programs on the developmental needs of adolescents they can do much to influence colleges to make further modifications of their entrance requirements. There should be no hesitancy to put new content into old labels where new experiences have real significance for the learners. A geometry credit at one time signified that the student had memorized the geometric propositions contained in the textbook. The best geometry teaching today provides opportunity for coping with actual problems of living in which a problem-solving approach is used to reach a conclusion based on relevant data. Secondary-school educators have an obligation to youth to examine the contents of courses to be sure that they satisfy the criterion of meeting the needs of life for the youth enrolled. Only after feeling confident of the validity of their response to this first requirement should schools turn to a consideration of college requirements.

Offerings in foreign languages and specialized mathematics and science should be available to satisfy special needs of students who plan to enter college where there are requirements in these fields that cannot be satisfied by the general-education offerings of the high school. These should be taken as near graduation as possible. There should be careful guidance before the election of these subjects and individualization of content in terms of peculiar needs of each student.

More and more, schools which follow either Type-Five or Type-Six programs (as outlined in the previous chapter) in meeting the common needs of students are recognizing that the last year, or at least the last half of the last year before a student leaves the school, ought to provide opportunities for the student to prepare specifically for his next steps in education. For example, if he has to take college-entrance examinations he ought to get ready for them in every way possible. If the college to which he plans to go maintains that knowledge of grammar (parts of speech and syntax) should be acquired for its own sake rather than for functional usage, the student should be helped to learn what the college will expect him to know. This procedure seems more and more necessary as colleges develop more variations in their entrance requirements. When one college requires no pattern of courses and another college not only requires a pattern of courses but also gives specific subject-field entrance tests, it would seem that the only sure way to help a student gain admission to the college of his choice is to give him an opportunity on an individual basis to get ready in those phases of education which the college stresses most.

Leisure and Creative Expression

There is general agreement that a human being will be emotionally stable and happy if he has an outlet for his emotions through some medium in which he can be creative in his own right. Over the years secondary schools have offered subjects such as dramatics, fine arts, and music. But generally these have been for the few who have special talents. Theoretically, opportunities for creative expression have existed not only in these special offerings but in many of the regular subjects such as English and science. Often the organization of a subject and the way in which it is taught have negated the development of creative expression. For example, book reports of a stereotyped nature in English classes or required speeches, regardless of whether the individual had anything he thought was worth saying, have caused students to want to have no more similar activities when they finish the class.

Secondary schools have an obligation to satisfy the need of every individual for creative experience. This can be done in two ways. First, classes in general subjects, if they provide environments conducive to expression, will help. The science class may provide the stimulus for a boy to develop a laboratory at home in which he will spend many interesting recreational hours. Out of the English class may develop several one-act plays which the students themselves have written and which they wish to give for their parents. An industrial-arts class often provides the impetus for a youth to develop a hobby which serves him well throughout life.

Second, in addition to examining the total offerings of the school to be sure that the organization of the class and the methods used encourage creative expression, special offerings should be available in drama, publications, creative writing, vocal and instrumental music, and the graphic arts and crafts.

In a small school it may not be possible to organize a special class. Where this is true it becomes even more important for teachers to permit individual activities to flourish in their classes. For example, there is no reason why teachers of English cannot encourage each individual to engage in some activity in the communication area which is highly creative and in which he can "lose himself" in some satisfying project.

Most schools have accepted the idea that boys and girls should have a chance to engage in physical activities throughout the years they are in school. It is suggested that schools ought also to recognize the importance of a continuity of offerings of creative experiences to each student. Experts in the field of child growth and development maintain that adults would be much happier and healthier if, from kindergarten through college, they had had the opportunity to engage continuously in experiences of a creative nature.

Secondary schools generally follow the traditional pattern of offering a subject five times a week for a period of about one hour. When there is a variation in this pattern it is usually to pair two subjects to make up a five-time a week combination. Makers of secondary-school programs might profitably consider blocks of time longer than an hour but which occur fewer than five times a week. For example, the arts might be offered to all students for one two-hour or two one-and-a-half-hour periods each week. Less time in the total week is taken up than if the subject were offered daily on an hourly basis. In addition, students would then have time to develop projects and do more before the end of the art period. With periods of an hour or less the time taken for getting ready and cleaning up cuts heavily into that available for doing constructive work.

In Grades VII through IX the offerings on the practical and fine arts (this term is used to include subjects such as dramatics, creative writing, music, or crafts which are offered primarily to give students an opportunity to be creative and to learn to enjoy activities of a leisure-time nature) should be of an exploratory nature and should give all youngsters a chance to become acquainted with the many possibilities for enjoying leisure time. Starting in about Grade X—some schools may wish to start in Grade IX, and others may wish to delay until Grade XI—the students should be able to intelligently elect an art subject which appeals to them. This elective may serve a vocational need for some students, but re-emphasis should be given to the point that the major purpose is to give all students an opportunity to grow in ability to enjoy life and to be more emotionally stable because of constructive, creative outlooks.

Home and Family Living

Secondary schools have traditionally neglected their duty in the area of home and family living. The typical secondary school has given girls not wanting to go to college an opportunity to take cooking and sewing. During the past few years some secondary schools have become aware of the need to go beyond this meager offering. They have broadened their home- and family-living program to include all phases of home living—foods and clothing, interior decorating, child care, and problems of family life such as buying a home and budgeting. Too often, however, these experiences are available only to a limited number of girls. The over-all design of a secondary-school curriculum should give all students, boys and girls, appropriate experiences to get ready for this most important part of their lives—a participation in family living. Much of this should be a part of the program to meet the common needs of students. Units in the core or common-learnings program in areas of home living should be provided. In addition, for exploratory purposes all students in their junior high school years should have opportunities to carry on activities in the home- and family-living laboratories of the school.

By Grade X students should be mature enough and familiar enough with the offerings in home and family living to elect subjects such as clothing, foods, child care, or home decorating. In some instances it may be desirable to have these subjects combined into one course. Girls who are going on to college should be encouraged to elect these courses. Through the guidance program, girls who will probably marry soon after high school should especially be urged to elect them. Some schools are doing pioneer work in discovering the offerings at the senior high school level which boys should be given a chance to elect. In general, the nature of this elective offering should center in activities which have a natural appeal to boys and which will get them ready to be homemakers. Camp cookery, the man's role in the care of the sick, problems of home buying, landscape designing, and budgeting should be included. Some opportunities to learn to understand the growth and development of children should be a part of the offerings. Many boys who expect to marry soon will be ready to give thought to ways in which marriages may be made successful.

Health and Physical Fitness

All secondary-school students should have an opportunity for continuing experiences throughout Grades VII to XIV in health and physical fitness. Here again, in the early years of the secondary school, possibly Grades VII through X, students should be able to participate in a sports program for all. Seasonal sports obviously would be the core of this program. Touch football, basketball, soft ball, hockey, and speed ball are illustrative. It should be remembered that an enjoyment of sports depends on the development of good body mechanics and attainment of sufficient skill to feel successful. Activities in this lower secondary-grade program should help students learn how to walk, run, dodge, sit, stand, and move with ease and poise. Equally important, it should help each boy and girl develop a zest for active participation in games of a physical nature. Many of these games should be the type which will encourage a student to want to be out of doors.

In the middle secondary-school grades—about ninth and tenth— sports such as tennis, archery, golf, bowling, swimming, horseback riding, folk dancing, modern dance, and social dance should be introduced to students while they are at the same time able to continue participation in team games. In Grades XI through XIV students should be able to elect individual sports.

Posture troubles and other physical defects should be spotted in the elementary grades. Always on the basis of a diagnosis by a competent physician, the school should give youngsters opportunities to overcome these physical difficulties. More emphasis ought to be given to training programs through which physical-education teachers become able to supervise boys and girls in programs of correcting defects. Attention to posture should be given in all physical-education classes, and some attention to individual needs can be given in any physical-education class if the teacher believes in taking care of individual differences. Everything possible ought to be done to keep students in need of corrective work from feeling atypical. Therefore, they should be taken out of their regular classes only when there is a clear need for work which should be done in a special group. Often the best practice is to have students attend their regular classes for three or four days of the week and then attend a special class the remaining periods. In a small school this may not be possible. Some physical-education teachers help students with real physical troubles before and after school.

Exceptional Students

In this section proposals will be made concerning programs designed to take care of the needs of the physically handicapped, the mentally retarded, and the gifted child.

The Physcially Handicapped. No case needs to be made that the secondary school has an obligation to help boys or girls with speech, hearing, or sight handicaps. Those with conditions such as cerebral palsy should also command our attention. When students are ill and must remain at home for a long period of time, society ought to give them a chance to learn if their illnesses permit study. A general principle to be followed in designing programs to meet these needs is that the student should be in the normal grouping of the school as much as possible. Small schools which have more difficulty than large ones in meeting these needs can profitably join together in providing facilities. Additional bus service will often be necessary, and special training is generally essential in order to be of service to these physically handicapped people. Obviously, a very small school cannot have on its staff an individual trained in each of the areas mentioned above.

Let us use the problem of providing for youngsters with speech defects to illustrate the manner in which a school can meet the problem of the physically handicapped. A well-trained teacher who understands how speech defects can be remedied should have a room in which to carry on his work. Students with speech difficulties should have this room as their home base in the school. They should be scheduled with other students for whatever subjects and activities they can manage in a group situation. For the boy or girl with a minor defect, a conference once a week with the special teacher may be enough. There may be some youngster whose needs suggest that he remain in the special room with the special teacher for all subjects excepting, perhaps, physical education and industrial arts. In a large school there may be enough students with difficulties to have one room in which those with the most serious troubles are placed and another room which resembles the description given above. Sight and hearing problems could be taken care of in the same manner as speech.

Those with cerebral palsy will definitely need a special suite of rooms in which proper equipment is available. Here again, whenever possible, students should be given an opportunity to take part in the normal on-going activities of the school. However, there may be those whose emotional stability will not be helped by such participation. In such cases the students will need to be given a total program in special rooms.

The Mentally Retarded. It is very difficult to generalize concerning an appropriate design for caring for the needs of mentally retarded children. The philosophy of the faculty is, of course, basic. The writers of this chapter take the position that students with an intelligence quotient of 80 or higher should be enrolled in the regular classes of the school. With good guidance, adequate electives, and individualized instruction, these students should not find themselves in situations with which they cannot cope.

The secondary school has an obligation, however, to provide appropriate educational opportunities for all students of secondary-school age who are not going to be institutionalized. For those with intelligence quotients from 70 to 80, it would seem that there should be a special suite of rooms with many laboratory facilities to make an activity program possible. The students, as in the case of the physically handicapped, should be in those regular classes where they can meet with success. They would be in a separate group, however, under a special teacher for a considerable portion of the day. Students whose intelligence quotients are below 70 should be put in a separate environmental situation especially designed to meet their needs. Opportunities for activities such as gardening and many other practical activities involving firsthand experience should be provided.

The Gifted Child. At the risk of too much repetition we wish to emphasize again the obligation of all teachers to individualize their work to the end that classroom experiences may be set up in relation to the wide range of individual differences of students. The development of the secondary school as a school for *all* American youth has brought with it the need to have standards which students can meet. Sometimes this has meant merely the lowering of a recognized group standard. What is needed is the individualization of standards in which case gifted students will be expected to contribute and produce more than some of their contemporaries.

Secondary-school teachers must borrow a page from the best practices of elementary-school teachers if they are to provide opportunities for each student to work in terms of his abilities. There is really no reason why a secondary-school teacher should not include in his teaching procedures the same methods that a superior second-grade teacher uses. In other words, several small groups should often be working on projects in which varying abilities are taken into account. Many different media of learning will be used. Often an individual will be engaged in an activity in which no other student in the class is involved. If these points are recognized, then the gifted student in the secondary school will have an opportunity to grow and develop in terms of his ability. Some schools accelerate gifted students as an aid to their adjustment. Some schools segregate them in order to place the gifted on a special track where they can learn faster and engage in different experiences. Both of these practices should be examined carefully. Acceleration should not occur at the expense of social adjustment. Segregation should not occur at the expense of developing democratic attitudes and values. With a program of electives such as has been described in this chapter, gifted students, with competent guidance, will take subjects which really challenge them. Other suggestions have been offered in a recently published monograph.

1. Encouraging an extra subject for the gifted with the purpose recognized as enrichment rather than acceleration.
2. Integrating the work in the regular classes of the more capable with experiences in fine arts, homemaking, or industrial arts.
3. Replacing an academic course with experience in other areas when achievement has already reached a high level, when the course is not specifically required by the college the student plans to attend, or when the course otherwise does not best meet his needs and interests.
4. After a conference of teachers, making time spent in a class more flexible in order to release the student at certain hours for needed experiences elsewhere.[5]

---

[5] *The More Capable Learner in the Secondary School*, pp. 34–35. Secondary Curriculum Monograph, M-72. Los Angeles: Los Angeles County Schools, 1951.

SUMMARY

In this chapter the authors have attempted to develop a point of view that the special needs of youth can be met adequately only when the faculty is continuously engaged in a curriculum-improvement program. This curriculum-improvement program involves a constant study of the adolescents in the school as well as keeping up to date on research concerning adolescents and how they grow and develop. It also includes a continuous and intensive effort on the part of the staff to understand the community and its demands on youth. Further, the faculty must be striving to clarify its own understanding of our democratic values and of the ways in which the school can be a laboratory for democratic living. With these as bases for curriculum development, the faculty is in a position to decide the offerings of the school in terms of the needs of the boys and girls enrolled. The individual teacher is given much latitude and freedom to carry on co-operative planning with the students in his classes, but he has the security of a framework of policy and practice which has been developed by the faculty and administration as a whole and in which he has had a part.

Community resources are capitalized upon as much as possible, especially the human element. Parents are recognized as partners. An evaluation program is carried on through discovering the extent to which students are growing in behavior characteristics which are recognized as important.

It is the viewpoint of the authors that a curriculum-improvement program, such as outlined above, will insure adequate attention to special needs through the following means:

1. The guidance program will identify and reveal these needs.
2. The teaching methods used by teachers throughout the school will provide many opportunities for special needs to be satisfied. Interrelationships between the general-education offerings and the offerings to satisfy special needs will be capitalized upon to the end that no sharp line will divide the two phases of the offerings.
3. Where a need exists, special classes will be set up. It is clear that such special offerings will generally be required in vocations (this includes preprofessional), in leisure and creative expression, in home and family living, in health and physical fitness, and for exceptional students.

CHAPTER IX

EXTRACLASS ACTIVITIES AND THE NEEDS OF YOUTH

J. Lloyd Trump

Professor of Education
University of Illinois
Urbana, Illinois

DEFINITION OF THE TERM

Extraclass activities are viewed in this chapter as that area of the total curriculum which includes experiences not usually provided in typical classes. Work experiences, out-of-school activities, and outdoor experiences, which ordinarily would be encompassed by the foregoing definition, are discussed in chapter x of this volume.

Such terms as clubs, debates, dramatics, assembly programs, variety shows, school publications, interscholastic and intramural athletics, student participation in government, glee clubs, band, orchestra, parties, dances, banquets, and many others, have become a part of the vocabulary of students, teachers, and the public generally. The concern of this chapter is with such activities as the foregoing regardless of the type of administrative controls exercised or the degree to which such activities have been included in the so-called regular subjects or common learnings of the school.

EXTRACLASS ACTIVITIES AND YOUTH NEEDS

The needs of youth, as discussed in foregoing chapters of this volume, may be met in different ways. Obviously some needs may be served best through the common-learnings area of the curriculum; other needs may be met by means of specialized, elective programs available to students; some may be adequately provided for through carefully developed and managed programs of extraclass activities.

Possible values which may accrue to students participating in extraclass activities have been indicated by many writers. The earliest, comprehensive compilation of these values was made by Koos in 1925.[1] The values most frequently mentioned were training in some civic-social-

---

[1] Leonard V. Koos, *Extracurricular Activities*, p. 11. Twenty-fifth Yearbook of the National Society for the Study of Education, Part II. Chicago: University of Chicago Press, 1926.

moral relationship, recognition of adolescent nature, socialization, training for leadership, improved discipline and school spirit, training for social co-operation, actual experience in group life, training for citizenship in a democracy, training for ethical living, and health. A more recent classification[2] shows more directly the relationships between possible values in extraclass activities and some of the youth needs described in earlier chapters in this volume. Strang classifies the values in activities under four principal categories: *developmental* (satisfy basic needs including social maturity, emotional stability, vocational security, aesthetic values, knowledge and skills); *diagnostic* (provide opportunities for studying individuals, also for individual self-appraisal); *therapeutic* (work out relations with others, develop new habit patterns, develop self-reliance, make students aware of problems); *group* (develop group morale or spirit, arrive at solutions to school problems). The close relationships between such values and youth needs are obvious.

A recent study by the writer[3] revealed major benefits which students, faculty, parents, and alumni believe are received from taking part in extraclass activities. The values rated highest by 3,525 secondary-school students were as follows: participation in activities resulted in the development of new friendships, made school seem more interesting, made possible learning how to win and lose in a sportsmanlike manner, created a greater loyalty to the school, gave something worth while to do in leisure time, resulted in more friendly relations with teachers, developed willingness to accept criticisms from others, and made available valuable information that would not have been received in a regular course. The benefits listed by 435 secondary-school graduates were similar, except that they listed as the second most important result of participation the development of more poise or ease in social contacts and also listed as important growth in skill in being able to speak before an audience. More than 200 faculty members listed similar values but also placed relatively high the outcome that students became more tolerant of the opinions and wishes of others. Almost 1,000 parents believed that similar values accrued to students. A value listed more frequently by parents than by students was that participation created a greater interest in regular school subjects.

The unusual appeal of extraclass activities to young people and adults makes them especially appropriate in meeting youth needs. For example,

---

[2] Ruth Strang, *Group Activities in College and Secondary School*, pp. 14–29. New York: Harper & Bros., 1941.

[3] J. Lloyd Trump, *High School Extracurriculum Activities*, pp. 111–23. Chicago: University of Chicago Press, 1944.

in an Illinois study,[4] 6,817 high-school students were asked to rate the following six types of activities in order of personal satisfaction: school subjects, extraclass activities, activities centering around the home, activities centering around noncommercial service agencies (such as the church, YMCA, and the like), activities centering around commercial agencies, and unplanned peer-group activities. These students uniformly ranked extraclass activities above regular school subjects from the standpoint of personal satisfaction; as a matter of fact, participation in extraclass activities ranked second only to commercial activities when data from all of the thirteen schools are considered, outranking even commercial activities in five instances. Moreover, parents and other adults attend basketball games, other athletic contests, plays, and other programs in large numbers, but they show relatively less interest in visiting or discussing the regular school subjects.

Several other characteristics of extraclass activities make them particularly effective in meeting youth needs. The flexibility and adaptability of extraclass activities, in contrast with typical class activities, make the former especially worth while. Students normally have a much wider degree of selection in activities than among class subjects. Also, more teacher-pupil planning is likely in extraclass activities, thus giving young persons opportunities to work co-operatively with older, more experienced individuals. Faculty members who may not be willing to encourage student participation in the planning of regular school subjects usually do not hesitate to accord students those privileges in connection with extraclass activities. Finally, the general lack of standardized content and methodology in the activities program, as well as freedom from college-entrance requirements, employment standards, and accreditation regulations, aid in making extraclass activities particularly effective in meeting youth needs. The usual barriers that teachers and administrators encounter in adapting regular school subjects more closely to youth and societal needs are not equally present in planning a program of extraclass activities.

EXTRACLASS ACTIVITIES AND DESIRABLE
TRENDS IN CURRICULUM EXPANSION

Extraclass activities may provide an unusually effective way for a school to make adaptations to youth needs which represent desirable trends in curriculum enrichment. Jones has shown, for example, that some phases of currently accepted regular subjects gained entrance into

---

[4] Earl Graham Pogue, "Participation in Extraclass Activities as Related to Socio-economic Classification," pp. 47–52. Unpublished D.Ed. dissertation, University of Illinois, 1949.

school programs as extraclass activities.[5] This evolutionary process appears likely to continue.

The following examples of possible relationships between desirable trends in curriculum enrichment and extraclass activities are cited not as an exhaustive list but rather for purposes of illustration:

1. Much emphasis has been placed in recent years on the importance of bridging the gap between the school and its community. Students in clubs, athletics, music, and speech activities, to mention only a few examples, have many opportunities both to present the work of the school to individuals and groups in the community and to seek community participation in school programs.
2. Learning to plan, work, and play together in coeducational activities provides wholesome experiences in preparation for family living and other adult activities.
3. Student participation in school policy-making and control through various forms of student-government organizations furnishes a much more realistic type of citizenship training than may be possible in regular courses in history and civics.
4. More effective appraisal of individual interests and capacities by students may result from observation of participation in extraclass activities than from noting experiences in the regular subjects of the school. A student may, for example, belong to several hobby or special-interest clubs, try out for different teams, participate in a variety of speech, music, and art activities, publications, and the like, in a way that will enable him to discover interests and capacities that cannot be explored in the usual program of limited elective subjects in high school.
5. In social and athletic activities, especially, students may have experiences that contribute to the development of sound mental and physical health.
6. Preparing activity budgets, as well as spending and accounting for activities funds, may be very realistic training in consumer economics as well as for citizenship.
7. Activity programs, especially in the case of clubs closely related to regular school subjects, may be planned to provide practical, useful applications of content learned in regular school classes.
8. The development of creative expression and appreciation of the creative efforts of others in music, art, and literature may be effectively developed in connection with extraclass activities.
9. Activities may provide experiences that help youth occupy their present leisure time more effectively and also prepare for adult leisure-time occupations. Although the "worthy-use-of-leisure" objective of secondary education has been emphasized repeatedly, it has found only limited expression in the regular subjects of the school; all too frequently, these subjects have had a voca-

---

[5] Galen Jones, *Extracurricular Activities in Relation to the Curriculum*, pp. 24–32. Teachers College Contributions to Education, No. 667. New York: Bureau of Publications, Teachers College, Columbia University, 1935.

tional or college-preparatory orientation. It is in the extraclass activities that the possibilities of training for leisure have found readiest expression.

10. Methods of evaluation are typically more flexible in extraclass activities; examinations calling for a demonstration of factual knowledge are seldom given. Although systematic evaluation of activities has been relatively infrequent in most schools—probably too infrequent—this lack of organized evaluation has resulted in a commendable minimum of overstandardization.

PROBLEMS ENCOUNTERED IN MEETING NEEDS
THROUGH EXTRACLASS ACTIVITIES

In spite of the apparent and desirable outcomes from the activity program, certain barriers must be overcome if those phases of the program which might naturally serve certain developmental needs of youth are to perform such service to good effect. Some of the most significant problems which must be recognized and solved are: (*a*) securing participation of all youth; (*b*) reducing the costs of participating in activities; (*c*) maintaining a reasonable balance in the activity program; (*d*) minimizing pressures for elaborate exhibitions and winning contests; and (*e*) providing more systematic evaluation in relation to youth needs.

Student Participation

If youth needs are to be met through participation in extraclass activities, it is obvious that such participation must reach *all* of the students in a high school. Studies of actual participation of students in different schools reveal diversified findings. Two generalizations, however, may be made. Lower classmen usually participate less than upper classmen. Students from lower-class homes tend to have fewer participations than those from upper-class homes.

In a study made by the writer involving 3,581 students in five selected Illinois high schools,[6] the number of activities participated in by these students during a given twelve-months period varied from 0 to 16. On the average, boys participated in 1.1 activities; the average for girls was 1.7. Approximately one-fourth of the students did not participate in any activity during the period. Forty-eight per cent of the boys and 39 per cent of the girls were in either none or only one activity.

Pogue's[7] recent study in thirteen Illinois high schools indicates that participants tend to come more largely from the middle and upper socio-economic classes than from the lower classes. It was not unusual in a school to find three or more times as many students from upper-class homes participating as from the lower-class homes. Of course, the findings vary considerably from one school to another. If the assumption made in

---

[6] Trump, *op. cit.*, pp. 75–77.

[7] Pogue, *op. cit.*, pp. 134–40.

chapter i of this volume is accepted, namely, that the secondary school should be designed to meet the needs of *all* American youth, limitations on participation constitute a serious problem which must receive the attention of educational workers.

Costs to Students

The cost of participation in extraclass activities constitutes one of the significant "hidden tuition" costs of secondary schools. Typically, it costs a considerable sum of money to play on the athletic teams, participate in the club program, attend school social functions, purchase school publications, attend dramatic presentations or be a member of the cast, be in good standing in class, or do many other things, either as a participant or as a spectator, that students like to do in connection with extraclass activities.

Recent studies by Hand,[8] for example, show the following illustrative median costs in representative Illinois secondary schools: class ring or pin—$13.00; playing on baseball team—$12.25, basketball—$2.80, golf—$50.00, or tennis—$15.00; membership in clubs—from $0.00–$19.30; attending basketball games—$2.50, football—$1.90, swimming—$0.75, and wrestling—$0.40; attending school dances—$2.45, parties—$1.20, banquets—$2.85; graduation—$14.35. Of course, the costs in some schools were much higher than the median figures shown here.

The student who comes from a marginal- or submarginal-income home finds it impossible to take part in the extraclass-activities program to the extent he would prefer. Not only does he lack the price of equipment, dues, or admissions but he probably must be busy at work earning part of the family income at a time when activities are scheduled. These costs of participation present a very significant problem encountered in meeting youth needs through extraclass activities.

Balance in Programs

Activity programs are sometimes not well balanced in relation to individual needs. Programs are less frequently planned, or conducted less adequately, for students possessing lesser ability and/or interest. Members of the varsity athletic team receive much free equipment of the highest possible quality in many schools; learners on intramural teams are not so well treated. Students possessing talent in dramatics receive much coaching on the part of the instructional staff; students with lesser ability are either eliminated entirely or receive relatively little attention in minor parts. Music instructors are too busy and equipment is inadequate to

---

[8] Harold C. Hand, *Principal Findings of the 1947–48 Basic Studies of the Illinois Secondary-School Curriculum Program*, pp. 54–63. Springfield, Illinois: Office of the State Superintendent of Public Instruction, 1949.

provide attention for those who would like to learn to play or sing or for those who would like to find out if they have interest in such activities.

Moreover, in a given school or community some activities receive an unusual amount of interest and support at the expense of other desirable activities. For example, basketball or band may be especially popular in a given community, and golf, tennis, or vocal music may receive relatively little time or money in the school program. Significant differences also sometimes exist between the stated aims of activities and what actually occurs in the operation of a program. For example, an activity may be designed to assist students in discovering and developing interests but be so operated that only those students already possessing considerable interest and ability are permitted or encouraged to continue membership.

Evaluation of Programs

Systematic efforts to evaluate the contributions of the extraclass program have been infrequent. An examination of the literature in this area reveals that nearly all writings are concerned with reporting the status of programs in operation along with arguments either pro or con for the continuance of or changes in given activities. Research has been limited primarily to comparisons between participants and nonparticipants or leaders and nonleaders. In general, such comparisons show the superiority of participants and leaders in scholarship, intelligence, citizenship in school, attitudes, interests, and selection of school subjects. However, there has been little disposition toward studies of behavioral changes resulting from participation; cause-and-effect relationships are not apparent.[9] Forty-four percent of the schools accredited by the North Central Association of Colleges and Secondary Schools recently reported that no specific steps to evaluate the program had been undertaken.[10]

This lack of systematic evaluation creates several problems. It is difficult to know which activities are of most potential worth in meeting youth needs. There is little actual supporting evidence to show what changes should be made in the management of activities. The comparative lack of evaluation has also resulted in relatively little attention being given to activities in preservice and in-service training programs of teachers. Moreover, the resultant lack of data presents a handicap in changing community attitudes toward what appear to be undesirable pressures and practices relating to extraclass activities.

---

[9] Carl W. Hansen, "Extracurricular Activities," *Encyclopedia of Educational Research*, pp. 424–28. Edited by Walter S. Monroe. New York: Macmillan Co., 1950.

[10] Trump, *op. cit.*, p. 157.

Improving the Management of Extraclass Activities

Several changes in the manner in which activities are typically managed in schools should be seriously considered. Among such needs are: (*a*) reaching consensus regarding purposes; (*b*) clarifying policy-making and administrative relationships; (*c*) encouraging student participation; (*d*) changing personnel policies; (*e*) providing adequate financial support; and (*f*) devising evaluation procedures. Educational leaders must accept responsibility for facilitating these changes.

Consensus Regarding Purposes

A fundamental task in improving the management of extraclass activities is reaching consensus in each local school regarding the role of activities in meeting youth needs. Agreement needs to be reached regarding: (*a*) what the school *should be* accomplishing in its extraclass activities program, (*b*) what the school actually *is* and *is not* accomplishing at the present time; and (*c*) what *changes need to be made* in order that the school may do a better job in meeting youth needs through the program. Such agreements should represent the results of discussion and consensus on the part of as many of the constituent groups of the school as possible, namely, students, teachers, parents, other lay persons, school administrators, and board of education members. These agreements should pertain to all phases of the extraclass program, including responsibilities for policy development, administration, sponsorship, nature of the program, scheduling of activities, participation of students, financial support, relationships between extraclass groups and organizations of the community, and evaluation of the program. Agreement should be reached not only on the level of general policies but also with respect to best methods of implementing such policies.[11] Unless these agreements are reached, there will be relatively little chance of major attacks on the problems indicated in the preceding section of this chapter.

Policy-making and Administration

A second necessary development is the clarification of policy-making and executive functions relating to the extraclass-activities program. Although the board of education is legally empowered with responsibilities for the development of policies regarding extraclass activities, boards of education should establish an advisory group to assist in this function.

---

[11] Eric H. Johnson *et al.*, *What Do You Think about Our School's Extraclass-Activities Program?* pp. 1–18. Illinois Secondary-School Curriculum Program, Consensus Study Number 1, Inventory A. Springfield, Illinois: Office of State Superintendent of Public Instruction, 1951.

Such an advisory group, including persons who would represent the various constituent groups of the school, should make recommendations regarding planning, managing, and evaluating the extraclass program. Some one qualified individual, however, should be designated executive director of the program. It is, of course, unwise for an advisory group to perform administrative functions. If management is to be improved, there must be executive leadership to look after a host of details which arise out of the program. The average secondary-school principal, even in the smallest schools, does not have the time to perform these tasks adequately. Therefore, usually some member of the staff should be given time to carry on these executive functions.

Student Participation

A variety of methods should be utilized to encourage student participation. Activities should be scheduled at different times of the day so that students may participate even if they are working part time or taking part in nonschool activities. Time allotments for the different activities need to be developed by the appropriate groups. Policies governing costs of participating in extraclass activities should be the same as for participating in class activities. For example, if instruction in Latin or United States history is provided without cost to students, instruction in social dancing, basketball, dramatics, and the like, should be similarly provided.

Activity programs should be made more interesting to students by planning activities which will actually involve all the students and by placing greater emphasis on service. Training programs for leaders and members should be developed. Frequently, a fallacious assumption has been made that students know how to be chairmen or presidents; they need to be trained in the functions of democratic leadership. Similarly, students need training as secretaries, treasurers, group members, and the like.

Qualitative as well as quantitative records of participation in activities should be cumulative and permanent. Students should know that the school has a continuing interest in them. Colleges and employers should realize that the school has information gained as a result of observing student participation in activities that will be helpful in guidance and employment. Rewards for participating in extraclass activities should be similar to those received for participating in class activities.

Finally, the significance of individual participation in relation to needs should be recognized by persons engaged in counseling and by teachers of common-learnings courses. Decisions regarding type and amount of participation by individuals should be based on counseling interviews rather than by automatic systems involving minimum and maximum participation.

Evaluation

Evaluation should be planned to reveal evidence regarding the extent to which the real life needs of students are being served. First, a systematic analysis of individual and group growth and developmental changes resulting from participation should be made. Such an analysis is possible only if measuring devices are carefully developed and adequate records are kept. The following seven steps in evaluation seem especially appropriate: (*a*) formulating objectives, (*b*) classification of objectives, (*c*) defining objectives in terms of behavior, (*d*) suggesting situations in which the achievement of objectives will be shown, (*e*) selecting and trying promising evaluation methods, (*f*) improving appraisal methods, and (*g*) interpreting results.[12] Students should be asked at the close of each season, semester, or year, for recommendations regarding future developments for each activity in which they have participated. Accomplishments in specific activities and the general program should be measured in terms of prior agreements regarding purposes and plans. Unless evaluation programs similar to those described in chapter xiv are followed, it will be difficult to know what contributions extraclass activities are making toward meeting the needs of youth.

ILLUSTRATIVE PRACTICES IN IMPROVING EXTRACLASS ACTIVITIES

Many suggestions for improving activity programs have already been provided in this chapter. Obviously, it is impossible within the space limitation of this presentation to describe all innovating practices that seem to promise improvement. An examination of recent issues of such periodicals as *School Activities, Student Life, NEA Journal,* and the various subject-matter journals will reveal many illustrations of practices in harmony with the suggestions provided here. The bulletins of the National Association of Secondary-School Principals describe many commendable administrative practices. The few practices mentioned here are illustrative rather than comprehensive. They have been chosen because the practices seem to be in harmony with the youth-needs concept emphasized in this yearbook.

Assembly Programs

Desirable trends in assembly programs may be illustrated under two classifications of programs, namely, student-centered and community-centered. Obviously, there are other types of programs that may be help-

---

[12] Eugene R. Smith, Ralph W. Tyler, *et al., Appraising and Recording Student Progress,* pp. 15–28. New York: Harper & Bros., 1942.

ful in meeting youth needs. However, the use of professional talent, moving pictures, and exchange programs does not ordinarily provide programs as responsive to local needs as those indicated here.

Learning experiences in both class and extraclass activities may result in student-centered assembly programs. For example, a home-economics, agriculture, or science class may put on a demonstration of work done in the class, or students in music, art, and the speech departments may combine to present a Thanksgiving program. Students in the Rochester, Minnesota, Senior High School have used the "town meeting" idea in assembly programs when they discussed student problems and responsibilities. At Drury High School, North Adams, Massachusetts, the students presented a panel discussion with audience participation on student interests in movies, radio programs, and comic books. Prior to the assembly program the eight hundred students in the school were polled to secure views on those topics. At Lincoln High School, Wisconsin Rapids, Wisconsin, an assembly on etiquette was presented the week preceding the Junior-Senior prom. In the East High School, Aurora, Illinois, an assembly program including use of ballet and pantomime depicted "A Day at East High" in which actual school situations and scenes were presented. Such programs as the foregoing may have considerable significance in the efforts of schools to meet more adequately youth needs.

Community-centered programs are similar to student-centered programs, the participants being members of the community who come to the school to present some particular message or entertainment of interest to the school group. Leaders in the community may be asked to present views on controversial issues. Representatives of a patriotic or service organization may provide a program in observance of a special day or to launch a project of special interest to youth. This utilization of community resources through school assemblies is a highly commendable activity. Those in charge of the assembly programs, however, must work carefully with community persons and groups to make sure that materials are presented in an organized, competent manner, that time schedules are planned, and that other essential elements of good assembly programs are followed.

Athletics

No part of the extraclass program attracts more participants and spectators, including persons from outside the school, or produces a larger amount of revenue and expenditures than the athletic program. Also, probably more controversies and problems have arisen in connection with athletics than with any other phase of the extraclass program. The present discussion touches only a few topics pertaining to this important phase of the program. Comments are given regarding both interscholastic and intramural athletics programs. Both are important elements of a successful program. In practice there seems to be no necessary division between the two; the strongest intramural athletic programs appear to be found where the interscholastic program is highly developed on a sound basis.

Many interesting practices in the area of intramural athletics are reported in the literature. Sometimes the games are played at noon, as in Holt, Michigan, where varsity players assist in directing the program. In the East Side High School, Paterson, New Jersey, a sport known as "Early Bird Basketball" is played to enable students who are not in the interscholastic program to participate; two to four games are played each morning prior to the opening of school. The Towson Junior High School, Towson, Maryland, has a compulsory intramural athletics program (exempting those physically unable to participate), including soccer tournaments, dodgeball tournaments, basketball, volleyball, and other sports. Recreational leisure-time activities are emphasized in the extensive intramural athletic program in the Galesburg, Illinois, Senior High School; sports having recreational and leisure-time value for both boys and girls are particularly emphasized. If the intramural program cannot be adequately supported from tax funds, an interesting method of raising money is that used in the Callahan Junior High School in Des Moines, Iowa, where a Dad's night is given over to an athletic show put on by the large number of boys that participate in the intramural program. The proceeds from an admission charge of twenty-five cents help finance the program. Emphases such as the foregoing, which result in increased participation, activities with more carry-over into adult life, attention to leisure-time activities, and provision for recreational activities, appear to be significant in efforts to provide more adequately for youth needs.

The goal in interscholastic athletics should be to provide for participation of a large number of boys, and possibly girls, in a wide variety of games in interscholastic competition during the year. Such a goal is possible only if a school provides more teams and fewer games per team in interscholastic competition. In all but small schools enrolling fewer than 150 students, there should be a minimum of four teams in basketball and football in interscholastic, league competition; in larger schools the number might well be as high as eight or ten. A step in the right direction is that followed by schools in the Suburban League near Chicago, where four teams from each school regularly meet four teams from the competing school on a given weekend. These four teams are freshman, sophomore, junior varsity, and varsity. A next step in such schools might be to provide first and second teams at each level, or to divide each level on a light-weight, heavy-weight basis. If proper controls are strictly exercised, there seems to be no logical reason why girls and junior high school boys should be denied the purported advantages of interscholastic competition.

Youth needs may be served by intramural and interscholastic athletics only if there is unusually careful supervision. State associations should strictly enforce rules regarding elegibility in terms of residence and school membership in good standing (but not necessarily "passing" a given number of subjects). Adequate physical examinations and health services must be provided. Quality supplies and equipment are important not only for varsity team members but for participants in intramural athletics as well. Safety precautions must be observed for students and spectators. School administrators and coaches must work constantly to involve members of the community in discussing athletic policies so that some of the evils resulting from undue pressure are minimized. A well-managed athletic program may be instrumental in improving community conduct at public meetings; loosely managed, it may actually contribute to low standards.

Class Organizations

Especially in small schools, class organizations are frequently used to provide experiences in group thinking, discussion, and action. Such activities may be very significant for individual youth, providing steps are taken to involve all of them in the activities being followed. Class organizations sometimes serve guidance functions also, for example, when Senior students select or are assigned "little brothers" or "sisters" among the incoming students.

Finances sometimes constitute a burden in connection with class activities. Class dues may be excessive. The cost of class rings, insignia, or special garb may also constitute an expensive charge to students. Some schools have standardized insignia and thus reduce costs to students. Such a practice has the added advantage that students can recognize school insignia easily and thus know that a given individual is a member or alumnus of his school. Similar arrangements with respect to commencement announcements and other class-organization costs may result in significant economies.

Students benefit from feeling a sense of loyalty to an institution. Loyalty not only to his present class but later as an alumnus of a given class and school may help satisfy that need.

Clubs

School clubs may function in many ways related to youth needs: providing services to other students, the school, and the community; furnishing enrichment of class activities; and assisting in the development of hobbies and special interests. No single pattern of recommended clubs or club activities may be described. The needs of individual students and of groups of students vary so widely that those in charge of planning and evaluating the club program in a given school will have to make specific plans in relation to local needs. A few examples of innovating practices are provided as illustrations rather than as a comprehensive treatment of the subject.

Service activities performed by school clubs are many and varied. The Publicity Club in the Mastbaum Technical School of Philadelphia collects and disseminates news concerning the school. The Crusader Commercial Club of Rural High School, Buhler, Kansas, handles the cashiering, advertising, ushering, and other tasks connected with the management of crowds at school and community functions, providing services for forty or more different activities per year. The Art Club of the Citrus Union High School and Junior College, Azusa, California, sponsors community exhibits of water colors and paintings. The Cinematography Club, Chattanooga, Tennessee, High School takes moving pictures of school events and activities to be shown to the student body and at community civic meetings. The East Junior High School, Duluth, Minnesota, has a student club called the Kid Kare Klub open to seventh-grade girls. The members learn duties of child care. A Home Visiting Club functions at William Howard Taft High School in New York City. Student members visit home-bound students bringing school news, books and materials, assignments, and the school paper.

School clubs also furnish enrichment of class activities. In the Anoka, Minnesota, High School, the Home Economics Club keeps several white rats, demonstrating the results of good and poor nutrition on their development. The Bloomfield, New Jersey, Junior High School has a Boys' Chef Club whose members experiment in the culinary arts. The Latrobe, Pennsylvania, High School, has an Ars Medica Club with 100 members who are interested in the medical profession. Activities include serving as readers to children in the local hospital and providing other experiences that would be helpful to students trying to decide whether or not they are interested in medical vocations. A Surveying Club in Central High School, Philadelphia, endeavors to utilize the mathematics learned in the classroom and to make practical applications in field situations. The Foreman's Club in the Hinsdale, Illinois, Township High School, made up of boys enrolled in industrial-arts classes, provides training and practice in appropriate leadership activities.

Clubs are also frequently organized to aid in the development of hobbies or special interests. The Boy's League Council, Parrish Junior High School, Salem, Oregon, promotes the building and racing of miniature, jet-propelled cars. In the New Trier Township High School, Winnetka, Illinois, a Magic Club provides students a means of sharing interest in the study and performance of tricks of magic. Members of a Bird House Construction Club in the James H. Smart Junior High School, Fort Wayne, Indiana, study birds and design and build nesting houses for birds. The Everett, Washington, High School has a student club called the Piscatorians. The functions of the club are to foster an interest in outdoor life and in such activities as hunting and fishing and to promote good practices in protecting game and fish.

Such activities as the foregoing, and many others which might be cited, show the extent to which youth needs may be met through school clubs, providing the sponsors and members show imagination, ingenuity, and interest. Much of the success of a club depends upon the competence of the sponsor. His ability to develop with the membership the notion that the organization should be one in which *all* of the members participate in every meeting, doing things which the students consider important, is fundamental if clubs are to be useful in meeting youth needs.

Commencement

While commencement as an end in itself is receiving less emphasis, programs are being planned to provide student participation so that the event may be a more meaningful one to the participants themselves and to the community at large. Because of the natural interest of many persons in the commencement program, an unusual opportunity is provided for presenting information on school progress and future needs. Such presentations may be made effectively by students. Practices which tend to limit costs attendant upon graduation should also receive serious consideration.

The National Association of Secondary-School Principals of the National Education Association publishes each November a volume known as *The (year) Commencement Manual*. This book contains a summary of high-school graduation programs, including complete scripts of both traditional and new-type programs. These descriptions are assembled from all sections of the country, representing a great variety of types of schools. Those planning a commencement program will find this book a valuable reference.

Contests

Each year a school is called upon to participate in many types of contests, both within and outside the school, in addition to those of an athletic nature described in a foregoing section of this chapter. Most of these contests are sponsored by an individual or group interested in furthering some favorite project or activity. Usually, such contests have some planned relationship to youth needs or a desirable program of the school, although frequently the timing and method of the contest may not be particularly appropriate. Obviously, those in charge of a school need to be alert in order to protect young people from exploitation through contests.

Contests may serve as significant devices in motivating desirable student interests. Some schools have established a joint faculty-student-parent committee which analyzes all requests for contest participation, contacts appropriate sponsors within the school, and develops principles of management for contests. Steps are then taken to involve as many students as possible in participation. For example, in the Bala-Cynwyd Junior High School, Ardmore, Pennsylvania, there is annually a student hobby exhibit, in which the emphasis is on contribution rather than competition although recognition awards are given for superior entries in the numerous divisions. The Art Club of Evanston, Illinois, Township High School sponsors an all-school art contest in which any student may enter drawings. In a recent year, more than 300 drawings and other art objects were displayed.

Homerooms

Homerooms vary so in organization and activities from one school to another that it is difficult to classify them. Their functions may be best described as administrative, guidance, curricular, extraclass, or a combination of those. Homeroom activities are used sometimes as a step toward the development of a common-learnings program. Where the homeroom period is of sufficient length, probably a minimum of thirty minutes daily, it is possible to include units of instruction closely related to the needs of youth that are not included elsewhere in the required curriculum of the school. The obvious problem in such a method of presenting common-learnings materials is that some of the teachers involved as homeroom sponsors may have relatively little interest in presenting these materials, even if well-organized by a homeroom committee or homeroom director. Use of the homeroom as a substitute for a common-learnings course should be recognized only as an intermediate step in the development of the program rather than as a solution to providing materials of that nature needed by youth.

Homerooms are, of course, used as a means of organizing the extra-class-activity program. In the Bellville, New Jersey, High School, for example, each homeroom is the basic unit of the activities program of the school. Whenever a need or interest is recognized, another group activity is created. Homerooms frequently serve as the basis for the organization of intramural, athletic, and nonathletic teams. Drives and campaigns are organized on that basis also. Not infrequently the homeroom serves as a basis of student participation in management of the school; students in homerooms elect representatives to the student government.

Music and Speech

Music activities should be characterized by more emphasis upon broader participation in community singing, appreciation of folk music as well as semiclassical and classical music, organization of small interest groups, and less emphasis on the winning of contests and lavish public appearances. Similarly, speech activities should be geared more to youth needs and less in the direction of preparation for specialized public appearances. In addition to school bands, orchestras, and glee clubs, there may be such activities as appreciation clubs, dance bands, operettas and operas, folk singing groups, harmonica and other special instrument clubs, drum and bugle corps, and many other types of special-interest groups. Dramatics, debating, discussion groups, radio- and television-presentation clubs, and speech contests are among the types of speech activities often found in secondary schools.

Almost everyone likes to act, to sing, or to play an instrument. Opportunities on a broad scale should be provided for all students along these lines. Although it may be desirable to have carefully selected groups in advanced music and speech activities, opportunities should also be provided for those who wish to learn. Opportunities for public appearances should be provided for less talented persons in such activities as small-group assemblies, activity meetings, and noontime entertainment. The emphasis on the talented few has in many schools been in direct conflict with the needs of all young people for creative and leisure-time activities in the arts.

Publications

Another outlet for the creative interests of young persons is provided through the various publications of the school. Such publications include the school newspaper, school magazine, school yearbook or annual, student handbook, and programs for various school performances. Innovating practices are in the direction of making these publications more student-centered with increased emphasis on youth needs and less on the use of the publication as a public relations device of the school.

Many examples of interesting practices in connection with school newspapers may be cited. Staff members of the *Panorama*, student newspaper of Central High School, Binghamton, New York, bring to the public a round-up of school news each Friday morning in a broadcast over the local radio station. Editors and feature writers of school newspapers in Portland, Oregon, hold a press conference with the president of the Portland Community Chest and plan a program of publicity that is a service to many community organizations which are members of the Chest.

The *Mathematics Student*, a magazine published every term by the Griffen Technical High School, Griffen, New York, Mathematics Club, contains articles on mathematics and its applications. Other school magazines provide outlets for creative productions for students in poetry, essays, short stories, book reviews, photography, music, and art.

Student yearbooks, taking a cue from the picture magazines, are presenting stories in pictorial form that will provide not only students but also adults with a better understanding of educational opportunities in the school. Such yearbooks may have considerable guidance value for incoming students as well as for those who have not participated as adequately in activities as might seem desirable. The *Waukegan, Illinois, Township High School Yearbook* recently was organized about the theme, "Meeting the Imperative Needs of Youth." During the year each of the ten imperative youth needs[13] was listed and the activities of the school, both curriculum and extraclass, were discussed in the frame of reference of youth needs.

Student handbooks are being written by students rather than for students. In the Benson High School, Omaha, Nebraska, the advanced journalism students have published a student handbook, "Let's Say 'Hi' to High School," which is of aid to new students. A committee of students at Technical High School, Oakland, California, published a book on student etiquette, "Modes and Manners," as a guide to dress and behavior at formal and informal events. When students do the writing, the style of writing is more likely to be easily understood and appreciated than when it is written by the faculty or school administrator. Pictures, cartoons, and other graphic materials make handbooks much more attractive. Since the student handbook is considered a part of the guidance program of the school, copies should be made available to all students without cost to them.

The use of programs for various school performances as an opportunity to present information regarding the purposes of such performances as well as interesting facts about their development is an innovating practice being followed in some secondary schools. The program, in other words, should include more than simply a list of the numbers and participants. The art and English departments may assist the particular department responsible for a given program publication.

---

[13] "The Imperative Needs of Youth of Secondary-School Age," *Bulletin of the National Association of Secondary-School Principals*, XXXI (March, 1947), 3–144.

Student Participation in Management

One of the significant student needs is for experiences in activities closely related to those of citizenship in a democracy. Participation in policy-making and control is being encouraged in secondary schools as a means of meeting this need. The goal of any such system of student participation should be that every student in school feels he has an appropriate voice in the development of policies that are recommended for adoption by the faculty, administration, and board of education of the school. Students must learn, of course, that many considerations and opinions other than their own go into the development of policies.

Studies should be made in the local school to determine the amount and degree of actual participation in policy-making by students. In the University of Illinois High School, an analysis was recently made of the policies which had been adopted in the school over a five-year period. For each year a chart was prepared showing the policies developed and the groups, i.e., students, faculty, parents, administration, and board, who had participated in the making of such policies. Thus, it was possible to chart the growth of student participation over a period of time and also to indicate quite dramatically areas in which it might be desirable in the future to provide for more student participation.

Many other examples of interesting practices involving student participation in management may be cited. The Shawnee High School, Louisville, Kentucky, has a Principal's Cabinet on which student representatives have membership. The Cabinet is an advisory group that discusses school matters and presents suggestions to the faculty and to the two student councils in the school. In the John Marshall High School, Richmond, Virginia, surveys of student participation, interest in activities, and reaction to assembly programs are used in planning the activity programs. Polls of student interests are used at the Thomas High School, Kearney, Nebraska, each year in order to develop the schedule of clubs for the year. Seven public high schools in Indianapolis, Indiana, have formed an inter-high-school youth council in an effort not only to assist in better relations among schools but also between the schools and various civic and governmental groups. The Farragut High School in Chicago has a student-guidance committee. Members of the committee visit elementary schools to furnish information about the high school and assist new students at the time of registering and in getting acquainted. In Cleveland, Ohio, student council members in the John Adams High School assist in reducing pupil tardiness. Every night a list of late sleepers is handed to appropriate students and the next morning at six-thirty they call on the telephone to awaken the sleepy ones. If no improvement is noted, the offenders are called before the council. All study halls are honor study halls in the Harvey High School, Painesville, Ohio. These study halls are supervised and governed by students elected for that purpose.

The foregoing recital of student participation in management could be extended almost indefinitely. Innovating practices are reported in large numbers in almost every educational publication. Important factors are that such participation is extended to all of the students of the school, that students are trained for such participation, and that the administration of student participation is genuine, with necessary limitations known to everyone.

Conclusion

The evidence and statements presented in this chapter appear to lead inevitably to the conclusion that extraclass activities possess unique qualities that make them particularly effective in contributing to the growth and development of youth. That there are certain barriers which need to be overcome if activities are to make the maximum contribution in meeting youth needs is also obvious. Innovating practices result when school officials, teachers, students, and communities are made aware of the potential contributions of activities and take steps to secure necessary improvements. Here as in other aspects of the curriculum the paramount need is to consider all needs of *all* students rather than the needs of a few, or only a few of the needs.

The importance of the educational leader in facilitating these desired developments is difficult to overemphasize. Unless provisions are made for the participation of all appropriate groups in planning, managing, and evaluating a program, and unless administrative arrangements are made to implement the plans developed through these deliberations, the program will be relatively ineffective.

Positive steps taken with respect to extraclass activities may be a relatively easy and rapid means of enriching the school's program in the direction of more adequately meeting youth needs. Many of the present extraclass activities will probably become recognized as a normal part of the regular class activities of the school. However, there will doubtless always be new types of activities emerging to replace those which have been curricularized. Thus, the school program may remain flexible and adaptable to changing conditions and needs.

CHAPTER X

PROVIDING FOR WORK EXPERIENCE AND OUTDOOR ACTIVITIES

WILSON H. IVINS

Associate Professor of Secondary Education
University of New Mexico
Albuquerque, New Mexico

INTRODUCTION

Making use of work and outdoor experience in adapting a secondary-school program to the needs of youth demands of us many things. First of all, we must recognize that the activities of work and outdoor recreation are in themselves fundamental needs of the maturing youth. Then we must realize that much of what youth do in work or in the outdoors contributes to their personal development, to fulfilment of their economic needs, to their need to become maturely social people, and to their need to learn about vocational life. Having recognized these things, we then need to understand what these experiences are, what forms they take, and how they may be used. Then we must ascertain the difference between the amount of these kinds of experience that youth are receiving and the experiences they actually need; this difference will be the amount that we in the school should provide. If we reach this point in our effort to provide work and outdoor experiences in a need-centered secondary-school program, the remainder of our task is to learn how to make the needed provision and then go ahead and make it.

The presentation of a chapter on work and outdoor experiences in this yearbook is an authoritative recognition of the importance for youth of such an extension of the usual classroom program of the secondary school. Although earlier analyses of the problems of modern secondary education have indicated a growing sense of the developmental values in work and outdoor programs for youth, the major writings have not usually recognized the potentialities of these experiences with the clarity that is exemplified in the preceding chapters of this volume. The conditions described in chapters ii, iii, v, and vi make this chapter vital to the unity of an approach to the major problem of meeting the developmental needs of youth. Provisions for these experiences in connection with secondary education represent a means to the end of personal development of youth. Because of their assistance to youth in the attainment of certain developmental goals, work and outdoor experiences may be analyzed in the light of the following categories of youth needs: (a) developmental and adjustment; (b) economic; (c) socialization; and (d) guidance, exploration and vocational. Actually, these are not distinct categories of youth needs because they are so closely related that they cannot be separated in the manner indicated. They are, however, useful as a basis of selection of various aspects of the needs of youth for consideration of the values of work and outdoor experiences.

The Relation of Work and Outdoor Experiences to Youth Needs

Developmental and Adjustment Needs

Studies of the growth and development of individuals tell us that work experiences and outdoor activities are necessary for the maturation of practically every individual. Thus, even in our modern culture, if boys and girls are to become men and women, they must have these kinds of experience.

The social acceptability of these experiences is well recognized. We have come to use the phrase, "hard worker," as one of praise. Secondly, we have come to realize that embodied in these experiences are outcomes which we call desirable character traits. There is little question of the need for providing these experiences in the hope that youth will be influenced by them in the development of traits of good character.

A third kind of need of youth is that of general physical development. An examination of the record will show that the burden of providing opportunities for this kind of development cannot be left entirely to the school.

Still another developmental need of youth is that for generalized or manipulative skills. Such skills are seldom learned by reading a book or engaging in any of the other study activities which are most often characteristic of the academic classroom. Also, examination of youth's current life situation reveals that there are fewer opportunities for practice and exercise of these skills than formerly. School provision of these experiences will contribute much to the acquisition of skills of this kind.

Since work and recreation are so important in adult life, youth need to develop also generalized work habits and recreational interests that are desirable. These habits can be developed effectively through example and practice in a work or camp program. They are, at the same time, habits for which the out-of-school environment makes insufficient provision and for which the formal school situation provides only verbalized instruction.

Economic Needs of Youth

The economic needs to be served by work experiences are in themselves deeply significant. They are not confined to the matter of provision of funds or resources for satisfaction of material desires. Indeed, many think that the most significant need of youth in the economic sphere is an awareness of the meaning of money and what it stands for rather than actual possession of money. One way of helping youth develop a sense of material values is to provide opportunities for them to earn money. Work experiences in connection with programs of secondary education would definitely enlarge the scope of these opportunities for many youth in the school.

We often hear, also, the idea that our youth should develop economic "literacy." Proponents of this view mean not only development of understanding of the meaning of a dollar but also a firsthand, concrete understanding and appreciation of labor, production, capital, distribution, economic organization, and their interrelationships. The assumption here is that actual experiences at work will sooner lead youth to a mature understanding of what makes the wheels go round than any other experiences the school can provide.

Finally, we should indicate that even in times of prosperity, young people have various needs for money. The hidden costs of secondary education have been shown to be beyond reach of many youth. Short of state, federal, or other subsidy of students in the high school, we see no other way for needy youth to get the money than by working for it. The suggestion here is that they do so at the same time that they engage in an educational experience under the supervision of the school work program.

Socialization Needs of Youth

Actually all that has been said of developmental and economic needs supports the view that youth need socialization. Yet, we should reiterate adult interest in the socialization of youth. We may talk to our youth in school as much as we wish about the values and imperatives in co-operation, interdependence of modern society, group effort, and enlightened self-reliance, but until we put youth in positions where they may experience these values and imperatives at first hand, they will not acquire an understanding of these concepts. In this connection, we wish to emphasize the suitability of work and outdoor experiences as means to the end visualized in school programs designed to promote the social adjustment of youth.

Practical and direct applications of the principles of democracy, stripped of clichés and verbalization, seem more common in the sphere of group work and recreative activities than any other in life. It is in this sphere, too, that we most often see the desirable trait of altruism coming to the fore. In such activities as team play on the football field, rebuilding of the burned-out cottage by neighborhood groups, construction of community projects by donated labor, and selection of recipients of such community favors as summer camp expenses, scholarships, and "good neighbor" awards we most often see the willingness to do or give something without the hope of material reward. In such activities, also, we most often see the fellowship, the maintenance of dignity and respect, the give and take, the co-operation, and the equality of opportunity which together make up so large a part of what we call democracy.

Guidance and Vocational Needs

With respect to vocational guidance and the exploration of vocational fields, the need is almost universal among youth. Typically, the school has tried to meet these needs through clinics, courses, career-day programs, and similar approaches. Although these approaches have unquestionable values, they cannot be compared with actual experiences in work and in outdoor activities. Among the needs in this sphere are: (a) need for help in wise choice of vocation (especially if the youth is ready to make such a choice); (b) need for help in the choice of recreational pursuits; (c) need for exploration of a wide variety of vocational *fields*; (d) need for exploration, participation, and learning in a wide variety of recreational fields; (e) need for a generalized introduction to the responsible world of work; (f) commonly shared needs of the individual for acquisition of a wide variety of items of vocational information; and (g) specialized needs of the individual for specific information and skills in specific vocations.

TYPES OF WORK EXPERIENCE

There is at present no unanimity about the meaning of the term "work experience." As with most concepts of this kind, the meaning is dependent upon the application. However, examination of the ideas expressed about it reveals certain characteristics with which most persons will agree.

Consideration of these characteristics suggests the following definition of work experience: Work experience is that experience which students obtain through participating in production of needed goods or services in a normal situation in industry, business, community at large, or school, under the direction of the schools.

Basic Forms of Work Programs

Most of the organized forms of work which have been developed in the schools satisfy the criteria in the definition just stated. A list of typical forms that have been developed would almost certainly include the following:

Co-operative Work Experience. This form includes experiences offered in such programs as co-operative distributive education (or occupations), co-operative diversified occupations, and co-operative office practice.[1] The main feature is the division of a student's day or school term into equal periods of school study and job instruction. The job instruction is provided by a co-operating employer and is supervised by him or by an employee. The school study consists of required general academic subjects, vocational subjects of the field in which he works, and subjects related to his vocational field.

In-school Work Experience. This form is organized in a greater variety of ways than any other. The work may be individualized or it may be performed by groups. Sometimes pay is given for the work and sometimes it is not. In any instance, however, the work will be performed in or around the school, for the school or members of the student body, and under the direct supervision of the teachers or other employees of the school.[2] This form could include such work activities as student library assistance, student clerical or janitorial labor, operation of motion-picture projector, cadet teaching or child care, participation in all-school or class-work projects in campus beautification, paper-grading, and summer gardening. In most instances direct vocational courses and courses directly related to the in-school work activities are not provided.

Institutional Work Experiences. This form is almost the same as in-school work. However, students not infrequently perform work in institutions on a co-operative basis like that used for co-operative work experi-

---

[1] S. Anderson, "A High-School Work-Experience Program in Action," *American School Board Journal*, CXXII (August, 1951), 18–19.

Kenneth B. Haas, *Co-operative Part-time Retail Training Programs.* United States Office of Education Bulletin No. 205. Vocational Division, Business Education Series No. 13, 1939. Washington: Government Printing Office, 1939.

Kenneth B. Haas, *Distributive Education: Organization and Administration.* United States Office of Education Bulletin No. 211. Vocational Division, Business Education Series No. 12, 1940. Washington: Government Printing Office, 1940.

H. T. Hearn, "The Baltimore Work-Study Plan in Business Education," *Balance Sheet*, XXXII (December, 1950), 148–49.

Arthur W. Ferguson, "Schools and Industry Co-operate," *Journal of Education*, CXXIX (January, 1946), 22–23.

[2] J. C. Adams, "Our Business Students Aid Our Entire Teaching Staff," *Balance Sheet*, XXXII (September, 1950), 4.

Wilson H. Ivins and Herbert Wey, "Capitalizing on Educational Values of Informal Work Experience," *School Review*, LVII (November, 1949), 485–89.

W. Wallace, James Chrielzberg, and Verner M. Sims, *The Story of Holtville.* Nashville, Tennessee: Wesley Hall, Vanderbilt University, 1944.

ence. It is differentiated on the basis of locale in which the work is performed.[3]

Camp Work Experiences. This form, which is of fairly recent origin, differs from the others in that the central purpose of the whole educational program at the time is built around work.[4] The work camp is what its name implies. The form is most common in states where crop harvesting requires large numbers of seasonal hands. Tobacco, citrus, and truck crops are frequently harvested by students in summer or fall work camps. The work aspect of the more general school camp program should also be mentioned here. In such camps, however, work is not the main part of the program and is concerned chiefly with camp maintenance or group projects designed to produce other primary learnings.

Developments in each of these four forms have been sufficient to provide numerous illustrations of actual school practice in educational literature. For more detailed descriptions of these four kinds of programs, including descriptions of actual programs, see *Work Experience in High School* by Ivins and Runge[5] and *Education for Life Adjustment*, edited by Harl R. Douglass.[6]

TYPES OF OUTDOOR EXPERIENCE

The phrase "outdoor experience" requires little definition. Yet it must be qualified with respect to the particular attributes it will assume when used as a basis for a school program. Actually, it is broad enough to allow the school to interpret it in any manner desired. Possibly this is not wholly desirable, yet it does make of the outdoor experience a very flexible means to the school's objectives.

The most significant aspect of the outdoor experience is the fact that it requires a shift of educational forces from the physical environment of the classroom to the outdoors. As the planners of the Michigan public school camping program have pointed out, this actually introduces a wholly new kind of education into the school curriculum.[7] They assert that it introduces new content as well as more direct and concrete meth-

[3] C. Hughes, "School of the Ozarks," *Coronet*, XXX (July, 1951), 92–95.

[4] *An Account of Eleven Experimental High-School Camps in Michigan, 1948–49.* Lansing, Michigan: Michigan Department of Public Instruction, 1949.

A. Morris and B. B. McCullar, "Georgia's F.F.A.–F.H.A. Joint Camping Program," *American Vocational Journal*, XXVI (April, 1951), 16–18.

[5] Wilson H. Ivins and William B. Runge, *Work Experience in High School*, chaps. i and iii; also pp. 242–48, 261–63. New York: Ronald Press Co., 1951.

[6] *Education for Life Adjustment*, chap. xviii. Edited by Harl R. Douglass. New York: Ronald Press Co., 1950.

[7] See publications of the Michigan Department of Public Instruction, especially *An Account of Eleven Experimental High-School Camps in Michigan, op. cit.*

ods. Teachers and administrators in our secondary schools of the past have shown a reluctance to leave the safe verbal confines of the classroom for a more challenging outside environment. This reluctance to explore new areas of motivation for learning has contributed to a failure to see the growing necessity for getting down to more practical lessons in the locale in which these lessons make sense. Consequently, some disturbance may be expected in the school which undertakes an adaptation of its curriculum to the facts of life which are involved in the establishment of an outdoor-education program.

School and Class Journeys, Field Trips, Picnics, and Similar Excursions

Some forms of outdoor experience have long been used by good schools to secure the advantages offered by their informality, their appeal to the interests and curiosity of the learners, and the freshness and realistic relevance of the learning experiences they provide. These opportunities are to be found in such familiar activities as journeys, field trips, picnics, and the like. In typical schools, little more than reorientation of philosophy and aims will be required to make use of them. Expense, time, and similar factors are relatively minor. What may hold up development of these forms of experience in the typical school are such factors as disruption of administrative and teacher routines, requirement of special planning and effort by teachers, and removal of restraints of the classroom in discipline.

We should note that the aims of outdoor activities may vary widely in such respects as formality, specificity, duration, and organization. The experiences themselves will vary just as widely. Such forms as interscholastic trips of athletic teams and other school groups and annual class trips of several days duration may become very comprehensive experiences, indeed. Yet these forms will exhibit one common characteristic; any of them will give access to kinds of learning which are virtually impossible in the classroom. They will define a unique environment for previously untaught but needed lessons.

With increasing frequency, we note the gradual decline of family outdoor activities. In its place we see more and more youth sharing the outdoors in such groups as boy and girl scout troops and clubs. Although we may deplore modern conditions which reduce family-group activities like picnicking, we must recognize that so far as the outdoors is concerned, the exact composition of the group in which the youth enjoys it is not so important as the fact that he does share the experience with someone in that environment. The school is composed of a tremendous variety of such groups in which the outdoor experiences may be developed.

School Camp Experiences

Work experience in crop-harvesting camps run by schools has been mentioned. Also, we need to recognize the fact that summer camps run by organizations and agencies other than the school have long existed and flourished. At the present time, however, we are aware of a growing trend in the direction of development of all-round camp programs which are integral parts of the school curriculum. This trend has developed for a variety of reasons. Among these are included the fact that the community has encouraged a lengthened school year. A lengthened year consisting of more of the same kind of school experiences has been rejected by most forward-looking educators. Also, we have come to recognize the imperative nature of such lessons as conservation, enjoyment of nature, and the development of skills of group participation in outdoor activities of many kinds. Accompanying recognition of these needed lessons has been awareness that they could be learned only in the environment in which they make sense, the outdoors.

In development, school camp programs have become integral parts of a general education core or they have been organized for special purposes like crop harvesting or for the teaching of certain special lessons like those listed. Evidence indicates that in the future the school camp program will become an essential part of a core program. In this, certain lessons of appreciation and enjoyment, group endeavor, and practical application of theoretical generalizations from the core classroom will be learned.

As was the case in describing the four basic forms of work experience, it seems that the purpose of revealing actual practice in developing high-school camp programs can be served best by referring to several excellent accounts of actual programs.[8]

INITIATING STUDENT PROGRAMS OF WORK EXPERIENCE OR OUTDOOR ACTIVITIES

Ascertaining the Need for These Programs

No administrator wishes to promote the cause of a new program that is not needed. In a small, rural secondary school, for example, needs for work-experience or outdoor-activity programs may be so simple that formal school programs in these fields would not be warranted. In such

---

[8] J. M. Clarke, *Public School Camping.* Palo Alto, California: Stanford University Press, 1951.

G. W. Donaldson, "Outdoor Laboratory School Camps: Tyler, Texas," *Survey,* LXXXVII (August, 1951), 357.

M. J. Gold and H. L. Robertson, "Classroom in the Cascades," *Clearing House,* XXV (October, 1950), 80–84.

L. M. Thurston, "Michigan High Schools and Their Camping Activities," *High School Journal,* XXXIV (February, 1951), 56–61.

cases, the administrator will wish to meet these simple needs within the existing framework of the curriculum.

Also, no administrator will wish to initiate the program alone, not even in the exploratory stage of ascertaining needs for it. Hence, he will enlist his faculty in the task. He will probably seek the additional assistance of a community advisory group. If he does not make the endeavor a co-operative one, it can have little prospect of real success. For the teachers, such co-operation will constitute a real in-service training. For the community, the co-operative effort will provide an opportunity for active support of school services and at the same time be a means of informing the adult population concerning the purposes of the school.

Surveys and study projects may be necessary to ascertain the nature of the needs for which formal programs should be organized. The following are types of activity that might be undertaken.

1. Survey of specific community needs voiced by special groups or observed in special situations
2. Survey of community resources—human, financial, physical
3. Study of the common needs of youth
   a) Publications of national associations or agencies
   b) Findings of specialists and groups studying youth development
4. Local survey of youth status and needs
   a) Studies of youth in school
   b) Analysis of youth activities
   c) Follow-up study of graduates, drop-outs, and other out-of-school youth

Obtaining Support of the Community

This is a continuing task of the school administrator. For any special type of program, some emphasis on the special characteristics of the needs involved will be necessary. Such activities as the following will be useful in developing this emphasis.

1. Explaining the program to the public by all available media of communication in the proposal stages of the project
2. Seeking advice and providing tasks for leaders and participants in community activities
3. Carrying on a continuing program of public relations and publicity

To obtain support for the introduction of new features into the program of the school, the administrator will observe two important principles of community-improvement procedures: First, the program should gain community support on the same basis as any other part of the total school program. Second, real and lasting support for the program can be obtained from the community only by giving the community an active part in its development.

Educating and Using the Faculty

The work experience or outdoor program of the school will require all faculty members to adopt new applications of methods that are familiar to them and to acquire some understandings that are new to them. Since teachers are the ultimate keys to success in the inauguration of these services, they should be given in-service or other preservice training. During the first group task, that of ascertaining the need for such programs, participation roles should be assigned to as many teachers as can be used. Soon after the completion of the preliminary steps, all teachers should be informed of the specific roles they are to play in the development of the program.

Establishing Aims and Standards

The school cannot rely wholly on local sources of information and values for the establishment of aims and standards. In most of the general aspects of the problem, much help will come from outside sources. In particulars, however, the community will be wise to rely upon local sources like the findings of the preliminary survey already mentioned. In any event, the need for establishment of aims and standards which will meet community approval and also be susceptible to a degree of comparison with more widely accepted aims and standards seems to be imperative.

In this effort to establish aims and standards, a minimum series of procedures would probably include the following:

1. Assigning responsibility for development of aims and standards
2. Studying the existing school program and considering needs for revision of
   a) Curriculum
   b) Methods
   c) Procedures, personnel assignments, organization
3. Stating program aims and correlating them with over-all aims of the curriculum
4. Developing full understanding of the meaning of the aims
5. Stating standards for the program and correlating them with over-all standards of the curriculum
6. Checking standards with statements from outside sources

Providing for Co-ordination of Faculty Efforts

These steps indicate, of course, that the experiences must be planned carefully and meshed with the other experiences which make up the curriculum. They must not become a haphazard series of activities for activity's sake; as such they will be meaningless. Only in the context of the whole curriculum will they produce the learning sought. To this end, the task of co-ordinating the efforts of the entire faculty should be assigned to an appropriate member of the staff.

Adapting Work Experiences to the Individual Student

This is one of the major and technical aspects of the co-ordinator's work. Not all students will find the same lessons in an experience; not all will have need for the same lessons. Also, we should note that as an experience becomes narrower and is organized for more specific outcomes, the need for assuring a good adjustment between students and experiences becomes greater. In the co-operative work experience, for example, the co-ordinator will discover that placement of the student in just the right experience suited to him is often a delicate and difficult task. Matching a group of students with an outdoor experience like a biology field trip requires, on the other hand, no more than an assurance that each student is a biology student who needs to learn what is to be taught by means of the trip.

In between these extremes are problems of matching students and experiences having varying degrees of difficulty. In this range, the guidance services of the school, especially those offered by the classroom teachers, have a most vital part to play. Not only will the guidance worker be able to make use of his special knowledge of the student and his needs but he will also be able to correlate the guidance service of the school with the experience programs involving student work or outdoor activities. Desirable individualization of education will result.

With respect to those features of the program regarded as integral parts of the general-education core, the process of matching particular students with selected experiences is eliminated because by definition the experiences offered in that core are supposed to meet commonly shared needs of all students. Hence, every student should have these experiences. However, even in this example, no two students will experience the lessons in quite the same manner. The necessity for individualization of instruction is just as great in the core program as in the special subjects. In these experiences, consequently, the teacher must be able to individualize the manner in which each student will participate.

OPERATING THE PROGRAMS FOR WORK AND OUTDOOR EXPERIENCES

The preliminary study and planning activities that have been outlined are all essential to the success of the school's program. However, they will not in themselves make it go on a continuing basis. After the preliminaries, various practices in operation of the program become vital to its success. The school must operate its program in a systematic and orderly manner, and we can at least outline some of the most essential steps that must be taken.

We should notice, too, that although some phases of these procedures will have had some attention in the preliminary organization of the pro-

gram, the greater portion of them must be done carefully and systematically month after month, if the program is to flourish. Each school will, of
course, develop its own approach to operating procedures. The procedures outlined in the following pages have usually been regarded as
necessary by the high schools that have had success in work or camp
programs.

Planning the Work or Outdoor Experiences

Naturally, the co-operative work program will require much more specific and detailed plans for job instruction than will an informal group
work project. Similarly, a camp program involving a program of two
weeks duration for thirty or more students will require more detailed
planning than a biology-class field trip. This suggests that specialists like
the co-ordinator will have heavy responsibilities in the planning. However, despite the leading role assigned to the specialists, we should underscore the necessity for teacher and pupil participation in this planning if
it is to be meaningful. We cannot outline here the details of planning in
each of the various kinds of work or outdoor experiences, but the major
elements can be indicated. Let us look first at the planning of the work-
experience or job-instruction program.

In planning the work to be done, the following things must be pro
vided:

1. A job or task to be performed must be identified.
2. A place or situation in which the job is to be done must be provided.
3. A means for placing the student or students in the situation must be provided.
4. The task to be performed must be analyzed and fitted to an outline of the instructional sequence which is to be followed.
5. Informational or instructional materials and devices must be selected, obtained, and organized.
6. Instructional method must be planned.
7. Plans for check-up and evaluation must be completed.

In general, these same elements would be basic in the planning of the
outdoor-experience program. However, because the outdoor experience so
often involves large groups of students in an environment that is usually
novel for them as well as for the teacher and the community, certain special aspects of planning for it should be mentioned. In the camp experience, for example, it can be seen that in addition to the elements just
listed, certain aspects of community support, transportation, and locale
will demand that planning include:

1. Staff planning of the total experience
2. Community planning for the sake of producing support as well as advice
3. Student planning (individuals and groups will have to plan for travel from

home, care of food, shelter, and similar needs while away from home as well as for the particulars of educational experiences in the outdoors)

4. Board of education planning, primarily requiring official approval of the activity
5. Resource-use planning, involving facilities and personnel often not ordinarily available to the school
6. Planning of daily activities
7. Student-teacher planning in the midst of the experience

As indicated, co-ordinators, teachers, and other resource persons will necessarily plan the experiences together in a general way. But after the experiences have been blocked out in a broad manner, the individual teacher or supervisor of the activity will find it necessary to include students in the more immediate aspects of the planning. In practice this is the way it has worked out both in work and in outdoor programs. In the Michigan public school camping program, for example, teachers found that the planning of the week's activities by the students in cabin groups was probably the most valuable single aspect of the whole program.

This does not imply that either the preliminary plans by the school staff or the more immediate plans by the teacher and students may be vague; quite the contrary. It does imply, though, that no one can tell another just how to do the planning. At best, he can indicate that it is an essential part of the total operation of the program. As such it will require superior supervision which will be challenged by the informality and freedom of the experiences. At the same time, supervisors are offered unusual opportunities for motivation of learning because of the stimulating effects of those same features of informality and freedom. The supervisor can tread no well-marked paths as he does in a subject field like mathematics. Although this situation has its undesirable features, it does provide the opportunity for the expression of high-order leadership.

Planning Related Instruction for the Classroom

The amount of detail involved in this planning will depend upon the particular type of work or outdoor experience to be supplemented by the classroom activities. In co-operative work experience, for example, the vocational and related classroom program is composed of carefully planned, self-contained subjects.[9] Group work or outdoor experiences of less formal nature, however, might be supplemented by units or even single classroom lessons in either core programs or special subjects. On the level of least formality, we would expect only a simple supplement of the experience. We might expect, likewise, that the orientation might be reversed—that the experience had been developed to supplement the

---

[9] Ivins and Runge, *op. cit.*, chap. xiv.

classroom teaching. A biology field trip to supplement classroom learning in an established course of study would be an example of this degree of informality. Even here, the necessity for planning of the classroom part of the instruction, to insure proper meshing with what is to follow out-doors, is clear. Although much more could be said of the techniques of planning related instruction in the classroom to supplement these experiences, all of it would merely reiterate this basic principle.

Providing for Correlation of Outside Experiences with In-School Learnings

Initial planning, especially with reference to co-ordination of faculty efforts in general, will have established a pattern for correlation. Planning of related instruction, which has just been described, will also advance the process. However, at this point, the need will arise for considering specific ways in which the fusion of theory and practice can be effected. Many secondary schools and higher institutions have worked out highly ingenious ways of doing this. These procedures are, however, so individual that each school usually finds it necessary to work out its own ways of performing the task.

Antioch College, for example, developed correlation of the student's learning on the campus with his learning in a job situation by requiring him to conduct field studies and write reports in which he was able to point out relationships between the two phases of his schooling.

The University of Cincinnati, on the other hand, typically makes use of a co-ordinator who observes the student on the job, confers with the student and his work supervisor, and then returns to the campus, either to teach the same student in his specialized classes or to instruct the teacher of the specialized class in what the student needs to learn in theory. This method, used in most high-school co-operative work programs would probably not be desirable in an outdoor-experience program. In the latter, some form of the Antioch College approach might be very effective.

Thus, it seems likely that exact specifications for correlation cannot be given. Instead, it is clear that teachers will necessarily sit down together, first in their own groups and later with their students, and plan to correlate the classroom experiences with those in the program by making revisions in content, seeking common emphases, and using common methods.

Administrative Aspects of the Program

The program will fail if it does not have vigorous support of the school administration; it will be weakened if the administration does not develop policies and procedures which will allow for efficient operation.

With respect to the matter of support, it seems that peculiarly administrative aspects of the program would include at least the following:

1. Assignment of sufficient personnel to do the work
2. Equitable distribution of personnel loads
3. Provision of adequate materials and facilities
4. Financing the program
   a) Estimating needs
   b) Providing for a budget
   c) Finding sources of funds
   d) Distributing and accounting for funds

Some of these elements are also relevant to administrative procedures which can contribute to efficiency in operation of the program. In addition, it will be necessary for the administration to make policy decisions regarding at least the following things:

1. Pay
2. School credit
3. Management of student time
4. Application of co-operative principle
5. Scope of programs
6. Revision of existing administrative procedures to provide for needs of the new program

As was suggested, these lists reveal a definite role which the administration must assume.

Evaluative Aspects of the Program

Most schoolmen are aware of the basic philosophy and principles of evaluation. These principles will apply to the work or outdoor program as well as to any other school program. Therefore, the following necessary evaluative procedures are listed to indicate that they are essential in the program and that they must be developed if hope is to be held for the success of the program.

1. Procedures for evaluation of the programs as wholes
2. Procedures for evaluation of work of administrative and supervisory personnel
3. Procedures for evaluation of individual student progress in experiences
4. Procedures for student self-evaluation of programs and own progress in group and individual experiences

In general, it should be noted that, in either work or camping programs, outcomes are quite likely to be most obvious in new skills acquired and in both old and new information applied. Clearly this will make possible new or increased use of the performance type of test as opposed to the more common paper-and-pencil test of information retained. At the same time there will be more or less intangible outcomes of these experi-

ences, despite their concreteness, in the form of attitudes and appreciations. Evaluation of the intangibles will challenge the imagination of
program administrators. In the field of evaluation we may expect many
extensions of such experimental procedures as film records of student
activities, oral critique sessions in which participants evaluate their own
activities, individual self-evaluative written reports, summation of actual
production or salary records, and the like. Certainly the schoolman will
recognize the need for keeping careful records of events because, if he
does, he is quite likely to discover that they lead in discernible fashion to
results that tell him what the experiences were worth.

Except from the standpoint of skills, production, earnings, or acquisition of information, evaluation of work or camping experiences is likely
to be more subjective than that for academic work. This is not particularly alarming, especially if the subject be provided with a clear understanding of what desirable standards and outcomes are.[10]

Finally, it should be noted that schools have made much progress in
their experiments with evaluation of work and outdoor experiences.
Study of sources and illustrations like those that have been cited will be
most productive of suggestions for imitation and improvement in a local
situation. Even better than reading about other schools' methods of
evaluation, however, will be the practice of actually visiting schools that
are experiencing success in their attempts to evaluate their programs.

Concluding Statement

Actually what has been said constitutes little more than an introduction to an area of education that has had slight exploration. Yet, one can
see even in this limited introduction some of the possibilities for meeting
new or heightened needs of American boys and girls. These needs constitute an important part of the things we really know now about the
problem of giving our youth the right kind of secondary education. It is
inconceivable that the high school of the future will not make use of these
work and outdoor experiences in the manner indicated or in some other
suitable manner.

---

[10] See Ivins and Runge, *op. cit.*, chap. xv, for a specific treatment of the problem
of evaluation in the co-operative work program.

CHAPTER XI

GUIDANCE TO MEET THE NEEDS OF YOUTH

RUTH STRANG

Professor of Education
Teachers College, Columbia University
New York, New York

In the preceding chapters we have seen how the needs of young people may be recognized, how they themselves can learn to meet these needs, and what the school can do to facilitate the process, largely through group experiences in class and outside of class. We have seen that these needs of youth are complex, interrelated, dynamic. Meeting them is essential to the best development of individuals and society. In addition to providing a "lush" and "benign" environment, it is necessary to guide individuals in the use of this environment and to help them, when possible, to take the initiative in making the environment more favorable to adolescent growth and development. This is the individualized aspect of education which we call *guidance*.

TODAY'S VIEWS OF GUIDANCE

The meaning of the word *guidance*[1] has become increasingly broad. By one writer or another, all the individualized procedures used in furthering the best development of youth have been included in the guidance program of the secondary school. Some leaders in the field emphasize the "choice" aspect, i.e., making plans for the future. Others stress child study, which involves collecting, interpreting, and synthesizing data about the individual; such study should lead to self-realization. Still others focus attention on the more effective adjustment of individuals in their environment. From another standpoint, guidance is viewed as a learning process. Let us first turn to the young people themselves for their views of guidance.

Guidance Young People Want

If anyone knows what guidance is needed today, it should be young people themselves. They speak from experience. On questionnaires, in freely written autobiographies and compositions, in interviews, and in

---

[1] In present usage the word *guidance* is used interchangeably with *student personnel work.*

group discussions, they tell us about the kind of guidance they want and need. Some of their statements have been tabulated; others are of more value as direct quotations.

Questionnaires. Questionnaires answered by a large sampling of youth in the high schools of several school systems[2] revealed certain needs for guidance. These students clearly lacked assistance in making educational and vocational plans. They were choosing courses solely because their friends were taking them, or because their parents or older brothers and sisters recommended them, or because a certain course seemed interesting. They were not considering these choices in relation to their abilities, their further education, or their vocational plans. In answer to the question, "Has anyone helped you in planning your future—getting into college, choosing a field of work, etc.?" many replied, "No one helped me," and one added, "but I wish somebody would."

These students were uncertain as to their plans after graduating from high school. Many who would profit by a college education had not even considered the possibility of going to college; others who were not likely to succeed were expecting to enter college. One boy recognized the need for this kind of educational guidance when he said, "I would like help in finding the best college for what I plan to do and the place where I can learn the most."

In choosing a vocational field, they were not canvassing their specific qualifications and interests, the openings in the field, the opportunities for growth, or the social value of the occupation. For example, one said, "I saw some nurses walking down the street, and they looked so nice in their white uniforms that I decided to be a nurse." Another decided to be a teacher because, "I've always liked to learn people."

At the head of the list of problems which these young people mentioned were concern about school and about the future. Next in order were economic, social, and home problems; personality problems such as self-consciousness, feelings of inferiority, and shyness; and physical defects. In answer to the question, "What sort of things would you like to talk over with an older person?" one pupil wrote, "My emotional self—explain the emotional point of view I have and why."

Personal Documents. Freely written compositions obtained from youth attending high school indicated the need for guidance in important areas of life adjustment—boy-girl relations, family relations, social acceptance.

---

[2] Division of Field Studies, Institute of Educational Research, Teachers College, Columbia University, *The Report of a Survey of the Public Schools of Pittsburgh, Pennsylvania*, pp. 236–37. New York: Bureau of Publications, Teachers College, Columbia University, 1940. Surveys of Newark (New York), Tenafly, and Montclair (New Jersey) show similar needs for guidance.

In compositions on "When I Felt at a Loss or 'All at Sea,'" approximately two thousand high-school pupils described the following kinds of problems on which they needed guidance:[3]

	Problems	No. of Pupils Reporting Problem
Educational Problems:		
	Failure, low grades	125
	Relationships with teacher	118
	Time budget	89
	College—selection, entrance, financing	82
	Choice of course, subjects	44
	Other: homework, etc.	39
Home problems:		
	Parental attitudes	197
	Finances	74
	Relatives	34
	Divorce	14
	Family car	9
	Others	58
Social Problems:		
	Friends, clubs, meeting place	181
	Fraternity, sorority	40
Emotional problems:		
	Boy-girl problems	191
	Other than boy-girl problems	161
	Vocational problems	131
	Part-time work, etc.	32
	Physical defects, illness	30
	Delinquency, police contacts, drinking	20

About three hundred did not mention any specific problem in these compositions.

No tabulation, however, can give so much insight into the nature of the attitude of these youth toward their needs as the original compositions,[4] one of which is quoted in full:

Recently I have been faced with a problem which seemed of great importance to me. I will graduate in February and have every hope of entering nursing school the same month. When I obtained information from the hospital where I hope to

---

[3] George D. Strayer, Director, *The Report of a Survey of the Public Schools of the District of Columbia*, p. 700. Washington: Government Printing Office, 1949.

[4] For examples of compositions obtained from various groups of secondary-school pupils, see:

Ruth Strang, "Inner World of Gifted Adolescents," *Journal of Exceptional Children*, XVI (January, 1950), 97–101; "Manifestations of Maturity in Adolescents," *Mental Hygiene*, XXXIII (October, 1949), 563–69; "Social Aspects of Vocational Guidance," *School Review*, LXIII (September, 1950), 326–34; "What Did You Get on Your Report Card?" *National Parent-Teacher*, XLIV (March, 1950), 26–28.

train, I discovered that I was lacking one credit in social studies. This came as a blow to me because I wanted so much to start in February instead of putting it off for a whole semester.

I don't believe that the lack of credit was my fault and I don't wish to put the blame on my adviser, but I had stated when I first came to this school that I either wished to enter medical school or nursing school. Since my adviser knew this, it seems to me that she should have made provisions for it in my long-range program.

When I spoke to the Director of Nurses about it, she told me that if my marks were high enough I would be able to enter the school and make up the credit during my training. I hope I will be able to do this. If not, I must wait until September.

I believe that the school should have persons well equipped to advise the pupils as to the subjects they should take. They should know the requirements for the different schools and their courses. If they are not sure, they should have the information at hand where it could be found easily, before giving the wrong advice.

A common attitude toward asking for help is expressed in the following excerpt from a composition by a fifteen-year-old girl:

I wonder if the problem I have in mind really has a solution. Can there be any truly complete answer? . . . Can a child of any age, in any school, *truly* feel he may pour his heart out to his teachers? Can he confront them with problems that concern only himself? Many times I have considered going to a teacher or a counselor for advice, but then I stopped to think: Why should this person be interested in helping me? Why should she listen to my sad tale? Though I may know the person as a teacher or counselor, she is really a normal everyday person with a job and a life of her own. What possible, earthly reason could there be for this person to be interested in me—a person she hardly knows?

This is many times true of parents, too. They have the burden of supporting you, caring for you. Why should they be burdened further with your comparatively petty problems? You picture them as becoming annoyed or amused with your problems instead of becoming interested. Because of this, many children work out their own problems and many times don't come to the best solution.

Interviews. In interviews, the individual's need for guidance is both revealed and met. In the permissive, accepting relationship of the interview, the student feels free to express his feelings and to gain a better understanding of his most acceptable self. For example, a high-school Senior, seventeen years old, said in the first interview with the counselor:

Gosh, I'm just an ordinary boy—I don't know what I should be, but my folks keep after me all the time. They look at me and say, "You're big enough to be deciding what you want to do—do you want to be a doctor or an engineer or what?" I guess I'm big enough, but I still don't know. . . . I'd like to please them, but if you're not made that way, you just aren't. . . . I guess I'm a disappointment to my mother because I couldn't ever be as bright and successful as her brother.

In a later interview, this boy considered with the worker all the information they had collected and began to see himself more clearly and realistically—a boy who was likable, good in sports, superior in mental ability but average or below in academic subjects, handicapped by poor study habits and poor instruction. During the series of interviews, he gained a better understanding of his relations with his parents and his conflicting desires to please them, and he began to move toward more clearly recognized goals in line with his own aptitudes and interests.

Group Discussions. Many of the same needs for guidance come out in group discussions. In the many panel discussions among high-school pupils which the writer has led, the following needs for guidance have been repeatedly mentioned:

1. Youth want more individual attention even in large classes—they want to feel that teachers are friendly and interested in them as persons.

2. They want opportunity to develop their talents; everyone has some contribution to make, and the teacher should give each a chance to develop and use his special ability. Some young people are too shy to take the initiative.

3. They want help in making out their high-school program, which involves looking ahead for three or four years, and in making sound educational and vocational plans: deciding whether to go to college, choosing a college, or surveying other educational opportunities. As one boy said, "You don't want to take a subject for three years and then find out that you have wasted your time as far as meeting college-entrance requirements is concerned." Another boy said, "I should like to get a picture of each kind of vocation, and I'd like to see, somehow, just what I would be getting into. I'd like to look at different possibilities before I make a decision. I haven't had much help like that." Many are most concerned with the war: "I think a lot of students need help in deciding what to do about the army. Should I go to college now and then go into the army or should I choose the Air Force now and then go to college after my two years are up? This is a great problem which many of us are trying to solve."

4. They want teachers to help them succeed in their studies and correct personality "fault lines"—behavior that would interfere with their success. One youth said, "If I were a teacher and a student is failing, I wouldn't wait until the end of the term to tell him. I would warn him that he was on the verge of failing his subject."

5. They would like to talk with teachers about many personal problems, although many of them feel this kind of guidance should be done by parents. One of the rural young people in the discussion group at the White House Conference said:

I think the people of my age need guidance in dealing with problems of sex, social relations, marriage, and vocations. Many cannot get this guidance in their homes. Parents seem to be afraid to talk to their children—afraid they can't answer them rightly. Many teachers are now asked about these problems, but they are not prepared to deal with them.

Case Study. If we synthesize personal data from various sources in a case study for each pupil, we get another view of the need for guidance. This was done in the survey of a suburban high school.[5] The following needs were most frequently indicated:

Needs	No. of Pupils Mentioning Services Needed
Help with study and reading problems	245
Educational guidance	202
Vocational guidance	163
Further mental or achievement testing	130
More social activities	123
Help with human relations	116
Counseling	113

Needs for Guidance Observed by Adults

Records of evaluation studies made by the Middle States Association of Colleges and Secondary Schools show lacks and deficiencies in present guidance programs and include recommendations for improvement. In 1948 Lois M. Gould[6] analyzed and summarized the results of 226 of these surveys of Pennsylvania schools. The needs most mentioned in order of frequency were as follows: adequate records; faculty participation in program; leadership; vocational guidance; accessible records; personal, social, leisure-time guidance; pupil participation in the homeroom; coordination; testing program; follow-up of pupils; educational guidance; adequate time for guidance; organized guidance program; use of specialists' consultation service; faculty awareness of service; occupational information.

Total Needs Met by the School Program as a Whole

Of the total needs of youth, some are met in each subject field and the common-learnings program, others in extraclass activities, and still others by special guidance services. The guidance specialist should help ad-

---

[5] Helen F. Williams, "A Case Study Approach to the Evaluation of Guidance in Tenafly High School," pp. 24–25. Unpublished Doctor's project, Teachers College, Columbia University, 1945.

[6] Lois M. Gould, "Suggested State-wide Standards for Guidance Services in the Secondary Schools of Pennsylvania," pp. 17–18. Unpublished Doctor's project, Teachers College, Columbia University, 1948.

ministrators determine how and by whom certain kinds of needs can best be met.

Along with the trend toward "making guidance an all-faculty function and toward co-operation between guidance specialists and classroom teachers" is a strong trend toward greater expertness and "increased use of objective measures in guidance programs."[7]

Contribution of the Classroom Teacher

Everyone on the school staff makes a contribution in meeting the needs of youth. The classroom teacher is most important because he is most directly in touch with the individual pupil. He makes his contribution by setting an example of personality and personal relations, maintaining a sensitivity to the needs of individuals in the class, conducting group discussions of common personal problems, realizing the special guidance values of his subject, developing out-of-class contacts, referring students to other sources of help, and exerting a wholesome influence on the school and community environment.

Guidance through Personal Relations

There are many ways in which classroom teachers can meet the emotional needs of young people. Pupils want teachers who treat them consistently,who are not changeable and unreasonable; who expect the best of them and look for the good in them rather than focusing attention on the wrong things they do; who build up their self-esteem rather than increasing their sense of failure and discouragement through critical or sarcastic remarks. They want teachers who listen, who see the pupil's point of view, who are "human," who keep abreast of the times, and who will admit that they have made a mistake. Most of all, they want teachers who understand them. In many schools present conditions are far from ideal. One boy commented on a situation that commonly exists: "In my school there are only two teachers of the seven that I have who know me by name. All they know us by is the card in their rollbook and what our marks are. Some of the teachers just don't care."

An ideal teacher-pupil relationship was described by a gifted high-school girl:

Miss A——— had the ability to develop every bit of innate talent, which I never suspected was there or which I was too lazy to cultivate by myself. . . . Often there are things which one finds hard even to confide to one's parents, and when questions like this arise I know this teacher has probably erased the same

---

[7] Arthur E. Traxler, "Emerging Trends in Guidance," *School Review*, LVIII (January, 1950), 14–23.

worry from the minds of many others. . . . She has given me a completely new outlook on life. . . . She has a gift of putting people's minds at ease while making them think at the same time. No one in any of her classes has ever been embarrassed or bored.[8]

Guidance while Teaching

The gifted teacher is sensitive to the individual members of his class. To John, who was lacking in self-esteem, the teacher gave encouragement by saying casually, "A few minutes ago John made a very important point, which we should discuss further." To Bill, who was cocky and careless in his statements, the teacher gave practice in careful thinking by helping him work through the question step by step. When he had arrived at the correct answer, the teacher said, "There, we knew you could do it, if you stayed with it."

Even in a large class it is possible to guide individual pupils as an intrinsic part of the teaching process, not only in their learning of school subjects but also in other aspects of their personal development. To do this requires an understanding of individuals, sensitivity to their needs at the moment, and resourcefulness in providing the experiences they need. Among these experiences are differentiated assignments, reading material that is on their level of comprehension, opportunities to work together in small congenial groups, and a chance to develop special interests and abilities and to use them for the good of the group.

Group Discussion of Common Problems

In various ways the teacher becomes aware of the common problems which his students are facing. Some normally come up in the discussion of the subject—juvenile delinquency in a social-studies class, or difficulties in family relations in a home-economics class. Other common difficulties, such as health deficiency and boy-girl relations, may be observed in any informal class. Compositions, as we have already suggested, may reveal adolescents' difficulties in moving toward maturity. When the teacher of any subject recognizes these needs and a general readiness for group guidance, he may well use class time for this purpose.

Various methods of group guidance may be used: the informal class discussion, the small problem-solving group which offers maximum opportunity for active participation by every member,[9] and the sociodrama, which has been used very effectively in English and social-studies classes.

---

[8] *The Gifted Child*, pp. 111–12. Edited by Paul Witty. Boston: D. C. Heath & Co., 1951.

[9] Herbert A. Thelen, "Group Dynamics in Instruction: Principle of Least Group Size," *School Review*, LVII (March, 1949), 139.

Guidance through the Content of Each Subject

As the curriculum is organized at present in the majority of secondary schools, each subject has special guidance value. For example, students may apply the scientific method to the solving of life problems. Gaining skill in sports may facilitate social adjustment. Much of the content of home economics can be used to improve health and personal appearance. In the study of literature, young people may gain insight into why they behave as they do and how other people may be feeling when they act in certain ways. In the social studies, they can learn how the present grew out of the past and can gain at least a little sense of direction in moving toward what seems to be an uncertain and ominous future. By studying the human relations in history, they may understand the influence of certain personalities on world events. Health education should help youth meet their personal health needs and make their local community a more healthful place for young and old. Music, fine arts, and all the practical arts and crafts have special therapeutic value in providing creative outlets for the psychological energy and pent-up feelings of adolescents. The knowledge and skill gained in every subject may be applied to individual needs.

Guidance through Contacts Outside of Class

One study showed that a group of teachers averaged thirty talk-contacts a week with individual pupils. To be sure, such contacts are short, but they may be very helpful if considered as part of the whole guidance process. Certainly the quality of these short contacts can be greatly improved. Following is a transcript of one of these five-minute interviews:

TEACHER: Will you tell me something of your high-school experience, mentioning especially how the school can help you?

ALBERT: There's nothing I care about. All I want is to get out and get a job. But I'm only fifteen. I have to wait another year.

TEACHER: You want to leave school now?

ALBERT: Yes, I don't like school, especially business training. It's mostly spelling, and I'm poor in writing and spelling. The teacher doesn't help, and I haven't asked.

TEACHER: Why not?

ALBERT: She thinks I can't do it, and I guess I can't.

TEACHER: What do you do outside of school?

ALBERT: My mother works, so I have to go home after school and take care of the house.

TEACHER: Do you belong to any clubs?

ALBERT: I belong to the patrol boys. I like it. I can't belong to the others because of the housework.

TEACHER: How do you get along with the reading?

ALBERT: I can read, but it's the words I can't pronounce. I read books outside sometimes—Boy Scout books. I take books from the library sometimes.

TEACHER: Have you gone to any parties in the school?

ALBERT: Went to two dances.

TEACHER: Do you know what you would like to do when you leave school?

ALBERT: I want to be an electrician. I don't see the use of the subjects I'm taking.

In this short contact, if the teacher had had more time and the boy had been ready to talk more freely, the teacher might have helped him gain insight into his dissatisfaction with school. Then they would have had a better basis for planning to make better use of his remaining required year in school. As it was, the teacher at least learned more about his attitude toward school, his home duties, his reading interests, and his desire for recreation with boys and girls of his own age. With this information, the teacher was in a better position to understand his school behavior and to try to provide in school more of the experiences he needed.

Co-operation with Other Members of the Staff

As the teacher works with guidance specialists on individual cases and participates in case conferences, he both contributes and learns. The case conference is a study group comprising the school principal, the nurse, any guidance specialists who may be available, and teachers who know the youth in question. Provision of time for these case conferences is the biggest problem. Some schools have used an unassigned period at the beginning or at the end of the school day, when teachers are expected to be at the school but have no scheduled classes. Other schools have used the lunch period, and, still others, the hour after lunch when a recreation or visual-aid program requires the supervision of very few teachers. The teacher-counselor presents all the information about the pupil which he has been able to collect; the others present the concrete information which they have obtained; all try to understand the pupil as a person and to determine what they can do to help him. The case conference not only helps everyone in contact with the subject to take a more understanding attitude toward him but also helps those present gain a deeper understanding of all young people and even of themselves and other adults.

The teacher should also use his understanding of youth in policy-making. No one knows better than the teacher what kinds of school experiences they need. He will have suggestions for curriculum modifications and for administrative changes to meet the needs of youth whom he has observed and tried to guide He should have opportunity to explain their need for guidance as he sees it and to recommend the specialized services which he thinks are necessary to round out his own guidance work.

Referral for Other Guidance Services

It is important for the classroom teacher to identify the young people who need more help than he has the time or skill to give. He should be prompt to recognize such signs of deep-seated and pervasive emotional disturbance as prolonged depression and unhappiness, withdrawal from social contacts, and "queer" or compulsive behavior.

If the teacher has a good relation with an individual pupil and is working with him successfully, he may become the teacher-counselor for this pupil. If the pupil needs more expert guidance than the teacher can give, the teacher's task is to prepare him for referral, talk with the person in the school responsible for referring cases for special help, and make an appointment for the pupil with this person. A skilful referral paves the way for successful treatment.

CONTRIBUTION OF THE TEACHER-COUNSELOR

Since it is impossible for any teacher in a departmentalized program to know intimately each of the pupils in all his classes, a small guidance unit is essential. The small guidance unit of about thirty pupils may take the form of a homeroom, core-curriculum group, life-adjustment class, extended period, or other type of organization. All these forms are characterized by the same objective—that every pupil should have someone who knows him as a whole and serves as his counselor. The teacher-counselor helps to meet the needs of these pupils both individually and through the group experience.

Gaining an Understanding of Each Pupil

Most of the teacher-counselor's understanding of his pupils is obtained in the informal group situation: He observes their behavior; listens to their discussions and conversations; studies their answers to questions about their interests, home backgrounds, relations with others; reads their autobiographical compositions and statements of their goals and purpose. He obtains additional information from interviews and home visits.

As the pivotal person in the guidance program, the teacher-counselor would naturally be responsible for the cumulative pupil-personnel records. He would help to develop the record form most convenient and useful; write in the quantitative information on marks, tests, and activities as he obtains it; collect and periodically summarize anecdotal records, reports of interviews and home visits, letters written about the pupil, statements of plans and goals written by the pupil, and other kinds of information about each of his counselees. These cumulative records should be kept in a place convenient to the teacher-counselor—either in his official room or in files in a centrally located office. The teacher-counselor obtains help from a guidance specialist, if one is available, in making a periodic summary of the records of each of his counselees. He uses the cumulative records as a means to an end—the pupil's better adjustment —not as an end in themselves.

Counseling Individual Pupils

The teacher-counselor's interviewing time is limited, and provision for privacy is often lacking. Many interviews have to be held in the guidance period while pupils are working independently or in committees. Sometimes the teacher-counselor holds longer interviews in his free period or after school. In these interviews a teacher-counselor can help each pupil build a clearer idea of his most acceptable self and of his relations with other persons. He should also be skilful in interviewing students regarding their educational plans, reading and study difficulties, and normal adolescent social and emotional problems of growing up. Skill in interviewing means willingness to listen sympathetically, desire to understand, ability to recognize cues that should be picked up and followed through, and self-control to resist the common tendencies to probe or pry, to tell what he thinks the pupil should do, and to jump to conclusions without adequate understanding of the pupil and his environment. Pupils very much need this kind of counseling interview.

Conferring with Parents

Despite the importance of contacts with parents, the teacher-counselor cannot be expected to have many interviews with parents or to make many home visits. However, he can make every contact count. As in interviews with pupils, he should realize that a friendly relationship is basic to everything else. He should be accepting, understanding, and sincere; he should make interpretations and give suggestions only as the parent is ready for them and needs them to think through the situation.

In the case of an adolescent who is struggling to gain psychological independence from the family, the teacher-counselor should guard against destroying a good relation with the pupil by seeming to ally himself with the parent. If there is danger of this, it would be better for another person to talk with the parent. The teacher-counselor may encourage the formation of child study groups in which parents may gain insight into the behavior of their adolescent children or, as one parent said, "at least recognize that they have a right to be understood."

Guidance through the Group

The teacher-counselor who meets his counselees daily not only in a special homeroom or guidance period but also in his other classes has a great advantage over the counselor who has free periods to see pupils individually but never meets his counselees as a group. Groups of Freshmen, for example, can learn about their new school, take tours of the building, interview "people of importance," learn about the extraclass activities, discuss the reasons for the rules and regulations in the handbook, become acquainted with the school and community resources which can help them succeed in high school.

In the group, the teacher-counselor can impart information about educational and vocational opportunities economically and vividly through the use of pamphlets, visual aids, and committee reports. Even a group discussion of individual educational and vocational plans may be of value to all the pupils, as well as of special help to the pupils whose plans are being discussed.

Guidance in human relations takes place in the process of living together. The learnings that result from working together in committees, from solving practical personal and school problems, and from engaging in service activities can be achieved in no other way. The role of the teacher-counselor is to recognize the group's needs; to help them observe, evaluate, and improve the group process; and to try to insure satisfaction for all in the group's success.

Group learnings may be reinforced by the discussion of cases representing common problems, by films such as some of the Coronet or McGraw-Hill series for high schools, and by mental-hygiene plays such as *The Ins and Outs*,[10] or by guidance plays such as "The Actor."[11] Equally effective are sociodramas based on situations described by pupils in the group.

These and other special techniques such as the sociometric test, question box, incomplete sentence or incomplete story may disclose common problems and help to meet young people's need to understand themselves, their social relations, and their changing world.

All of these group procedures require skilful leadership. The teacher-counselor should not be expected to be an expert in all of them. Gradually, however, he will become more and more skilful as he studies this field and learns from the group itself.

---

[10] Nora Sibling, *The Ins and Outs*. New York 19: New York Committee on Mental Hygiene of the State Charities Aid Association in association with the National Committee for Mental Hygiene (1790 Broadway).

[11] M. Jerry Weiss, "The Actor," *Journal of the National Association of Deans of Women*, XV (October, 1951), 16–31.

Contribution of the Club Sponsor

In follow-up studies and on questionnaires answered while still in school, pupils give a prominent place to the extraclass program. Many value these activities more highly than their regular classes. Their suggestions for the improvement of guidance through informal groups are sound. They want club leaders who give members of the group responsibility for planning and carrying out plans; who suggest ideas, as consultants and resources, but do not dominate; who are concerned with the best development of every member of the group and help members work together in flexible subgroups, not always with the same group or clique. Members of the student council want to know in what areas they can make decisions and carry out plans and in what areas they may serve only in an advisory capacity. They would like to think things through and plan with the sponsor and the principal from the beginning—not go ahead on their own and then have their plans arbitrarily vetoed. Establishing constructive, friendly relationships with pupils is often less difficult for the club sponsor than for the classroom teacher. Some of the most important guidance of individuals has been done through this relationship.[12]

Group activities meet many adolescent needs. They learn to state and clarify a problem, suggest and evaluate solutions, make and carry out a plan of action. They learn how to work together toward a common goal and to get personal satisfaction from the success of the group. Their personal development is also furthered through the opportunity to build special skills and to use them in the service of the group. For example, pupils have made progress in music as a result of being in the school orchestra or band; they have developed interest and aptitude in science through the science club.

The club sponsor is also alert to use the opportunities for guidance offered by school and community services. This involves maintaining close relations with other members of the staff and possibly with a community council, interclub council, or advisory committee of faculty and students.

Contribution of the Administrator

The administrator holds a key position of leadership. From the pupils' standpoint, the principal should be friendly and interested. The replies of high-school pupils to the question, "How can the principal meet students' needs?" suggested that the principal may make these contributions to the guidance program:

---

[12] See Chap. ix for a much fuller treatment of extraclass activities.

Suggestions to Principal	No. of Pupils Responding
Show more interest and friendliness toward individuals	101
Encourage student activities	27
Plan better assemblies	14
Arrange more interviews	14
Bring faculty and students together	9

These contributions to the guidance program in a high school can be most clearly seen in the day-by-day account of how one principal co-operatively developed a guidance program.[13] It was an up-hill job to get effective guidance started in a run-down school. For the principal himself, it was a growth experience. The courses in guidance and secondary education which he took each summer increased his understanding of the needs of the situation and acquainted him with procedures to use. In the beginning the school was so dirty and poorly equipped that immediate attention had to be given to this aspect. Pupils worked with the principal in cleaning, redecorating, painting a mural, and beautifying the school grounds. As the teachers gradually changed their attitude toward pupils, corporal punishment was no longer used and the detention room was discontinued. As pupil needs were more clearly recognized, better shopwork was offered, and attention was given to the solution of real health problems. Most important was the principal's relationship with his staff. Through casual contacts and longer interviews, committee work, case conferences, study groups, and faculty meetings, the principal created the feeling that they all had a vital part in a going concern.

The limited time for faculty meetings was spent in discussion of immediate guidance problems such as how to improve the homeroom period, how to understand and treat troublesome pupils, how to use test results and cumulative records. Role-playing and films were introduced in the discussion. Gradually the teachers' attitudes began to change; they began to look at their pupils with more sympathy and understanding. Through the student council, pupils were given opportunity to use initiative and to take responsibility. The role of the principal was to recognize and use the resources in the pupils, teachers, and members of the community. The result was a guidance program that grew as everyone concerned developed personally and professionally.

CONTRIBUTION OF THE SPECIALIST

Since most of the teachers now in service and many prospective teachers are poorly prepared for their guidance responsibilities, they need the help of more expert persons—well-qualified counselors, deans, psycholo-

---

[13] Glyn Morris, *Practical Guidance Methods for Principals and Teachers.* New York: Harper & Bros., 1952.

gists, school social workers, psychiatrists, and medical personnel. This technical leadership may be provided in each high school by its own staff, in the school system through a guidance department or bureau of child guidance, in the county by the supervisor of guidance, or in the state department through its special services. Placement of the specialist is determined by the size of the school or school system and the demand for this service by the staff and the community.

There are many ways in which the guidance specialist can help teachers improve their counseling and group work:

1. Working with teachers on individual cases
2. Holding case conferences
3. Encouraging the formation of groups of teachers for child study
4. Providing information on educational and vocational opportunities, on personal appearance and other aspects of personality development
5. Assisting the teacher-counselor to make a periodic synthesis of the information in the cumulative record folders of his counselees
6. Conducting institutes, workshops, seminars, or faculty meetings on practical aspects of guidance, using demonstrations, dramatizations, sociodrama or role-playing, small group discussions, committee work, guidance films, and panel discussions by pupils and parents
7. Serving on policy-making committees with teachers and administrators, and applying the guidance point of view to problems of administration, instruction, and the curriculum.

Working Together To Meet the Needs of Youth

Co-ordination of the individual's education is best achieved when the person who serves as his counselor keeps his cumulative record up to date, periodically summarizes the information in it, and takes responsibility for seeing that the pupil gets the experiences and special help that he needs. In most instances this person will be the teacher-counselor; in other instances, it may be a teacher with whom the pupil has an especially fine relation, the principal or vice principal, or the full-time guidance worker. The important thing is that the designated person be recognized as the pupil's counselor and that all important information and recommendations be cleared through him.

Co-ordination of the school staff is facilitated in many ways. A physical plant provides contiguous health, guidance, and administrative offices and adequate files and interviewing rooms. The teacher-counselor should also have an opportunity to present some or all of his counselees for discussion in case conferences. In one school this was done in a guidance council of about fifteen teachers representing all departments of the school. They met once a month to prevent problems from arising, to deal with present difficulties, and to make the changes in school policy and procedures which were indicated by study of individual pupils. The high-school principal served as chairman of the council, which also included an elementary-school principal and guidance specialists of the school system. Other aids to co-ordination include forms for the convenient exchange of information about pupils, news letters or bulletins that bring information about different aspects of the problem to all members of the staff, and the methods of in-service education already mentioned. The development of a common philosophy and guidance point of view in the staff as a whole is the best basis of all for co-ordination.

Co-ordination of school and community agencies is achieved by similar methods. Guidance of young people can be promoted by a community council or a council of youth-serving agencies which includes representatives from the school. The method by which this co-operative action is secured largely determines its success.

EVALUATION OF GUIDANCE OF YOUNG PEOPLE

The results of guidance can never be fully evaluated. Changes in the individual's idea of himself may not become evident in his behavior until some time after graduation. Many of the criteria of successful adjustment elude measurement. Nevertheless, all the members of the school staff should continuously try to see whether they are moving toward the goals of guidance.

Several kinds of evidence may be collected. The first is evidence of change of attitude and point of view on the part of the school staff. This may be noted in the remarks which teachers make about the pupils in group meetings and in individual conferences. Do teachers show more desire to understand the pupils, to look for the good in them, to view their behavior as caused?

Evidences of changes in groups may also be observed: Does the chairman or leader of the group help the members to learn to work together? Does he listen more? Is there more general participation by all the members? Are they more successful in stating and accomplishing group purposes? Is there active participation by all through committees and other subgroups? Does every member of the group grow as a result of the group experience?

Pupils' growth may best be noted in the cumulative record or the case study. From these records changes in scholastic achievement, extraclass activities, goals and purposes, social relations, and other aspects of adolescent development may be summarized and related to the guidance procedures. The case-study approach to the evaluation of guidance is direct and sound; it uses the same techniques and data as the guidance program itself.

Another kind of evidence is to be found in the opinions of the recipients of the service—the pupils themselves. In surveys of guidance in secondary schools the pupils have been asked to answer anonymously such questions as the following:

How did you come to take the subjects you are now taking? Did anyone help you? If so, who helped you? What kind of help did you get? What kind of help did you want? (Similar questions are asked with respect to further educational plans and choice of vocation.)

What sort of things would you like to talk over with an older person? Have you talked about these things with anyone in school? What have you liked about the talks you have had with teachers or other persons in the school? How could they be made more helpful?

What have you liked about the clubs or activities to which you belong? What have you disliked? How could they be made better?

If you were a teacher what would you do to help pupils make the most of themselves?

Follow-up studies of drop-outs and graduates give valuable opinions about the way in which the guidance program is functioning in the lives of the pupils after they have left school.

PREPARATION FOR GUIDANCE RESPONSIBILITIES

The effectiveness of guidance in the future depends a great deal on the institutions for the education of teachers. Since effective guidance depends so largely on the personality of the administrator, the teacher, and the counselor, the first task of the teachers' college is the personality development of the students selectively admitted. Every student in a teachers' college would probably benefit by at least fifty hours of expert counseling during his four years of study. The second task of the teachers' college is to build understanding of children and young people through observation and through child study groups and classes. Its third responsibility is to help students see the guidance program as a whole and become conscious of the way in which every member of the school staff contributes to it. In this introductory guidance course students should also begin to acquire skill in the guidance techniques they will use as teachers, teacher-counselors, and club sponsors. Finally, in the course of their practice teaching they should have practice in guidance. They should learn (*a*) to recognize and use opportunities for guidance while teaching, (*b*) to observe significant behavior and record it objectively, (*c*) to keep, interpret, and use cumulative records, (*d*) to recognize cases of serious maladjustment and learn how to refer them for more expert help, (*e*) to make the best use of short contacts with students and parents, (*f*) to improve the quality of discussions and committee work, and (*g*) to work together with other members of the school staff and of the community.

CONCLUDING STATEMENT

The central need of adolescents is to grow toward maturity in their own best way. Other needs stem from this. To meet this need, guidance procedures in the context of the total educational program should be provided.

Through counseling, testing, and guided group experience, the individual gains understanding of himself and his relations with others in this changing world. This understanding leads to the making of realistic plans and the learning of techniques for meeting life situations.

Through his own initiative and the resources within himself, aided by the unified efforts of all members of the school staff, every pupil can develop his best potentialities. Guidance services are not just for the "problem cases" or those who are going to college.

Essentials of the guidance process are respect for every person, sensitivity to how he is thinking and feeling, a positive attitude with attention focused on his assets, encouragement to take initiative and responsibility and to be self-directive. Some control of the environment is usually indicated. Adjusting the environment to the needs of the individual may take many forms, such as modification of the school program, interviews with parents, membership in a congenial group, opportunities for service through which he gains a sense of worth and belonging. This is developmental guidance.

In some cases remedial guidance is needed. Seriously disturbed adolescents need more intensive and expert counseling and psychotherapy. This service should be available in each high school. In rural communities a county guidance service or a full-time worker serving several high schools helps meet the needs of indivduals who have not learned to deal with reality in constructive ways.

The end results of effective guidance are persons who can and will use their abilities to serve society and who can and will attain happiness through the realization of their best potentialities.

SECTION III

PROBLEMS OF THE CLASSROOM TEACHER

CHAPTER XII

TRANSLATING YOUTH NEEDS INTO TEACHING GOALS

RALPH W. TYLER

Dean, Division of Social Sciences
University of Chicago
Chicago, Illinois

PURPOSE OF THE CHAPTER

The previous chapters have dealt with the problems of adapting the secondary school to the needs of American youth at the level of planning the over-all design of school programs. This chapter and the two following are directed to the work of the classroom teacher in carrying out such a program.

The classroom teacher, in the last analysis, plans and guides the learning experiences of students. Even when the needs of youth have been identified by the school and an over-all school program has been designed to meet such recognized needs, unless the teaching program is also worked out in these terms, the school does not meet the requirements of youth needs. The identification of the needs of youth can provide only material with which the teacher can work, while a design for the school program can furnish only a structure which facilitates more effective teaching. To attain in fact a curriculum which helps meet the needs of youth, the teacher must employ his knowledge of youth needs in an appropriate fashion and use the design of the school program in a way to contribute to this end in his own teaching. The purpose, then, of this chapter is to suggest how the classroom teacher may utilize data regarding the needs of his students so as to define appropriate and significant goals for teaching, that is, to formulate statements of desired behavior patterns which students may be helped to develop.

How TEACHING MEETS THE NEEDS OF YOUTH

The function of the school is not to meet student needs directly. It is quite clear, for example, that American schools are not set up in order to give students food, shelter, love, friendships, and the like. These are among the basic needs of youth, and the school is able to help its students meet these needs, but not by giving specific suggestions directly to the students. Instead, the function of the school is to educate students in such a way that they themselves are better able to meet their own needs. That is to say, the school as an educative agency has the responsibility of helping students acquire those patterns of behavior which assist them in meeting all of their basic needs. Using the illustration of the need for food as an example, although the school's role is not to give students food, the school can help students meet their needs for food in a variety of ways. The school may help students develop the competencies required to earn a living and, thus, to assure the financial resources for obtaining food. The school can help young people understand principles of nutrition and, thus, be able to select, prepare, and utilize food more wisely. The school can help young people develop a constructive attitude toward food, so that they are not subject to the restrictions of dietary practices which are harmful, nor are they an easy prey to new food fads which develop from time to time. In other words, the function of the school is to help learners change their own behavior patterns, that is, acquire understanding, skills, habits, attitudes, interests, and ways of thinking which are important constructive resources enabling them to meet their need for food.

In a similar fashion, it is easy to see that the function of the school is not primarily to provide love and friendship to students, but to enable them to meet their own need for love or friendship by helping them acquire those patterns of behavior which facilitate the meeting of this need. For example, when the school helps students develop a more adequate understanding of human relations, the ability to enter sympathetically into the lives of other people, a sensitivity to the concerns, hopes, and aspirations of others, skill in communicating informally and intimately with others, or a range of interests which can be shared with other people, then the school is enabling its students to acquire the resources by which they can effectively meet their need for love and friendship.

Since the role of the school is not to meet the needs of youth directly, but indirectly through helping them acquire understanding, ways of thinking, attitudes, interests, appreciations, skills, abilities, and habits, which are useful in meeting these needs, it is necessary to translate information about the needs of students into teaching goals which represent the patterns of behavior by which the students can meet their own needs more effectively.

How the Teacher Guides Learning

In suggesting procedures by which the classroom teacher may utilize knowledge of student needs and translate them into teaching goals, some attention should be given to the general picture of the way in which the teacher carries on teaching activities. Teaching is commonly viewed today as a purposeful activity guided by general principles of learning toward goals which have been selected because of their significance to the students being taught. The teacher is not viewed as one who slavishly follows a textbook or a course of study without adaptation and without clear understanding of basic purposes. Instead of following a rigid outline and set of procedures, the teacher is guided by a conception of the educative process which provides general direction for his work. A common way of thinking about the educative process is in terms of objectives, of learning experiences that are organized so as to maximize their effect on the learner, and of evaluation procedures which provide a continuing check on the adequacy of the educative process. In these terms, the teacher's work is guided by his conception of the objectives, that is, the patterns of behavior which he seeks to help students acquire. He utilizes learning experiences as the means by which students may acquire those desired patterns of behavior. The learning experiences are chosen because they provide an opportunity for the students to practice the desired behavior patterns and because they are of such interest and meaning that the students participate in them actively, with interest and with increasing understanding of their significance.

The teacher is also conscious of the importance of organizing these learning experiences, seeking to arrange them in such fashion that the experiences of today build upon those of yesterday and those of tomorrow will build upon those of today, thus providing a sequence of learning which contributes to the broadening and deepening of the student's understanding, attitudes, and skills. The teacher also seeks to arrange learning experiences in such a way that what goes on in his classroom has some relationship to the experiences the student is having in other classes and in life outside the school. This integration of learning experiences also helps, as does the sequential organization of them, to increase the cumulative effect of learning and to maximize the results achieved.

Because the teacher is not following slavishly a course of study outline or a textbook, flexibility is possible. He is not without direction. He is guided by his conception of teaching goals and by his understanding of the conditions under which effective learning takes place. He is conscious, however, of the wide range of individual differences in his students and of the fact that the experiences students are having cannot be completely determined from the teacher's control of the external environment. The student brings his own feelings, his past experiences, his knowledge, his background of abilities and interests to the learning experiences of the class. These individual backgrounds and predispositions make the actual experience each student is having different in some respects from that which is being had by other members of the class. As a result, the teacher realizes that he cannot predict with great precision the results of the learning experiences which he has helped to initiate. Hence, he seeks continuously to appraise the effects of learning in his classes, seeking to find out what changes are actually taking place in the students' ways of behaving, that is, in their understanding, attitudes, skills, and the like. To such a teacher, evaluation is a continuous process which uses a variety of appropriate means such as observation, tests, interviews, informal discussion, and examples of products made. Through his conception of teaching goals, his knowledge of how learning takes place, and his continuing evaluation, he can give necessary direction to learning yet retain considerable flexibility in his teaching.

Two Kinds of Youth Needs

This brief explanation of one of the common ways of thinking about the educative process is outlined here in order to indicate the way in which the needs of students enter into the planning and conduct of the work of the classroom teacher. Knowledge of the needs of youth is of great value in choosing educational objectives or teaching goals, in planning learning experiences, in developing an effective organization of these experiences, and in evaluating the effectiveness of the educational program. However, as was pointed out in chapter ii, the concept of student needs includes two types: those representing the active and, in many cases, conscious efforts of students; and those which grow out of the expectations and requirements which modern society places upon its members. The twofold nature of needs, that is, those derived from the drives and tensions of the adolescent and those derived from the demands of society, may be a confusing rather than a clarifying notion for the teacher. On the one hand, where the student is conscious of his need, this concern provides both motivation for learning and an assurance of continuing practice of the learning behavior, so that it becomes a fairly permanent educational achievement, while, on the other hand, the needs of youth which are not now sensed by youth but are demands of society must be considered carefully to identify other sources of motivation and appropriate opportunities for current use if the learning is to be effective.

For the first type of needs, that is, needs growing out of the drives and tensions of the student, there are several implications for the classroom teacher. In the first place, to focus teaching attention upon those behavior patterns which help the student to resolve his tensions and to satisfy his drives means that the classroom learning experiences are not in continuing conflict with the persistent concerns of the students. Instead of the student being distracted from the classroom experiences by his worry over getting a date or being accepted by his classmates or some other need of this sort, the classroom experience itself utilizes such concerns and makes them an integral part of the learning experiences.

In the second place, objectives derived from a study of student needs do not have to be justified by some long chain of reasoning to relate the classroom activities to some deferred values of adult life. The meaning of these objectives and their significance to the student are easily seen, and they give the teacher a clearer notion of the functional value of what he is teaching.

A third implication of this type of student needs in the work of the classroom teacher is the increased likelihood that there will be a great deal of carry-over from what is learned in school to actual application in life outside of school, because the areas of life in which the learning is to be used are involved in the actual learning experiences and the student is under a certain degree of tension to meet his needs and to use what he is learning in school to satisfy needs outside of school. This is an important value because of the great waste of school learning when there is little carry-over and youth in school acquire knowledge, attitudes, skills, and the like, which are not utilized widely in life outside.

The other type of needs, those that are derived from the demands of society upon the individual, are not so easily motivated and require more planning with regard to the readiness of students for learning experiences related to some of these needs, more experimentation in identifying sources of motivation, and considerable resourcefulness in providing suggestions for ways of continuing to use, in the lives of youth outside of school, that which is learned in school. In other words, the use of the second type of need, without such planning, may result in a course which has some of the characteristics of the often criticized teaching which was planned for the future without reference to any explicit study of students and society. However, since these are real needs which are now being experienced or will be faced by students in our society, their functional value can be seen, and it is possible to help youth understand and appreciate their importance as well. Nevertheless, the classroom teacher needs to recognize the differences between needs derived from these two sources because of the differences in the planning they may require.

PROCEDURE FOR TRANSLATING NEEDS INTO TEACHING GOALS

In translating needs of either type into teaching goals, the following generalizations are useful in guiding the procedure: (*a*) Youth needs imply educational goals when youth is not able to meet the needs satisfactorily without developing new patterns of behavior. If youth is able to meet his needs without further learning, then such needs do not suggest significant teaching goals. (*b*) Teaching goals can be derived from the needs of youth by identifying the patterns of behavior which will help students meet these needs. (*c*) The patterns of behavior thus identified are appropriate teaching goals if they are consistent with the educational philosophy of the school and are capable of being learned in the school. These generalizations provide a basis for outlining procedures that can be followed by the classroom teacher in translating needs of youth into teaching goals.

The teacher's first step in this procedure is to assemble the information about the needs of the youth in his classes. As suggested in chapter ii, some of this information will have been derived from studies of large groups of young people, and they will suggest needs which are characteristic of most, if not all, American youth. Others will have involved studies of young people in the teacher's own school and perhaps still others will have been data collected by the teacher regarding the students in his own classes. These data will indicate needs of students, some of which are common to all or most all young people, some of which are common to certain groups only, such as male youth in contrast to female youth, and some of which will be characteristic only of the particular students in the particular classes taught by this teacher.

In the second place, the teacher will need to assemble studies regarding the needs of students that have been made by examining our society and identifying the demands and expectations which society makes of young people. These will probably be more general needs and less highly individualized than in the case of the first group obtained from studies of students themselves, but there are differences from one part of the country to another and from rural to urban life and from one social or ethnic group to another which are worthy of consideration.

With such statements of youth needs before him, the teacher considers each need in turn as well as groups of needs, seeking first to identify needs which his students are already able to meet satisfactorily without further education or learning. In his community, for example, it may very well be that high-school students are already well equipped to meet the need for food, or perhaps it will be apparent that his students are having no difficulty in meeting the need for friendship and for acceptance by members of both sexes. If he finds any needs which are being adequately met or which the students are able to care for without additional education, these are eliminated from further consideration in setting teaching goals.

For those needs which remain, that is, those which students have difficulty in meeting without further education, the teacher considers next what patterns of behavior could be developed by students which would help them meet these needs. Such patterns of behavior, if appropriate for his teaching goals, will need to be in harmony with the school's philosophy and relevant to the field in which he teaches, that is, patterns of behavior which are desirable and can be learned in this field and in the high school.

An Illustration of Procedure in Relating Teaching
Goals to Student Needs

To illustrate this step, suppose the need under consideration were one of those cited in chapter ii and obtained from Havighurst's list of "developmental tasks of adolescence," namely, "achieving emotional independence of parents and other adults." Let us suppose that in a middle-class suburban community the students are having considerable difficulty in achieving emotional independence from parents. Few students have jobs, and the parents set up fairly strict codes of conduct to guide the high-school students in their behavior. Let us suppose, too, that the teacher examining this need is a teacher of English in the eleventh grade. He begins to list behavior patterns which, if acquired, would help students in achieving this emotional independence of parents and other adults. He includes the following in his list: ability to take responsibility for significant group activity, attitude of confidence in participating in activities involving both youth and adults, an understanding of the changing conditions of family life, an objective attitude toward his own tendency to vacillate between dependence on parents and efforts to achieve complete independence, an understanding of the probable stages through which he will pass in going on from high school until he becomes a responsible head of a new family. These behavior patterns would be helpful to students who are striving to achieve emotional independence from parents and other adults, and they are in harmony with the philosophy of the school in which he is teaching, a philosophy which places a great deal of emphasis upon intelligent behavior, upon understanding rather than blind obedience, upon the development of a democratic society in which members are able to solve problems for themselves. The philosophy of his school also holds that thought, feeling, and action are all significant aspects of human behavior and that the school has the responsibility of developing students who are able to guide feeling and action by intelligent understanding.

These suggested behavior patterns are also in harmony with what the teacher knows about the psychology of learning. He knows that students can learn new attitudes and points of view; they can develop a broader and deeper understanding; they can acquire increasing skill and ability in planning and conducting activities. In checking these possible behavior patterns against other factors involved in learning, he recognizes that these are behavior patterns which have not yet been acquired but for which there is readiness because of the students' concern about emotional independence from adults. He recognizes that time can be made available for his classes to make progress toward such teaching goals. He recognizes that there is sufficient freedom in his classroom to plan learning activities in which students will take a good deal of responsibility so that there will be opportunity for them to carry on the activities implied by these objectives.

Next, the teacher checks these suggested behavior patterns against his conception of what is involved in the field of English. In his school, English is defined as including all four aspects of communication, namely, reading, writing, speaking, and listening. He sees the possibility of selecting reading material of good literary quality which would help young people understand more adequately the urge they have for emotional independence as well as the attitudes of parents toward the independence of their children. He sees also the possibility in the field of English to work out a dramatic presentation of some material relating to emotional independence, either something already written, such as a cutting from Booth Tarkington's *Alice Adams*, or having students write an original script which might serve to dramatize the feelings and issues involved and at the same time give students in the planning, staging, and performing of the play a great deal of responsibility for managing the details themselves and for arranging with the various school people and community representatives to bring the play to the attention of an adult group. In this way, the teacher satisfies himself that he can properly, in the field of English, make a contribution to meeting this need for achieving emotional independence from parents and other adults through aiming at the teaching goals suggested and by using the study of English as an appropriate field in which such objectives may be emphasized. Finally, he checks these teaching goals against the general outline of curriculum sequence in the school to see that they are in harmony with the plan for sequential development.

This illustration indicates the primary steps involved in translating student needs into teaching goals. These needs do not automatically give rise to suggested teaching goals. They require careful consideration by the teacher, who must infer from his understanding of the needs and his understanding of the learning possibilities of his own field the types of teaching goals that can appropriately be provided in his classroom to help students meet the needs that have been identified. In this sense, translating needs into teaching goals is a creative process.

Teaching Goals Involve Both Behavior and Content

The foregoing illustration may also have indicated certain other points in the procedure. A teaching goal which is really helpful to the teacher in guiding the selection of learning experiences, in planning the organization of these learning experiences, and in giving a basis for evaluation, is a goal which indicates both the kind of behavior which the student is being helped to acquire and also the content with which this behavior deals. In the illustration above, several kinds of behavior were suggested as important in helping students achieve emotional independence from parents and other adults. One kind of behavior involves such activities as perceiving ideas, recognizing their relationship to his own experience, being able to compare and contrast related ideas, stating them in his own words, and the like. This behavior, often called understanding, is an important kind of behavior in intelligent action because action guided by intelligence is action guided by understanding of the situation and of the consequences of particular behavior. Hence, the development of understanding is a significant kind of behavior to achieve in connection with the meeting of many needs of youth.

A second kind of behavior mentioned in this illustration is that of attitudes. They represent ways of looking at things, beliefs, points of view, feelings about the significance of things, or feelings of attraction or aversion. In connection with the achieving of emotional independence from parents and other adults, the way students feel about their behavior and about the behavior of their parents and other adults, is very important. If they feel guilty about their efforts toward independence, this feeling restricts and inhibits the development of such an independent status. If they feel resentful toward their parents or other adults, that, too, is a factor which greatly hinders the effective meeting of this need. Hence, the emphasis upon developing an objective attitude and being able to enter sympathetically into the points of view of parents and other adults is an important one.

A third kind of behavior in the foregoing illustration is that of ability; actual competence in taking responsibility for significant group activity. There are many abilities, such as those of reading, writing, and the ability to communicate effectively in a social group, which are of great importance in meeting needs and which can be developed through education. This list of types of behavior does not exhaust the kinds of behavior which the teacher may set up as teaching goals, but it serves to illustrate what is meant in saying that every teaching goal involves some type of behavior to be developed.

On the other hand, none of these types of behavior develops in a vacuum. The student does not develop understanding apart from understanding something. The content of this behavior, namely, what he is learning to understand, is also an important part of the teaching goal. Hence, in the illustration above, several kinds of content were suggested as important for the student to understand. These were understanding changing conditions of family life and understanding the probable stages through which he will pass in going on from high school until he becomes a responsible head of a new family.

Correspondingly, attitudes are not developed apart from the content of these attitudes. Attitudes in this case include confidence in participating in activities involving both youth and adults, an objective attitude toward his own tendency to vacillate. This indicates the content of the attitudes sought. In the same way, every ability implies certain content. An ability suggested in the previous illustration was the ability to take responsibility for significant group activity. This implies content regarding the direction of group activities.

Summary of Procedure for Translating Needs into Teaching Goals

This illustration outlines the way in which a teacher may begin with a need of students and identify types of behavior patterns which, if acquired by the students, would help them meet this need. It indicates the way in which the behavior patterns suggested can be checked against such criteria as their consistency with the educational philosophy of the school, their appropriateness to the field of the teacher's work and to the maturity of the students involved, and the extent to which they could probably be attained under the conditions possible in the school. This illustration also shows how the desired behavior patterns can be stated so as to indicate the type of behavior to be developed and the kind of content which would be involved in it. The type of behavior is particularly useful in suggesting the sort of learning experiences needed since the learning experiences required to develop understanding will differ somewhat from the kind of learning experiences useful in developing attitudes or in developing skills or habits. On the other hand, the outline of content involved will indicate the content to be dealt with in connection with the learning experiences that can be selected and organized for this purpose. This, then, is the process by which the teacher can utilize knowledge regarding the needs of students in setting up possible teaching goals for his work.

Establishing Priority of Teaching Goals

As the teacher examines a number of possible youth needs, he is often able to suggest many more desirable patterns of behavior than he could possibly have time to develop. One of the common weaknesses of the secondary-school curriculum is the tendency to crowd it too full, that is, to aim at more goals than can reasonably be attained or that can be attained to a high enough level to provide some guarantee that what is learned will continue to be used in the subsequent lives of students. It is, therefore, important as one develops a list of possible teaching goals to arrange them in some priority of importance. A way of making this judgment is to consider the significance of the goal in the light of the school's educational philosophy. To illustrate the way in which the school's philosophy implies priority of importance, several matters commonly included in current educational philosophies can be listed. Great emphasis is currently given to the importance of developing youth who can solve new problems that arise, who can think clearly and critically, and who can deal understandingly and intelligently with the issues that come up in home, community, and work. Such an educational philosophy will give great priority to objectives having to do with understanding, problem-solving, and critical thinking.

Another current philosophical emphasis is upon wide participation on the part of students in the common activities and problems of mankind. This idea grows out of the importance in a democracy of getting wide and responsible participation of all people in the common life of the group. This philosophic emphasis will give considerable priority to those teaching goals which emphasize the attitudes, habits, and skills involved in effective group participation.

The philosophies of many schools also include a third major emphasis, namely, the importance of respect for human personality. Value is placed upon human beings regardless of their race and their economic, social, or cultural background. This philosophic emphasis would give priority to objectives which help young people develop attitudes of respect for the common man. Although these are only three of a larger number of issues commonly treated in a school's philosophy, they are probably sufficient to suggest the way in which the teacher may use the philosophy of the school in assigning priority to possible teaching goals. Additional illustrations may help to clarify the procedure of translating student needs into teaching goals in harmony with the purposes of the school.

Illustrations of Procedure in Selecting Teaching Goals That Conform to the Philosophy of the School

Another need mentioned in chapter ii and taken from Havighurst's list of "developmental tasks of adolescence" is that of "accepting one's physique and accepting a masculine or feminine role." A science teacher, in considering this type of student need, would probably suggest several behavior patterns which might be developed through science that would help students in meeting this kind of need. Understanding the growth processes of adolescence and the variety of individual growth patterns may help a student in accepting his individual physique and his particular role, either masculine or feminine. Such knowledge may help him understand that every youth passes through the adolescent growth cycle and help him realize that the marked changes in growth rate and the wide individual differences among youth are perfectly normal manifestations. Although science is not the only field which can contribute to an objective attitude toward physical growth and toward the differentiation of sex role, it is possible in science to make comparative studies among animal species and reduce the highly subjective feelings which young people often develop regarding growth changes in their own bodies. This will, of course, be supplemented by learning experiences in English and in other fields which can also contribute to the development of more objective attitudes in this area. In considering the importance of these objectives, the science teacher would probably note that they are in harmony with a school philosophy that places great emphasis upon understanding and critical thinking and would, therefore, be given priority among a group of possible teaching goals for science. A science teacher would also need to consider the appropriateness of the objective in terms of the previous experience of the students, their present readiness, and the way in which it fits into a sequential program of educational development. In terms of readiness, such teaching goals would be most appropriate in the early stages of the adolescent growth cycle around the later years of the junior high school. And if this were also in fair agreement with the general sequential organization of the secondary-school curriculum, it would seem that these teaching goals are worthy of emphasis in planning actual learning experiences in the junior high school science program.

Another illustration might be drawn from the need of youth to prepare for marriage and family life. A teacher of home economics considering this need is likely to recognize a number of possible teaching goals which could help students meet this need effectively. Among these would be an understanding of the changing role of the family in modern life, an understanding of the kinds of personal values and satisfactions to be obtained from marriage and family life, an understanding of some of the common problems of the modern family, interest in being an effective and constructive family member, an attitude of concern for the success of the family and for the happiness of individual family members, ability to carry on some of the common activities of family life, including such things as preparation of food, decoration and care of the home, family recreational activities, and the like. These teaching goals indicate both the kinds of behavior to be developed (understanding, interests, attitudes, and abilities) and the content appropriate for each of the types of behavior. In considering these possible goals in the light of the educational philosophy of the school, the home-economics teacher is likely to conclude that the objectives dealing with understanding are in harmony with the emphasis the school places upon critical thinking, problem-solving, and understanding. The objectives emphasizing interest and unselfish attitudes are likely to be in harmony with the school's emphasis upon respect for the dignity and worth of every human individual. It is also likely that the objective of ability to participate effectively in some of the common activities of family life would be in harmony with the school's educational philosophy. This, then, would suggest that these teaching goals are important and have fairly high priority. The home-economics teacher would then check them against the background of the students in particular classes as well as against their maturity and readiness for work of this sort. They would also be checked against the general plan for the sequential organization of the curriculum. It may very well be that information about the particular classes would suggest that these objectives are especially appropriate for senior high school students at the eleventh- or twelfth-grade level, since they may have an adequate background for goals of this sort and they are increasingly concerned about the impending new family responsibilities.

An additional illustration may be based on the analysis in chapter ii of the needs of youth to use leisure time wholesomely and enjoyably. This analysis indicates that several community needs are involved, such as the need of the community to support well-balanced programs of recreation which appeal to individuals of widely varying interests and talents, the need of the community to demand that commercial amusements comply with acceptable standards of taste and physical and mental health, the need of the community to be alert to protect citizens through law and the pressure of public opinion from undesirable influences which undermine and cheapen character. It is also pointed out that the individual needs to learn to plan his leisure carefully and to use acceptable standards of tastes in terms of which he makes intelligent choices regarding leisure time.

From this analysis of student needs growing out of the community and the individual's responsibility, several teaching goals are suggested which would be appropriate teaching goals for a course in social studies. They include understanding why the use of leisure is a social problem, understanding the kinds of responsibilities which communities have in this area, understanding the individual's role in providing for and participating in the recreational life of the community, and becoming familiar with the range of leisure activities that are possible. Other goals that are likely to occur to a teacher of social studies would include interest in a variety of wholesome recreational pursuits, skill in several types of recreational pursuits, ability to apply appropriate standards in the selection of movies, radio programs, television shows and other commercial amusements, appreciation of the extent and range of satisfactions to be obtained from a variety of wholesome recreational pursuits. As is pointed out in chapter ii, English, science, mathematics, physical education, art, and music would all have some contributions to make to meeting these needs, but in the present illustration it is assumed that the social-studies teacher is examining the need for suggestions regarding teaching goals appropriate for his field. These possible teaching goals would then be considered in the light of the school's philosophy to identify those which have high priority because they are in harmony with the major values recognized by the school.

In terms of typical philosophies of American public schools, it is likely that those teaching goals relating to youth's understanding of the need for wholesome recreation, understanding of the community's responsibility for helping to provide such recreation, and understanding of the individual's role in making wise selections would be given high priority. It is also likely that high priority would be given to the development of skill in choosing one's recreation by applying appropriate standards of taste and value. The other objectives would probably be given somewhat less priority, but none is likely to be greatly out of harmony with the educational philosophy of most schools.

The social-studies teacher would also consider these possible goals in terms of their appropriateness for his particular students. In this connection, he would consider their maturity, their background, and the extent to which the needs implied had been directly indicated in their own behavior. He would also consider these goals in terms of the general outline of curriculum sequence in the school to see that they were in harmony with the general plan for broadening and deepening the student's understanding of major concepts, his commitment to social values, his command of important skills. In considering organization, he would also need to consider the problem of integration, how these teaching goals could be related to the work going on in other fields in which these same students are engaged so as to provide opportunity for the integration of learning among the various school subjects. Consideration of the way in which possible teaching goals may be woven into the sequential and integrative organization of the curriculum is necessary in achieving maximum results in developing the kinds of behavior patterns which would enable students to meet such needs as the one for the use of leisure time wholesomely and enjoyably.

SUMMARY

These illustrations should have clarified several important points. In the first place, it should be clear that the needs of youth are not themselves teaching goals but rather that the problem of the classroom teacher is to infer the kinds of behavior patterns which can be developed in students that are likely to help students meet their needs. In the second place, it should be clear that the statement of these behavior patterns or teaching goals should indicate the kind of behavior toward which learning experiences should aim and the kind of content to be dealt with in connection with this behavior. In the third place, these illustrations should make clear that the selection of teaching goals involves continuing reference to the school's educational philosophy, so as to give priority to those types of behavior patterns which are consistent with the philosophy of the school and to eliminate from the teaching goals those behavior patterns which are in conflict with that philosophy and those which do not represent major features of that philosophy. In the fourth place, it should be clear that teaching goals are also considered in the light of what is known about the psychology of learning so that goals which are selected for teaching emphasis are attainable, appropriate for the subject field involved, appropriate to the background and maturity levels of the students, and possible of attainment under the conditions available in the high school. The purpose of this consideration is to eliminate as teaching goals those that are inappropriate for the maturity of the students, those that are unlikely to be attained under the conditions of the school, and, thus, to focus upon significant attainable objectives appropriate for the background and maturity of the students. Finally, it should be noted that these possible teaching goals are considered in the light of the general plan for the organization of learning in the school to see that they are in harmony with the accepted principles of sequential development and of integration, so that they can be woven closely into the fabric of the high-school curriculum and can do their part in providing for a series of highly effective learning experiences which lead on sequentially and provide some degree of unity in the total high-school experience of the student.

When a teacher has such goals clearly in mind so that he sees both the kinds of behavior he is seeking to develop in students and the content involved, he is in a position to plan learning experiences that are useful in helping students to attain these goals and, in this way, ultimately, to meet their own needs. The next chapter develops in greater detail the procedures for selecting learning experiences to attain teaching goals which have been identified from studies of student needs.

CHAPTER XIII

ADAPTING CLASSROOM ACTIVITIES TO THE NEEDS OF YOUTH

NADINE I. CLARK

Chairman, Social Studies Department, and
Director, Curriculum Materials Center
Evanston Township High School
Evanston, Illinois

and

GERTRUDE M. AITCHISON

Teacher of Unified Studies
Evanston Township High School
Evanston, Illinois

PURPOSE OF THE CHAPTER

If the school is to meet the needs of youth, one of its most important concerns must be the selection and use of classroom activities appropriate to that end. In this chapter the authors will consider the role of the teacher in the determination and direction of such activities, ways and means of developing a desirable classroom climate, and the selection and organization of learning experiences and materials. It is assumed that the reader is familiar with the discussion of the needs of youth in the first two chapters of this yearbook and with the discussion of how youth learn to meet their needs in chapter iii. The philosophy of those chapters is basic to the discussion which follows.

THE ROLE OF THE CLASSROOM TEACHER IN MEETING THE NEEDS OF YOUTH

Much of the school's success in meeting the needs of youth will depend upon the skill and understanding with which each teacher adapts classroom activities to the needs of a particular group of students. The techniques involved in the adaptation are independent of the subject taught, the grade level of the students, or the particular curriculum involved. They will, however, be influenced by three important factors.

One factor influencing teaching procedures is the teacher's conception of how learning takes place. The needs of students cannot be met by classroom techniques based on the idea that learning and verbalization are synonymous. Learning takes place most effectively when the student accepts the goal of his activity as one which is satisfactory to him. The learning objective is supposed to have been achieved when the learning experience causes modification of the learner's behavior. This modification is the result of purposeful activity which involves the practice of the skill, or the practical application of the concept, to be learned. Also, learning occurs only when the activities of the student are geared to his previous learning; that is, when his new experiences are based on the understanding and abilities he already possesses. For a further development of this concept the reader is referred to chapter iii.

Another factor which will help determine a teacher's classroom techniques is his own ingenuity and skill. Even in a school where the course of study is prescribed and the major emphasis is placed on the acquisition of textbook information, a skilful and resourceful teacher can do much to meet the more important needs of the students. In fact, in any specific classroom situation, the degree to which learning takes place and needs are met depends largely on the teacher's ability to apply his own knowledge of the learning process.

A third factor which will help determine the effectiveness of classroom techniques is the personality of the teacher. The climate of any classroom is very largely the result of that most significant of personality factors, the emotional maturity of the teacher. No matter how earnest in intention, theoretically well informed, and skilful in the use of a variety of classroom techniques, the teacher may find his best efforts unsuccessful if he is emotionally immature. Good human relationships, which are dependent in large part on the emotional maturity of the individuals concerned, are more important than techniques and are a prerequisite to the success of even the most skilfully conceived techniques.

DEVELOPING A DESIRABLE CLASSROOM CLIMATE

A prime consideration in adapting classroom activities to the needs of youth is the climate of the classroom, the class itself being a major part of peer society. The relations of students to one another affect most, if not all, of their emotional needs. The learnings which result from these relations greatly influence their growth as persons, since the satisfaction of common emotional needs is a part of the developmental tasks which are the most pressing and immediate concerns of youth. Many of these emotional needs will be met concomitantly as the individual becomes functionally integrated into the group of which he is a part. Security in the classroom situation can do much to prevent some of the emotional maladjustments which affect adversely the scholastic achievements of many pupils.

In attempting to promote good group spirit, a teacher should continually be aware of the central importance of the group as a possible source of the approval and recognition which each individual seeks. The group will affect its individual members for good or ill. Their status in the group will either aid or inhibit their learning. The group can enhance the importance of the individual by making him feel wanted. If the group feeling is strong enough, it can absorb individual hostilities. The group will develop standards which are realistic, though some of these may not be consciously recognized. It can define areas of responsibility for both students and teacher, thus helping to avoid misunderstanding. Hence, the teacher will regard his efforts to promote desirable group processes as fundamental to the success of the year's work.

One of the teacher's first objectives, then, should be to create an atmosphere of friendliness and belongingness to aid the growth of the "we" spirit which will help a class become a group. He will begin by making certain that the students become acquainted with one another, starting with the simple procedure of introductions at the first session of the class. This might well preface a get-acquainted period, in which everyone, including the teacher, tells something about himself. The well-adjusted teacher can often establish a tone of honesty and acceptance by free expression of his own hopes and even failures. Adolescents are quick to catch such feelings and respond whole-heartedly. As the year progresses, the group might set up standards for its behavior, perhaps on trips— "We act this way." It might put on an assembly program or a courtesy drive, or challenge another class to a baseball game with a coke party afterward. Even the constant use of the terms *we* and *our* helps.

The understanding teacher will realize that the youngster who does not conform, especially for emotional or social reasons, frequently becomes an isolate. His nonconformity may be due to any one factor or a combination of factors in himself, his home, or the school. Some emotional factors might include: lack of affection; denial of recognitions he feels are his due; retarded interpersonal relations; failure to accept his abilities, limited or exceptional; and continual frustration. The degree to which he can be helped in the classroom will be dependent on the skill and understanding of the teacher in interpreting his motives. Perhaps the easiest way to describe some techniques is to give a brief case study.

Tall, well-built, and attractive Mark was the brunt of some class humor because of his noisy and uncontrolled throat tic. The constant gulp-cackle was annoying to everyone. He was partially rejected by all and completely rejected by some few who, themselves, had difficulty in adjusting to the tenth-grade class.

Investigations of Mark's background revealed him as the youngest of three boys, frantically trying to keep up with the exploits of his two brilliant, athletic brothers. Although Mark was above average in intelligence and had a fair degree of athletic ability, he was blocked in both directions by his anxiety. Two years before entering this particular class, he had been withdrawn from school by request of the classroom teacher and put under the care of a psychiatrist. His entrance, then, into this tenth-grade class was shadowed by fear of his reception by the teacher and the students. The teacher's casual acceptance of his tic and interest in his love of trains soon established a pleasant teacher-pupil relationship, but it was obvious to both that his acceptance by the group would be slow.

When some of the boys began to imitate the tic, the teacher decided that the time for action had arrived. She chose a time when Mark was not in class and when the group was particularly cohesive. They had been reviewing a story of Lou Gehrig's gallant fight against multiple sclerosis. The teacher quietly suggested that each of us has problems to solve, both physical and social in nature. The pupils eagerly responded with comments about some of their difficulties. Gradually she led them to a discussion of mannerisms that might create problems in the classroom. She spoke of how the class had cured her of twisting a lock of her hair when she was excited and wondered if any of them had had similar experiences.

Ginny exploded with, "How about Mark? He's awful!" Other pupils agreed and spoke at length about the tic. The teacher pointed out that while adults can help young people by friendly efforts to understand them, any real help must come from classmates. Only they can make the individual feel wanted and a part of the group. In warm-hearted adolescent fashion, the class responded by wanting to make Mark everything from chairman to homeroom student-council representative.

Mark did not magically become cured through the class's attempts to understand and to accept him, but he was freed from their antagonism and enabled to forge ahead more successfully, assured that his relationships with them were improved.

The utilization of the co-operative atmosphere, the sympathy already aroused, and the momentary assumption of the pupil role by the teacher when she admitted her own nervous mannerism, led, in this case, to a consideration of behavioral changes. The pupils were not only learning to understand Mark's problem and to help him solve it but were also learning a most important social factor: the responsibility of the group to its individual members.

We referred earlier in the case of Mark to the complete rejection of him by those who themselves had problems. Among the rejecting pupils was Deanna, the daughter of the local bank president. Deanna's every move was directed by her domineering mother. The child was docile with and eager to please any adult, but, with other children, she was an agressive, bullying person. She was the instigator and, often, victor in many verbal battles. By a bit of subtle maneuvering, the teacher had Deanna elected chairman of the "committee-to-call-to-order." At first Deanna punished her fellow students for minor infractions of the rules, but as she found that her decisions were not challenged, she began to use persuasion instead of dominance; friendly understanding instead of impatience.

Chores such as cleaning boards, emptying wastebaskets, opening windows, passing out paper, and the like, are useful ways to use the pent-up energies of youngsters whose span of attention is short or whose need for physical movement is great. Aggression may be channeled through debate, panels, and discussions. Psychodrama is a most exciting technique for working off, in a socially acceptable way, the problems students face. The teacher with quick emotional understanding will see and utilize hints from such creative activities.

A teacher should always be aware of the pupils' need to form friendships within the group. Sometime during the first few class sessions, sociometry might be used to determine seating arrangements, for there is probably no better way to make certain that pupils are near their own choices. Telling pupils to sit where they please will not overcome the inhibitions which always prevent many from showing their real preferences; and the few, almost inevitable, isolates should not become conspicuous. Also significant is the fact that the most recent research indicates that children's choices often show them reaching for a greater degree of maturity in their associations. Any socially acceptable method which makes free association possible, then, is desirable.

Valid results from the use of a sociometric question are dependent in part on the manner in which the question is put to the group and on its specificity. The teacher can explain in a matter-of-fact way the purpose of the question and then request the students to write, after the numbers one to three, the names of the classmates with whom they would most like to be seated during periods when the class is working as a group. He will make it clear that these first, second, and third choices are for no other purpose, such as committee work, that they will be kept confidential, and that everyone will probably get one of his choices, though not everyone can have his first choice.[1]

A teacher must be alert to the presence of the tensions which will arise in any class group from time to time. He should not assume that the reasons for tension are apparent in surface behavior. If the group seems to be using Wally Evans as a scapegoat, for example, the reason may be rooted in some frustration common to most of the students. This frustration might even be the result of the teacher's own assumption of too authoritarian a role. Or it may have resulted from the unconscious dissatisfaction of some students with their own achievement in an individual or class project. If the teacher can identify and remove the cause, perhaps

---

[1] For a fuller discussion of the sociometric technique and a clear explanation of how to use it, see Helen Hall Jennings, "Sociometric Grouping in Relation to Child Development," *Fostering Mental Health in Our Schools*, chap. xiii. 1950 Yearbook of the Association for Supervision and Curriculum Development. Washington: National Education Association, 1950.

through a frank discussion with the group about why their progress seems slow, he will be solving a school-achievement as well as a group-process problem. These problems frequently coincide, so that attacking one may have much the same effect as attacking the other. The teacher's own emotional maturity is particularly important here. If he can accept both himself and his students as they are, he will have a better opportunity to foster an atmosphere in which free interchange of opinion is possible and where everyone is respected for whatever contribution he can make.[2]

The teacher must keep in mind the fact that adolescents, like younger children, are quick to spot weaknesses, especially emotional ones. Unlike their younger selves, however, a growing sense of fair play and protection can lead secondary-school pupils to surprising degrees of kindness. Once they understand their responsibility toward others, they usually respond whole-heartedly, as in the case cited above. To the adolescent, however, adults are legitimate goals for cruelty. Witness the usual treatment of substitute teachers. The authors have stressed the importance of the teacher's own emotional maturity, whereby he can accept not only the hostilities of the pupils but also his own constantly shifting role as an ideal, parent-substitute, and the like. The following instance may serve for illustration.

Seventeen-year-old Peter, overage and oversized, often flatly refused to obey his teacher's instructions or requests. She found that he had been refused admittance to three of his classes because of his surly attitude. Now and then she feared that she, too, must "get rid of him" as some of the other teachers advised.

Further investigation revealed that in a five-room shack by the river lived Peter, his parents, four brothers and sisters (Peter was the third child), and two grandparents. No English was spoken in the home; the women of the family lived in terror of the drunken, unemployed father. He frequently beat the youngest child but, recently, had been leaving Peter alone physically, at least, because the boy had knocked him down.

The teacher had several conferences with the school psychiatrist, to whom she had referred Peter. He helped her see that perhaps Peter felt that a surly, rough dominance was the male role and, therefore, treated his women teachers as he saw his father treat the women in his home.

The teacher then enlisted the aid of the two strongest boys in the class. All requests and instructions were given to Peter through them. Her only contacts with the boy were when she praised him for any good work that he did. Weeks

---

[2] For a valuable discussion of the group and its problems, see Herbert A. Thelen and Ralph W. Tyler, "Implications for Improving Instruction in the High School," *Learning and Instruction,* chap. xii. Forty-ninth Yearbook of National Society for the Study of Education, Part I. Chicago: University of Chicago Press, 1950. See also Henry Maas, "Understanding Group Processes," *Fostering Mental Health in Our Schools,* chap. xvii, *op. cit.*

of patience and self-control on her part began to show evidence of progress. Peter never became a model, but his attitude became more pleasant, and, after a time, he was able to respond to his teacher's instructions.

The mores of any adolescent group must also be carefully considered. Standards, especially in clothing, diet, and speech, change according to locale. If the girls feel that anyone with a dogtag is a "gone goon" and the boys think a "lush brush" haircut is the sign of manhood, the teacher will accept these standards and reserve his corrective procedures for more important mores.

The teacher should also be aware of the background of his students through a study of records as well as personal interviews, themes, and individual comments made during discussion. He will discover economic and social differences not only among the students but also between the students and himself, for the school's standards and mores are predominantly middle-class and, consequently represent different value systems from those of some of the students. The teacher, however, must be careful not to leap to conclusions about the mores of students. Youth cannot be typed even when the general background of their subgroup is known. Individuals show wide variations. This is due partly to the strong influence of the peer group concerned. Hence it is important for a teacher to know who are the friends of his students.

Conflicts in value systems are also potential sources of misunderstanding between the home and the school. Many schools have attempted to remedy this through the use of "back-to-school nights," or a P.T.A. meeting where the parents go to the classes of their youngsters and learn what the teacher is attempting to accomplish in a particular class. These and other methods will contribute to that development of a good classroom climate which should be a major concern of all teachers.

Selection and Organization of Learning Experiences

In selecting learning experiences, the teacher in most schools is keenly aware of society's expectation that the school will enable students to understand social, political, and economic life and that it will teach the skills necessary to participate in these areas. Some of the spontaneous interests of youth—their curiosities about their world—are the same as many societal expectations. Other expectations of society coincide with the developmental tasks of adolescence, such as increasing mastery of communication skills, improving reasoning ability, and acquiring a satisfying philosophy of life or code of values.

Intellectual needs, of course, cannot be considered entirely apart from other categories. The level of achievement in any need area affects and is in turn affected by the level of achievement in other areas. Thus, an individual's failure to satisfy scholastic requirements may result in aggressive acts which damage his status in the classroom group. Or, on the other hand, an individual's status in the group may be strong enough to prevent scholastic failure from causing a serious emotional reaction.

In the main, the selection and organization of learning experiences, like all teaching techniques, will be determined by the teacher's conception of how learning takes place. If he agrees with the point of view of this yearbook, he will be mindful of the fact that he must not identify the learning process with the group process. His instructional methods are largely group methods, but the group learns as individuals, not as an entity. The outcomes of the learning experiences will, therefore, be as varied as the personalities of the students concerned.

The teacher will attempt to make sure that the activities in which his students engage are such as to promote learning. This objective results from a refusal to consider as desirable "action for action's sake." An activity becomes a learning experience only if the participant has some insight into the whys and wherefores of what he is doing. The teacher, for example, will not lead youth to engage in "democratic practices" under the illusion that they will automatically become adherents to the democratic way of life. They must understand the purpose behind the practices they use. This will mean that they must understand democracy itself. No matter what the title of his course, he will include this as one of his objectives. And he will continually evaluate with his group their progress toward its attainment.

He will also be guided by the conviction, as expressed by Bayles,[3] that:

Taking the curriculum as a whole, democratic education requires that learn*ing* be considered primary and learn*ings* secondary in the sense that each unit, although designed to promote immediate learn*ings* of that unit, shall also be handled so as to promote learn*ing*—the ability to think, or to learn independently.

The teacher will attempt, then, to provide opportunities for youth to acquire the skills of reasoning, or problem-solving. This will be true regardless of the subject area with which they are concerned.

The teacher will understand also that a student's knowledge of facts about a certain subject is no guarantee that he can solve problems in connection with that subject. The importance of the citizen's ability to handle problem situations independently and intelligently in a democratic society makes it imperative that the learning experiences of youth be directed toward the acquisition of this skill. The teacher must also remember that providing pupils with a rich variety of learning experiences

---

[3] Ernest E. Bayles, *The Theory and Practice of Teaching*, p. 133. New York: Harper & Bros., 1950.

is essential if they are to become competent in the use of problem-solving techniques. Unless their experience is wide, they will be unable to recognize the existence of many problems whose study, if not solution, is important to them.[4]

How Will Problems Be Selected for Study?

In selecting problems for youth to study, a teacher will have to consider the aims and policies of the school or college as well as his own philosophy of method. If he is expected to follow a previously determined course of study which emphasizes subject-matter content, his success in meeting the individual needs of the students will depend primarily upon his own personality and his skill in providing desirable learning experiences. Required subject matter can be organized into units of work centered around the solution of problems which capitalize on many of the spontaneous interests of students without neglecting course requirements. Students will co-operate in "covering" required work if this situation is explained frankly.

The teacher's success in adapting a predetermined course of study to a particular group lies most of all in his ability to plan co-operatively with the students. This does not mean that he abdicates his position of responsibility as a teacher and as an adult with superior knowledge and skill. Nor does it mean that he plays at planning, concealing an authoritarian hand in a velvet glove. It does mean that the teacher, having clearly preplanned objectives in terms of understandings, attitudes, and skills, works with the group to choose activities so geared to individual interests, needs, and aptitudes, that they result in desirable learning. The group first plans its own objectives in co-operation with the teacher, bearing in mind that these objectives are neither sacred nor fixed. There will also be continuous evaluation by the group of its progress and much replanning of procedures in the light of experience.

In this kind of planning, the teacher functions as a leader rather than as a dictator. If his role in the group has been well established, his leadership is accepted and his opinions are respected. The objectives finally achieved by the group may differ from those the teacher originally had in mind. Whether they are more or less desirable will be determined by the effectiveness of the group processes and of the methods used to capitalize on individual interests and abilities. We would agree with Bayles[5] that:

---

[4] For further elaboration of this point, see Robert L. Thorndike, "How Children Learn the Principles and Techniques of Problem-solving," *Learning and Instruction*, chap. viii. Forty-ninth Yearbook of the National Society for the Study of Education, Part I. Chicago: University of Chicago Press, 1950.

[5] Ernest E. Bayles, *op. cit.*, p. 130.

What we want is in reality pupil-teacher planning—neither pupil planning nor teacher planning alone, the one to the exclusion of the other. We would expect a teacher's influence to be dominant, but we would also expect the original plans of the teacher to be distinctly modified by pupil contributions as each study progresses.

The latter must occur when a teacher really works with a peer group in a permissive setting.

How Will Problems Be Organized for Study?

Several methods of organizing problems or learning experiences for study are possible. As in the selection of problems, organization can be preplanned in entirety by the teacher; it can be preplanned in part by the teacher, then decided in co-operation with students; or it can be left to the decision of the students. The authors believe that the second alternative is preferable. Youth generally do not have sufficient knowledge to make such choices on their own. However, aided by the teacher, who can point out alternatives and help establish criteria, they can gain familiarity with materials and also give the teacher clues to their own needs.

The organization of learning experiences is also dependent on whether a teacher follows, for the most part, the organization of a particular textbook or whether he uses a broad-areas approach or a problem approach. If the latter, his choice of materials is less restricted and, as previously indicated, more likely to meet the intellectual needs of young people. This is true particularly in the social-studies field. Almost all history textbooks, for example, are organized chronologically. Materials dealing with recent problems may be left, for the most part, to the latter weeks of the course which uses a strictly chronological study of events. If not, they are often interposed arbitrarily according to some convenient, if illogical, treatment of current events, perhaps by setting aside one day each week for such study. This plan is widely used, though deplored by most authorities.[6]

Probably the best type of teacher-pupil planning takes place when a course of study becomes a series of experience units. An experience unit differs from others in that it describes what actually took place in a class group. It cannot, then, be written in advance of the particular learning experience. It may include the preplanning of the teacher, but most if its content is a step-by-step description of how this preplanning was carried

---

[6] For further information on the teaching of current affairs see *The Teaching of Contemporary Affairs*. Edited by John C. Payne. Twenty-first Yearbook of the National Council for the Social Studies. Washington: National Council for the Social Studies, 1951.

into the classroom to become a part of the co-operative planning and carrying out of activities by class and teacher. Like other kinds of units, the experience unit also contains a description of outcomes and evaluation methods.

The following experience unit is included by the authors as an example of teacher-pupil planning. The teacher who submitted this illustration was required by the Freshman course of study to include a unit on home life. As can be seen, the teacher had already decided on certain limits to the scope of the topic, i.e., that the class would not study the history of family living, but, rather, would study their own families and their possible future families. With such limitations in mind, the teacher planned the procedures to be employed with the group.

I. Teacher's objectives:
   A. That the pupils should understand that
      1. Each member of the family has a part to play in the life of the group.
      2. Pleasant, happy homes depend upon the understanding, sympathy, and co-operation of the individual members.
      3. All members of the family are different in temperament and interests, but they have much in common.
      4. The techniques developed now for getting along with the family are those that will probably be used in one's future home.
      5. As the children in the family grow up, their responsibilities increase and their roles change.
   B. That the pupils should gain skill in
      1. Getting along with others.
      2. Understanding themselves, their strengths and weaknesses in personality and abilities.
      3. Participating in social activities, especially dating.
      4. Interpreting one's self to others, especially to parents, brothers, and sisters.
      5. Using reference materials.
      6. Practicing interview techniques.
      7. Writing and speaking.
      8. Letter writing, especially letters inviting someone to be a speaker, and thank-you notes.

II. Planning:
   A. There was a preplanning session, as is customary, of the teacher, the student chairman, and the class secretary. They discussed some comments from themes and "bull sessions" which showed student unhappiness or dissatisfaction with home life. The chairman and secretary decided to copy some of the comments on the board in order to stimulate class discussion of how the group would approach the study of the unit.
   B. The class session started with the first quote: "What can you, a ninth-grader, do if your parents won't tell you the truth?" Many questions

were asked and comments made. Finally the secretary was asked to write on the board all the statements or questions called out. When the fifty or more were jotted down, the class took time to consider whether there was any natural grouping of problems. As a class, they voted that the student objectives in this unit would be to find out:

1. How to get along with brothers and sisters. Typical questions were:
   a) Do I seem as bad to my brothers and sisters as they seem to me?
   b) When my sister and I hit each other, my brother sticks up for her. Does this mean he likes her better than me?
   c) Why is my brother such a swell-head and so bossy when I try to be decent?
2. How to get along with parents. Typical questions were:
   a) Do you think it is right to be able to confide more easily in your best friend than in your parents?
   b) What can you do if your parents get mad when you bring home a bad report card even though you did the best you could?
   c) What about parents who act differently when other people are around so that when you tell them of something your parents did, they won't believe you?
3. How to make and use a budget; what recreation is good for ninth-graders.
   Typical questions were:
   a) Should we get paid for work we do around the house?
   b) Should your parents give you an allowance or just hand out money when it is needed?
4. How to behave in public and how to date.
   Typical questions were:
   a) What can I do if I am not allowed to stay out as late as the other guys?
   b) Is it better to go steady in high school or to "play the field"?
   c) Is there any way we can make kids behave on the busses without being called sissies?

III. Formation of committees:
   A. It was agreed that there would be a committee for each major objective as listed above. Everyone listed his first, second, and third choices for working on these committees. The secretary, two appointed students, and the teacher made the decisions about committee assignments.
   B. Preliminary assignments
   Each committee met during class time and decided to assign the following to its members:
   1. Bring in clippings from magazines, newspapers, and business-house organs on our subject for reference and bulletin-board displays.
   2. Review regular and special radio and TV programs.
   3. Report on movies and plays.
   4. Make lists by name, author, catalogue number, and subject of all reference books and fiction in the school and public libraries on the topic.

IV. Special activities: As the following committees worked, these special activities were planned, carried out, and the results reported to the class:

A. Brothers and sisters: Made up a questionnaire on attitudes toward sisters and brothers, duplicated it, and gave it to six ninth-grade groups. The results were tabulated, and some attempts made to explain the possible reasons for the answers.

B. Getting along with parents: Made a survey of parent opinion on, "What I like and dislike most in my ninth-grader." Family Service, a community organization, was consulted on what areas create the most conflict between parents and children.

C. Budget and recreation: Made a survey of three classes to find out (a) how much money, on the average, each student had per week; (b) where he got it, from allowance or work; and (c) what was to be paid for out of it.

D. Public behavior and dating: Made up a questionnaire to be given to bus drivers, movie managers, and store managers on their attitudes toward teen-agers.

V. Presentations to class by committees (in addition to above):

A. Brothers and sisters: Presented an original tape-recording of a family at dinner, their quarrel over the family car and baby-sitting. By role-playing, they demonstrated how the problems might have been settled more reasonably.

B. Parents: Invited a school psychiatric worker and two fathers and mothers to be on a panel with the five committee members to discuss questions handed in by the class as a whole on getting along with parents.

C. Budget and recreation: Presented a model budget and methods of earning money, etc. Invited a representative from an insurance company to talk about establishing credit, savings, and types of insurance.

D. Public behavior and dating: Drew a series of cartoons with verses about behavior in public places. Had a movie manager in to discuss the behavior of ninth-graders in public places and in the movies in particular.

VI. Final evaluation:

A. Class discussion of the success of the unit brought out the fact that the group had learned:

1. Some techniques for getting along with brothers, sisters, parents, and grandparents.
2. How to make up a questionnaire, do surveys, and tabulate results.
3. How to use reference materials in the library.
4. How to write thank-you notes to adults.
5. How to interview people.
6. How to make outlines and make reports.
7. How to introduce speakers and guests.
8. That adults like to work with young people.
9. How to talk to a group.

B. Administration of a teacher-made essay test with questions to evaluate factual learnings from readings and ability to apply these learnings to specific situations.[7]

One difficulty in planning genuine experience units with students is the rigid separation of subject areas found in most schools. No one who has taught in high school can be unaware of the resulting compartmentalization in the minds of adolescents. An alert teacher can help to overcome this. He can call attention to the understandings, skills, and attitudes which apply not only to his own course but also to others. He can lead the pupils to watch for these carry-overs and to describe examples of them. He can inform himself about the work being done in other classes and consult with other teachers in an effort to achieve as much correlation as possible.

Teacher-pupil planning is not limited to the working out of experience units. It can be used to solve and to capitalize on many other classroom problems. For example, one teacher of a tenth-grade Spanish class was considerably disturbed when he walked into the classroom one morning early in September to find an excited group of students surrounding two boys who were "slugging it out." When the bloody noses were ministered to and the general air of excitement was dissipated, the combative pupils stared with a kind of scared expectancy at the teacher, waiting for their punishment. They were puzzled when, instead of reproaches, he said that fights do happen now and then but the important thing is to know *why* they occur. Friendly questioning elicited the information that one boy had called the other a "dirty greaser." Since the latter youngster was a Mexican, he retaliated immediately.

After the class had freely discussed the meaning of "greaser," they suggested other national stereotypes such as "dago," "gringo," etc. Together with the teacher, the group began to plan how by studying Spanish-speaking people, particularly those in Latin America, and Spanish life, they might find some evidence to support or disprove at least the stereotype "greaser." (Interestingly enough, the Mexican lad proved to be one of the most ardent workers on a committee which specialized in the derivation of Mexican-Spanish words.) Such capitalizing on emotional situations is especially good motivation for study.

In addition to the experience unit, the resource unit can be helpful to all teachers regardless of their philosophy of method. A resource unit differs from others in that it contains suggestions for many class and

---

[7] For further discussion of evaluating the success of a unit, see J. Paul Leonard, *Developing the Secondary-School Curriculum*, pp. 482ff. New York: Rinehart & Co., 1946.

individual activities, and for the use of a wide variety of materials, but does not prescribe the specific ones to be used with a particular class. It is intended to serve as a storehouse from which individual teachers can draw and adapt what they need for their own classes.

Many resource units have been prepared by professional organizations such as the National Council for the Social Studies and the National Council of Teachers of English. They offer not only the activities and materials mentioned above but also the results of the latest research in and information about the various topics concerned. Other resource units have been compiled by workshop groups such as those sponsored by the Joint Council on Economic Education. Individual teachers and small groups within a single school have also written resource units. These are especially helpful to new or inexperienced teachers in the same system.

Whether resource units are written in advance to serve as guides for classes or are largely descriptive of past experiences, they usually have certain of the same characteristics. These include a statement or list of the purposes or objectives of the unit, a description or outline of the subject matter covered, a list of student activities, and a bibliography of written materials and visual aids. More helpful are units which also include suggestions for introductory and culminating activities and for methods of evaluation.

Other Criteria for the Selection and Organization of Learning Experiences

Reference has been made previously to the need for providing widely varied activities in order to extend and enrich the learning experiences of youth. Why are so many teachers content with so few of the many possibilities? Information about these possibilities can be found in innumerable sources such as the many professional books available, the resource units, magazines, and other publications of professional organizations, bulletins issued by state departments of education, and publications of local school systems.[8]

Unless a class is to be held to a single standard of achievement, provision must be made for youth of greatly varying abilities. When adolescents are encouraged to give their own preferences, they are found to enjoy doing things which involve working with one another and developing new skills and abilities. Thus, they are able to discover new interests and to gain greater recognition from both peers and adults. Young people seldom have to be convinced that the best way to learn something new is

---

[8] For an unusual number of specific illustrations, see Paul R. Mort and William S. Vincent, *Modern Educational Practice.* New York: McGraw-Hill Book Co., Inc., 1950.

to practice doing it. Once they understand the objective, they welcome the use of laboratory practices in courses other than science. This has been amply demonstrated by Columbia University's Citizenship Education Project.[9] The "incidental" learnings from experiences of this sort often turn out to be the real learnings.

Teachers in all subject areas should have as one of their objectives providing experiences to widen the sympathies and interests of pupils. Teaching understanding (not necessarily approval) of other people's beliefs or methods of behavior includes the use of literature, movies, discussions, TV programs, trips to museums, visits from parents or townspeople from other countries, and studies of the contributions of scientists, mathematicians, and linguists. If some of the class are interested in music, for instance, a study of Paderewski might increase interest in Poland. If there is a Polish settlement near by, the group might attend a Polka.

Members of a science class might well be stimulated to explore French character by their study of the Curies. One tenth-grade geometry class "came alive" through the Pythagorean theorem. Practical geometry exercises developed as they reconstructed the physical world of the early philosophers and mathematicians. This last type of activity is especially recommended for the nonacademic pupil. Construction, laboratory exercises in the community, and the like, often enable him to find a measure of success sorely needed but too often denied him within the four walls of the classroom.

Frequently adolescents do not recognize, or are unable to verbalize, their deep need for institutions, schools, clubs, and other groups on which they can expend their emotions in the form of loyalties. The teacher will be quick to dramatize emotionally situations which develop school spirit and patriotism. Each member of the class may be able to repeat the inalienable rights of man, or the Four Freedoms, but the teacher will try to make sure that each one feels their significance in his heart. Brotherhood Week, Memorial Day, Thanksgiving, and similar occasions will be rich celebrations wherein each child honestly finds meaning and emotional satisfaction.

No matter what type of unit is used, the teacher will remember that in addition to student needs in the emotional, social, and intellectual areas, there are, of course, common physical needs, such as nutrition, rest, exercise, and recreation. Some other physical needs are of special concern because they are directly involved in the developmental tasks. In the period of adolescence, with which we are here concerned, youth face the

---

[9] *Improving Citizenship Education.* A Two-Year Progress Report of the Citizenship Education Project, Publication No. 29. New York: Teachers College, Columbia University, 1952.

necessity of learning to live with what is really a new physical self. Self-consciousness and anxiety naturally accompany their efforts to control their new bodies. If teachers ignore the physical basis of these emotional reactions, they are likely to meet frustrations in their efforts to help students achieve other objectives.

When planning to meet the physical needs of a class group, the teacher will not make the assumption common to many teachers that the home is already meeting most of those needs. He will acquire the habit of looking at his students to see whether they appear rested and well. He will notice a flushed face or too-bright eyes. His quick, searching glance, perhaps while attendance is being taken, will note signs of a tired or sick child and will do much to ward off mild epidemics or contagious illnesses before they become serious. If Frank sleeps through a third of the class period, the teacher's reaction will not be a sign of annoyance but that of an effort to discover the reason.

The good teacher will also be sure that lesson assignments require only a reasonable amount of out-of-school preparation. He will not rely solely on his own judgment of the time required but will consult the students and be willing to take into consideration assignments made by other teachers. He will also be alert to possibilities for units of work or activities to promote better understanding of physical needs. He may have the experience of one tenth-grade social-studies class, for example, which had been engaged in a unit on Germany between the two world wars. Ken and Martin, who were especially fond of sports, had been fascinated by the athletic program of the Hitler youth. Hostels and bicycles, games and marching, seemed to them a fine idea. In the discussion that followed their report, there were many comments about the lack of recreational facilities in their town. The class decided to enlist the aid of their mathematics teacher (eight of the pupils were taking business mathematics) and work out a survey of community recreation. Possibilities for follow-up were found to be almost limitless.

The teacher will also take advantage of every opportunity to help students understand the nature of the physical changes which they are undergoing. If he teaches general science or biology, his task will be relatively easy. If the class is studying English or social studies, he will also find possibilities for including an understanding of physical development among the objectives of even a largely mandated course of study. Simple observation may indicate whether or not the students need help in this regard.

Criteria for Choosing Learning Materials

As materials available for classroom use appear in ever increasing quantity, the problem of their selection and organization becomes as difficult as it is important. Added to the usual textbooks, designed for use throughout a specific course of study, is a variety of books and pamphlets devoted to special problems and topics. Newspapers and magazines are also included among the printed materials which students can use in learning experiences. Audio-visual aids enrich the variety of materials and complicate the task of selection. Pictures, slides, filmstrips, films, recordings, charts, diagrams, graphs, specimens, maps, gloves, dioramas, models, posters, and cartoons are audio-visual materials available to some extent for use in any classroom.

In establishing criteria for the selection of materials, the teacher must consider their source. Whether specifically designed for school use or not, materials may be divided, first, as to whether they come from commercial publishers or from private nonpublishing sources, such as organizations or businesses. Those with which teachers are usually most familiar are the textbooks, pamphlets, and other books written for students and sold by publishing firms. Many private businesses and business organizations distribute materials for school use. Some of these are free of charge, others are sold at a small cost. Among the best known are the maps and pamphlets available from airplane and railroad companies and the pamphlets distributed by the National Association of Manufacturers. The governments of our own country and many other countries also offer publications for school use. Additional sources are organizations such as the League of Women Voters, B'nai B'rith, and other private groups.

The question of the source of materials is important in the case of those which contain nonfactual or interpretive information. Then the teacher must ask whether the information is slanted to favor the viewpoint of the supplier. If the supplier is a textbook publisher, the question will be applied to the author. Especially is this true when publications in the field of social studies are being considered. The teacher's concern will be to make sure that all major points of view on controversial topics are included among the materials he uses. Also, materials should include some of the most recent ones available.

Another important criterion is the level of difficulty in the reading ability required and in the interpretation of content. Most classes contain pupils of varying ability in reading and in understanding. The materials available to them should vary accordingly. The major difficulty, especially in high school, is to supply pupils of low reading skill with material suitable to their intellectual maturity.

Variety in kinds of teaching material is also important. Textbooks should be accompanied by pamphlets, magazines, newspapers, films, and other materials among the possibilities already listed. The particular subject area will only partially restrict the possibilities. Teachers of all subjects can use at least several of the many kinds of material at hand. Nor is the cost factor an adequate reason for failure to offer variety. A resourceful teacher will find it possible to secure some, if not all, of the aids available. Most professional journals publish lists of free and inexpensive materials. Any class can pool its resources and gather from its own community many interesting and helpful aids to learning.

The attractiveness, or eye-appeal, of teaching materials should not be ignored. Publishers are paying increasing attention to this factor. Inferior reading matter should not, of course, be preferred because of its format or visual appeal. But in many cases, the choice is between a book which has visual appeal for pupils and one which does not. Interest gained first through such attractiveness can often be held by content.

Also important is the fact that classroom materials should give pupils opportunities to grow in both the breadth and the depth of their interests. Youngsters who care only for fiction should have opportunities to read other kinds of literature. Those interested only in science stories should be introduced to others. Those accustomed to read only juvenile books should, if their mental abilities permit, be challenged by exposure to more mature material. The school or public librarians are invaluable aids in steering children toward more mature reading matter.[10]

MODERN CONCEPTS OF METHODS OF TEACHING

As one studies the role of the teacher and his procedures for adapting classroom techniques to the needs of students, it becomes evident that scholastic competence on the part of the teacher is not the only requirement for success. One cannot overstress the fact that the use of modern teaching methods requires understanding of the learning process. Indeed, concepts of teaching method result from knowledge of how pupils learn. This indicates, first, that the teacher will see each student not only as a theoretical individual but also as a very real and personal entity. Without this knowledge of the individual a teacher cannot hope to meet the needs of that individual. Nor can he deal with the individual apart from his social environment. The teacher must obtain all possible information about the community background of pupils. There is no substitute for firsthand knowledge of the community in its physical, economic, social, and political aspects.

Modern teaching methods also require the ability to adapt subject matter to the needs of students. Hence, the teacher must be competent in the use of audio-visual materials and other means of teaching those who

---

[10] For further discussion of criteria for selecting learning materials see W. G. Brink, "The Selection of Curriculum Materials and Experiences," *The High School Curriculum.* Edited by Harl Douglass. New York: Ronald Press, 1947.

cannot learn well by reading. The teacher must also be able to provide experiences in which students may apply verbal concepts to specific situations. For instance, if in social studies they learn about their city council and the duties of its members, a trip to a council meeting and following council activities via the local newspaper will allow them to test out their book knowledge.

What do these requirements imply for the teacher? Certainly the teacher must be creative and versatile in handling classroom situations and subject matter. No one method is adequate for dealing with all situations. The question-answer type of teaching, for example, must be supplemented by class discussions of problems, by the presentation of committee reports, by panel discussions, and so on. The teacher must be ready to seize upon current happenings, assembly programs, club activities, and the personal excitements in the lives of pupils as springboards for learning. If Phillip's father is building a new house, his mathematics class might study architectural principles in home-building, costs of construction, and sizes of rooms; or his social-studies class might study zoning ordinances, building permits, labor unions, and contracts; or his biology class might survey health laws and requirements for adequate health and safety measures in the home.

The classroom, then, becomes a laboratory rather than a lecture hall, with the teacher a director, a co-worker, and a learner in problem-solving situations. This implies that narrow subject matter preparation on the part of teachers is hardly adequate for the task of helping today's youth. Prospective teachers should be encouraged to gain a broad, liberal-arts background in their academic preparation. Those teachers who are already in the field should be stimulated to widen and deepen their interests and, when possible, to indulge in some refresher courses outside their specialized fields. Thus, they will be better prepared to demonstrate the type of versatility in the use of methods and techniques which is required by the needs of youth in the world today.

Summary

In summary, the authors have tried to emphasize these major ideas:

1. Classroom techniques are determined primarily by a teacher's conception of how learning takes place, by his ingenuity and skill, and by his emotional maturity.
2. A good classroom climate is necessary for optimal learning and is dependent upon the development of group spirit, the recognition of the mutual responsibility of group and individual, the successful handling of group and individual tensions, and the recognition of pupil mores.
3. Learning experiences seem to be selected best by means of the co-operative planning of teacher and pupils.

4. Learning experiences are most effective when organized around the solution of problems.
5. Teaching materials should be selected according to their source, viewpoint, level of difficulty, variety, visual appeal, and opportunity for growth of pupil interests.
6. The modern teacher must be versatile in the use of a variety of procedures.

CHAPTER XIV

EVALUATING PROGRESS TOWARD THE SATISFACTION OF NEEDS

VERNER M. SIMS

Professor of Psychology
University of Alabama
University, Alabama

INTRODUCTION

A program for evaluating the progress being made in learning is inherent in any intelligently planned teaching-learning situation. Educational evaluation is a matter of passing judgment on the learnings of pupils and is done for the purpose of aiding in pupil growth. As such, it is an integral part of the process of learning and teaching. Without it, both teacher and student work in the dark, and ineffective learning will surely result. The issue is not one of whether we should evaluate; it is one of how best to do it.

Steps in Evaluation. Satisfactorily done, evaluation always follows a fairly uniform course:

1. The several learnings, all of those sought through the schooling, are identified.
2. The extent to which these learnings have been or are being achieved is determined as accurately as possible.
3. In light of the pattern of achievement thus revealed, the question, "How are we doing?" is answered; and next steps are planned in terms of what is best for the learners.

Purpose of the Chapter. These three steps constitute the essence of sound evaluation whether our concern is with the growth of the "whole child" or with his growth in a more restricted area such as a subject-matter field. They describe good evaluation whether it is to be done by the student himself or by his teacher; and they describe good evaluation whether the school assumes responsibility for all the learnings of all American youth or for some of the learnings of some of these youth. This chapter is concerned with what this conception of evaluation will mean for a secondary school which sets about trying to build its instructional program in terms of the needs of youth as set forth in the preceding chapters. The reader should find it particularly helpful to relate the problem of evaluating progress toward the satisfaction of needs (the present chapter) to the determining and discovery of needs (chaps. ii and iv), the translation of needs into teaching or learning goals (chap. xii), and the planning and carrying out of teaching and learning activities adapted to these needs (chap. xiii). This series of chapters, together, encompass the job of teaching. Let us begin the consideration of evaluation with the first step in the process, the identification of the learnings sought by schooling.

IDENTIFYING THE LEARNINGS SOUGHT

Evaluation Contingent on Identification of Learnings Sought. Logically, it seems self-evident that any valid scheme for evaluating learning would of necessity proceed from a careful identification of these learnings, which, in the case of evaluating school learnings, would be those which are being sought through the teaching. Actually, however, the typical teacher's evaluation is poor because he never makes this basic first step. Instead, having identified (or assumed) some needs of his pupils, he works diligently for a time at helping them meet these needs and then decides that it is time for a test. If he is a "modern" teacher, he, of course, uses objective tests! But what kind? "Well, last time I gave a true-false test, so I think I will make this one multiple-choice." If he be "old-fashioned," he lets it go for five or ten essay questions. In either case, he begins, not with an identification of the learnings being sought, but with the decision to use some type or types of instrument. Therefore, he will sample for testing only those learnings which can be measured by the type of test decided upon.

Contrast the approach used above with the teacher who, knowing that he has been trying to teach his pupils to understand the rules of punctuation, to acquire skill in punctuating, and to form the habit of using appropriate punctuation in their everyday writing, proceeds systematically to collect evidence relating to improvement in the three areas; or the health teacher who, having been encouraging his pupils to eat a balanced diet, sets about collecting evidence of change in the actual food consumption for a sample of days.

A Complex Job. In the actual school situation, the matter of identifying the outcomes sought through teaching is a complex one. In the conventional school of today, not only do the outcomes vary from level to level and from teaching field to teaching field but two teachers of the same subject may seek very dissimilar outcomes. The particular teacher assumes the needs of his pupils, is told what their needs are, or finds those of their needs which he feels competent to help in the acquisition of, and proceeds to teach. In a school where the program is to be built in terms of all the learning needs of its pupils, it seems inevitable, too, that the outcomes sought will vary for the several pupils within a given classroom. It is beyond the scope of this chapter to consider all of these outcomes

It seems clear, however, that they will be of a great variety. Even in the present-day secondary school, with its limited assumption of responsibility for meeting the needs of youth and with its relatively restricted curriculum, the number and kinds of outcomes sought in teaching are vastly greater than the number commonly tested for.

To complicate matters still further, outcomes are not usually taught for or acquired separately, in serial order. In teaching science, as an example, the same learning experience may be and often is so planned as to contribute to pupil growth in areas as varied as knowledge of the world about him, appreciation for the scientific method, tolerance for differing opinions, and the practice of making accurate observations. Moreover, the pupil learns as a unitary whole, and, consequently, learning situations, whether so planned or not, will almost surely have some influence on the learner's total behavior, his feeling, thinking, and doing. In terms of the conception of learning developed in chapter iii, it should be clear that a boy learning to solve algebraic equations is at the same time acquiring likes or dislikes and ways of behaving which may have profound influence on his total development. Viewed from the standpoint of the learner, kinds of learning are in reality aspects of total learning, and we cannot judge the goodness or badness of one aspect of learning without studying it in relation to the total. For purposes of evaluation, however, it is quite appropriate to analyze the total learning into its component parts. The important thing is to remember that the analysis is made for convenience only, and before judgment can be passed on the learning the pieces must be fitted back together to make the whole.

Total Learning Analyzed. However varied the learnings sought through schooling may be, a simple classification will comprehend them. This classification is fivefold:

1. Pupils will be expected to memorize many facts.
2. Pupils will be expected to learn many meanings.
3. Pupils will be expected to acquire skills and abilities of various kinds.
4. Pupils will be expected to develop numerous attitudes, appreciations, interests, and ideals.
5. Pupils will be expected to form habits of behaving in certain ways.

The first group, memory for things learned, real and symbolic—names, places, events, processes, qualities, relations, rules—constitute the most obvious of the outcomes. Although the importance of acquiring information is often overemphasized, there are many facts which youth must know if their needs are to be met. Moreover, the meanings associated with many of these facts are more or less arbitrarily determined. Particularly is this true in the field of symbolic learnings where we arbitrarily

assign symbols to the elements, relations, and qualities of the real world
and expect young people to remember the symbols.

More essential to proper functioning in life, however, is a great group
of meaningful learnings with which education must be concerned. The
understanding of simple concepts, of principles, of processes and relationships generally, and of complex data of all sorts, in large measure, constitutes what we know as intelligent behavior. A good part of successful
learning and teaching, as well as evaluation, depends upon the identification of the particular understandings to be acquired. Actually, for much
of what we commonly call factual learning, investigation will show that
the major concern is with understanding, although often neither the
methods of teaching nor those of testing would convey that impression.
In the teaching and testing of vocabulary, for example, the pupil is expected not only to learn and remember the word but also to understand
its referent; yet too seldom does the teaching or testing concern itself
with the understanding.

A school which undertakes to meet the needs of youth will also find itself involved in the development of many intellectual, manual-motor,
and personal-social skills or abilities. Skills for making a living and skills
for living will be needed. Students will be striving, and teachers will be
helping them, to acquire occupational skills, skills essential to the wise
use of leisure, skills needed in personal adjustment and in straight thinking, skills needed in getting along with people and living in a democracy,
as well as skills needed for continued learning.

The secondary school of the future will not, however, confine its efforts
to the development of the *abilities* of its students. Many of the needs of
youth involve their feelings. They need to like some things, to dislike
others. Interests and ideals must be developed and cultivated; loves and
hates as well as understandings and abilities will become "fundamentals"
of learning. To assume that affective learnings, such as a love of freedom,
tolerance of others, respect for truth, vocational and avocational interests, or appreciation of the beautiful, are intangible by-products of schooling will probably result only in their being poorly achieved.

Educators have too often assumed that given understanding and
ability to do, with perhaps some modicum of appreciation, habits of
doing will take care of themselves. This just is not true. One may have
all the understandings necessary to good health, be master of the skills
needed, even have a strong desire for health, yet not have acquired the
habits essential to healthful living and, therefore, not be healthy. People
may understand democracy, accept as their faith "immortal belief that
mankind, if it so desired, could be free," yet have habits which make

them dictators. In a very real sense, these habits of conduct and performance constitute the ends of education; the teacher must know that this is so and, as teacher and tester, must attend directly to them.

All Aspects of Learning Must Be Identified. Evaluation might well begin, then, by asking the questions: What facts need to be remembered? What understandings and skills are we trying to develop? What attitudes should be fostered or changed? What habits should be built up or strengthened? Whether through asking these questions or through some other means, however, the first step in good evaluation is to identify all the learnings desired and being sought. The appraisal of learning will be valid to the extent that it is based upon evidence relating to the total learning of the pupils. The school can do a satisfactory job of assessing progress in learning only when this first step has been taken. Those schools which attempt to serve all the learning needs of all youth will be concerned with a greater number and variety of outcomes.

Collecting Evidence of Achievement

A Broadened Conception of "Test" and "Testing." Having defined the learning outcomes being sought, the next task in evaluation is one of devising means for determining success and collecting evidence of the success being realized in learning. The basic rule to be observed here is the assumption that all learning is reflected in changes in what people say and do (or don't say and do). Collecting evidence of learning is, therefore, a matter of collecting positive and negative signs of changed behavior from observation of, or records of, the doings and sayings of pupils. Stating the principle in these broad terms serves to call attention from the outset to the demand in a school which is to be concerned with meeting all the learning needs of its pupils for a broadened conception of the words "test" and "testing." Once the school has accepted such responsibility, it can no longer put its sole dependence for evaluation in paper-and-pencil tests; until technological developments are more advanced, we may even have to forego the convenience of turning all of our scoring problems over to a machine! We will search for signs of learning in all sorts of formal and informal, problematic and free situations, where the testing may or may not be disguised; and we will search for them among oral or manual-motor responses as well as written, among the nonstructured as well as the structured, including those which may and those which may not be presently quantifiable. Our tests will, therefore, include such instruments as rating scales, check sheets, questionnaires, attitude scales, anecdotal records, observation schedules, and "situational," projective, and performance tests, as well as the more conventional devices.

No Absolute Standards for Reliability and Validity. Furthermore, the magnitude of the job is such that we will undoubtedly have to be satisfied with less refined evidence of learning than would be desirable under ideal conditions. The writer is confident that better appraisal of learning will result from relatively crude testing of *all* the aspects of learning than from highly refined measurement of *a few* of the aspects. In other words, the English teacher who is concerned that youth understand and come to like certain pieces of literature as well as learn facts about them will do better evaluation if he has before him some evidence, even though it be crude, of change in likes and in understanding than he will if he depends on factual learning tests, however reliable these may be. This does not mean that we will give no heed to the reliability and validity of our tests. It does mean, however, that we can set no absolute standards for reliability and validity; we can only choose the most reliable and valid technique available at the time for testing the particular aspect of learning with which we are concerned.

Seek Aid of the Educational and Psychological Testers. For aid in collecting evidence of learning, the school will need to refer to the work of the educational and psychological testers. For a half century now, a considerable number of men have been engaged largely in trying to test for the kinds of psychological characteristics which schools are concerned in developing. The results of the work of these men, not only the instruments which they have devised but more particularly their methods, are available for use. Many of their instruments are designed to test specifically some of the outcomes which will be sought in schools and, where no instruments are available, a study of the methods used in test construction will provide suggestions which the teacher can readily adapt to his particular needs.[1] Let us survey the possibilities. For convenience in treatment, we will consider in order the problems of testing for the several aspects of learning considered in the preceding section (pp. 252 ff.)

Testing for Facts Remembered. The measurement of factual learnings would appear to be best done by means of the short-answer, so-called "objective" types of test. There are available many standard instruments of this sort, although they are mainly of the survey type, and their usefulness is, therefore, limited to giving an over-all, summary picture of the factual learning in a particular field. All that is required for the use of these tests is for one to familiarize himself with available sources, learn something of how to judge the worth of tests, how to give and score

---

[1] The reader should find it helpful to examine one of the more recent comprehensive treatments of psychological testing, such as L. J. Cronbach's *Essentials of Psychological Testing* (New York: Harper & Bros., 1949) or Florence Goodenough's *Mental Testing* (New York: Rinehart & Co., 1949).

them, and how to interpret the results.[2] If tests cannot be found to meet the particular need, there are good treatises on the construction and use of such tests.[3] The chief problems involved are: first, adequate sampling of the facts taught; secondly, selecting types of tests appropriate for the particular learnings to be tested; and, finally, a willingness to work at acquiring skill in making items which conform to known rules of good item construction. To undertake to use any other technique (such as essay examinations or daily recitations) to measure factual learning seems uneconomical. For equivalent testing time, the adequacy of the sampling can never be comparable to that of the objective test, the time for scoring is much greater, and the factor of subjectivity in estimating amount learned is inevitably introduced.

Testing for Understanding. The teacher who is concerned about the need of youth for acquiring information will do well to ask himself whether he does not also want his students to gain understanding, either of the symbols or of their referents. Inquiry will often show that the concern is over meaningful learning as well as memory. One cannot infer understanding from evidence of memory for the facts, but one can assume that if the pupil understands he must have adequate information. Factual learnings, therefore, need not always be measured directly and separately from understanding.

Short-answer tests, of both the multiple-choice and the free-response types, readily lend themselves to testing many of the meaningful learnings (understandings) which are sought through schooling. The prime rule in testing for understanding is the demand that the test situation have some element of "newness" in it. Understanding of simple concepts can be measured by presenting the concepts in new words or by requiring that students react to them in new ways. Understanding of principles, rules, laws, and other generalizations can best be tested by some of the many adaptations of "Application of Principles" tests. Many short-answer types are suitable for testing understanding of relationships once the relations to be understood are identified. The analogies and rear-

---

[2] The series, *Mental Measurement Yearbook* (Edited by Oscar K. Buros. New Brunswick, New Jersey: Rutgers University Press, 1938, 1941, 1949), gives valuable aid in locating available tests and in judging their worth.

[3] For example: *Educational Measurement* (Edited by E. F. Lindquist. Washington: American Council on Education, 1951) gives a very comprehensive treatment but is directed more to the professional tester than to the classroom teacher; R. W. M. Travers' *How To Make Achievement Tests* (New York: Odyssey Press, Inc., 1950) presents a brief but good treatment of paper-and-pencil test-making; and *Measuring Educational Achievement*, by W. J. Micheels and M. R. Barnes (New York: McGraw-Hill Book Co., 1950) contains many ingenious suggestions for testing a great variety of learning outcomes.

rangement types of test seem to be the most neglected of the useful ones. The understanding of more complex data can be tested either by presenting new samples of the data and asking questions about them or by presenting "old" data and asking new questions about them. The data presented may be valid or they may be invalid with the questions taking the form of "What's wrong with this picture?" Variations of the "Interpretation of Data" tests have unlimited possibilities here.

If one is not ingenious enough to develop an "objective" technique for testing understanding, essay questions (that is, questions demanding a free and extended response) may be used with assurance that fairly dependable evidence can be obtained if the teacher will give thought to framing questions which call for understanding on the part of the pupil and will follow approved procedures for judging the response.[4]

In the broadened curriculum that would be required to meet youth needs which are not now accepted as the school's responsibility, we cannot expect to rely on paper-and-pencil tests alone for appraising factual learning and understandings, as is now almost universally done. In such testing the medium of impression is reading, that of expression is writing. These are media particularly suited to people with high scholastic ability; but high scholastic ability will not characterize all youth. We will, therefore, need to explore other methods of presentation and other means of response. Some pupils will be better listeners than readers, and orally administered tests will better fit their abilities; other pupils will need to be presented with concrete or pictorial materials rather than abstract verbal materials. Some pupils will talk better than they can write, and oral responses will more validly measure their learning; others can handle things better than words, and testing them will require manipulative rather than verbal responses.

Testing for Skills. For evaluating the skills or abilities with which schools will be concerned, only a limited number of instruments are now on the market, but the experience of other persons who have faced the same problem offers many suggestions which can be adapted to the task. Particularly from the field of testing in business, industry, and government, many ideas are available. Simple verbal skills which are additive in nature, such as spelling ability, sentence comprehension, and skill in using the dictionary or an index, can be measured by the same techniques described for testing factual learnings and understandings, that is, through the summation of responses to sample situations. In this same way, many mathematical skills can be tested. Even some simple manipu-

---

[4] The best single source for aid in testing for understanding is *The Measurement of Understanding.* Forty-fifth Yearbook of the National Society for the Study of Education, Part I. Chicago: University of Chicago Press, 1946.

lative-motor skills, such as typing, archery, or reading a micrometer, can be tested in a quite similar manner by controlling the method of response and "counting-up" the output. Nothing new is introduced in this testing except perhaps control of the time factor in the case of skills where speed is considered an important aspect of the performance. In skill tests, too, the measure of output will often need to be corrected in some manner for quality; but a satisfactory, if arbitrary, rule for doing this can usually be worked out. The typical speed test in typing is a good illustration. Such tests can be, some have been, developed for measuring simple additive skills.

For appraising complex, integrated skills (such as skill in basketball, in construction work, in composition-writing, in laboratory technique, in use of the library, in dealing with people), the most dependable known method is through the use of rating scales for judging either the performance or the product of the work. If one is to evaluate progress toward the satisfaction of youth's needs, one must be trained in the construction and use of rating scales. Even in the current high school there is serious need for such ability if evaluation is to be satisfactory. In physical education, art and music, home economics, shop, agriculture, and to a lesser extent in other fields, teachers commonly seek to develop complex skills yet have little or no training in judging progress. The result is that they either make no judgment or pass judgment in a disorganized, unsystematic manner which is of little value or which may even be harmful.

A treatment of the construction and use of rating scales is beyond the space limitations of this chapter, and anyone who proposes to use such instruments can find help in available literature.[5] One comment does, however, seem in order. Rating scales are of two general types: "relative," where the pupil's achievement in the several aspects of the skill is compared with that of other members of his group; and "absolute," where his achievement in the several aspects is compared with predetermined and described levels of performance. For purposes of evaluation both types will be found useful, but as a teaching-learning device the "absolute" scale is always to be preferred because it more accurately describes the skill and its aspects for the learner and his teacher. As an illustration, to describe a boy's stance in boxing as comparable to that of the top one-tenth of his class will give neither him nor the other members of the class as much help in learning as to check him in a category which reads: "He leads out with his left hand, shoulder and left foot advanced,

---

[5] *Rating Employee and Supervisory Performance* (Edited by Dooher and Marquis. New York: Management Association, 1950), particularly Parts I, II, and VI, will be found useful by anyone interested in the construction and use of rating scales.

and is slightly crouched in a well-balanced position at all times"—this being the description of the stance of an "expert."

Testing Affective Learnings. When it comes to appraising growth in the emotional-attitudinal-motivational realm, the school can expect help from the psychologists who have worked in this area.[6] There are some instruments available for use in measuring attitudes, ideals, and interests (appreciations which we have grouped under this general head should probably be treated as composites of "understanding of" and "feeling for," with testing of the two variables done separately). The best help comes, however, from adapting the methods of those who have worked in the field to the specific outcomes with which the school is concerned.

Attitudes which pupils will freely reveal, where awareness of the intent of the tester will have no distorting effects on the response either because of compulsion to hide one's feelings or because of self-consciousness over responding, can be measured relatively easily. For example, in case of learnings such as preferences for poetry or prose (providing the teacher himself is not too biased), recreational interests (providing one deals only with socially acceptable activities), attitude toward the United Nations (providing the teacher has not made it appear disgraceful to be against it), liking for foods (providing the teacher has not made it clear that pupils *must* like all foods), or choice of medium for musical expression (providing the media are all equally respectable), we can probably assume that expressed opinion is synonymous with attitude. There are several practical testing devices which teachers can make and use for testing such attitudes. If only crude information on feelings for or against some issue is wanted, a simple polling technique may be satisfactory. If more refined measurement is desired, a teacher can learn to construct attitude scales or questionnaires without too much trouble. Thurstone's paired-comparison technique of scale construction is not very practical because of the labor involved, but a quite similar although cruder scale using a simpler method of ranking the items will usually serve the teacher's purposes. The writer has found, for example, that a selection of statements which a few judges (two or three) agree vary along a continuum from "most" to "least" favorable, but not necessarily in equal steps, will give a fairly reliable measure of attitude, and the labor of construction is not prohibitive even if the scale is to be seldom used. Simple attitude questionnaires, where agreement with favorable and disagreement with unfavorable statements related to various aspects of the issue in question are to be summated, may also be found useful. Such teacher-

---

[6] One who seriously proposes to investigate this field could well begin with Quinn McNemar's general review and summary, "Opinion-Attitude Methodology," in *Psychological Bulletin*, XLIII (July, 1946), 289–374.

made attitude tests will probably compare about as favorably with standardized instruments as a teacher-made factual learning or skills test does with a standard test. Pupil participation in the construction of such instruments has the added advantage that the experience will help them crystalize their opinions. Self-inventories, modeled after such instruments as the *Strong Vocational Interest Blank*, the *Kuder Preference Record*, or the *Allport-Vernon Study of Values*, also lend themselves to evaluating interests and ideals if there is no compulsion to deceive. Tests of this type are not difficult to make.

One cannot always determine whether pupils can and will freely reveal their attitudes—the teaching situation, itself, being a determining factor. Some teachers can develop an atmosphere wherein pupils freely discuss their feelings on most any matter; other teachers are not so successful. The teacher who encourages free expression, who is quick to defend the right to differ, who is not too free in revealing his own feelings, can expect that many attitudes, the expression of which would usually be inhibited, will be freely revealed. There will, however, almost surely be some attitudes with which teachers are concerned which are of such a nature that we may expect distorting effects resulting from the obvious approach. In the typical school situation, the interest of pupils in mathematics might not be freely revealed to the mathematics teacher; a preference for hillbilly music might well be kept from some music teachers; prejudices which were characteristic of only a minority of a class would probably be hidden; attitudes or interests in opposition to the moral or social codes would certainly be inhibited. Other attitudes and feelings may never have been verbalized, and agreement or disagreement with verbal expressions would not give valid evidence on attitudes.

The best leads for evaluation of affective learnings come from the field of projective testing.[7] Although the currently popular projective tests are generally designed to get at highly complex personality patterns, usually call for unstructured responses, and are complicated to make and use, these factors are not inherent in the method. The essential characteristic of a projective test is the fact that the subject unconsciously projects his personality into his response. This he may do because the purpose of the test is disguised or he may do it simply because of the freedom he is allowed in response. "Free association" tests, popular many years ago, many variations of sentence completion tests, or such a simple instrument as the "Guess Who" test, developed by Hartshorne and May around 1925 to measure reputation, are all projective tests. Once the teacher gets the

---

[7] *An Introduction to Projective Techniques* (Edited by Harold and Gladys Anderson. New York: Prentice-Hall, Inc., 1951), studied for its implications for the evaluation of pupil learning, should be found a very rewarding experience.

idea, pictures, cartoons, verbal sketches, movie strips, staged incidents, and many other types of data may be presented to pupils for the purpose of eliciting responses which reveal attitudes. Pictures of Negro and white children together in varied situations (perhaps mixed in with other "neutral" pictures) presented with the request, "What is this picture about?" or "Do you see anything wrong in this picture?" might well reveal attitudes toward the Negro when verbal attitude scales or questionnaires would not. Choice of reading matter during a "free" reading period (providing a great variety was available, and providing the pupil was not aware of being observed) possibly would give a better indication of reading interests than would an interest inventory. Sociometric techniques, which are essentially "projective" in nature, will also be found useful for testing many social attitudes as well as other interpersonal learnings. Even psychodrama would appear to have possibilities for use in collecting evidence of learnings in this general field. Interpretations of signs collected through projective methods can often be quantified by determining the per cent of all signs revealed which are favorable. This percentage technique is usually required since the number of signs observed will not be the same for all pupils.

The teacher who has facilities and time for keeping anecdotal records, providing he has opportunity to observe the pupils in free situations and is clear with reference to the attitudes he is concerned in developing, can accumulate "signs" of attitudes, interests, and ideals through this means. Trying to keep anecdotal records is not too practical in a secondary school so organized that the teacher has to assume responsibility for guiding the daily learning of many pupils (from 120 to 200 or more), but if the school is to meet the learning needs of its pupils we will almost surely have to reduce the daily pupil-teacher ratio even if this demands that the teacher assume responsibility for guiding learning in wider fields. At any rate, all that is needed to make anecdotal records useful is opportunity to collect signs and some system for analyzing and interpreting the signs collected.[8]

If we propose to meet youth's educational needs we must attend to the affective aspects of pupil development, and there is no excuse for the common assumption that such outcomes are not susceptible to appraisal.

Testing Habit Formation. The school which becomes concerned over the in-school and out-of-school habits which its pupils are acquiring will also need to include in its evaluation program evidence relating to growth in

---

[8] J. Krugman and W. Wrightstone's *A Guide to the Use of Anecdotal Records* (Brooklyn, New York: Bureau of Reference, Research, and Statistics, Board of Education of the City of New York, 1949) is a useful, brief reference and contains a good bibliography for one who wishes to pursue the subject further.

this area. Theoretically, such appraisal raises no serious problems, but evidence is difficult to obtain, particularly that relating to out-of-school habits. Where a faculty is willing to tackle the job co-operatively, in-school habits are relatively easy to evaluate; but in modern schools where the population is drawn from a considerable geographic area and the contacts of the teacher with most of his pupils is limited almost entirely to the school, the task is great. The importance of this evidence is such, however, that the school must attempt to collect it. Sooner or later, the secondary school is going to be asked to justify its existence in terms of carry-over to out-of-school life, and this carry-over is largely a matter of habits. It is not so much what one *can do* as what one *does do* that counts.

For estimating the extent to which pupils are forming desirable habits, or breaking undesirable ones, we must depend heavily on observation of behavior. There are two principles to be followed if this observation is to result in valid evidence: First, the pupils must be observed in "free" situations, where there is no artificial compulsion to behave in a "proper manner." You cannot tell what a pupil's normal speech habits are by observing him in the presence of his English teacher or judge his eating habits generally by watching him when his girl has invited him to a "home economics" dinner. Secondly, to insure that observation will furnish valid evidence of learning, a systematic plan of organizing and interpreting the data collected must be adopted. Objectivity here, as in measurement generally, is obtained by having a defined set of rules which are followed. Observation may be done incidentally and informally or be done formally if this principle is observed. Generally speaking, the most satisfactory means of accumulating the evidence is through anec-dotal records. Systematizing the data accumulated is generally best done by the use of rating scales.

Projective techniques would also seem to offer possibilities for getting evidence on out-of-school habits. Interviews, subtly handled, or written material, carefully planned, could be very revealing.[9] For evidence in such cases, the purpose of questioning might be hidden or one might de-pend on the freedom of response. Many teachers have found that they can get valuable insights into the habits of their pupils from autobio-graphical writings. The writer has successfully used a formalized diary technique to study the ways in which junior high school students spend

---

[9] Persons interested in reading further on this subject might like to see this writer's article, "The Essay Examination as a Projective Technique," which appeared in *Educational and Psychological Measurement*, VIII (Spring, 1948), 15–31, and cer-tainly should read G. W. Allport's monograph, *The Use of Personal Documents in Psychological Science*, Social Science Research Monograph, No. 49. New York Social Science Research Council, 1942.

their out-of-school time. A standardized blank, presented at the opening of the school day as a test of the accuracy of memory and reporting, called for information on what the pupil had done, where he did it, why he did it, and with whom he did it, for half-hour intervals from the closing of school the previous day. Tests made by checking with parents and cross-checking the pupils' reports indicated that, at this age range at least, the method gave valid evidence.

The job of testing for habits is a difficult one, but, if a school faculty will tackle it together, satisfactory evidence can be accumulated. Habits, like factual learnings, understandings, skills, and attitudes, are reflected in changed behavior, and evidence of change in all these aspects of learning will be needed in the secondary school which proposes to build its program to serve all the learning needs of youth.[10]

Testing for Multiple-Learnings. As a matter of convenience, we have treated the problems of testing for the several aspects of learning separately, but this does not imply that each will of necessity be tested separately. Just as the child learns as a unitary whole, so he performs in a test situation. Many tests can be so planned as to yield evidence relating to learning in several areas. In fact, many teachers plan such tests, then destroy the evidence which they have collected through unsystematic analysis and crude, mathematical summations of their data. An essay, to illustrate, may be planned to reveal evidence of skill in the mechanics of English, ability to organize one's thoughts, understanding of some social issue, and attitude toward the issue; yet the interpretation of the data, the grade or mark given, hides these important facts. If we are to test widely as will be demanded in a school which seeks learning outcomes on a wide front, the problem of economy in testing becomes an important one. One way to save time would be to plan test situations which yield evidence on several of the outcomes being sought. Tyler and his associates made important beginnings in this direction in some of the tests developed for use in the Eight Year Study of the Progressive Education Association. Other means will probably have to be explored, but they await investigation by scholars in the field. Simplified versions of "situational tests" such as those used by the Office of Strategic Services for the selection of men for military intelligence work, for example, would appear to have promise.[11]

---

[10] Good suggestions on observation techniques in the study of children will be found in Ruth Strang's *Introduction to Child Study* (New York: Macmillan Co., 1951) and in *Helping Teachers Understand Children*, a handbook developed by the staff of the Division on Child Development of the American Council on Education (Washington: American Council on Education, 1945).

[11] Office of Strategic Service Assessment Staff, *Assessment of Men* (New York: Rinehart & Co., 1948). This is a stimulating account of a very clever testing program

Testing the Instruments. Finally, the reliability and validity of all "homemade" instruments for testing learning outcomes will need to be established. For some learnings, particularly out-of-school habits, the task of getting an adequate sample is considerable. Some instruments will have "face validity"; that is, the items will obviously be elements of the total being tested, and their summation will obviously reflect the total. Such cases would be a test of understanding of technical vocabulary (providing the content was "new"), a typing test, or a check sheet for "school citizenship habits." For tests where items are random samples from a homogenous body of materials, a crude test for internal consistency will probably satisfy the demand for evidence of validity; at least such evidence is commonly accepted. The validity of other instruments, (projective tests; analyses of anecdotal records; rating scales for complex, integrated skills or habits; self-inventories) will need to be checked against some outside criteria. The teacher who is "validity conscious" will think of many ways of getting such evidence.

Through the several means considered here, perhaps through others which resourceful teachers will develop as they work at the job, information will be assembled as to the total learning of the pupils. From an interpretation of these data we can evaluate progress and plan intelligently for next steps in learning and teaching.

INTERPRETING EVIDENCES OF ACHIEVEMENT

Weakness of the Conventional Interpretation. Teachers' tests are currently interpreted primarily for the purpose of getting a summary description of the level of performance or achievement of the pupil. This is done by summating points earned (or by averaging percentages) and converting this total (or average) into a grade (or mark). Such interpretations are more or less meaningless, are often deceiving, and at best have limited usefulness. Their meanings are usually vague because each school adopts its own set of symbols and each teacher makes his own definitions of the symbols. Furthermore, the illusion of accuracy created, particularly by percentage grades or by the generous use of pluses and minuses, combined with the tendency of everyone to interpret the grades in terms of his own definitions rather than in terms of the definition of the person who gave them, means that grades are often misleading. Even assuming that we could overcome these weaknesses in the grading system, we still have left the fact that any summation or average of achievements as varied as those sought in the modern school hides more than it reveals. When we average up "book learning" and laboratory technique in a sci-

and should be read by anyone who wishes to undertake the evaluation of learning on a broader front than the schools ordinarily consider.

ence course and come out with a mark of *C* for three different pupils we
may easily cover up the fact that one of the pupils is average in both
verbal learnings and laboratory technique, the second is skilled and
ingenious in the laboratory but poor in verbal learning, while the third is
just the reverse. And this information may be exactly what we need to
advise the pupils intelligently as to the next steps. If the school undertakes to meet yet other needs of its pupils, matters will become even
worse. Attempting to describe with a single symbol achievements as
diverse as those we have considered in previous sections of this chapter
would seem to be next to impossible.

The secondary school which proposes to develop a satisfactory evaluation program will need to find means other than grades for interpreting
the evidence of achievement which it collects. We can undertake here
only to point out in general terms what some of the characteristics of an
adequate approach will be.[12]

Two Aspects of the Job. First of all, the fundamental reason for making
any interpretation of evidences of learning is to get information which
will help the pupil, or help the teacher in working further with him. Once
this fact is accepted and appreciated, the inadequacy of any grading system for doing the job becomes obvious. Instead, the task involves (*a*)
making some meaningful interpretation of achievement in each of the
several aspects of learning which are being sought, and (*b*) examining
these several achievements and their interrelations for clues as to next
steps in working with youth. In a sense, what we should work toward is a
profile of achievements rather than a summation. Even when used intelligently, a summation of varied evidences of learning hides most of the
information which would be of value to one who proposes to use the results of evaluation procedures in meeting the needs of youth. It is the
configuration of achievements which yields the most useful information
for this purpose.

Interpreting Evidence in a Particular Aspect of Learning. Let us make
some further analysis of the process. First, what means for interpreting
measures of achievement in a particular aspect of learning are available?
Grades, assuming that they are carefully defined and their definitions
understood and accepted by everyone concerned, do constitute one possibility; but only one. When standard tests are used, the standard score
is usually a much more meaningful and useful device. When one knows
that a student's reading skill is at the sixty-seventh percentile in a large

---

[12] The approach to interpretation which is made here closely parallels that presented in the *Assessment of Men, op. cit.* Although the writer had the ideas previously,
had, in fact, written concerning them, nevertheless he is indebted to the OSS Assessment Staff for a considerable clarification of his thinking on the problem.

sample of pupils of similar status, why bury the fact by converting it into a *B* or *C* grade? The social-studies teacher who feels that her students should be tolerant toward racial minorities has her work cut out for her when she finds by means of Hinckley's *Attitude-toward-the-Negro Scale* that Johnny, in terms of the norms, is *very unfavorable* in attitude.

For other types of learning outcomes, a meaningful interpretation may be made by comparing the pupil's performance with some predetermined standard or standards of performance. If a typing rate of 40 words per minute is the minimum Civil Service requirement for a junior typist, to say that a girl types at the rate of 47 words per minute is certainly more meaningful than to say she makes a *B* in second-year typing. The English teacher who assumes that his pupils should be able to spell all of the "100 spelling demons," knows what the job before him is when he finds that Johnny spells 57 of them correctly. The shop teacher needs no relative interpretation, a grade or any other, in order to determine whether a particular pupil can operate a machine in such a manner as to reduce to a minimum the chance of losing a finger.

For other purposes which the teacher or pupil may have, the only interpretation of test results required may be done in terms of the pupil's own needs, his capabilities, or his previous performance: This pupil can't extract the square root, we teach him and find that he can now do it; this boy, with an intelligence quotient of 75, is now reading good comic books with understanding; an accompaniment of this girl's work in fingerpainting has been a reduction in her nervous tensions; in typing, this girl has at last moved off a plateau and is increasing her speed. Interpretation of learnings such as these can be made by the teacher or pupil without any direct reference to the accomplishment of others.

For yet other learnings and purposes, the best interpretation may be an expression of position in the class, some "man-to-man" or "order-of-merit" rating. Grading "on the curve" is a special case of such rating; but a simple arrangement of the class from high to low is another. For any such rating to be useful, the quality or qualities being rated must be clearly defined and the steps in the scale must be understood by all concerned. For most purposes, perhaps a simple quintile ranking (or when groups are larger, decile) is the most satisfactory one to use, and it has the advantage that its meaning is easily grasped and accepted for what it is.

The point we have tried to make is that instead of seeking a uniform method of interpreting all learnings for all purposes, we should seek the most meaningful interpretation of the particular learnings for the particular purpose.

Examining the Pattern of Achievements. Having obtained some interpretation of learning in the several areas with which the school is concerned, the final step in evaluation consists of laying out these data in a pattern which makes possible an examination of the relations of each to the other and to the total. From a study of this design and its relation to student needs will come the best leads as to next steps for learning and teaching.

Let us see what such interpretation will be like in a typical class situation. A science class has just finished a series of "small group" projects. In preparation for a planning session where decisions will be made as to next steps in their study, the teacher is reviewing the folders of his pupils. Here is a boy with high academic intelligence (intelligence quotient, 130), from a socially mobile family, who wants to be a scientist. Although seemingly he is not aware of it, he is more or less rejected by the group and, at the age of 17, has no girl friend. He is still sloppy in his work and has a tendency to make snap judgments. He reads widely in science and is at the 97th percentile on a science-information test. He is one of a group of five which has just completed a study of the history of the atom bomb. His understanding of the bomb and its history far surpassed that of anyone else in the group, but the other members refused his leadership, and, partly at least, as a result, the group did a mediocre job.

In light of these facts, the teacher makes notes as follows:

1. Ask for written personal evaluation of his achievements in last project, and have conference.
2. Suggest he work out rating scale to judge own work before submitting it.
3. Try to interest in independent study of scientific method—might begin with Dewey's *How We Think*.
4. Seek help from some of more mature girls in class.
5. At beginning of next group project, raise question with him concerning his procedure, and talk to some members of group concerning him.

Such interpretations of learning will be highly flexible, varying from pupil to pupil and situation to situation; within the limits of practicality, they will always be inclusive; and the focus will be on planning next steps, on further growth. They obviously will demand considerable skill on the part of the teacher, but they are the essence of good guidance.

Failure to consider the total pattern of achievements and its relation to needs results in such one-sided growth as we commonly see in schools: learning the facts concerning English Literature but at the same time learning to hate it; spending more and more time "among the books," which are already being used as an escape mechanism; memorizing the rules of good health but making no application of them; acquiring the abilities and skills for vocational success and along with them developing antisocial habits which preclude the possibility of useful citizenship. And one of the most serious blocks to such interpretation has been the insistence that we have a uniform grading system where the total achievement of a pupil is expressed by one of a limited number of symbols. This is not to say that there may not be need for a summary statement of learnings, but this summary will be in the form of one or more paragraphs, not in terms of a single letter or number.

THE ROLE OF PUPIL AND PATRON IN EVALUATION

The Role of the Pupil. If evaluation of learning is done well, it will require the co-operation of teachers, pupils, and parents. We have so far presented the problem primarily from the standpoint of the teacher; but this should not be construed as meaning that evaluation is the sole responsibility of the teacher. Ideally, evaluation is as much an integral part of learning as it is of teaching. Youth in the secondary school of the future will surely play a much more important part in the process than they currently do. Whenever in the teaching-learning situation the pupil's purposes coincide with those of the teacher, evaluation should be a joint enterprise. That is, pupils should share in identifying the learnings to be sought, in planning means of determining success, and in the collection and interpretation of evidence of learning.

This co-operative approach not only makes for better evaluation but also means that teaching and learning will be at their maximum effectiveness. Participation in identifying the learnings to be sought aids in the clarification of the pupil's own purposes; having a part in planning the means of determining success requires that he translate his purposes into observable changes in behavior, sharing in collecting and interpreting evidence of learning has the added advantage that it contributes to the kind of rapport that is so essential for good learning situations. The teacher who develops with his students a good rating scale for judging some skill, in effect, places a copy of his "final examination" in the hands of those students long before examination day. They can see the essential qualities which make up the skill and can judge themselves throughout the course of learning; they will know and accept the bases upon which their teacher proposes to judge them.

The reader is cautioned not to interpret the above statements as indicating advocacy of the practice in which some teachers engage, of having pupils determine their own grade or the grades of one another. Such practices result from a misconception of the role of evaluation in learning and teaching. In the preceding section of this chapter the writer has taken the position that grading as commonly done has no place in a good evaluation program. Until such time as more satisfactory means of reporting on learnings are adopted, however, the responsibility for making summary judgments of learning is placed on the teacher and he cannot rightfully shirk it. Although the teacher may well include among the data which he takes into consideration the pupil's own judgment of his learning or even the judgment of his classmates, nevertheless, the final decision is the teacher's to make.

Furthermore, there will undoubtedly always be some learnings that the teacher seeks for high-school youth which they are not yet mature enough to recognize and accept as purposes of their own. Teachers will naturally anticipate needs of their students and work toward their achievement. The teacher who sees among his students signs of intolerance, poor reading skill, habits of evading reality, too low standards of work, or a confusion of correlation with causation is apt to be concerned, even when the students are not conscious of the condition. In fact, many times the teaching is directed toward creating an awareness of weaknesses, and the measure of success would then be in terms of the extent to which the young people become aware of their needs and concerned about them. At other times, the teacher may decide that creating awareness would not contribute to learning, might even interfere with it, and he would work by indirection. In all such cases the teacher must carry the burden of evaluation alone. Student participation, even consciousness of the fact that they are being judged, may have such distorting effects on their responses as to completely invalidate any evidence collected. The rule to follow is this: To the extent that the student accepts as his own the goals set for him by the teacher, he should participate in the evaluation; if the teacher's goals are not the student's then the teacher must of necessity accept the responsibility.

The Role of the Patron. If anything like a complete evaluation of pupil learning is to be achieved, the teacher will also need to solicit the aid of parents and patrons generally in evaluating pupil growth. Particularly will such help be needed in collecting evidence on the out-of-school carry-over of learnings. Much evidence of learning, or lack of learning, can be observed and reported on not only by parents but by recreation directors, scout leaders, Sunday-school teachers, employers, and others having contacts with pupils, but valid use of such aid requires reliable judgment on the part of the teachers.

The rule for deciding what part in evaluation these out-of-school adults should play is the same as that stated above for determining pupil participation. To the extent that the patrons' purposes are harmonious with those of the teacher, evidence which they collect and report can be accepted. If the mother's aim is the same as that of the teacher (to help the daughter, for example, to learn to take care of her own room and clothes), then the mother can assist in collecting evidence of progress; if her aim is to make her daughter appear well in the eyes of the teacher, it is another matter. If the boy's employer is concerned over helping the boy acquire the skills of a trade, his observations can be useful; if he is only interested in exploiting the boy or in contrasting the present-day school with schools in the "good old days," his contribution to evaluation will have limited value.

The fact is that, in many present-day schools, aid in evaluation from adults of the community is sought by teachers. Agriculture and home-economics teachers, for instance, depend heavily on parents for reports concerning certain learnings, and teachers of such work as diversified occupations (where pupils spend half the day on a job) turn to the pupil's employer for aid in evaluating learning.

As parents and others come to realize that the teacher's evaluations are made for the purpose of helping the child learn, we can expect that they will play a larger and larger role in the process. The truth is, of course, to date most of our so-called evaluation has not been done for the purpose of helping pupils.

The Demands of Such an Approach to Evaluation

Need Trained Teachers. The practical implementation of a program of evaluation such as has been set forth in this chapter makes heavy, new demands on the secondary school—demands which the school is not at present equipped to meet. In the first place, it demands a type of training which most teachers in service have not had and which most teachers in training are not now getting. Probably the majority of teachers in American secondary schools have had no training of any sort in evaluation, and most of these who have had training had nothing more than a narrow study of standard tests with perhaps a unit (or chapter) on teacher-made, paper-and-pencil tests. The same sort of limited treatment of evaluation seems to characterize most of the courses in tests and measurements offered in teacher-education institutions today. Textbooks in the field, by and large, make an equally limited approach. The type of training which would seem appropriate would be roughly that outlined in this chapter; that is, it would help teachers to identify *all* the learnings which they were seeking through their teaching, it would give them practice in developing and using instruments of all sorts for getting evidence concerning the varied kinds of learning which were sought, and train them in interpreting these data to the end that the progress of youth toward their goals will be bettered.

Need Expert Assistance. Giving teachers a different type of training will not, however, solve all the problems. There is not time in the education of a teacher to make an expert in evaluation out of him, yet he will face many problems which require the help of an expert. So far as the writer can see, the only practical solution is to provide such assistance through the consultative staff of the school. A person broadly trained in evaluation, who is familiar with available instruments and techniques and is skilled in working with individual teachers and teacher-groups, should be able to furnish the necessary "expertness" for a considerable group of teachers. The trouble here is that such "evaluators" are not plentiful. Few schools have persons so trained on the supervisory staff, and but few teacher-education institutions are training them. It seems that if we are to have better evaluation the place to start is at the teacher-education level. In view of the resistance to change, which characterizes most institutions for the education of teachers, perhaps the best practical point of attack would be pressure from the consumers of their products, the leaders in secondary education.

Need a "Faculty" Approach. Adequate appraisal will demand, too, a co-operative (or faculty) approach, rather than the individual (or teacher) approach which is presently customary. Although each teacher will almost certainly be seeking some learnings which are his concern alone, many learnings will be the common concern of several teachers, and approaching evaluation individually is wasteful. Take, for example, ability to do straight thinking, the habit of assuming responsibility, skill in expressing one's self effectively, or understanding of the scientific method. These are outcomes which we would surely find not one but several teachers concerned with. Moreover, better evidence of learning can often be collected by teachers other than the one directly responsible for the teaching. Many of the so-called "tool" subjects are of this sort. Habits of using acceptable English and the transfer of mathematical skills to fields not primarily mathematical are good illustrations. Actually, one's fellow-teachers are often in the best position to collect evidence of the extent of transfer of any learning. A co-operative, give-and-take arrangement would seem to be the sensible means for appraisal of this learning.

Need New Instruments and Aids. If, and when, any number of schools undertake educational evaluation in a manner such as has been outlined here, it is to be hoped that we would find a broadened attack on the testing of achievement by professional test-makers and test publishers. At the present time, aside from tests of factual learning, of simple skills, and to a lesser degree of understandings, but few instruments are to be had. It would seem reasonable to assume that when numbers of teachers become concerned over the teaching of and testing for other learnings, new instruments will become available. Standardized and unstandardized instruments, more carefully and skilfully constructed and validated than can be expected from the ordinary classroom teacher, for testing commonly sought-for attitudes, complex skills, and habit systems would serve a useful purpose and at the same time should be profitable to publishers.

Need Reorientation in Research. Finally, satisfactory implementation of a sound evaluation program will require a reorientation on the part of many researchers in the field of measurement and evaluation. There are any number of problems crying for investigation. The possibilities of projective techniques (both disguised and free-response testing) for getting evidence of achievement, adaptations of rating techniques to the testing of school learnings, the influence of the medium of testing (both the medium of impression and of expression) on observed achievement in varied fields of learning and for youth of varying psychological make-ups, the possibility of developing "situation" tests which will yield evidence of the learning of varied types of outcome, the implications of factor analysis for more efficient measurement of learning outcomes of the type the secondary school is concerned with, the development of satisfactory means for interpreting school learnings in terms of the "profile" rather than the "summation" concept, and the educational effects of pupil and patron participation in evaluation are among those which have occurred to the writer as he has prepared this chapter. If one would criticize current research in the field it would be in terms of the fact that too much of it seems to be directed toward getting more and more refined measures of more and more limited outcomes of learning. In the meantime, teachers even now work diligently to develop many learnings for the appraisal of which they get little or no help.

Conclusion

Let it be said the writer is well aware that a program of evaluation such as has been outlined here imposes a big job on the school. Probably most schools will but approach it as a goal. This is well and good, providing they do so with the realization that to the extent they do achieve such a goal, and to that extent alone, can they intelligently develop a school program in terms of all the needs of youth.

CHAPTER XV

EDUCATION OF TEACHERS TO MEET THE NEEDS OF YOUTH

J. G. Umstattd[1]

Professor of Secondary Education
University of Texas
Austin, Texas

The Task Set for Teacher Education

The preceding chapters and the one that follows impose a twofold task upon teacher education. New orientations and new practices will be required in preservice teacher education if the young graduate is to be able to teach, to counsel, or to administer in the manner specified in this volume. Also, the in-service leadership of teacher education must help to redirect the thinking and the efforts of those now teaching who were prepared for the subject-centered high school if they are to work effectively in the needs-serving program for youth as proposed by this yearbook.

The final draft of the present chapter was prepared after a careful reading of twelve other chapters of the volume that were available at the time. The writer has attempted to treat only those aspects of preservice and in-service teacher education that appear to be of greatest importance in the light of the other discussions. Some of the ideas involved in this treatment were specifically stated by the other contributors, others were implied, and still others seemed to emerge of their own accord. Implied throughout the volume is the demand for superior personal qualities in the entire school staff. Of no less significance is the constant implication that general institutional prerequisites must be met if the total job of teacher education is to be well done. Repetition has stressed the need for school personnel to be both broadly educated to understand and to interpret life and specifically trained to determine pupil needs and to satisfy them through teaching, counseling, and administration. Frequent mention is made of new concepts of curriculum, method, and evaluation. As many as possible of these and other rich and varied suggestions have been

---

[1] The writer is grateful to L. D. Haskew for helping prepare the preliminary outline of this chapter and for making additional contributions after the first draft of the manuscript had been completed. He is also indebted to J. Earle Grinnell for reading the original manuscript critically and for making numerous suggestions for its improvement.

treated as space permits. Only bare reference is made to those fully treated in other chapters. The reader is referred to other sources for those aspects of teacher education that have little relationship to the theme of the yearbook.

The Kind of Person Needed

The kind of person required as teacher in the secondary school under discussion is of fundamental importance to teacher education. High intelligence is needed to detect and to differentiate needs as described in chapter ii. A vivid imagination is required to design the programs suggested in chapters vi through x and to devise experiences to serve the changing and varied needs therein discussed. The broad gap in teaching between what has been done and what one feels must be undertaken by the secondary school challenges the inventiveness of the most creative of persons. Increasing initiative and insight are demanded by the ever broadening responsibility assigned the modern teacher as counselor (see chap. xi). The growing tension of life requires that the teacher possess emotional stability, poise, and self-reliance. It may be possible to develop some of these essential personal traits during the period of professional training, but the latent qualities must be there at the beginning.

Once the candidate has been admitted to teacher education, additional attributes of a personal nature are essential. High in the list is the willingness to accept the pupil. He must gain understanding, too, of the effect of emotion upon learning and the effect of social class upon the attitudes a child brings to school. His own prejudices, bred and nourished in him by his own social group and causing him to reject persons of another class or creed or race, must give way to social maturity. A primary goal of teacher education, then, is that each prospective teacher gain the social development, or call it spiritual growth if you will, that will give him the sincerity of purpose and humility of spirit needed for the spontaneous and complete acceptance of all pupils placed under his care.

No less a goal of teacher education is that all prospective teachers develop a high degree of professional zeal. When Dr. Seagrave, the Burma Surgeon, was released from jail in the spring of 1951, his first thought was to get back to work in his hospital in Northern Burma. The medical interne accepts in good spirit the two years of intensive postdoctoral professional work, without pay, beyond his seven years of college preparation; in fact his zeal for his profession seems to increase in proportion to the rigor of his training. It is such a zeal that must be engendered during the period of teacher education. Anything less than complete dedication to teaching will fail to meet the personal requirements for the teacher in the kind of secondary school anticipated by this volume.

General Institutional Prerequisites

The quality of the institution should parallel the quality of the prospective teacher. Ways must be found to improve more rapidly the work of institutions that hold teacher education to be one of their aims. Two lines of thought will suggest the need for the more rapid growth in effectiveness. First, a brief sketch of the struggle for the professional education of teachers during the last seventy-five years will show how slow the growth has been. And, secondly, an appraisal of the present-day quality of teacher-education institutions will indicate the distance yet to go to achieve excellence. Our purpose here will be served by a paragraph to each point.

The resistance of college faculties to courses in "pedagogy" was a barrier at the beginning and has persisted in some places throughout the life of the teacher-education movement. Like other fields, education has been forced to prove itself before being accepted among the disciplines of the college. Near the turn of the century the almost-universal reaction to the new field of education was a contemptuous "bag of tricks." The only recognized preparation to teach was the mastery of the "liberal" arts. Gradually, as substance was added to the field and as the critics became better informed, education became recognized in the college catalogues. But the pace has been so slow that even today one may hear reverberations of the struggle. At this rate another century might be needed to achieve the excellence in teacher education required to equip teachers for the tasks contemplated by the programs described in this yearbook.

A glance at the current scene will suggest the distance yet to be traveled. The layman's appraisal of our teacher-education institutions is given in the headline across pages 146-47 in the October 16, 1950, issue of *Life:* "Their Scorned and Neglected Colleges Are Appallingly Ill Equipped for Job." Only the very best institutions approach the standard of quality that all must attain to bring to life the secondary-school program envisioned by other writers of this yearbook. The worst are rendering a disservice by perpetuating obsolete and even deleterious practices. Only in recent years has teacher education attempted to appraise itself.[2] At the moment no one can say how good teacher education is because results of qualitative measurements of more than a sample of the institutions do not exist; in fact, we cannot define "good" in this context. If the kind of teaching required for the task herein described is good teaching, then those teacher-education practices which prepare students for that

---

[2] American Association of Colleges for Teacher Education, *Revised Standards for Accrediting Colleges for Teacher Education.* Oneonta, New York: The Association (11 Elm Street), 1951.

kind of teaching are good practices and the institution that develops and uses those practices is a good institution. By this criterion, there are now very few good institutions, and the present pace of progress toward this standard of goodness is indeed slow.

There seem to be several prerequisites to an increased rate of improvement. First, it would help if all members of the education staff were persons who reflect rich, liberal education. They might well possess those refinements of taste and personal living that through even casual contact impart similar qualities in some measure to others. Broad knowledge, intellectual integrity, and personal charm would enable them to win the esteem and confidence of colleagues both outside and within the education faculty. Of great significance would be their ability to demonstrate the skill and quality of teaching that their students will need as teachers of modern youth.[3]

A second prerequisite is that liberal-arts faculties appreciate that the problems of teacher education are their own problems. This prerequisite is valid because prospective secondary-school teachers of academic fields obtain about four-fifths of their college training in liberal arts. If the faculty which has the student four-fifths of the time is antagonistic to the other one-fifth of the student's curriculum, it becomes impossible for the one-fifth to succeed. It is fortunate for modern teacher education that co-operation is gradually replacing conflict on the campus. Faculties of all colleges in some institutions are studying their own materials and their own problems of teaching. Regional groups are pooling their efforts to improve curriculum and instruction.[4]

A third general institutional prerequisite essential to the success of any program of teacher education is that the entire faculty of the institution have frequent contact with secondary schools. No person on an education faculty is qualified whose mental image of secondary education is that of his own high school of ten, twenty, or forty years ago. It is also important that members of other faculties keep a contact with high school somewhat more intimate than that which comes from having their own children in high school. No institution in our society has changed more than

---

[3] Fred J. Kelley, *Toward Better College Teaching* (United States Office of Education Bulletin, No. 13. Washington: Government Printing Office, 1950); Fred J. Kelley, *Improving College Instruction* (Washington: American Council on Education, 1951); see also Edward M. Palmquist and Donald F. Drummond (editors), *Toward Better Teaching* (Columbia, Missouri: Committee for the Improvement of Instruction, University of Missouri, 1951).

[4] Russell M. Cooper, *et al.*, *Better Colleges—Better Teachers.* Published by the Committee on Preparation of High School Teachers in Colleges of Liberal Arts of the North Central Association of Colleges and Secondary Schools. New York: Distributed by Macmillan Co., 1944.

the secondary school during the last quarter century, and the need for even greater changes is indicated in this volume. This fact can be fully comprehended only by contact with the school. Faculty members who do not make such contact are likely to become obstructionists to progress in teacher education.

Still another prerequisite for the institution to meet if it is to prepare teachers for the modern school is that it be constantly alert to social change and to advances in all areas of knowledge. If the institution itself does not move along with society, it cannot prepare teachers to cope with the problems of youth today. If members of the staff show ignorance in their respective fields, they cannot hold the respect of youth eager to become teachers in the modern school. Teacher-education institutions must continually follow the frontier of social progress, and their faculty members must not only be informed of new knowledge but they must themselves contribute to it in their respective fields.

Finally, the general administrative and budgetary policy of the institution must be such that the professionalization aspects of teacher education can be given their place in the sun. The proper study of children requires laboratory facilities as surely as does the proper study of bacteria. Adequate supervision of student teaching cannot be run on a shoestring. Good in-service education cannot be provided in summer sessions by herding all comers into large sections for financial profit; nor can good in-service training be provided by lecturing to such large sections about "not lecturing to" high-school students.

DEVELOPMENTS IN PRESERVICE TEACHER EDUCATION

A number of significant elements in teacher education are suggested by the content of other chapters. The need for a knowledge of changing social forces, for example, is made clear in chapter i. The need for professional zeal and the demand for personnel of superior quality are implied throughout. Specific learnings are required for the work described in such chapters as ii, iv, vii, xii, and xiv. The attempt is made here to draw the more important of these suggestions from their places in the several chapters and to treat them as proposed developments for preservice teacher education.

A Dynamic and Modern Point of View

It is most imperative that those institutions which seek to improve society should themselves be most sensitive to its course. In the vanguard of those institutions is the college or university which prepares the teachers for the next generation. It is inconceivable, then, that the point of view of teacher education be any other than that which reflects the dynamics of the present. To achieve this standard the institution itself should be democratic in its administration, in its staff relationships, and in all its dealings with students.

A second way in which the institution may reveal sensitivity to societal change is to promote freedom of discussion of the controversial issues of the day. No institution is qualified to educate teachers for the modern world whose governing board restricts the right of free discussion in the search for truth, be the source of the restraint social, political, economic, or religious. No selfish or partisan motive can be permitted to lend bias to the education of teachers if they are honestly to serve the needs of youth. In a world demanding freedom of the spirit there can be no enslavement of the mind.

A Continuous Process of Professionalization

Since professional zeal is the motive power of the teacher, it is important that professionalization be a constant aim of the institution, one to which well-planned and continuous effort is given. The procedures might well begin in the secondary school with activities for the recruitment of superior youth. Co-operative effort between the public schools and the teacher-education institution would soon result in a number of mutually advantageous practices, all directed toward interesting young people in teaching and stirring within them the beginnings of professional spirit. More direct means of recruitment and preprofessionalization would include sponsoring high-school chapters of Future Teachers of America, supplying professional leaflets and posters for use in school libraries and corridors, and promoting visits of high-school students to the college campus.

The first courses in teacher-education carry a heavy responsibility for professionalization. They should be planned to reveal the compensations of teaching as a way of life. The courses should be taught by teachers whose knowledge and skill win the admiration of the embryonic teacher and whose zeal for the work inspires emulation. The courses should have very little of the customary dry, tabular encyclopaedic and a great deal of the attractively written and well-illustrated information. Laboratory experiences, visual aids, and contact with school should supplement the discussion. Teachers of marked success and others in their first year of teaching could be brought before the beginning classes for consultation. A college committee on the introductory course should be constantly at work to devise ways of making this first course a professional experience of first order.

Organizations for students of education provide another important means of professionalization. On many campuses these organizations starve for lack of a faculty sponsor with time to devote to the development of the organization. This situation could be corrected by relieving sponsors of a part of their load as teachers. A sufficient number of national campus organizations already exist to serve the purpose of professionalization if time and effort were devoted to their local development. Still another avenue is afforded by national and state associations which encourage students to become members at reduced rates. This plan has the merit of making the journals of professional organizations readily available to students and of giving them the opportunity to attend conventions.

The demands of professionalization require that the total curriculum of the teacher-education institution be under constant study and be continuously subject to revision. The needs of teachers become the guidelines for such revision. To keep abreast of such needs some institutions use advisory committees from the field; others employ studies by committees from their own staff. Particularly valuable are the studies conducted through the National Commission on Teacher Education and Professional Standards of the National Education Association, and through the various state advisory councils on teacher education. All-college or all-university curriculum committees for teacher education are becoming quite common and are proving of value in professionalizing the total program for prospective teachers.

Selective Admission

As stated above, the type of teaching and counseling described in the other chapters of the yearbook require persons of superior ability. Since selective admission is designed to raise the level of teacher-education candidates, it might well become a standard part of teacher education.[5]

A well-designed plan of selective admission probably should begin with selective recruitment in the high school. A guidance program such as the one described in chapter xi would be an effective aid to the selective recruitment. Here again, there is need for co-operation between high-school and college leaders in the development of practices that will be mutually advantageous, resulting in better service to high-school youth and the assurance of obtaining competent students for teacher education. It is probable that a system of scholarships would be needed to make teacher education possible for many able youth who could not otherwise go to college.

The techniques of selection should be repeated as the student seeks admission to the professional program in college. The standards for selec-

---

[5] The Curriculum Committee of the School of Education, Syracuse University, *A Functional Program of Teacher Education*, chap. iv. Washington: American Council on Education, 1941.

tion might well become progressively more exacting and in time be applied universally to public and private institutions alike, as is now true in medical education. In order that the program of selection may be administered effectively, the student should be under the guidance of the education division from the time he first enters college whether his first education course be taken in his Freshman, Sophomore, or Junior year. It is also important that the process of selection be continuous throughout the Bachelor's program, but the mode of guidance throughout should be positive in order to protect the mental health of the student and to give him confidence.

The procedures used by the College of Education, Wayne University, Detroit, illustrate the essentials of a superior program of selective admission.[6] Data are collected on "intellectual qualities," "physical qualities," and "qualities of personality" when the student applies for admission to teacher education. ("Students desiring to teach art, health education, music, homemaking, and industrial education" apply at the beginning of the Freshman year; all others apply at the beginning of the Junior year.) Evidence on intellectual qualities includes scholastic records in high school and college, a score on a mental test, and scores on handwriting, spelling, arithmetic, and English usage tests. A physical examination includes vision, hearing, speech, tuberculin, blood, and basal metabolism tests. The procedures used to obtain estimates of personality qualities include ratings by the student's former high-school principal or counselor; personal data and personal history forms which "give a complete picture of the life history of the student, with information concerning family, home life, economic status, interests, extracurriculum and club activities, and many other items of personal information"; ratings on qualities other than scholarship by four faculty members, including the pupil's official college adviser, with whom he has had work during his Freshman and Sophomore years; a rating by his prospective College of Education adviser based on an interview; ratings from employers if the student has been employed; an appraisal by a psychiatric physician where such a procedure is indicated; ratings from at least two youth-serving community agencies of different types with which the student must have served approximately one hundred clock hours during his Freshman and Sophomore years; and, in doubtful cases, an interview with the dean or assistant dean.

Selective admission to the teacher-education program at Wayne University, a public institution, has been in operation more than a decade.

---

[6] The writer is grateful to Robert M. Magee, Assistant Dean, for supplying the information about their program and for checking this statement for accuracy.

Between September, 1947, and May, 1951, of the 4,475 applicants for admission to the senior college professional work, 3,037 were admitted. Thus, about a third of the applicants either fail to complete their tests and interviews after filing an application blank or find themselves rejected upon the basis of the evidence collected. It is not known how many other students, wishing to become teachers but knowing of the standards to be met, do not apply for admission. It is probable that some of those who fail to finish their admissions tests and others who never apply might possess superior qualities for teaching; but it is almost certain that many in both groups have rendered education a service by not attempting to enter the profession.

Areas for Study and Experience

The insight and ability required for the job of serving the needs of the adolescent seem to the writer to be dependent upon prior study and experience in several important areas. Either by implication or by direct statement these areas are spotlighted in the accompanying chapters. The more widely accepted will be only barely mentioned here. Those closer to the frontier of practice will be given somewhat fuller treatment.

The Role of General Education. The general-education movement in curriculum making is a reaction against the extreme to which the elective system was carried. Its means and motives, however, delve deep into the sources of human living. Its basic content is the western civilization and its chief purpose is the conservation and promulgation of the values that lie at the foundation of that way of life. It is hailed as an antidote of humanism for an illness caused by a science and a technology that have lost value control. The role of general education in teacher education is at once apparent. It provides a faith by which to live and to help others live more richly. It carries the inspirational values that give motive power to a strenuous task. It becomes the chief instrument for the cultivation of those personal qualities of refinement fundamental to the teacher's mission. It supplies the content for many areas of teaching and the common force for the integration of all fields of knowledge.[7]

Broad Social Orientation. Closely related to general education are the social foundations of education. The relationship is almost that of parent to offspring because a large portion of the foundation is an integration of the changing environment. Add to the ingredients of general education,

---

[7] *General Education* (Fifty-first Yearbook of the National Society for the Study of Education, Part I. Chicago: University of Chicago Press, 1952); and W. Hugh Stickler, James Paul Stokes, and Louis Shores (editors), *General Education: A University Program in Action* (A report of the program at Florida State University. Dubuque, Iowa: Wm. C. Brown Co., 1950).

previously stated, the elements of the biological and psychological sciences which reveal the nature of man, and the social foundations of education are complete.

The *process* of integrating elements from general education and other sources into social foundations is of itself significant. The process of drawing related elements from a variety of sources around a new focus may be called the method of integration. It may be considered a part of social foundations of education since it is the general method that concentrates social meanings upon the problems of education. It should be noted that the integration will not occur without conscious and skilful effort on the part of the prospective teacher and his instructor. A study of the process is essential to its effective use.

It is obvious that social foundations are more than this process of distillation. They are, in addition, the product of the process and, as such, provide permanent insight into the problems of the teacher. In their totality, the social foundations should be given a significant position in the common core of teacher education.[8]

A Scientific Base for the Understanding of Children and Youth. Stressed throughout this volume as fundamentally important in teacher education are recent findings in educational psychology and other sciences in the area of child growth and development.[9] The new knowledge provides a scientific base for understanding the student as a person, thereby contributing to a fuller understanding of him as a learner. The prospective teacher must gain a full appreciation of recent results of studies in perception, motivation, and maturation. The basic theories of learning that have gained experimental support must be comprehended. It is imperative that the teacher understand the role of emotion in learning. He must learn the principles of mental health adequately to apply them in all his teaching. To some degree he should become able to detect symptoms of mental illness. The list might be extended, but it is clear that teacher education must be supported by scientific findings in human behavior. The following section provides further elaboration of this principle.

The Significance of Home Environment and Background for Meanings and Understanding. Every prospective teacher would profit from a full appreciation of the importance of past experience to present learning and development if he is to serve the diverse needs of children from vastly

[8] Harold Rugg (chairman), *The Emerging Task of the Social Foundations of Education.* Ann Arbor, Michigan: Report of the Committee on Social Foundations, National Society of College Teachers of Education, 1950.

[9] Marian E. Breckenridge and E. Lee Vincent, *Child Development.* Philadelphia: Saunders Co., 1943. Also: Robert J. Havighurst and Hilda Taba, *Adolescent Character and Personality.* New York: John Wiley & Sons, Inc., 1949.

different backgrounds. The key to the teacher's success in serving any child is frequently his knowledge of the social class from which the child came and his understanding of how the attitudes, mores, language habits, prejudices, and beliefs of the child's home environment affect his reactions at school.[10] The teacher must realize that words learned under different situations carry meanings that reflect the environments in which they are learned, thus making common vocabularies convey different ideas. He must understand that the concepts he seeks to develop are colored by understandings the child brings to school. In short, the elements of social psychology which have recently made clear the significance of social class for human behavior should be given an important place in the program of teacher education.

Understanding the Community. As the site of education moves out from the four walls of a schoolroom, and as the participation of citizens in the education of youth becomes greater, the teacher finds increasing need for a keen insight into community life. He should become aware of the many ways in which community agencies and influences other than the school are educating youth. He should develop skill in locating pressing needs of the community that can be met by adjustments in the school program. He needs an understanding of the social structure of the community, of its various agencies and institutions, and of the nature of public opinion in a community.[11]

Modern Concepts of Curriculum Development and Organization. An understanding of modern curriculum development and organization is so strategically important to the task of satisfying the needs of youth that an entire section of this yearbook is devoted to the problem. The reader is referred to chapters vii, viii, ix, x, and xi for thorough treatments of its various aspects.[12]

The Broadening Concept of Method. Method is the process that transforms potential into power. In industry it is the know-how of skill and management that transmutes raw labor and material into finished product. In painting it translates the vision into the masterpiece. In athletics it is the difference between sand lot and stadium. Excellence everywhere

---

[10] W. Lloyd Warner and Paul S. Lunt, *The Social Life of a Modern Community.* New Haven, Connecticut: Yale University Press, 1941. Also: W. Allison Davis and Robert J. Havighurst, *Father of the Man.* Boston: Houghton-Mifflin Co., 1947.

[11] See the companion volume of this yearbook, *The Community School.* Fifty-second Yearbook of the National Society for the Study of Education, Part II. Chicago: University of Chicago Press, 1953.

[12] See also Henry Harap (editor), *The Preparation of Teachers in the Area of Curriculum and Instruction.* Ann Arbor, Michigan: Monograph Number Two, National Society of College Teachers of Education, 1951.

is the result of superior method, because it is through method that the negative is inhibited and the positive applied.

Method is the synthesis of relevance, activated toward new creation. It focuses upon the situation all pertinent theories, principles, insight, knowledge, and skills from one's experience, and it becomes more potent with effective use. Thus broadly conceived, method is the foundation of art and the tool of science.

In education, method is the process through which theory enters practice. Good method is the determiner of good teaching. Identical twins teaching in the same field may have the same beliefs, the same motives, the same personal qualities, and the same subject knowledge; yet one succeeds while the other fails, because only the one has mastered method.

If the preceding treatment carries validity, the place of method in teacher education should be evident. (Its importance is stressed in chapter xvi.) Since it is the process by which the prospective teacher is to achieve the aims of instruction, its elements should be accorded an important place in teacher education. The learning of method requires conscious effort, and its mastery comes only with diligent practice. Its acquisition cannot be left to intuition or casual observation. Method does not invariably accompany knowledge. Genius may contribute to education without the aid of classroom method, but the classroom teacher will fail to serve the needs of youth without a mastery of method. And that mastery can come only through rigorous study and practice.

Evaluation Broadly Conceived. The results of the teaching-learning process were long taken on faith. What seemed reasonable in the educative process was considered good. It was reasonable, for example, to have "failures" remain in a grade several years because it seemed certain they would learn in time. When put to test, this assumption has been proved false, some children having been found to retrograde during retention.

The scientific movement in education has substituted evaluation for untested faith wherever measurement is possible. To serve the needs of youth intelligently, the teacher should be able to discern change in all aspects of growth and development. A clear and concise treatment of this highly important aspect of teacher education is given in chapter xiv of this volume.

Expanded Professional Laboratory Experiences

Laboratory experiences that afford the prospective teacher the opportunity to apply to real situations the theory and practice of modern education is the critical factor in teacher education.[13] It is essential to both

---

[13] John G. Flowers (chairman), *Social and Community Laboratory Experiences in Teacher Education* (San Marcos, Texas: Subcommittee of the Standards and Sur-

understanding and skill. The amount and variety of laboratory experience now afforded in teacher education is a small fraction of that currently required in engineering education, dental education, or medical education, yet the work of the teacher is more complex than that of any other profession. Only a few teacher-education institutions approach the standard for laboratory experience that must be attained by all if the teacher is to become prepared for the task imposed by this volume.

The scope of the laboratory experience should be such as to include all aspects of the teacher's job in the school and in the community. Simpler experiences could be afforded during the recruitment period for "student aids" while the prospective teacher is still in high school, such as assembling and setting up laboratory or visual-aid equipment, assisting with field trips, helping keep the classroom attractive, and taking care of much classroom routine. With the first course in education the opportunities should be broadened to the degree possible with the school contacts available.

The initial stages of laboratory experience rarely, if ever, involve the student's having even partial charge of one class over a period of time. Such an assignment, however, is an essential part of the prospective teacher's laboratory experience. The "student teacher's" work during the period of assignment is not limited to his teaching of the one class which has, in varying degrees of reservation, been turned over to him. It also includes as many as possible of the other aspects of the work of the regular teacher in his field. The observation stage of his assignment will have involved a study of the records on each pupil in the class to gain an understanding of the child's home background, interests, abilities, and experiences. It will also have acquainted the neophyte with the pattern of the regular teacher's job in all its facets, including staff relationships, community contacts, committee work, record keeping, and so forth, almost without end, as well as the nature of experiences to be designed for the class and the methods of guiding the classroom, laboratory, and field work. As the student teacher emerges from the observation stage into the participation stage and eventually into full charge of the class, his preprofessional experience will become more and more intensive and complex. It will absorb almost all his complete time and personal resources.

The length of the period of assignment will depend upon the facility desired in the numerous tasks involved. Certainly it should be increased

---

veys Committee, American Association of Teachers Colleges, 1948); and E. M. Tanruther (chairman), *Professional Laboratory Experiences* (Twenty-seventh Yearbook of the Association for Student Teaching. Lock Haven, Pennsylvania: Association for Student Teaching, State Teachers College, 1948).

beyond the median of 5.5 semester hours found by Michaelis in 1949.[14] A full semester in complete charge of one class, preceded by observation and some participation, plus two additional hours per day throughout the semester in other work within the school should provide an adequate minimum. Second and third assignments should be available for those needing or desiring them. The possibility of additional assignment is of considerable importance where no internship program is available.

The failure of public schools to develop superior programs of in-service education for beginning teachers suggests the need for a period of internship under the guidance of the college to facilitate the induction of its graduates into the profession. The need is also suggested by the demands for higher professional performance by teachers, such as those implied in the preceding chapters. The elements of a superior program of internship have been rather clearly defined in recent years. A few scattered institutions now have the program in operation and others have it in their immediate plans. To hasten its application, an interne program might well be one of the standards for the accreditation of teacher-education institutions.[15]

A Five-Year Program

As in the case of the internship, which is one type of fifth-year work, the five-year program for prospective secondary-school teachers has been widely accepted in theory but rarely applied to practice. According to Stinnett, in 1950-51 there were 868 institutions in the United States with teacher-education programs for secondary-school teachers.[16] Of that number, Stinnett found that 191 offer graduate work through the Master's degree and 109 others offer work beyond that level, but it was not possible to ascertain how many have the kind of fifth-year program here recommended. It would probably be safe to say that less than 10 per cent of the institutions have well-integrated five-year programs.

Of particular significance as reasons for the five-year program are the size and nature of the task now imposed upon teacher education. Almost every one of the other fifteen chapters in this volume adds new areas to be mastered and suggests new modes of procedure for the prospective

[14] John U. Michaelis, "An Overview of Teacher Education in State Universities." Berkeley, California: University of California, 1948 (mimeographed).

[15] R. L. Goulding (chairman), *Handbook on Internship.* Tallahassee, Florida: Teacher Education Advisory Council, 1944; see also Morton S. Malter and Troy L. Stearns (co-chairmen), *Off-Campus Student Teaching.* Thirtieth Yearbook of the Association for Student Teaching. Lock Haven, Pennsylvania: Association for Student Teaching, State Teachers College, 1951.

[16] T. M. Stinnett, *The Accreditation of Institutions of Teacher Education.* Unpublished Doctor's dissertation, University of Texas, 1951.

teacher to learn. Some of the essentials of teacher education have been sketched in the present chapter. It should be noted that not only have new content been added and new skills proposed but a new point of view has been advocated as well. Thus the prospective teacher is not only confronted with learning more fields and mastering more skills than his own high-school teacher experienced but he must also use both the learning and the skills in a new setting and for a new purpose. It is extremely doubtful that he can become prepared for this job in four years.

The nature of the five-year program is implied throughout this volume. One essential principle for its construction, however, has not been clearly set forth. The five-year program must be organized as a well-unified series of general and professional experiences. Simply to tack on a fifth year of work unarticulated with the previous four years will not do the job.

The In-Service Program of Teacher Education

As the preservice program of teacher education approaches the standards of quality required to serve the needs of youth as outlined in this volume, the in-service program will change accordingly toward higher levels of professional performance; but the amount of the in-service effort will not decrease as preservice increases, because the continual development of educational theory will require constant in-service exploration and experimentation to prevent an increasing lag in practice. Several types of services will be needed almost continually, and the general procedures for rendering them will require little change in framework as new theory brings new demands on practice.

Inasmuch as in-service education is discussed to some extent in other chapters, particularly chapter v, the treatment here has been restricted to little more than an outline.[17]

Specific Services to the Beginning Teacher

The services required for the proper induction of new teachers will vary in accordance with a number of factors, including the differences among their respective college programs. Three general devices likely to be of service to most beginning teachers are a lighter than normal load, supervisory service, and a study program suited to need.

A Lighter than Normal Load. While the smaller assignment is obviously not within itself an aspect of in-service training, the practice facilitates the in-service program in three ways. First, it reduces the need for help by placing the beginner in a less complex situation for a warming-up

---

[17] See also Charles E. Prall and C. Leslie Cushman, *Teacher Education in Service.* Washington: American Council on Education, 1944.

period; secondly, it provides extra time for the newcomer to prepare materials and to plan appropriate procedures; and thirdly, it affords the time for him and his counselor to hold conferences needed to solve new problems as they arise.

In determining the load for the beginner, at least three points should be considered. First, all assigned classes should be within his major field of preparation. Secondly, during the first semester of work the new teacher should not be given the normal number of committee assignments. And, in the third place, the number of classes he is to teach should be one less than the standard for the school. Under these circumstances the load of the beginning teacher during his first semester would be four classes in his own teaching field, perhaps one student activity, no study hall, and no responsible committee assignment.

Supervisory Service. The aid needed by the beginning teacher closely resembles that given by the college supervisor during the student teaching period. It should, therefore, involve all tasks of teaching included in the preservice program. Since a relatively small proportion of school systems have adequate supervisory programs, it is suggested that teacher-education institutions lend assistance in the following ways: Provide a program for the preparation of superintendents and principals which includes a minimum of eighteen semester hours in the theory and practice of supervision; provide an adequate graduate program for the training of supervisors; hold Saturday seminars for near-by beginning teachers; co-operate in a program of visitation to beginning teachers, planned by all institutions within a state or a region so that each beginner will be aided by the institution nearest him regardless of where he graduated; encourage the beginning teacher to correspond freely with his student-teacher supervisor of the preceding year; encourage small school systems co-operatively to arrange clinics at local centers to focus upon the problems of the beginner with consultative aid from the institutions; develop an internship program such as that previously described; and provide consultative service to school systems.

A Study Program Suited to Need. A study program to serve the needs of the beginning teacher is an essential part of in-service education. It may be conducted entirely by the school system, entirely by the college, or by the school and college co-operatively. College credit may or may not be involved in any of the programs.

Special Consideration of the Older Teacher

The teacher who has been out of touch with educational developments for a decade or more poses a problem for in-service education in some ways more serious than that of the beginning teacher. The teacher who has let time slip by unnoticed faces the needs both of unlearning the old concepts and procedures and of learning the new, whereas the beginner has to deal with only the new. Also, the older teacher is often as firm in his convictions about his way of work as the supervisor and consultant are in their points of view, whereas usually the young teacher is more favorably disposed toward the modern than the traditional, and is, therefore, eager to accept the preferred help.

Ways in which the local administrator may help the teacher who has not had the opportunity to keep abreast of the times are suggested in chapter v. It may also be added here that a number of the institutional aids listed above for the beginning teacher would require only minor changes to serve the older teacher as well.

Continuous Growth of the Entire Staff

From the foregoing discussion it is clear that the special provisions to serve the beginning teacher and the older teacher are highly important aspects of the in-service program; but they do not constitute the whole of it. The professional and personal growth of the *entire* staff requires continuous planning and persistent effort. Several prerequisites are essential to the successful operation of the complete program.

A Sustained Morale. Basic to any successful enterprise are such elements of a high *esprit de corps* as abundant zeal, faith in the mission, hope of achievement, and radiant confidence. These qualities of mind upon which success is dependent are the same wherever high achievement is recorded. In a program of in-service education, in particular, a high morale is the determiner of success because there more than almost any other place are human associations closest and mental states most infectious.

Procedures designed to create and sustain morale should, therefore, both precede and accompany the in-service program. Applicants from the preservice institutions should be screened for promise. Prior to employment they should become well informed about the practices of the school system, including in-service study, and about its points of view. Treatment of the staff should follow sound personnel management, embodying such qualities as fairness, clear lines of authority and responsibility, clear channels of communication, encouragement of initiative, recognition of meritorious service, and great care in giving credit where credit is due. The use of these principles of good human relationships will produce an emotional climate favorable to continuous high-level achievement. Only in such a climate is first-class in-service education possible.

Democratic Action. It is not to be assumed that teachers could become highly motivated and skilled for democratic education in the classroom by a process that is not democratic itself. The rules of democratic practice should prevail throughout the program: before signing his contract, the teacher should understand that in-service study is involved, thus entering the program by choice; the policies and regulations pertaining to the program should be determined by the group and subject to its modification; the goals of the program should be dictated by the needs and interests of the group; the practices should provide for the interplay of democratic values; evaluation should be in terms of the promotion of democracy in the school and classroom; and the appraisal of individual teacher growth should be self-administered.

Released Time on Pay. The usual load of the modern teacher absorbs all his time and energy during the days school is in session, and, in the long haul, weekends are needed for the personal pursuits essential for wholesome living. Therefore, too great a toll would be assessed against the teacher's resources, particularly the resources of teachers no longer young, if the in-service educational activities were added to those of the already overloaded day. It is realized that current practice generally violates this principle, but the principle is nevertheless valid. Pioneering school systems are realizing its validity and are applying it in several ways. For example, many schools dismiss an hour early once a week for the committee work. Some school systems have added a tenth month to the pay year of the teacher and use it for in-service activities.[18] Other schools operate on a twelve-month contract, at the monthly rate of the ten-month contract, with the summers devoted successively to teaching, local workshops, attendance at college, or travel.

Added pay for additional work seems to be the rule already in all lines of work except education. The schools should get abreast of the times in this regard, at least to the extent of providing released time, on pay, for certain specified types of in-service education.

The Use of a Variety of Devices

All practices that might contribute to the professional advancement of the staff should be woven into the long-time plan of in-service teacher education. For any given year, the school system alone or in co-operation with a teacher-education institution should use as many different devices as possible within the time limits imposed by the teaching and administrative loads of the staff.

Several prerequisites or characteristics are common to all devices for in-service education. Careful planning is of primary importance. High-level action doesn't just happen. The planning should be co-operative in

---

[18] *In-Service Program for Teacher Personnel, 1951* (Summer). Austin, Texas: Board of Education, Austin Public Schools.

nature, involving all persons concerned with the endeavor. It should begin several months in advance of the program, and it should be continuous throughout the period of the experience. The plan itself should be built to satisfy needs discovered and felt by the persons to be associated in it.

Participation in any given activity should be limited to those persons who need and want the experience it offers; that is to say, participation should be voluntary. Earlier discussion has indicated that released time should be provided, on pay, and that other types of financial support should be adequate. Evaluation should be continuous throughout, and its findings should provide the basis for the planning of each successive stage of the enterprise. Given the morale-building type of personnel management, all phases of the in-service program that meet the standards just named will be highly successful. Without these requisites, any device would be mechanical and therefore likely to fail.

Several of the more valuable types of in-service education are treated in chapter iv of this yearbook. Valuable descriptions may also be found in recent publications on such features of these programs as preschool and post-school conferences,[19] the all-system evaluation program,[20] and summer workshops.[21] Two devices the writer believes to be of considerable value to in-service education, neither of which is to be found generally in the literature, are given brief treatment below.

Periodic All-Day Conferences during the School Term. Immediate needs may be met more specifically by concentrated effort in five or six all-day work sessions distributed throughout the year than by conferences held before a school opens in the fall or after it closes in the spring. In particular, these single-day sessions give teachers the opportunity to carry on such curriculum work as the planning of procedures and the preparation of materials of instruction.

Inasmuch as the work-sessions are limited to one day, the preplanning must be even more carefully done for them than for other aspects of the in-service program. The jobs to be done must be clearly defined, the

---

[19] Lavone A. Hanna (chairman), *Group Processes in Supervision.* Washington: Association for Supervision and Curriculum Development, National Education Association, 1948.

[20] J. G. Umstattd, "Implications for the Use of the 1950 Criteria by State Departments of Education and Local Schools," *Bulletin of the National Association of Secondary-School Principals,* XXXV (March, 1951), 229–40.

[21] Earl C. Kelley, *The Workshop Way of Learning* (New York: Harper & Bros., 1951); Paul B. Diederich and William Van Til, *The Workshop* (New York: Hinds, Hayden & Eldredge, Inc., 1945); Charles E. Prall and C. Leslie Cushman, *Teacher Education in Service* (Washington: American Council on Education, 1944); and E. S. Evenden (chairman), *The Improvement of Teacher Education* (Washington: American Council on Education, 1946).

work groups organized, the materials made ready, the meeting places equipped and designated, the local leaders prepared, the outside consultants obtained and assigned, and the entire staff made mentally and emotionally ready for a day of profitable work. When these precautions are followed, the one-day work-conference can become one of the most valuable devices for professional study.

In passing, a peculiar value of the single-day session may be mentioned. The session carries a public relations significance in that it brings to the public mind the fact that the teacher's job includes much work outside of class hours when pupils are not around comparable to that of the banker out of banking hours. It also emphasizes the policy of paying for work done beyond the class day.

A Materials Laboratory. A materials center or laboratory in each building is a valuable asset in the in-service program. Its facilities and equipment provide a constant demonstration of learning aids to teachers of lesser experience, and its resources continually supply the needs of the pre- and post-conferences, the curriculum-development program, and the day-by-day demands for instructional materials.

Among the resources required by the laboratory to render these services are a wide variety of well-catalogued collections of previously and currently used resource units for all areas and levels; up-to-date bibliographies for pupils and teachers in all fields; files on local resources, including both materials and people; subject indexes to books for different grade levels (American Library Association); vertical file catalogues (H. W. Wilson Co.); numerous well-indexed vertical files of pamphlets, bulletins, circulars, and flat pictures; materials and tools for the making of mock-ups; objects and specimens of all types not constantly used in given classrooms; maps and charts of all usable types; all projection equipment not permanent fixtures in the regular classrooms; recording apparatus; slides, film strips, films, and recordings owned by the building; facilities for making the best use of visual and auditory aids stored centrally for the system; copies of the regular and supplementary textbooks; periodicals that stress current curricular materials such as the *Scholastic Magazines* group. In addition to these materials already available there should be supplies and facilities for the preparation of new materials as they are needed.

The management and upkeep of the center is of primary importance. The person in charge should have broad training in library service and in the use of instructional aids. He should have the active co-operation of a committee representing all areas and levels. Sufficient clerical assistance should be available to keep the materials circulating and in order. Preferably, the laboratory should be adjacent to the library and under the general control of a properly trained librarian. Its sections should be organized by such broad fields as social studies, language arts, and science, with working facilities near by for both students and teachers. The budget of the system should provide each school with funds for the purchase of a reasonable amount of materials and supplies to keep the center up to date. In short, the school official contemplating the setting up of a materials laboratory should realize that its effective operation will require a highly trained manager, active co-operation of the faculty, competent assistants, and adequate funds for keeping the resources current.

A critical part of the in-service program, so far as the value of the materials laboratory is concerned, is the training of the teacher to use the resources effectively. Such training should be included in the induction experiences for beginning teachers and others new to the system.

SUMMARY

The attempt has been made in this chapter to discuss ways of adapting both preservice and in-service teacher education to conform with the implications and direct suggestions carried in the other chapters of the yearbook. References are cited liberally for further elaboration of these points and for treatment of other aspects of teacher education.

It has been made clear that an increasingly high quality of person will be needed as teacher in the kind of school discussed in this volume, and it is also stated that the teacher-education institution should parallel the competence of the students in its general qualities. Thus, it is important that the institution have a modern point of view and that it seek to professionalize its students. Also, it should be safeguarded against incompetent individuals by a selective admission program. Experiences given students should include broad general education socially oriented, the opportunity to gain scientific knowledge about children and youth, frequent contacts with local communities, and a thorough study of modern thought and practice in curriculum, method, and evaluation.

The professional laboratory experience for prospective teachers should be continuous through the professional training from the time the prospective student chooses teaching as a calling, and it should culminate in a well-designed program of internship. To meet this requirement in addition to the others implied in this volume, it seems to the writer that a five-year program will be essential.

Inasmuch as in-service education was treated to some extent elsewhere in the yearbook, limited treatment was given it in this chapter. Attention was given to the specific needs of the beginning teacher and to those of the teacher with long experience. It was suggested that continuous growth of the entire staff may be based upon high morale that is sustained by sound personnel management and that the growth might be effected through such devices as democratic action, released time on pay, and good financial support to the in-service education program. Reference was made to a number of techniques for in-service education treated elsewhere, and descriptions were given of periodic one-day conferences and the materials laboratory.

The central idea of this chapter is that, if the kind of teaching implied in this volume is to be done in the American secondary school, numerous changes will have to be made in programs for the education of teachers. Some of the needed changes already apparent have been pointed out. Still others may be expected to emerge from future developments in the secondary school envisioned by the yearbook.

SECTION IV

SECONDARY SCHOOLS AND THE FUTURE

CHAPTER XVI

CHARACTERISTICS OF A SECONDARY SCHOOL MEETING THE NEEDS OF YOUTH

WILL FRENCH

Professor of Education
Teachers College, Columbia University
New York, New York

STATEMENT OF CHAPTER PURPOSE

The typical secondary school is the product of many diverse and sometimes conflicting influences. In it one can see the educational patterns of the past modified by the pressures of the present. Few if any secondary schools present clear-cut examples of what they would be were they true either to the philosophy and psychology of traditional secondary education or to the more soundly based principles and practices of the modern school. Most of them are a mixture of many things that secondary education has been, now is, and hopes to be.

Therefore, as the closing chapter of this yearbook, the committee presents a series of word-pictures of what happens to the functions and structure of secondary schools when they make a forthright effort to meet the needs of all youth of secondary-school age in their communities.

The previous chapters of this yearbook have dealt with the necessity of meeting youth needs better in the future than in the past (chap. i); with the methods of identifying the needs of youth (chap. ii); with the importance of adult understanding of how youth learn to meet their needs (chap. iii); with the study of the extent to which youth needs are now being met in secondary schools (chap. iv); and with the process of discerning how action to improve the prevailing situation may be carried out (chap. v ff.). It is proposed in this chapter to point out some of the chief characteristics secondary schools must assume if they accept the meeting of youth needs as their major function and develop the structure —organization, administration, and program—required for the performance of this function. Much of the content of this chapter can be inferred from what has been said in previous chapters. Many of the suggestions presented here have been drawn from best current practice in selected secondary schools.

The aim of the present chapter is to high light some of the features which seem to be most directly associated with efforts of secondary schools to meet youth needs. The chapter does not, however, attempt to relate particular features or characteristics of secondary schools to each of the principal youth needs. Special functions or structures which a school may have developed as a means of meeting a certain need may be found helpful in meeting other related needs as well. It would be unrealistic to prepare separate lists of the chief characteristics of a school which is endeavoring to satisfy each of a number of the important youth needs dealt with in the yearbook. Instead, the chapter will group some of these important needs under four general headings and then describe programs and procedures which appear to be associated with a secondary-school's efforts to meet the related needs included in each group. This fourfold grouping makes it possible to discuss some of the most significant characteristics of schools with a minimum of repetition.

From what has been said, the reader should not infer that we want to present a set of exact specifications to which we think all schools should conform. Far from it. We do not want uniformity, but neither do we want variety for the sake of variety. We want to point up some of the *different* characteristics secondary schools might adopt with confidence that youth needs may be more fully met than if these conditions and procedures are lacking. We hope to suggest some characteristics which, if possessed by a school to a pronounced degree, will make that school a more benign habitat for youth growth and development than it otherwise would be.

BASES FOR DECIDING WHAT CHARACTERISTICS SECONDARY SCHOOLS SHOULD HAVE

The characteristics which secondary schools are being encouraged to develop can be seen by a study of some of the standards and criteria which have been established by various organizations interested in promoting improvements in the programs of the secondary schools. Many state departments of education have either directly or indirectly set up standards for secondary schools in their respective states by their selections of bases for deciding what schools they will approve. Some regional associations accredit secondary schools within their territory and seek to mold them into a pattern which is considered to be a good one. The Co-operative Study of Secondary-School Standards[1] represents the joint endeavor of all regional associations to develop criteria by which schools can be guided in their efforts to improve themselves. Some of these ef-

[1] *Evaluative Criteria.* Washington: Co-operative Study of Secondary-School Standards, 1950 edition. For comparison see 1940 edition.

forts stress characteristics important in meeting youth needs; some do not. None base their standards as specifically or as completely on meeting youth needs as this yearbook indicates to be desirable.

Secondary-School Standards and Criteria

Originally the efforts of both the regional associations and the state departments of education to upgrade the secondary schools were almost wholly concerned with attempts to make them better college-preparatory institutions. They dealt almost exclusively with those aspects of the secondary-school's programs and administrative practices which were considered to affect the character of the work involved in preparing students for college. Both the states and the associations were chiefly concerned with the number and arrangement of college-preparatory courses, their content, and the amount of time to be required for a credit in any subject.

More recently, due in part to a loss of faith in the validity of some of these standards, in part to increased state support of education, and in part to a growing recognition of the fact that the states must be more concerned with the secondary school as a whole than with its college-preparatory curriculum, the standards set by some of the states for approval have been broadened and made more flexible. The North Central Association took the lead in encouraging the other regional associations to join in an effort to improve the selection of criteria by which secondary schools should be appraised. As a result, the Co-operative Study of Secondary-School Standards emerged as an effort to improve both the bases and the means of accrediting secondary schools. The publication of the resulting *Evaluative Criteria*[2] has supplied more objective bases for ranking various aspects of any secondary school in relation to the attainments of similar secondary schools. Also, these criteria provide the opportunity for more participation by the faculty of a school and by school representatives generally in the process of evaluating a given secondary school, and they reduce the chances that influence may be exerted by others less directly concerned with the administration and supervision of secondary education. The work of the Co-operative Study in developing these criteria and the influence of the regional associations and state departments of education in promoting their use have stimulated interest on the part of many principals and faculties in the problems of school improvement and have pointed out the strong and weak points of the schools as gauged by these criteria. These criteria not only encourage a secondary school to consider the needs of its student body in deciding what it ought to be doing but also serve as a measure of how well the school is succeeding.

---

[2] *Ibid.*

The criteria, first published in 1939, have been revised from time to time. The 1950 edition offers many improvements over the original publication. The full effects of this continual revision can be evaluated only after a period of use.

Valid Standards and Secondary-School Functions

The most valid standards to use in rating an institution are those which are most directly related to the performance of its essential functions. The problem of deciding whether or not secondary schools are good is one of defining their functions and of determining whether these functions are being performed well or poorly. The profession is in general agreement upon the principal function of the American secondary school. It is, broadly stated, "Education for ALL American Youth." There is also quite general agreement that this education is best reflected in youth's increasing competence for "responsible living in a free society" to use the Harvard Report's well-known phrase. Earlier chapters of this yearbook describe effective ways of helping students develop as much of this competence as it is possible to acquire through learning experience in school.

Most sets of standards and criteria now in use recognize this over-all function of the secondary school. Yet, they also reflect in considerable measure the objectives of earlier periods when (*a*) the secondary school was a selective institution and (*b*) the most effective way of "educating" these selected youth was assumed to be the intensive study of basic fields of knowledge. To whatever degree these limitations still prevail, the standards are less valid than they should be, from either the sociological or the psychological standpoint. If one assumes that the secondary school should endeavor to meet the basic needs of all youth as far as they can be met by schooling, he will want to know what available standards to use in evaluating a school's ability to perform this function. He will also want to know what characteristics or features of a secondary school will provide the best assurance that it is likely to succeed in performing this function well for all youth. These are the characteristics which secondary schools should be concerned to develop, and these are the ones on which they should be evaluated.

The Beginnings of Youth-Needs Evaluation

Chapter iv has shown that, during the last decade of rising interest in the secondary-school's task of meeting youth needs, principals and teachers have been trying out various ways of performing this task. For several years, the National Association of Secondary-School Principals, through its Committee on Curriculum Planning and Development, has been gathering information about the programs of those secondary schools that were making an earnest effort to meet the basic needs of their youth. *Planning for American Youth*[3] was in reality an effort to describe hypothetical secondary schools in Farmville and American City which were assumed to have programs which are oriented to youth needs. Subsequently, this Committee of the Association tried to move from the hypothetical to the actual situation by asking member schools to send in reports on any new programs or patterns of organization and administration which they had found helpful in their effort to meet some particular youth need better. A summary of the reports from a large number of schools was published in the *Bulletin of the National Association of Secondary-School Principals.*[4] In a later issue of this publication Ransom reorganized the descriptions of the programs of these schools into lists of characteristics which he considered important for any secondary school which is trying to meet each of "the imperative needs" of youth.[5]

Against the background of these studies of the "imperative" needs of youth, the following effort is made to high light the essential characteristics of a secondary school with a youth-oriented program. For the purpose of this chapter youth needs which have been set out in more detail in previous chapters are considered under four broad headings. It is recognized that the facilities and resources to be described under any one of these four areas may also be serviceable in meeting the needs classified under another area. Our point here is not to show that any facility or resource is needed exclusively for the meeting of any given need but, rather, to show that, having initiated certain activities and procedures because of its interest in meeting a particular youth need, a secondary school then finds itself better able to meet other needs also.

CHARACTERISTICS OF A YOUTH-ORIENTED SCHOOL
Satisfying Physical- and Mental-Health Needs

The most obvious essential for a secondary school which is seriously concerned with attempting to meet the health needs of youth is a physical setting which lends itself to the achievement of this objective. The school site and plant should be such as to contribute toward good physical and mental health of school personnel. Many good secondary-school plants

---

[3] National Association of Secondary-School Principals, *Planning for American Youth*. Washington: National Education Association, 1944.

[4] "The Imperative Needs of Youth of Secondary-School Age," *Bulletin of the National Association of Secondary-School Principals*, XXXI (March, 1947), 3–144.

[5] W. L. Ransom, "How Well Does Your High School Rate on the Ten Imperative Needs of Youth?" *Bulletin of the National Association of Secondary-School Principals*, XXXIII (October, 1949), 8–46.

help maintain the physical health of students because they are safe and easily kept clean. Relatively few make an equally telling contribution to the mental health and well-being of the young people in school. But the youth-oriented school tries to prevent blocks to good mental health by providing learning experiences that are appropriate to each student. It attempts to develop a good program based on self-discipline as well as group discipline and evaluates student progress in terms of self-growth rather than in terms of group competition. It provides an active social life for students and leisure-time activities of a nonphysical-recreation type that help to satisfy the social and emotional needs of youth.

When groups of people are in close contact through long periods of intensive work, every effort should be made to see that the stresses produced by these working conditions are kept to a minimum. By the use of resources known to well-qualified designers of school plants, a physical setting can be produced which promotes all phases of health. This school building by its over-all design contributes to the health and safety of students. There is proper lighting. Building materials facilitate cleanliness and are conducive to the quiet operation of a school. The use of a variety of appropriate colors overcomes the deadening effects of color monotony.

Desirable physical facilities, school plants, and sites do not invariably make adequate provision for the school's program of health instruction. The amount of space required outside of the building for a good program of health and physical fitness is often grossly underestimated. Sites are inadequate to provide for the many types of activities which could be well carried on out-of-doors. To offset such deficiencies, indoor facilities are sometimes provided, but because of the expense involved these are frequently insufficient to make up fully for the small site. This forces a reduction in program to points far below what is required if the need is to be fully met. Only the impossibility of providing a large site should cause schools to undertake to house indoors those health and physical-fitness activities which can be better and more cheaply provided for outdoors. Other needed aspects of the well-housed school will become apparent in the succeeding paragraphs as other phases of the physical- and mental-health program are discussed.

Health Education a Pervasive Emphasis. Health education in the youth-oriented school is not considered the exclusive responsibility of any one department. It is a school-wide responsibility. To be sure, many of the physical-health activities center in the programs of the health- and physical-education teachers, but other members of the staff recognize their responsibility for furthering health education. Wherever opportunity presents, the health aspects of any problem under consideration are developed in all classrooms. The school offers students appropriate learning experiences in the fields of safety, first aid, child care, and personal hygiene and health. It also provides opportunities for students to learn about the work of local, state, and federal health services, group health plans, and health and hospital insurance.

The health service of the school is not limited to treating a "patient," but regards each contact with a student as an opportunity to further his education in matters of health. This service is competent to meet any need for health service not effectively met by the community's other health agencies. Among these agencies, and under the leadership of the school health service, students' needs are easily met and they come to feel that their health is considered to be one of the important concerns of both school and community.

Health Included in General-Education Program. The school's program of general education is built around the more common needs of all its youth. Thus, health becomes a center for various units of work in this required program. Year by year there is a recurring emphasis on different health problems and situations with which students of different ages are faced. These include situations of personal psychology and mental hygiene as well as those of physical health. The work is also planned to underscore health not only as a matter of personal, individual concern but also as a matter of group concern. Good health is thus seen as a situation upon which those who are members of the school and community can work together to everyone's advantage. To plan and promote this program, a student-teacher school-wide committee works in close co-operation with other health-serving agencies of the community. This committee is responsible for encouraging students to recognize that what the cafeteria service provides is determined by what is good health practice. Thus, the school does what it can to help each student achieve a better physical and mental growth than he otherwise would. There are also specialized and elective health-education activities and courses for the students. These courses may be elected by any students who are interested and may be required of students who reveal a health need which can be met by such courses.

Comprehensive Physical-Education Program. The physical-education program itself provides an opportunity for participation in a wide variety of activities designed to build physical fitness and provide interesting physical recreation. The building facilities and the campus equipment and staff are adequate to provide each student the equivalent of an hour a day in health and physical-recreation activities of some kind. A full program of well-supervised interscholastic activities is offered not only to provide competition between "first" teams but also between "seconds" and "thirds" with other schools. Students who are not interested in competitive sports are not deprived of opportunity for such types of physical recreation as they may care to follow. Facilities for recreation are available throughout the year, including "vacation" periods. The health- and physical-education programs are co-ordinated with the school's health-service programs. Health service thus has a chance to advise the physical-education staff of any special health needs of any student, and the physical-education department has easy access to the comprehensive records of health service for needed information regarding referrals.

As a result of this comprehensive program of physical and mental health, students of the youth-oriented school recognize the health- and physical-education program as one of the basically important educational opportunities provided by their school.

Meeting Youth Needs for Life-Work Competency and for Economic Literacy

These two related needs are here grouped together because they both center around the economic aspects of living in our kind of world, and thus the type of program which a school must have in order to meet either need will also help meet the other. To teach a life work without insuring the attainment of a high level of economic literacy on the part of the student is to substitute a training program for an educational program; to attempt to teach for economic literacy without relating the studies to life work is to make an artificial study out of what needs to be a very realistic experience.

The School's Concept of Work. The secondary school that undertakes to meet youth needs well accepts work—manual, intellectual, or artistic— as intrinsically worth while. People need to work, to have purposes, causes, and ends to serve even when they do not need the money which can be secured by work. People need to be taught to do work well; to respect the products of others' work; to recognize the interdependence of workers and to appreciate the contributions of all workers to the social and economic welfare of society. Since all work well done is worth while, and since youth can learn to work well, the youth-centered secondary school has abandoned the old point of view that young people need to be *educated* for some kinds of work but for other kinds they need only to be *trained.*

In the youth-oriented school, both the "college-preparatory" students and the "vocational" students are taught that a large part of what they are doing in school is life-work education. The "college-preparatory" group learn to be critical of the studies they are required to pursue in secondary school and of what colleges ask them to do to secure admission to higher levels of professional education, and they resent any college-entrance requirements which are obviously nonfunctional in terms of the work they are trying to get ready to do. The school reinforces this idea of the value of all work by eliminating from the school program and records everything that implies a hierarchy of educational values; such as "academic" vs. "nonacademic" subjects, "half-credit" and "full credit" courses, "solid" and "nonsolid" courses, higher honor for achievement in an academic field than in a vocational or artistic field, and different kinds of diplomas at graduation. Every activity engaged in by any student with the approval of the school and under the supervision of the school stands on its own feet, equal to every other activity carried on by any other student. The college-preparatory group gets experience in basic occupational processes and with common tools and machines. The school stresses with all its students the worth-whileness of both essential and creative labor.

A School-Work Program. Thus, quite logically, the school has developed a school-work program which encourages students to regard the work they can do in or out of the school building or the school day as part of their education. The school has developed a community organization which works in conjunction with the guidance staff in finding out what work the community affords which can be appropriately engaged in by youth as a part of their education. The opportunities include work in industry, business, professional offices, the school itself, community social agencies, and the homes. Where it is customary for the work to be paid for in money when performed by adults, the students are paid for their services; if it is work for which adults customarily contribute their services, the students do so, too. Learning still goes on whether students are earning or serving, so both types of situations are used by the school. In all cases the school provides supervisors—"co-ordinators"—because the primary purpose is not production of goods and services but of higher levels of skills, of better understanding, and of insights and appreciations. These supervisors are also responsible for advising the school as to any weaknesses in youth they observe "on the job" which can be overcome by modifications in the work done by the pupils while in other school classes. This applies not only to the school's technical and vocational classes in the shops and laboratories, called for by the types of work available to its graduates in the community and region, but to its general-education program as well. A major concern of this general-education program is that of providing opportunity for "vocational" guidance (meaning work-guidance) and for building such economic competence as will enable youth to participate more intelligently in life as producer-consumer. In fact, the school's general-education program is based primarily upon the need of all youth for a "life-adjustment" program which will help them meet health needs, work needs, and social-group needs in school, home, and community.

That the youth-oriented school's approach to life-work education is a broad one is indicated by the fact that the general oversight of the whole program is vested in a co-ordinator of life-work education. He has associated with him a faculty committee drawn from the whole area of life-work education—"college preparatory," "vocational" education, and the school-work program. This committee is guided by continuing studies of work opportunities which are available to its students. The school's interest is centered on a broadly conceived program of life-work education for all rather than on a narrower program that offers a high level of technical competence to a few students in a few commercial and vocational fields. These more technical courses are also available, through the school's program of adult education, to those older, more experienced workers in the community who have need for such courses. This school wants all of its students to have experience with work, under actual working conditions, if possible; it wants all to recognize much of what they do in the school building as a work-connected activity; and it wants all youth to be familiar with some of the basic work processes and tools, to see work broadly defined as essential to personal mental health as well as to national economic health, and thus to get a firsthand respect for work and for all workers.

Establishing Leisure Interests and Standards

The youth-oriented school differs from many in that it does not draw a sharp line for its students between work activities and leisure activities. Unwilling to regard work as a necessary evil, the school tries to teach students that finding and doing work in which one is interested is the first step toward making life enjoyable. It cannot logically, therefore, regard leisure activity as a therapeutic by which one repairs the damage to his intellectual, emotional, and physical self that the necessity of having to work has caused. It prefers to teach its students that "good living" requires that one be interested in and have some competence in a variety of action-possibilities in which one engages from time to time.

Since we live in a world where living can be made better for all if each person produces goods and services beyond his own needs, each person ought to devote a substantial part of his time to some productive, creative activity which he likes and is able to do reasonably well. This we call his "work"—his way of "making a living." Beyond the time used for this work he will want to be engaging in other activities not primarily "to make a living" but because he likes to do these things, too. The difference between work activities and leisure activities in school is that the student chooses to learn one of them with the intention of using it as a means of earning a living. So this secondary-school's program is not divided into two parts—one part for work and one for leisure, or one part curricular and the other extracurricular; neither can one part be a "credit" program and the other a "noncredit" program; nor can one part be considered as belonging in the schedule of the school day and the other outside of it. Whatever is considered worthy of a place in the school's program is not halfway in it but wholly in it. Some students are likely to be engaged in a certain part of the program as life-work education while others are in it because they have discovered that they enjoy that particular kind of activity and want to learn more about it in the company of others who enjoy it. The school regards this part of the program as life-work education for those students who are enrolled in it in preparation for making a living; but the school regards this part of the program as leisure-time education for those who select it as a leisure-time activity while in school.

Scope of Leisure-Time Offering. So the school's program is as broadly representative of the various kinds of activity which are of interest to students as the community can be encouraged to support financially, with each activity as well provided with equipment, supplies, and teaching personnel as any other. Every activity—hour for hour—is considered equal to every other for any student whom the school registers for it. In the earlier years the school provides opportunity for transfer from one to another activity during the year, thus encouraging development of a breadth of interests. The school uses a variety of means, such as orientation courses, aptitude tests, and observations of student-interests, to encourage the development of special interests and aptitudes. Some of the activities operate on a broken-week schedule so that a greater variety of activities may be undertaken than if everyone were engaged in them every day of the week.

Co-operation with Other Youth-serving Agencies. The school recognizes that it is not the only institution providing worth-while educational opportunities for the youth of the community. Through close co-operation with other youth-serving agencies much needless duplication of activity is avoided. Between the school's and the community's resources these youth have a program of recreational, leisure, and cultural opportunities broad enough to meet personal, home, and community needs. The school does not try to fill all the waking hours of youth with *its* program. In fact, its first effort is to encourage other institutions and agencies to schedule programs of worth-while activities so as to make them available to the young people attending school. Having done this, it cannot take the position that the only legitimate use of "out-of-school" time is on assigned homework. It makes good use of the time it has, but it does not assume that it has or ought to have *all* of youth's time. The school freely offers the use of its own facilities to other organizations for any worthwhile activity that cannot be as well carried on elsewhere in the community. The school uses its own staff as much as possible to provide services other agencies in the community cannot perform and to coordinate the programs of various youth-serving groups.

The school recognizes that some activities of interest to youth in the community are operated on a commercial basis and that some of these do not always maintain as good standards as might be desired. The school encourages parents and students to join in an effort to promote good standards in these commercialized activities. If this effort fails to get the co-operation of the owners, the school initiates its own programs, open freely to all youth, where standards approved by parents, students, and the teaching staff can be maintained. The school takes a liberal attitude with respect to proprietary recreational and leisure interests, but its influence in the community and with the students is definitely on the side of encouraging high moral, ethical, and cultural standards in the recreational and leisure-time aspects of personal and community life.

The youth-centered school undertakes to develop a school plant which augments the other youth-serving facilities of the community. Classrooms which are in fact group workrooms, laboratories, studios, shops, reading rooms, social rooms, little theater, and gymnasiums are supplemented by such outdoor facilities as garden plots, play fields, a stadium, picnic areas, nature-study preserves, and outdoor theater, if such facilities are not otherwise available for youth's use in the community. Money is not spent on the building or site for the sake of architectural and landscape artistry as such, but the plant as a whole effects a functional beauty which makes itself felt by all who live and work in these surroundings. The entire effect tends to cultivate respect and appreciation for public property, for education, and for the school as a community institution.

Evaluation in Terms of Results. This school and community program of developing broad and worthy youth interests is subject to frequent modification on the basis of study and evaluation by a youth council whose membership is representative of youth, adult citizens, and the school staff. Much responsibility for the operation of this phase of the school's program, as well as of other phases, is carried by representative members of the student body. They are, therefore, qualified to evaluate the program and to contribute to its improvement. There is a formal annual evaluation of the school work. This covers not only the program offered at the school but also existing community facilities for recreation and the constantly changing pattern of leisure-time needs of youth and adults in the community. It also covers the services rendered by the guidance counselors in helping each student to analyze his total year's experience as a means of self-development and in helping students cultivate new and higher interests and aptitudes.

Developing Competence in Group Living and in Civic Affairs

Unless our youth can come by a greater willingness and ability to act effectively together on the problems of group living, all else we do for them by education may be wasted effort. A personal commitment to value-standards and the willingness and ability to act in accordance therewith have applications to small face-to-face group-living such as prevails in the school and in the home. The value of such abilities and attitudes is also evident to young and old alike in the way different persons in a community act in relation to problems affecting community welfare. Whether we approach this area of human relationships from the point of view of the happiness and welfare of each person involved or from that of the preservation of our cultural heritage, we come out at the same place. It is a matter of deepest concern to the youth-centered school and a problem so urgent that education and other competent resources at our command must be concentrated on its solution.

The School as a Benign Habitat for Good Living. So our secondary school which is fully oriented to youth needs must be the kind of place for youth to live that facilitates good living and habituates youth in the appropriate practices of good living. It must have the kind of leadership that exemplifies the best kinds of personal relationship based on the respect of person for person. This leadership must be evident in the way the school is managed and in the way the whole staff goes about the task of studying ways of improving the school. It must be evident in the attitudes of teachers to students and in the types of student relationship the school cultivates. It must be evident in the emphasis the school puts upon learning situations and activities where the quality of human relations and effective ways of reaching group decisions are involved. This area of learning is so important that everything the school does or teaches must augment the ability and willingness of youth to participate more effectively in the activities of the different groups with which they are identified.

The staff takes the pragmatic approach to the problems of standards in personal and group life, allowing each person or each small group all the freedom of action that can be exercised without depriving others of corresponding freedoms to which they are entitled. The staff commits itself also to a method of reaching decisions which starts with free discussion of proposals, followed by as much study and investigation as is necessary for persons to become informed about the matter and to "think it over" prior to bringing it to a decision.

These basic commitments to value-standards and to methods of group thinking and action color the relations of the principal with the teachers; they give tone to faculty and committee meetings and to meetings with parents; they affect the way a teacher or counselor approaches a conference with a student; and they guide decisions as to what classes will do and how they will go about their work. Wherever the school as an institution touches the life of a student, he sees these values in control and these methods of work being followed. Concurrently he sees them in operation in school life and student organizations. He knows students have a responsible part to play: that they are organized to think through and to act upon affairs of interest to them, both in the school and in the community; that he as a student belongs to small groups and to the organized student body and, as a member, has a chance to play a responsible part in the thinking and acting of these groups. He knows that where his life touches the lives of others these value-standards and methods of group work are the best ones to use—and he comes to feel that they ought to be used.

The Part Played by General Education. The required general-education program is the focus for much of the study and activity through which knowledge of the problems of modern group living and the methods of studying them are gained. Teachers and students plan for the study of problems which grow out of daily living in school and community. There are, too, elective courses in the social sciences and related fields, broadly defined, which are offered as the needs and interests of the student body demand. The work of the general-education program ranges from large-group problems of the world in general and of the United Nations down through the situations in the local community and school that need attention or that are being attended to by the agencies of local government. The parts of the school-work program which involve activity with social service agencies or with divisions of the local government serve the purposes of good civic education as well as of work experience.

Home and family living comes in for an appropriate allocation of time and for continuous emphasis. Various aspects of the personal relationships involved in living in a home with parents, in planning for the establishment of one's own home, and in child care are open for study and discussion. The school provides situations designed to develop wholesome boy and girl relationships. Supervised experience in child care in the community's nursery schools and kindergartens is provided for as many students as possible where their own homes do not furnish an opportunity for such experience. Student projects designed to help improve their own homes are encouraged. At appropriate levels of maturity, units concerned with the over-all growth and development of the individual are included. The basic elements of this home-education program are included in the general-education program with the more specialized activities carried on by the home-making teachers. A parent committee in co-operation with the teachers involved in this home-education program evaluates this program and offers suggestions for it just as an industry committee does in the corresponding vocational-education programs.

Evidence of Success of Program in the School and Community. The final evaluation of the effectiveness of such a program of group and civic education is made in terms of the kind of behavior that ensues. This is especially true in the field of human relations. A school does not have to wait a decade to see what kind of citizens it is turning out, because if the program is effective it will begin being so at once; and teachers, students, and parents can begin to see evidence of modified personal and group behavior, interests, and activities right in the school, the home, and the community. The number of students actively interested in local social and civic affairs touching on youth life, the number carrying on responsible activities in school, home, and church, and the amount and character of student-initiated self-control are evidences of the extent to which the school's program of personal and group-life improvement is taking root. Teachers should be able to note fewer instances that reveal attitudes or conduct on the part of individual students or of student groups born of intolerance or unwillingness to accord to others differences in points of view. There should be more evidence of good will, of understanding and acceptance of differences arising from different racial, religious, social, or economic backgrounds. There should be more evidence of personal self-control, of acceptance of the standards of control set by the governing student bodies. There should be more evidence that student organizations accept more responsible parts in the conduct of school affairs. Decisions as to what to do should be reached on a basis of free discussion and study with recognition given to the consequences of alternative courses of action.

Parents and other adults should be able to note increased willingness to "give-and-take" in the home relationship. There should be evidence of a youth's efforts to help make his home a better home for all members of the family. His relationships with younger brothers and sisters should be improved, and he should be better able to understand why young children act the way they do. There should be some evidence that he knows that some underlying causes may provoke the untoward conduct of individual members of the household and that the best way to change the behavioral pattern is to uncover the causes. It should be evident that he is more fully assuming the responsibilities of membership in the various youth organizations to which he belongs as well as accepting the privileges of such membership. The youth of the community and their organizations should be found taking positions that are basically right on moral and ethical questions related to their interests and practices. Larger and more responsible parts should be taken by youth in various civic and social projects which are dependent upon the service of volunteer workers. In sum, the over-all test of the effectiveness of a community's program of social, civic, and moral education for its youth is the extent to which these youth generally show that they know what actions and decisions are desirable and are disposed to respond to them.

As long as high-school youth have a need for social and civic education, that need will be evidenced by immaturity of thought processes and unseemly choices among possible courses of action. Even when they have a sincere desire "to do the right thing," there will be failures, for they are learners, not experts. Accordingly, the committee in charge of the school's program for developing competence in group living and in civic affairs always studies both failures and successes of the students. It notes facts connected with both and studies them for guidance in the further development of the program. Within a few years these notes and observations begin to show how the personal and group thinking and acting of youth are gradually being affected by learning experiences specifically oriented to their needs.

Summary Statement

We can expect a central purpose which dominates any institution to modify its concept of functions and its structure; to give it different characteristics just as differing dominating purposes make individuals think differently, act differently, and eventually develop different characters. A secondary school fully oriented to youth's needs cannot be like a school fully oriented to some other central purpose. It will also have some different characteristics from many existing secondary schools which are often dominated by several purposes not always compatible with each other. That this country needs the fully grown and developed capacities of all of its youth seems self-evident. That organized education can be an effective instrument in facilitating and achieving this growth and development is generally admitted. As experimental psychologists study the growth of children and youth, it becomes increasingly clear that methods of teaching and of working with youth which provide opportunity for them to meet their own needs better are most effective in producing desirable kinds of growth and development. As schools and communities accept the commitments implicit in the growth and development concept of the function of secondary education and as they learn the best methods of work in performing these functions, they will develop different characteristics from those of the secondary schools of the past and even of the existing high schools in this country. They ought to do so. And they ought to be judged, rated, and evaluated by standards and criteria valid in terms of their purposes and methods. They cannot be justly evaluated by instruments which accept these purposes and methods only in part. We need to develop, on the basis of experience and research, new standards for deciding upon what constitutes a good secondary school which are wholly compatible with the basic function of youth education in our democratic world. Only under such conditions will our secondary schools feel as free as they should feel to develop or will they get as much help as they should get in developing those characteristics essential to a youth-needs oriented school.

INDEX

INFORMATION CONCERNING THE NATIONAL SOCIETY FOR THE STUDY OF EDUCATION

1. PURPOSE. The purpose of the National Society is to promote the investigation and discussion of educational questions. To this end it holds an annual meeting and publishes a series of yearbooks.

2. ELIGIBILITY TO MEMBERSHIP. Any person who is interested in receiving its publications may become a member by sending to the Secretary-Treasurer information concerning name, title, and address, and a check for $5.00 (see Item 5).

Membership is not transferable; it is limited to individuals, and may not be held by libraries, schools, or other institutions, either directly or indirectly.

3. PERIOD OF MEMBERSHIP. Applicants for membership may not date their entrance back of the current calendar year, and all memberships terminate automatically on December 31, unless the dues for the ensuing year are paid as indicated in Item 6.

4. DUTIES AND PRIVILEGES OF MEMBERS. Members pay dues of $4.00 annually, receive a cloth-bound copy of each publication, are entitled to vote, to participate in discussion, and (under certain conditions) to hold office. The names of members are printed in the yearbooks.

Persons who are sixty years of age or above may become life members on payment of fee based on average life-expectancy of their age group. For information, apply to Secretary-Treasurer.

5. ENTRANCE FEE. New members are required the first year to pay, in addition to the dues, an entrance fee of one dollar.

6. PAYMENT OF DUES. Statements of dues are rendered in October for the following calendar year. Any member so notified whose dues remain unpaid on January 1, thereby loses his membership and can be reinstated only by paying a reinstatement fee of fifty cents.

School warrants and vouchers from institutions must be accompanied by definite information concerning the name and address of the person for whom membership fee is being paid. Statements of dues are rendered on our own form only. The Secretary's office cannot undertake to fill out special invoice forms of any sort or to affix notary's affidavit to statements or receipts.

Cancelled checks serve as receipts. Members desiring an additional receipt must enclose a stamped and addressed envelope therefor.

7. DISTRIBUTION OF YEARBOOKS TO MEMBERS. The yearbooks, ready prior to each February meeting, will be mailed from the office of the distributors, only to members whose dues for that year have been paid. Members who desire yearbooks prior to the current year must purchase them directly from the distributors (see Item 8).

8. COMMERCIAL SALES. The distribution of all yearbooks prior to the current year, and also of those of the current year not regularly mailed to members in exchange for their dues, is in the hands of the distributor, not of the Secretary. For such commercial sales, communicate directly with the University of Chicago Press, Chicago 37, Illinois, which will gladly send a price list covering all the publications of this Society. This list is also printed in the yearbook.

9. YEARBOOKS. The yearbooks are issued about one month before the February meeting. They comprise from 600 to 800 pages annually. Unusual effort has been made to make them, on the one hand, of immediate practical value, and, on the other hand, representative of sound scholarship and scientific investigation.

10. MEETINGS. The annual meeting, at which the yearbooks are discussed, is held in February at the same time and place as the meeting of the American Association of School Administrators.

Applications for membership will be handled promptly at any time on receipt of name and address, together with check for $5.00 (or $4.50 for reinstatement). Applications entitle the new members to the yearbook slated for discussion during the calendar year the application is made.

5835 Kimbark Ave. NELSON B. HENRY, *Secretary-Treasurer*
Chicago 37, Illinois

i

PUBLICATIONS OF THE NATIONAL HERBART SOCIETY

(Now the National Society for the Study of Education)

PUBLICATIONS OF THE NATIONAL SOCIETY FOR THE STUDY OF EDUCATION

Distributed by
THE UNIVERSITY OF CHICAGO PRESS, CHICAGO 37, ILLINOIS
1953